AFTER
POSITIVISM

AFTER POSITIVISM

*New Approaches to Comparison
in Historical Sociology*

EDITED BY
NICHOLAS HOOVER WILSON
AND DAMON MAYRL

Columbia University Press
New York

Columbia University Press
Publishers Since 1893
New York   Chichester, West Sussex
cup.columbia.edu

Library of Congress Cataloging-in-Publication Data
Names: Wilson, Nicholas Hoover, editor. | Mayrl, Damon, 1977– editor.
Title: After positivism : new approaches to comparison in historical sociology /
    edited by Nicholas Hoover Wilson, and Damon Mayrl.
Description: New York : Columbia University Press, [2024] | Includes index.
Identifiers: LCCN 2023040238 | ISBN 9780231208222 (hardback) |
    ISBN 9780231208239 (trade paperback) | ISBN 9780231557320 (ebook)
Subjects: LCSH: Sociology—History. | Positivism.
Classification: LCC HM435 .A428 2024 | DDC 301.09—dc23/eng/20230922
LC record available at https://lccn.loc.gov/2023040238

Cover design: Milenda Nan Ok Lee
Cover art: PON-PON / Shutterstock

This volume is dedicated to the memory of Xiaohong Xu ⌣

CONTENTS

ACKNOWLEDGMENTS

This volume has its origins in a working group on "Critical Realism and Comparative Methods," convened between 2016 and 2018 in a series of meetings in New Haven, Connecticut; Ann Arbor, Michigan; and Berkeley, California. We thank Phil Gorski for encouraging us to convene that group, the Templeton Foundation for funding it, Laura Donnelly for invaluable organizational support, and Carly Knight, Dan Lainer-Vos, Xuefei Ren, and Tim Rutzou for their contributions to our collective reflections. At Columbia University Press, we are grateful to Eric Schwartz for shepherding this volume to completion; and to Zachary Friedman, Lowell Frye, Kalie Hyatt, Marielle Poss, and the rest of the production team for making it a reality. Finally, our greatest thanks go to Luis Barcena and Julie Huang, two patient and supportive souls who are truly incomparable.

AFTER POSITIVISM

COMPARISON AFTER POSITIVISM

DAMON MAYRL AND NICHOLAS HOOVER WILSON

One of the problems we salsa-dancing social scientists face is that we have to address the connection not only between the forest and the trees, but the connection of the bark to the trees, the trees to the forest, and the forest to the whole ecosystem. Well, the kinds of questions that historical and comparative methodologists are inclined to ask almost always presume *that the real question is the key one, namely how the bark relates to the ecosystem. (Kristin Luker,* Salsa Dancing Into the Social Sciences, *2010, 192)*

Big structures, large processes, and huge comparisons enter the analysis at precisely this point. They provide the stanchions to which we lash our historically contingent statements. (Charles Tilly, Big Structures, Large Processes, Huge Comparisons, *1989, 60–61)*

Historical and comparative sociologists have long pondered how to connect individual bits of evidence (the bark, to say nothing of the trees themselves) to some of the largest social processes that exist (an ecosystem and its niches). One of the most useful tools we possess to make that connection is *comparison*, an act of anchoring our empirical statements to concepts, theories, and larger phenomena. Yet the way we think about comparison is rapidly transforming. This volume aims to synthesize key themes of these shifts and suggest some ways of reimagining what comparison is and what it can do for us.

Before we describe our own approach, however, it is useful to first articulate what we (and many others) position ourselves *against*. After that, we relate our approach in this volume to other postpositivist threads, before describing the volume's contents in greater detail.

The Long Shadow of Positivism in Contemporary Sociology

As Philip Gorski (in the Afterword to this volume) notes, "positivism" has a long history as a philosophical position. Within sociology, its roots can be traced back to Auguste Comte's "positivist philosophy" in the mid-nineteenth century, but it rose to dominance within sociology a century later as the logical positivism of "Vienna Circle" philosophers such as Karl Popper and Carl Hempel was taken up by important mid-century sociological evangelists like Paul Lazarsfeld and David Lundberg (Halfpenny 1982; Levine 1995; Platt 1996). Today, however, few sociologists would claim the label "positivist." Instead, "positivism" as it is often invoked now stands less for any single philosophical or methodological position—and much less a coherent scientific/intellectual movement (Frickel and Gross 2005)—than for a *set* of sometimes-implicit postures that still serve as a foundation to conduct and communicate a great deal of social-scientific research.

We follow George Steinmetz (2005b, 281; see also Hacking 1981) in defining positivism as "a cluster of specific ontological and epistemological positions" regarding causality and the nature of the (natural or social) world. At the heart of this set of positions lies a *regularity theory of causation*—that is, the belief that causation occurs through a series of invariant, regular, law-like relationships called "constant conjunctions of events" by David Hume (Hume and Selby-Bigge 1896), which can then be formulated into general scientific "covering laws" (Hempel 1942). The goal of social science, from a positivist point of view, is to identify social laws and regularities that operate across time and space, with the ultimate goal of using those laws to predict and control (Porpora 2015).

This theory of causation is further linked (in various formulations) to *scientism*—a vision of research that seeks to "remake the social sciences in the image of the natural sciences" (Steinmetz 2014, 421). Scientism entails a belief in the "unity" of the natural and social sciences such that they can be investigated through a common method (ideally, the experimental method as imported from natural sciences such as physics). Scientism thus privileges quantification over hermeneutics or narrative and encourages hard-science styles of presentation (e.g., propositional theories and formal hypothesis testing). It also entails an empiricist emphasis on the observation of events over theory.

One of scientism's most important tenets is its insistence on *a stringent notion of "objectivity" that severs the relationship between fact and values*. Positivist methods are designed to reinforce this distinction by distancing researchers from the "object" of study and carefully attempting to exclude emotions, ethics, and values from the research process (Collins 1990; Harding 2015; Steinmetz 2005b). Objectivity in this sense is possible, for positivists, because they treat social phenomena (like natural phenomena) as time-, space-, and concept-in-dependent—that is, they assume the independence of ideas from their social context. Good researchers, they claim, need only set their values aside to gain a disinterested perspective on their "objects of inquiry," and any good researcher who successfully does so should be able to come to the same conclusions.

Positivism, in short, makes a set of claims about the social world and how it may be investigated: that the social world is governed by invariant, regular laws; that these laws can be unearthed through the use of methods copied from the natural sciences; and that good researchers both can and must be "objective" in how they approach their research. All of these claims, however, have been roundly criticized over the years.

Two Critiques of Positivism

One prominent set of critiques has targeted positivism's *epistemological* claims and, in particular, its claims about the possibility of objective knowledge. These critiques have largely fallen along two interrelated lines: (1) a *power critique* stating that social scientists cannot be objective because all knowledge is inter-twined with power relations; and (2) a *standpoint critique* stating that the pro-duction of knowledge is inherently subjective and perspectival. Whereas the former questions the possibility of knowledge as *disinterested*, the latter ques-tions the possibility of knowledge as *universal*.

The power critique starts from the premise that science, as a form of knowl-edge, is inseparable from the societies in which it is formed; and, as a result, the knowledge that gets produced for those societies both reflects the biases and inequalities prevalent therein *and* helps to reproduce them. Power rela-tions shape the kinds of questions scientists ask and the purposes to which their findings are put. Antiracist, Black studies, Indigenous, and postcolo-nial scholars, for instance, have pointed out that important positivist methods developed to produce knowledge that allowed racial and colonial regimes to better know and understand the populations they were attempting to control (Bonilla-Silva and Zuberi 2008; Go 2016; Quisumbing King and White 2021; Tuhiwai Smith 1999). Katherine McKittrick (2020, 4) poetically summarizes how epistemology and resistance meet as she introduces her book, *Dear Science and Other Stories*:

Black people have always used interdisciplinary methodologies to explain, explore, and story the world, because thinking and writing and imagining across a range of texts, disciplines, histories, and genres unsettles suffocating and dismal and insular racial logics. By employing interdisciplinary method- ologies and living interdisciplinary worlds, black people bring together various sources and texts and narratives to challenge racism. Or, black people bring together various sources and texts and narratives not to capture something or someone, but to question the analytical work of capturing, and the desire to capture, something or someone.

Feminist scholars, meanwhile, have demonstrated how sexist biases and blind spots compromise every phase of "objective" research, from the selection of topics to research design to the interpretation of data and findings (Harding 2015; Sweet 2018). Values and interests inevitably seep into scientific findings, even when the strictest scientistic methods are used (cf. Gorski 2013a). More than this, however, scholars working in critical traditions have shown how the ideal of objectivity has been used to exclude or dismiss women, people of color, and the poor, by casting them as deficiently "rational" or insufficiently "objective" as compared to the unmarked white male scientists of the positivist imagination (Go 2020; Harding 1992, 2015; Tuhiwai Smith 1999). Claims to objectivity themselves thus should be seen as political claims with political effects (Proctor 1991).

Though related to the power critique, the standpoint critique challenges the ideal of objectivity from a slightly different angle. Differences in social power, from this point of view, matter for the production of knowledge because they generate different experiences, which in turn inform interpretations of the world. All knowledge is thus unavoidably partial and perspectival—or "situ- ated knowledge," in Haraway's (1988) famous formulation. Standpoint theorists draw on a longstanding tradition of scholars who have emphasized how those in subordinated positions often have special knowledge of the workings of power that eludes the powerful (e.g., Collins 1990; Du Bois 1903; Harding 1986; Hartsock 1983; Smith 1974). The important corollary to this is that positivist scientists (who were overwhelmingly white, male, and Western) also have a standpoint—one that they have unjustifiably tried to universalize under the rubric of "objectivity." Postcolonial scholars, for instance, have shown how the scientific knowledge Western scholars produced about the Global South both reflects and reproduces a metropolitan understanding of their former colonies *and* relies on concepts and categories that travel poorly or not at all beyond the Western settings in which they were produced (e.g., Chakrabarty 2007; Go 2016; Said 1973).

The implications of these epistemological critiques are profound: because subjective meanings are both context dependent and shaped by social location, universal laws and even universal interpretations are impossible. Universal, objective knowledge therefore cannot exist; there is only knowledge from an unacknowledged standpoint whose uncritical deployment only tends to reproduce power relations. Consequently, claims to "objectivity" merely elide the standpoints (and, typically, power) of the scientists making them and act as a form of epistemic violence against those with other standpoints.

However, in addition to these epistemological critiques of positivism, positivism has also been challenged on *ontological* grounds. That is to say, it has been challenged not simply for the claims it makes about how knowledge is produced, but for its assumptions about the nature of the social world. Positivism's desire to uncover universal laws is premised on the idea that the social world is essentially homogeneous and can be treated as a set of stable entities for the purpose of study. Such a vision assumes that the social world is analogous to the natural world, meaning inter alia that social structures do not depend on the meanings people apply to them; that social structures are essentially the same everywhere; and that social causes will always have the same effects everywhere (Gorski 2013b). Andrew Abbott (1988) has famously referred to these assumptions as a "general linear reality" model of the social world, which treats social phenomena as a great storehouse of equivalent cases that can be treated as independent and fundamentally equivalent units for the purposes of causal inference.

Yet the failure of social scientists to uncover anything like a covering law despite decades of trying suggests this vision of the social world is flawed (Little 2013). Instead, positivism's ontological critics have argued that the social world is "heterogeneous" and "dappled," characterized above all by diversity and variation that preclude the possibility of covering laws (Cartwright 1999; Little 2009). This heterogeneity is inherent in the objects social scientists study. Social entities are not fixed, but instead are born, die, merge, and divide. They are frequently entangled with one another. Social causes are not constant and often do not have consistent effects. And the organization of and meanings ascribed to social phenomena can vary dramatically across time and space (Abbott 1988; see also Steinmetz 2005b). Positivism takes none of these considerations into account. As a result, it struggles to account for contingency and conjunctural explanation, time- and space-specific concepts, and the way social causes are culturally constituted.

Although we do not intend to ignore or minimize the epistemological critique of positivism, this volume instead centers the ontological critique. We do so because, as we elaborate below, these ontological critiques pose particularly difficult problems for the classic comparative method in historical sociology (e.g., Skocpol 1979; Skocpol and Somers 1980). Consider the case of race. An analyst interested in undertaking a comparative historical study of the development of racial inequality must attend to the fact that modern race is a category that only emerged in the early modern era, that the meaning of "race" itself (and the classifications that instantiate it) varies globally and historically, that ideas of race have diffused across colonial relations of power in both directions, and that official racial categories often do not match the racial identities of those to whom those categories are applied (Quisumbing King and White 2021). The positivist approach to comparison, which haunts the classic comparative method, provides few tools for such a project, which must take the passage of time, connections between cases being compared, the multiplicity of potentially relevant causal factors, and the shifting meanings of the central analytic construct into account.

Today, few historical sociologists would subscribe to the entire positivist program without qualification—indeed, the whole point of discussing comparison *after* positivism is that there are disputes about each. Yet, in going about their daily work, many social scientists struggle to live *without* some semblance of them. As Michael Mann (1981, 548) summarizes, "in practice sociological researchers have operated with a kind of 'as-if positivism,' acting *as if* they could apprehend and describe reality through the process of operationalization, and *as if* they could rely on absolute standards of scientific proof for their results to be evaluated."

In this volume, we seek ways for social scientists to make sense of, plan, conduct, and justify their research without having to adopt a compromising "as-if" stance. Our goal is to reconstruct the most important parts of the positivist approach without abandoning their felicitous and productive aspects. More simply put, our goal is to pursue a *post*positivist way of conducting comparative and historical social science. Before that, however, we will first ground our discussion more specifically in the role positivism has played in historical sociology and especially how it has invoked comparison.

Who Wants to Be a Millian Heir? Positivist Comparison in Historical Sociology

Sociology as a whole has felt the influence of positivism throughout its entire history—an influence that intensified for American sociology beginning in the 1940s when the discipline found congruence with larger "Fordist" social structures (Adams, Clemens, and Orloff 2005; Steinmetz 2005a). But one key vector by which positivism entered historical sociology was via comparison.

Positivist comparison in historical sociology is indebted to the inductive method formalized by John Stuart Mill in his massive *A System of Logic*, first published in 1843. Mill was a fierce defender of empiricism—the doctrine that

"no informative assertion about the world is *a priori*" (Skorupski 1998, 35)—
and hence spent much of *A System of Logic* spelling out (he thought for the first
time) rules for induction, or "the operation of discovering and proving general propositions" that formed not only "a complete logic of the sciences [but]
also . . . of practical business and common life" (Mill 1974, vol. I, 284).[1] At the
same time that Mill fought against transcendentalism and idealism by defending the centrality of direct observation (the core of "empiricism"), he also centralized a paradox introduced by David Hume: that although causes can never
be observed (only matters of fact accessible to empirical observation), people
nonetheless infer causal connections among "constant conjunctures of events"
(Hume and Selby-Bigge 1896, 13).

The key contribution of Mill's *Logic* for comparison are the methods, which
Mill calls "canons," for establishing causes by comparing cases or instances of
things to one another (see especially Mill 1974, vol. I, book III, chaps. 6–8 and
book VI). In the method of agreement, which applies to cases that are otherwise different but display similar outcomes, one tries to identify a common
causal factor amid differences; whereas in the method of difference, to be used
in cases that are otherwise similar but display different outcomes of interest,
one tries to identify a causal difference. Moreover, Mill thought that these two
methods were particularly powerful when used in conjunction to discriminate
among a multitude of causes with relatively few cases.[2]

As one of the fiercest proponents of historical sociology's "second wave,"
Theda Skocpol was instrumental to importing Mill's comparative method into
historical sociology. Both in her monumental *States and Social Revolutions*[3]
(Skocpol 1979) and in an important methodological article coauthored with
Margaret Somers (Skocpol and Somers 1980), Skocpol argued that the methods of agreement and difference could be employed on macro-social phenomena (canonically social revolutions) to identify relevant factors as "variables"
that can be assessed and ruled in or out as causal factors through systematic
comparison.

Skocpol's explicit reasons for employing Mill's methods were that social revolutions are inaccessible to experimentation and could only be studied using a
method capable of addressing the problem of "too many variables and not enough
cases" (Skocpol 1979, 36). But Millian methods also supplied crucial legitimacy for
historical sociology as social *science*. Skocpol and those inspired by her approach
thus "elected to play on the turf of their mainstream colleagues" (Calhoun 1996,
309) and brought positivism into historical sociology through the comparative
method. Indeed, as Bargheer (chapter 1 in this volume) notes, today's continuing
fusion of "comparative" and "historical" is largely a legacy of this attempt to legit-
imize historical inquiry through the "scientific" comparative method (see also
Abbott 1991).

Problems with Positivist Comparison

The internal logic of historical analysis, however, meshes poorly with many positivist premises. Thus, the invocation of Mill's method was subject to a number of criticisms. One line of critique came from the positivist mainstream and emphasized how Millian methods are ill-suited for analyses with few cases (Lieberson 1991, 1994).[4] In this sense, these criticisms emerge from within the positivist framework and center around whether and how historical comparisons can (or, more typically, cannot) adequately meet the standards for variable-centered social research in the pursuit of lawlike generalizations. From a similar, mainstream positivist standpoint, Millian comparison was also criticized on practical grounds; in "second wave" historical sociology, it tended to rely on reading secondary histories of its cases (Bollen, Entwisle, and Alderson 1993) and thus raised questions about whether its data sources comported with anything resembling direct empirical observations of the historical record (Goldthorpe 1991, 2000).

Yet at the same time, a variety of additional criticisms have emerged from beyond the boundaries of the positivist framework. These criticisms—many of which we introduced earlier—reject important assumptions underlying not just the Skocpolian program of comparative historical sociology but also positivist sociology more generally. We elaborate them further here.

One of the strongest critiques is the argument that positivist comparison assumes a "general linear reality" model of social life (Abbott 1988). General linear reality reflects Hume's (Hume and Selby-Bigge 1896) ideas about causality and, in particular, the principle that anything approaching a causal "law" in the natural or social sciences must exhibit a "constant conjunction of events."[5] The central idea, that effects will be regular and that causes will always precede effects, is basic to both variable-based regression analysis and the logic of Millian comparative methods.

These assumptions are highly questionable, however. The regularity of effects is unlikely, particularly in historical research, because society is an open system whose conditions and meanings change over time (Sayer 1999). Moreover, a regularity view of causes and effects and constant conjuncture cannot explain the emergence of new phenomena (Gorski 2009; Hirschman and Reed 2014) or the destruction of old ones (Steinmetz 2008). Similarly, causal complexes are increasingly understood to be conjunctural and contingent, such that the effect of variables is not regular (Ragin 1987; Steinmetz 1998). And just as the effects of causal factors may not be regular, causes do not always precede their effects—either in a strict sense or even probabilistically. This is particularly true of historical phenomena, where causes and effects may emerge simultaneously (Gorski 2018). For these reasons, regular or covering laws are essentially unknown in the social sciences—positivist efforts and protestations to the contrary.

A related critique targets the positivist idea that cases are independent of one another. In reality, and again in a way that is particularly germane and problematic for historical research, events in one case regularly influence others (Steinmetz 2014). Famously, the Russian and Chinese revolutions analyzed by Skocpol (1979) were themselves influenced by another one of her cases, the French Revolution. Thus, positivist assumptions that each case is independent are deeply suspect in historical research. The meaning of a variable X at one point in time may be entirely different from the meaning of that same variable at another time (Sewell 1996).

Scholars have also questioned the premise that observable regularities are where causal action actually lies. It is known that there can be multiple causal pathways to the same outcome (George and Bennett 2005; Mahoney 2000) and that important causal factors may be present even if they are not active or necessary in a particular case (Danermark, Ekström, and Karlsson 2019; Decoteau 2017). For this reason, many critics have argued that surface-level or "actual" comparison needs to be supplemented, if not replaced, by comparison across mechanisms (Steinmetz 2004; see more below).

Finally, because positivism is premised on the idea of regularities rather than events, it is impossible to use positivist comparative methods to explain rare events. Yet many events that are substantively important in the world, such as revolutions, are relatively rare yet demand explanation. In this sense, historical sociology must find ways of explaining rare events (and even singularities, such as the Holocaust) that do not rely on problematic positivist assumptions (Steinmetz 2004). In other words, these critics insist, *contra* positivist premises, that rare events and singularities may be explained even if they are not made fully generalizable (Gorski 2018).

Beyond problematic assumptions about regularity, positivist approaches to comparison have also been critiqued for misrepresenting the research process. In contrast with the classic "scientific" model where the research process is simply the carrying out of formalities in a "context of justification" (Popper 2005), actual historical research is messy and iterative (Abbott 2004; Feyerabend 1975; Somers 1998; see also chapter 2 in this volume). If important clues and insights emerge from within the research process itself, this complicates positivist assumptions that comparison—particularly variable-oriented Millian comparisons—does what its proponents claim it can do.

Beyond Positivism

Today, there are two main threads of postpositivist comparison in the social sciences, each of which has proponents adopting their positions with greater and lesser degrees of qualification.

One major family of postpositivist social science attempts to directly reconstruct and defend the central positions of positivism. The more emphatic variety of this approach can be found in positions such as King, Keohane, and Verba (1994), who argue that the social sciences have a fundamental unity around variable- and regression-based methods; Morgan and Winship (2014, especially chap. 10), who argue similarly for an architecture of causal inference derived from the counterfactual analysis of mechanisms (see more below); and Sanchez-Jankowski and Abramson (2020), who seek to defend what they call the "conventional scientific tradition" in participant-observation. Each retains the ambition to generalize to more or less law-like or predictive statements from a smaller number of cases. Meanwhile, a more qualified version of this approach still seeks generalization but acknowledges more directly the "scope conditions" on any generalization emerging from comparison and tends to emphasize the multiplicity of possible causes for the same phenomenon or event (Goertz and Mahoney 2012; Mahoney 2000; Ragin 1987, 2000; Ragin and Becker 1992; Ragin and Zaret 1983). Set-theoretic versions of this approach further selectively abandon aspects of the positivist program (e.g., the possibility of fully objective knowledge) while strongly affirming others (e.g., regularity causation; see Mahoney 2021).

The second major family of approaches, which again is represented by more or less emphatic proponents, departs from central assumptions of positivism more decisively. Many question positivism's sharp division between fact and values, insisting upon the need to account for the researcher's position in the knowledge-production process and calling for greater attention to descriptive and other forms of noncausal analysis (Abend 2006; Abend, Petre, and Sauder 2013; Besbris and Khan 2017; Collins 1990; Go 2016; Gorski 2017; Haraway 1988; Itzigsohn and Brown 2020; Riley, Ahmed, and Emigh 2021). Scholars in this camp have also reconsidered the relationship between theories and observation, on the one hand, and the role played by case analysis, on the other. In "strong" varieties of this position, the acts of comparison, especially case selection and analysis, are indissoluble from their theoretical significance, and that significance further permeates empirical observation (e.g., Bonnell 1980; Burawoy 1998; Somers 1998). Although they are sympathetic to such notions of concept dependence, those holding a qualified version of this position, meanwhile, still hold that different theories are adjudicable through various forms of case analysis (George and Bennett 2005) or through the subjection of claims to a democratic "community of inquiry" (Tavory and Timmermans 2014).

However strong their emphases, these works collectively attempt to either reconstruct or transcend the positivist goals of comparison. And although in our view all these lines of thought have been valuable, this volume goes in another direction. At base, we recognize that the previously discussed postpositivist approaches fundamentally work "downward" from epistemology and ontology to methods themselves and remain epistemologically *pessimistic* (focused, above all, on how to avoid error in our theories and in our search for "the truth of the matter"). By contrast, we start with a different set of convictions: actually practicing social scientists, in muddling through the difficult research process and its dialogue with data with a deep ethical commitment to "getting the story right," have developed a variety of productive and insightful methods with their origin in a multitude of research traditions, theories, and perspectives.[6] As such, the task of a volume such as this is less to *prescribe* or derive a logical set of "best practices," but rather to *describe* and develop a vocabulary that is sufficiently capacious to enable and potentiate excellent work already going on. Our way of thinking through comparison and its meaning for social scientists participating in a healthy scholarly ecology, in other words, is fundamentally epistemologically *optimistic* and *inductive*.

A Postpositivist Toolkit for Comparison

Because our perspective in this volume is self-consciously pragmatic, pluralist, and averse to mapping a "royal road" to comparison, we adopt an eclectic approach to the earlier postpositivist threads. In other words, we take to heart the spirit (if not the anarchist letter) of Paul Feyerabend's (1975) exhortation "anything goes!" and seek to employ whatever elements of postpositivism produce interesting new substantive results and insights. Collectively, those elements group (however roughly) into four families.

A Turn to Research Practice

If there has been one fundamental shift in the philosophy and history of science in the past seventy-five years, it has been the recognition that the *practice* of science is as important as its findings (Kuhn 1996; Latour 1987; Latour and Woolgar 1979; Pickering 1992). When we peer into scientific practices, we often find a far messier terrain than described in publications themselves (Pickering 1995).

Although this observation may seem self-evident and trivial, it has enormous consequences for the comparative method. Above all, it invites us to *embrace the act of research as a core part of the comparative method.* Writings on comparative historical methods have long been metatheoretical, emphasizing abstract principles and ideal-typical approaches. As a result, they have too long neglected the actual nuts and bolts of comparative research—that is to say, its actual lived practice (Mayrl and Wilson 2020). We believe that attending more closely to the concrete steps that comparison entails can offer clues into the strengths and advantages of the method (e.g., its abductive and recontextualizing value for the researcher) even as it may explode some old myths about why comparison "works" (e.g., allowing the researcher to "rule out" variables in causal explanations; see Przeworski and Teune 1970; Skocpol and Somers 1980). Methodological reflections are essential to historical sociology, but we should build them from the ground up, based on the actual lived practice of comparison, rather than the top down, based on logical abstractions that may or may not adequately capture that lived practice.

Communities of Inquiry and Concept Dependence

The observation that research is an *act*, and not an abstract ratiocination, also implies that it is fundamentally *social*. That is, whether in providing a democratic community of critique, questioning, and support over the course of the research practice (Tavory and Timmermans 2014); a disciplinary boundary where explanations "bottom out" at a consensus foundation (Morgan and Winship 2014, 346–47); or an anticipated readership for research conversant in an "analytic architecture" for presenting findings (Mayrl and Wilson 2020), *every* scholar marshals their comparisons and analytic strategy, at least in part, with reference to a community (Shapin 1994). By extension (though this point remains controversial, sometimes tarred with the shibboleth "relativism"), these communities may even supply basic theoretical perspectives and paradigms that imbricate themselves with the very observations scholars make, or at least the significance they make of those observations (see, *inter alia*, Hacking 2004; Kuhn 1996).

These points, too, have direct consequences for comparison in the social sciences. They encourage us to *embrace a multiplicity of warrants for comparison*. Comparison has important roles to play in causal analyses, but causality does not exhaust the entirety of the purposes for which comparison is well suited. Comparison can help generate constitutive arguments, insights into emergence, and productive theoretical ruptures. Even among causal analyses, comparison may play important roles beyond efficient causation, providing insights into formal or ultimate causes as well. Comparison plays many roles in the research process, and the savvy historical researcher will be attuned to how those roles may be parlayed into generative insights. Indeed, comparison's role may vary from time to time within the same research project, to the scholar's benefit.

Theories of Explanation and Causality

Finally, and perhaps most importantly, the postpositivist landscape has seen a tectonic shift *away* from Hume's radical empiricism (which privileges events and matters of fact that are directly observable above all else) and toward a direct examination of causal mechanisms (see Aviles and Reed 2017; Elster 1989; Gross 2009; Hedström and Ylikoski 2010; and Morgan and Winship 2014 for key statements).[7]

Of course, a variety of positions have emerged in the wake of a seismic shift like this one. Although there are radical and consequential differences among them that are beyond the scope of our discussion here, one distinction is especially important for comparison. Some approaches retain the basic ontology of variables and properties and use the language of mechanisms to facilitate more precise analytic decomposition of phenomena—and with it, eventually, more trenchant general law-like statements (e.g., Hedström and Ylikoski 2010; Morgan and Winship 2014). Others similarly maintain the variable-and-property language but more strongly emphasize multiple causation (where the same events might be caused by different mechanisms or the same mechanism may, in combination, produce different effects) (Bertalanffy 2003, 132; Mahoney 2008) and the ongoing influence of mechanisms (sometimes even cumulative) on future events (Mahoney 2003; Pierson 2011).[8] Still others push this insight further, emphasizing mechanisms as "generative" sources for "actual"—that is, empirically observable—phenomena (Steinmetz 2004).

This last strain of mechanism-based analysis carries a radical implication: rather than using mechanisms as an *epistemological* conceit to better establish law-like regularities (whether deterministic or probabilistic), some have insisted that mechanisms have an *ontological* reality and that our imagery of reality is best represented by "entities" and their powers and properties. This view orients us to various different things in the world—individual people, organizations, and material objects—and emphasizes their potential or actual abilities to bring about states of affairs—that is, their causal powers (see Jacobs 2017 for a good overview; also Elder-Vass 2010; Harré and Madden 1975; Varela and Harré 1996). Some proponents of this perspective emphasize how causal mechanisms are composed into new entities that, in turn, have emergent causal properties (Emirbayer 1997; Hirschman and Reed 2014) compatible with key classical theoretical stances, such as Elias's (2000) "figurational" sociology and the Marxist notion of "totality" (Jay 1984)[9]; others embed the insight in a full-fledged alternative theory of causality derived from Aristotle (Greco and Groff 2017; Lear 1988); and still others emphasize the "affordances" granted by entities—that is, the way that they invite, encourage, or enable certain lines of action (Keane 2014).

There are thus many different points of emphasis on what mechanisms are and do in our scholarship—even as some question the language of mechanisms in the first place (see especially chapter 10 in this volume). From our vantage, however, we believe that the general emphasis carries two important implications for comparison. First, we should *embrace a broader array of comparisons*. Classic positivist approaches to comparison suggest a fairly limited set of criteria for case selection. One of the great advantages of postpositivist approaches is their ability to open up new kinds of comparison, including comparison across mechanisms, comparisons across sequences, comparison across narratives, and comparison of cases that may, at first blush, appear not to be comparable at all. Our advice in thinking about comparison is that a much wider array of comparisons may be generative, assuming they are theoretically motivated and designed to reveal mechanisms, processes, and sequences that are essential to historical explanation. As an open system, the social world is messy. Historical researchers interested in comparison should embrace that messiness and the wider array of comparisons that come along with it. As reviewers, we should not hold comparisons to be fatally flawed for "failing to control" for some factor. Rather, we should judge each proposed comparison on its own terms, in terms of its theoretical motivation, the underlying mechanisms and processes it reveals, and how well suited the comparison is to generating insights into those mechanisms.

Second, we ought to *permit comparison to serve an accessory or complementary role in causal analysis.* Comparison, by itself, offers many strengths for researchers, but it is not always the best candidate for developing strong causal analyses. Yet when conducted in tandem with other kinds of methodological strategies, comparison may be ideally suited for synthetic or evaluative causal analyses (see chapter 12 in this volume). Rather than treating comparison as a unitary phenomenon or singular method, comparison should be treated as a tool that can be used in primary or accessory ways, depending on the research question being asked.

Rethinking Comparison: An Overview of the Volume

This volume is organized in three parts, each of which takes the postpositivist scholarship above into account and mobilizes it toward rethinking the why, what, and how of comparison.

Why Compare: Warrants for Comparison That Are Not About Causality

Part I examines the question of *why* to compare. Classic positivist approaches argue that causal analysis and identification are the primary warrants for comparison. Yet this warrant has been savagely criticized over the past forty years (e.g., Goldthorpe 1991; Lieberson 1991, 1994). Postpositivist comparison must justify its position in the toolkit of sociological analysis on other grounds. In this section, the authors provide a set of alternative warrants for comparison that do not assume that its primary function is to identify causality. Instead, the contributors focus on comparison as a practice, the engaging in which shapes the perceptions and phenomenology of researchers in ways that make them more creative. And although comparison may be ill suited (on its own) to making convincing causal inferences, it can be leveraged for other kinds of arguments or repositioned as an adjunct to other techniques in making causal arguments.

Stefan Bargheer's contribution (chapter 1) sets the stage for part I by making the case that comparison is only accidentally relevant for historical sociologists. Bargheer argues that the union of comparative and historical sociology as a "method" and an organizational section is a historical accident that reflects traces of the field's reconstitution in the 1970s. Because sociology at that time was organized around a strong quantitative/qualitative divide that echoed the rise of computing, novel statistical packages such as SPSS, and new datasets like the General Social Survey, its champions latched onto comparison as a capital-building strategy oriented toward the field's dominant player, multivariate regression analysis. Today, however, Bargheer argues that statistical analyses have developed in new directions that complicate the "general linear reality" assumptions of multivariate regressions (Abbott 1988). Although these developments raise new potential points of encounter between statistical and historical researchers, they have also rendered comparison only one among several methodological tools available to historical sociology, and one that is not essential to the enterprise.

In his contribution (chapter 2), Damon Mayrl argues that comparison plays an important role in historical research not for its ability to identify causality, but instead because it acts as a structuring technique that maximizes the analyst's abductive capacity. Examining the practice of comparison, he argues that comparative designs—with their emphasis on deep immersion in specific cases and the iterative revisiting of those cases in light of one another—act as heuristics that allow historical sociologists to notice important features of their cases and generate creative explanations for them. While the causal heavy lifting in historical work does not belong to comparison, Mayrl argues that comparison is nevertheless an indispensable tool for developing causal explanations in an auxiliary capacity.

Xiaohong Xu adopts a macro-phenomenological approach in chapter 3, arguing that the primary warrant for comparison should be thought of as a means of creatively refreshing and updating uninteresting theorizing. Comparison, Xu argues, provides a means of problematizing existing relationships between the case and its reference group, allowing new relationships to be centered and analyzed. Xu argues that comparison plays both a deconstructive role (in disrupting existing associations and theoretical assumptions) and a reconstructive one (in suggesting new connections and theoretical relationships). By recasting familiar situations as "interesting" new problems to solve, comparison provides a spur to improving sociological theorizing.

Finally, Josh Pacewicz (chapter 4), looking at parallels between historical sociology and ethnography, argues that comparison's primary warrant should be to make *constitutive* rather than *causal* arguments—that is, arguments geared toward describing the essential characteristics of a phenomenon, rather than those oriented toward pinpointing its causal origins. Pacewicz argues that the single-case tradition in historical sociology shows that comparison in practice has been superseded by increased attention to processes within cases and to constitutive claims-making. Examining exemplary works of ethnography, he argues that particular kinds of cases lend themselves to constitutive arguments; and suggests that, for historical sociologists, this insight suggests the need to move beyond the strictures of causal arguments, to select cases for comparison that allow scholars to ask "what" before "why."

What to Compare: New Objects of Analysis to Address Issues of Concept Dependence

Part II examines the question of *what* to compare. Classic positivist approaches treat units of comparison as stable things whose meanings do not vary across time or space and that can thus be compared against one another with ease. Postpositivist comparison, by contrast, must grapple with phenomena that are constituted by cultural meanings and external contextual factors that vary over time. Our contributors to this section of the volume each mark out new objects of analysis that can help address these entanglements, in the process drawing our attention to ways of comparing that bring contextual factors to the center.

In her contribution, Natalie Aviles (chapter 5) considers what it would mean to adopt an ontological view of social life that centers processes rather than entities. Aviles considers shortcomings in dominant theories of social process and argues that they may be remedied by incorporating insights from pragmatism. One consequence of this, she argues, is that historical sociologists interested in social change should prioritize identifying and *comparing problem-solving sequences* that can better capture the looping nature of social life. Comparing problem-solving sequences allows scholars to analyze how actors' practices are structured in relation to situational contexts whose meanings change alongside them. Because those sequences depend on the meanings actors attach to situations and objects, she argues, sequential comparison transforms contextual variations into an asset for the identification of the meso-level processes and mechanisms that produce change.

For her part, Laura Ford (chapter 6) argues that two new senses of comparison need to be taken seriously by historical sociologists. First, extending the work of Margaret Somers (1998), Ford argues that narrative methods reveal new and different modes of causality as compared to narrower positivist methods (like Millian comparison). Second, focusing on *formal* causation (as opposed to the *efficient* causation more familiar to positivists), Ford next explores the application of narrative methods to the sociology of law and demonstrates a set of principles to govern narrative analysis, especially the ongoing *comparison among narratives* and their alignment with relevant aspects of what is being described.

Finally, in his contribution, Nicholas Hoover Wilson (chapter 7) suggests a new path forward for comparing morally weighted phenomena. Focusing on the difficulties analysts face in comparing "corruption," Wilson observes that although "corruption" in general supplies moral energy and potential to social struggles, its meanings and effects cannot be understood apart from how it is incorporated into other mechanisms to produce empirical regularities. To overcome this difficulty, Wilson introduces Nancy Cartwright's (1999) concept of a "nomological machine" as an organizing principle for comparison. To compare nomological machines, he argues, is to at once compare the potentialities of its constituent mechanisms (like corruption in general); how those mechanisms' effects change in combination, producing new powers and capabilities; and, finally, how the comparative practices of the analysts themselves are embedded in fields of scholarly production.

How to Compare: Improving Causal Comparison Through Novel Methodological Strategies

Part III examines the question of *how* to compare. Whereas positivist approaches to comparison treat cases as independent and outcomes as determined by decontextualized variables, postpositivist approaches to comparison must grapple with the embeddedness of cases in time, space, and culture. What strategies of case selection and causal tracing best reflect, and best permit us to analyze, the "dappled" and "heterogeneous" nature of the social world (Cartwright 1999; Little 2009)? Several of our contributors to this section examine how causal analysis may require combinations of comparative approaches, or comparison in combination with other analytic techniques, to adequately capture the nature of causality across time and space. They also think about the relationship between time and comparison and discuss how best to develop strategies that account for temporality and emergence of historically constituted phenomena.

George Steinmetz's chapter (chapter 8) examines the interpenetration of social (lay) and sociological comparison, the problems this interpenetration poses for the comparative method, and potential solutions to that problem.

Steinmetz reviews the inescapable centrality of comparison to both social and scholarly life and shows how "spontaneous" social comparisons shaped socio-logical approaches to comparison. Drawing inspiration from the critical realist tradition, Steinmetz argues that comparison is essential to build confidence in the plausibility of inferences and may take one of two forms: a comparison at the level of "real" mechanisms, potentially in dramatically different times and places; or a comparison of empirical regularities, suitable for identifying contingencies as well as regularities. He argues that the use of these two forms of comparison can improve sociologists' ability to reflexively break with the spontaneous comparisons that structure their scholarly visions.

In his contribution, Jonah Stuart Brundage (chapter 9) takes up the question of what it means to undertake a *historical* comparison. Stuart Brundage hones in on the problem of emergence as it relates to contingency: namely, analyzing change over time means potentially dealing with epochs where explanatory mechanisms in one era did not apply and, indeed, might not have existed at all. Through a critical reading of three canonical "classics" from historical sociolo-gy's second wave, he shows how the authors treat "politics" as a distinct causal force without satisfactorily accounting for how politics was embedded and entwined with other social forces at earlier points in history, ultimately yield-ing tautological claims about modernity. The solution, he argues, is to think of historicization as a comparative strategy that involves comparisons not just of classic causal forces but *also* of their conditions of possibility. This approach, he argues, is particularly useful for questions of specification, case selection, and problem definition—and thus has particular relevance for historical studies of the transformations characteristic of modernity.

Simeon Newman, in chapter 10, questions how different comparative strate-gies measure up to the realist goal of empirically adequate explanatory models. Newman evaluates four different comparative strategies—the Millian method, "inference from absence," the negative-case method, and the alternative-factors approach—and finds that the latter two best accord (though imper-fectly) with realist standards for explanation that emphasize empirical accu-racy and adequacy. At the same time, on their own, each method falters when pushed to its logical conclusion. Newman argues that judicious use of negative-case and alternative-factors comparative approaches, and using them together, can yield more empirically sound conclusions that furnish firmer grounds for aggregating accounts of social change.

Yang Zhang's contribution (chapter 11) considers how new approaches to comparison may emerge from new approaches to causal explanation. Arguing that leading models of causation continue to neglect the temporal and sequen-tial aspects of historical change, he argues instead for a sequential theory of causation that emphasizes periodic confluences, simultaneous and nonlinear causality, iteration, and reflexivity. This approach requires treating sequences as the fundamental unit of analysis, and Zhang supplies a typology of "temporally sensitive comparisons" to judge them.

Finally, chapter 12 by Rebecca Emigh, Dylan Riley, and Patricia Ahmad reimagines Mill's methods of comparison by regrounding them in the philosophy of dialectical realism. Against positivist presuppositions that emphasize comparisons across events or things, their dialectical comparative approach instead centers the causal power of relationships and mobilizes comparison alongside narrative methods to evaluate and explain how changes in relationships produce outcomes over time. Comparison, in their approach, is maximally effective when used across cases whose outcomes are present or absent in expected or unexpected ways according to theoretical expectations. In so doing, it provides degrees of support for or against a theory without requiring the identification of a single ultimate causal factor. By extracting the comparative method from a positivist framework, they show how it may be paired with narrative methods such as process tracing or negative-case methodology to fruitfully evaluate theoretical claims.

The volume concludes with an afterword by Philip Gorski, who reflects on the chapters' ambivalent relationship to the project of critical realism, extends that agenda in response to new developments in sociology and beyond, and proposes a tempered meta-theoretical framework for further work to follow.

***

Our main aim in this introduction has been to provide an overview of the vibrant landscape of postpositivist comparison, especially in historical and comparative sociology. But the fissures and tensions our introduction has noted also suggest two major directions for further thought and research.

First, we can continue to probe the structure of the communities of inquiry that loom large in the postpositivist landscape. This would entail investigation into the theoretical paradigms and assumptions that shape the production and evaluation of knowledge, often in ways that have slowed the introduction of important insights from those outside those communities (Go 2016; Hammer 2020; Itzigsohn and Brown 2020). In addition, it would entail a more concrete understanding of which specific communities and which groups of interlocutors shape one's comparative toolkit (see, e.g., Beck 2017; Mayrl and Wilson 2020). Linking these two aspects of the community of inquiry back to the production of knowledge (and ignorance) would be salutary not only for our understanding of how knowledge is produced in comparative research but also in social scientific knowledge more generally.

Second, the recognition that there are a multitude of ways to do "good" comparison and that an orthodox return to positivist principles seems impossible carries enormous risks. To paraphrase Winship and Morgan's pungent phrase, without a standard to adjudicate truth claims by scholars practicing very different modes of comparison, the risk is a kind of "warlordism," wherein factions savagely defend their interpretations against all comers. Addressing this question head on and identifying strategies for overcoming or taming these potential conflicts loom as crucial scholarly tasks in the years to come.

Even given this risk, we believe that our epistemological optimism remains warranted. But continued work needs to be done to establish the concrete conditions of intellectual production that would allow dialogue among scholars from different traditions to flourish and also to work out the most fecund structure for that dialogue to take place.

Notes

1. It is ironic that Mill's argument here is for the *unity* of scientific and nonscientific reasoning, given how strongly subsequent positivists have argued for the privileged position of science relative to common sense.
2. Mill also described two more canons of induction—that of "residues" and of "concomitant variation"—which have been less influential among comparative social scientists.
3. An entire volume could be written about the influence of *States*, and it has been the subject of many critical revisitations (e.g., Skocpol 1994). For our purposes, let it be noted that two influential reflections on the book dispute the core reading that its method is *actually* indebted to Mill (Goodwin 1996; Sewell 1996).
4. Critics pointed out that Mill himself had warned against applying the methods of agreement and difference to the social sciences (Lieberson 2004; see also chapters 8 and 12 in this volume).
5. Notably, Hume himself was a radical empiricist skeptic, so in his view, it was impossible to ever actually observe causality directly. Thus, the constant conjuncture of events was the keystone to his understanding of the growth of scientific knowledge.
6. Of course, such a turn is *not* to renounce the search for a better understanding—even "the truth"—about the social world in the name of an intellectual free-for-all. It is instead to recognize that the source of error correction is less often from methodological prescriptions themselves and more often from dialog among theory, method, and data, and "rigor and imagination" (Abbott 2004, 3) undertaken by as wide and inclusive a community of social scientists as possible (Tavory and Timmermans 2014, chap. 7).
7. There is dispute around the language of "mechanisms," and the extent to which it should be directly tethered to the traditions of American pragmatism or analytic sociology. Throughout this section, we use the term capaciously to include causal processes of scholarly interest.
8. In his most recent work, Mahoney (2021) develops a set-theoretic approach to social scientific inquiry that explicitly rejects an ontology of variables with essential properties in favor of an ontology of sets (categories) understood as conceptual spaces within the mind. Mechanisms in this model are not conceived of as having causal powers, but instead are understood as links in causal chains, where causality is understood in terms of the logic of set theory. As discussed earlier, this formulation departs from some aspects of the classic positivist approach while retaining others; for our purposes here, we only need note that Mahoney's use of the language of mechanisms—despite the

abandonment of variable language—is still epistemological, unlike the more ontological uses of the concept discussed later in the chapter.

9. Mill himself emphasized the distinction between forcing causation and what he called "chemical" causation in *A System of Logic*.

References

Abbott, Andrew. 1988. "Transcending General Linear Reality." *Sociological Theory* 6:169–86.

——. 1991. "History and Sociology: The Lost Synthesis." *Social Science History* 15(2):201.

——. 2004. *Methods of Discovery: Heuristics for the Social Sciences*. New York: Norton.

Abend, Gabriel. 2006. "Styles of Sociological Thought: Sociologies, Epistemologies, and the Mexican and U.S. Quests for Truth." *Sociological Theory* 24(1):1–41.

Abend, Gabriel, Caitlin Petre, and Michael Sauder. 2013. "Styles of Causal Thought: An Empirical Investigation." *American Journal of Sociology* 119(3):602–54.

Adams, Julia, Elisabeth Clemens, and Ann Shola Orloff, eds. 2005. *Remaking Modernity: Politics, History, and Sociology*. Durham, NC: Duke University Press.

Aviles, Natalie B., and Isaac Ariail Reed. 2017. "Ratio via Machina: Three Standards of Mechanistic Explanation in Sociology." *Sociological Methods and Research* 46(4):715–38.

Beck, Colin J. 2017. "The Comparative Method in Practice: Case Selection and the Social Science of Revolution." *Social Science History* 41(3):533–54.

Bertalanffy, Ludwig von. 2003. *General System Theory: Foundations, Development, Applications*. New York: Braziller.

Besbris, Max, and Shamus Khan. 2017. "Less Theory. More Description." *Sociological Theory* 35(2):147–53.

Bollen, Kenneth A., Barbara Entwisle, and Arthur S. Alderson. 1993. "Macrocomparative Research Methods." *Annual Review of Sociology* 19(1):321–51.

Bonilla-Silva, Eduardo, and Tukufu Zuberi. 2008. "Toward a Definition of White Logic and White Methods." In *White Logic, White Methods*, edited by Tukufu Zuberi and Eduardo Bonilla-Silva, 3–26. Lanham, MD: Rowman and Littlefield.

Bonnell, Victoria E. 1980. "The Uses of Theory, Concepts and Comparison in Historical Sociology." *Comparative Studies in Society and History* 22(2):156–73.

Burawoy, Michael. 1998. "The Extended Case Method." *Sociological Theory* 16(1):4–33.

Calhoun, Craig J. 1996. "The Rise and Domestication of Historical Sociology." In *The Historic Turn in the Human Sciences*, edited by Terrence J. McDonald, 305–38. Ann Arbor: University of Michigan Press.

Cartwright, Nancy. 1999. *The Dappled World: A Study of the Boundaries of Science*. New York: Cambridge University Press.

Chakrabarty, Dipesh. 2007. *Provincializing Europe: Postcolonial Thought and Historical Difference*. Revised edition. Princeton, NJ: Princeton University Press.

Collins, Patricia Hill. 1990. *Black Feminist Thought: Knowledge, Consciousness, and the Politics of Empowerment*. New York: Routledge.

Danermark, Berth, Mats Ekström, and Jan Ch. Karlsson. 2019. *Explaining Society: Critical Realism in the Social Sciences*. New York: Routledge.

Decoteau, Claire Laurier. 2017. "The AART of Ethnography: A Critical Realist Explanatory Research Model." *Journal for the Theory of Social Behaviour* 47(1):58–82.

Du Bois, W. E. B. 1903. *The Souls of Black Folk*. New York: Signet Classics.

Elder-Vass, Dave. 2010. *The Causal Power of Social Structures: Emergence, Structure and Agency*. Cambridge: Cambridge University Press.

Elias, Norbert. 2000. *The Civilizing Process: Sociogenetic and Psychogenetic Investigations.* Revised edition. Oxford: Blackwell.

Elster, Jon. 1989. *Nuts and Bolts for the Social Sciences.* New York: Cambridge University Press.

Emirbayer, Mustafa. 1997. "Manifesto for a Relational Sociology." *American Journal of Sociology* 103(2):281–317.

Feyerabend, Paul. 1975. *Against Method: Outline of an Anarchistic Theory of Knowledge.* London: Verso.

Frickel, Scott, and Neil Gross. 2005. "A General Theory of Scientific/Intellectual Movements." *American Sociological Review* 70(2):204–32.

George, Alexander, and Andrew Bennett. 2005. *Case Studies and Theory Development in the Social Sciences.* Cambridge, MA: MIT Press.

Go, Julian. 2016. *Postcolonial Thought and Social Theory.* New York: Oxford University Press.

——. 2020. "Race, Empire, and Epistemic Exclusion: Or the Structures of Sociological Thought." *Sociological Theory* 38(2):79–100.

Goertz, Gary, and James Mahoney. 2012. *A Tale of Two Cultures: Qualitative and Quantitative Research in the Social Sciences.* Princeton, NJ: Princeton University Press.

Goldthorpe, John H. 1991. "The Uses of History in Sociology: Reflections on Some Recent Tendencies." *British Journal of Sociology* 42(2):211–30.

——. 2000. *On Sociology: Numbers, Narratives, and the Integration of Research and Theory.* Oxford: Oxford University Press.

Goodwin, Jeff. 1996. "How to Become a Dominant American Social Scientist: The Case of Theda Skocpol." *Contemporary Sociology* 25(3):293–95.

Gorski, Philip. 2009. "Social 'Mechanisms' and Comparative-Historical Sociology: A Critical Realist Proposal." In *Frontiers of Sociology*, edited by Björn Wittrock and Peter Hedström, 147–94. Leiden, Netherlands: Brill.

——. 2013a. "Beyond the Fact/Value Distinction: Ethical Naturalism and the Social Sciences." *Society* 50:543–53.

——. 2013b. "What Is Critical Realism? And Why Should You Care?" *Contemporary Sociology* 42:658–70.

——. 2017. "From Sinks to Webs: Critical Social Science After the Fact-Value Distinction." *Canadian Review of Sociology/Revue Canadienne de Sociologie* 54(4):423–44.

——. 2018. "After Positivism: Critical Realism and Historical Sociology." *Political Power and Social Theory* 34:23–45.

Greco, John, and Ruth Groff, eds. 2017. *Powers and Capacities in Philosophy: The New Aristotelianism.* New York: Routledge.

Gross, Neil. 2009. "A Pragmatist Theory of Social Mechanisms." *American Sociological Review* 74(3):358–79.

Hacking, Ian. 1981. *Scientific Revolutions.* New York: Oxford University Press.

——. 2004. *Historical Ontology.* Cambridge, MA: Harvard University Press.

Halfpenny, Peter. 1982. *Positivism and Sociology: Explaining Social Life.* Upper Saddle River, NJ: Gregg Revivals.

Hammer, Ricarda. 2020. "Decolonizing the Civil Sphere: The Politics of Difference, Imperial Erasures, and Theorizing from History." *Sociological Theory* 38(2):101–21.

Haraway, Donna. 1988. "Situated Knowledges: The Science Question in Feminism and the Privilege of Partial Perspective." *Feminist Studies* 14(3):575–99.

Harding, Sandra. 1986. *The Science Question in Feminism.* Ithaca, NY: Cornell University Press.

——. 1992. "Rethinking Standpoint Epistemology: What Is 'Strong Objectivity?'" *Centennial Review* 36(3):437–70.

——. 2015. *Objectivity and Diversity: Another Logic of Scientific Research*. Chicago: University of Chicago Press.

Harré, Rom, and Edward H. Madden. 1975. *Causal Powers: A Theory of Natural Necessity*. Lanham, MD: Rowman and Littlefield.

Hartsock, Nancy. 1983. "The Feminist Standpoint: Developing the Ground for a Specifically Feminist Historical Materialism." In *Discovering Reality: Feminist Perspectives on Epistemology, Metaphysics, Methodology, and Philosophy of Science*, edited by Sandra Harding and Merrill Hintikka, 283–310. Dordrecht, Netherlands: Reidel/Kluwer.

Hedström, Peter, and Petri Ylikoski. 2010. "Causal Mechanisms in the Social Sciences." *Annual Review of Sociology* 36(1):49–67.

Hempel, Carl G. 1942. "The Function of General Laws in History." *Journal of Philosophy* 39(2):35–48.

Hirschman, Daniel, and Isaac Ariail Reed. 2014. "Formation Stories and Causality in Sociology." *Sociological Theory* 32(4):259–82.

Hume, David, and L. A. Selby-Bigge. 1896. *A Treatise of Human Nature*. Oxford: Clarendon.

Itzigsohn, José, and Karida L. Brown. 2020. *The Sociology of W. E. B. Du Bois: Racialized Modernity and the Global Color Line*. New York: New York University Press.

Jacobs, Jonathan D. 2017. *Causal Powers*. Oxford: Oxford University Press.

Jay, Martin. 1984. *Marxism and Totality: The Adventures of a Concept from Lukács to Habermas*. Berkeley: University of California Press.

Keane, Webb. 2014. "Affordances and Reflexivity in Ethical Life: An Ethnographic Stance." *Anthropological Theory* 14(1):3–26.

King, Gary, Robert O. Keohane, and Sidney Verba. 1994. *Designing Social Inquiry: Scientific Inference in Qualitative Research*. Princeton, NJ: Princeton University Press.

Kuhn, Thomas S. 1996. *The Structure of Scientific Revolutions*. Chicago: University of Chicago Press.

Latour, Bruno. 1987. *Science in Action: How to Follow Scientists and Engineers Through Society*. Cambridge, MA: Harvard University Press.

Latour, Bruno, and Steve Woolgar. 1979. *Laboratory Life: The Construction of Scientific Facts*. Princeton, NJ: Princeton University Press.

Lear, Jonathan. 1988. *Aristotle: The Desire to Understand*. Cambridge: Cambridge University Press.

Levine, Donald. 1995. *Visions of the Sociological Tradition*. Chicago: University of Chicago Press.

Lieberson, Stanley. 1991. "Small N's and Big Conclusions: An Examination of the Reasoning in Comparative Studies Based on a Small Number of Cases." *Social Forces* 70(2):307–20.

——. 1994. "More on the Uneasy Case for Using Mill-Type Methods in Small-N Comparative Studies." *Social Forces* 72(4):1225–37.

——. 2004. "Comments on the Use and Utility of QCA." *Qualitative Methods* 2(2):13–14.

Little, Daniel. 2009. "The Heterogeneous Social: New Thinking About the Foundations of the Social Sciences." In *Philosophy of the Social Sciences: Philosophical Theory and Scientific Practice*, edited by C. Mantzavinos, 154–78. New York: Cambridge University Press.

——. 2013. "Disaggregating Historical Explanation: The Move to Social Mechanisms in the Philosophy of History." *Social Epistemology Review and Reply Collective* 2(8):1–7.

Mahoney, James. 2000. "Strategies of Causal Inference in Small-N Analysis." *Sociological Methods and Research* 28(4):387–424.

——. 2003. "Strategies of Causal Assessment in Comparative Historical Analysis." In *Comparative Historical Analysis in the Social Sciences*, edited by James Mahoney and Dietrich Rueschemeyer. New York: Cambridge University Press.

——. 2008. "Toward a Unified Theory of Causality." *Comparative Political Studies* 41(4–5): 412–36.

——. 2021. *The Logic of Social Science*. Princeton, NJ: Princeton University Press.

Mann, Michael. 1981. "SOCIO-LOGIC." *Sociology* 15(4):544–50.

Mayrl, Damon, and Nicholas Hoover Wilson. 2020. "What Do Historical Sociologists Do All Day? Analytic Architectures in Historical Sociology." *American Journal of Sociology* 125(5):1345–94.

McKittrick, Katherine. 2020. *Dear Science and Other Stories*. Durham, NC: Duke University Press.

Mill, John Stuart. 1974. *A System of Logic Ratiocinative and Inductive*. Edited by J. M. Robson. Vol. VII. *Collected Works of John Stuart Mill*. Toronto: University of Toronto Press.

Morgan, Stephen L., and Christopher Winship. 2014. *Counterfactuals and Causal Inference: Methods and Principles for Social Research*. 2nd edition. New York: Cambridge University Press.

Pickering, Andrew. 1992. *Science as Practice and Culture*. Chicago: University of Chicago Press.

——. 1995. *The Mangle of Practice*. Chicago: University of Chicago Press.

Pierson, Paul. 2011. *Politics in Time: History, Institutions, and Social Analysis*. Princeton, NJ: Princeton University Press.

Platt, Jennifer. 1996. *A History of Sociological Research Methods in America, 1920–1960*. Cambridge: Cambridge University Press.

Popper, Karl. 2005. *The Logic of Scientific Discovery*. New York: Routledge.

Porpora, Douglas. 2015. *Reconstructing Sociology: The Critical Realist Approach*. New York: Cambridge University Press.

Proctor, Robert. 1991. *Value-Free Science? Purity and Power in Modern Knowledge*. Cambridge, MA: Harvard University Press.

Przeworski, Adam, and Henry Teune. 1970. *The Logic of Comparative Social Inquiry*. New York: Wiley.

Quisumbing King, Katrina, and Alexandre I. R. White. 2021. "Introduction: Toward a Global Historical Sociology of Race and Racism." *Political Power and Social Theory* 38:1–21.

Ragin, Charles C. 1987. *The Comparative Method: Moving Beyond Qualitative and Quantitative Strategies*. Berkeley: University of California Press.

——. 2000. *Fuzzy-Set Social Science*. Chicago: University of Chicago Press.

Ragin, Charles C., and Howard Saul Becker. 1992. *What Is a Case? Exploring the Foundations of Social Inquiry*. Cambridge: Cambridge University Press.

Ragin, Charles, and David Zaret. 1983. "Theory and Method in Comparative Research: Two Strategies." *Social Forces* 61(3):731–54.

Riley, Dylan, Patricia Ahmed, and Rebecca Jean Emigh. 2021. "Getting Real: Heuristics in Sociological Knowledge." *Theory and Society* 50(2):315–56.

Said, Edward. 1973. *Orientalism*. New York: Vintage.

Sanchez-Jankowski, Martin, and Corey Abramson. 2020. "Foundations of the Behavioralist Approach to Comparative Participant Observation." In *Beyond the Case*, edited by Corey Abramson and Neil Gong, 31–56. Oxford: Oxford University Press.

Sayer, Andrew. 1999. *Realism and Social Science*. London: Sage.

Sewell, William H. 1996. "Three Temporalities: Towards and Eventful Sociology." In *The Historic Turn in the Human Sciences*, edited by Terrence J. MacDonald, 245–80. Ann Arbor: University of Michigan Press.

Shapin, Steven. 1994. *A Social History of Truth: Civility and Science in Seventeenth-Century England*. Chicago: University of Chicago Press.

Skocpol, Theda. 1979. *States and Social Revolutions: A Comparative Analysis of France, Russia, and China*. Cambridge: Cambridge University Press.

——. 1994. *Social Revolutions in the Modern World*. Cambridge: Cambridge University Press.

Skocpol, Theda, and Margaret Somers. 1980. "The Uses of Comparative History in Macrosocial Inquiry." *Comparative Studies in Society and History* 22(2):174–97.

Skorupski, John. 1998. "Mill on Language and Logic." In *Cambridge Companion to John Stuart Mill*, 35–56. Cambridge: Cambridge University Press.

Smith, Dorothy. 1974. "Women's Perspective as a Radical Critique of Sociology." *Sociological Inquiry* 44:7–13.

Somers, Margaret R. 1998. "'We're No Angels': Realism, Rational Choice, and Relationality in Social Science." *American Journal of Sociology* 104(3):722–84.

Steinmetz, George. 1998. "Critical Realism and Historical Sociology. A Review Article." *Comparative Studies in Society and History* 40(1):170–86.

——. 2004. "Odious Comparisons: Incommensurability, the Case Study, and 'Small N's' in Sociology." *Sociological Theory* 22(3):371–400.

——. 2005a. "The Epistemological Unconscious of U.S. Sociology and the Transition to Post-Fordism: The Case of Historical Sociology." In *Remaking Modernity*, edited by Julia Adams, Elisabeth S. Clemens, and Ann Shola Orloff, 109–57. Durham, NC: Duke University Press.

——. 2005b. "Scientific Authority and the Transition to Post-Fordism: The Plausibility of Positivism in U.S. Sociology Since 1945." In *The Politics of Method in the Human Sciences*, edited by George Steinmetz, 275–323. Durham, NC: Duke University Press.

——. 2008. "Logics of History as a Framework for an Integrated Social Science." *Social Science History* 32(4):535–53.

——. 2014. "Comparative History and Its Critics." In *A Companion to Global Historical Thought*, edited by Prasenjit Duara, Viren Murthy, and Andrew Sartori, 412–36. New York: Wiley.

Sweet, Paige L. 2018. "The Feminist Question in Realism." *Sociological Theory* 36(3):221–43.

Tavory, Iddo, and Stefan Timmermans. 2014. *Abductive Analysis: Theorizing Qualitative Research*. Chicago: University of Chicago Press.

Tuhiwai Smith, Linda. 1999. *Decolonizing Methodologies: Research and Indigenous Peoples*. London: Zed.

Varela, Charles R., and Rom Harré. 1996. "Conflicting Varieties of Realism: Causal Powers and the Problems of Social Structure." *Journal for the Theory of Social Behaviour* 26(3):313–25.

PART I

WHY COMPARE?

CHAPTER 1

THE QUALITATIVE-QUANTITATIVE DIVIDE IN COMPARATIVE HISTORICAL ANALYSIS

STEFAN BARGHEER

W
hen the American Sociological Association (ASA) created
its Section on Comparative and Historical Sociology in
1983, its intent was not just to stake out a field of inquiry
but also to establish a new research method. In the making since the late 1970s,
it was first called the Section on Comparative Historical Sociology (Abbott
1991, 215–16; Rosich 2005, 154). As the original name indicates, at the time,
scholars assumed that studying history and engaging in comparative analysis
were one and the same thing. At times, the assumption of the complete identity
of comparative analysis with historical inquiry within the social sciences was
further underlined by using a hyphen and defining the new research method
as the "comparative-historical" method (e.g., Mahoney 2004). In recent years,
however, this tie has loosened. Today, it is called the Section on Comparative
and Historical Sociology, and research in this section can be either historical or
comparative but does not necessarily have to be both. (On single-case studies
in historical sociology, see chapter 4 in this volume.)

The loosening of the tie between comparative and historical research, once
epitomized by a hyphen, raises the question of why these two methodological
orientations were initially perceived to be one and the same thing. The connection is everything but inevitable, if viewed across disciplines. Historians, for
instance, who are by profession conducting historical research, do not routinely
engage in comparative research (Baldwin 2004); nor do comparative anthropologists show an intrinsic predilection for historical inquiry (Gingrich 2012).

Why then, one may ask, was historical research in sociology designated to be comparative and why predominantly so in the late 1970s and early 1980s?

The following section provides an answer to this question by looking at the ways that statistical research practices transformed during this period as a result of the introduction of statistical software packages such as SPSS. I argue that the initial methodological debate on comparative historical methods reflects an effort to position the field in relation to regression analysis, by either emulating it or by rejecting it. This methodological debate was built on the assumption of a timeless divide between quantitative and qualitative research. The subsequent section shows that this divide was in reality a mere artifact of the historical moment and lost plausibility in subsequent decades. Statistical analysis has since developed beyond regression analysis and now coincides with many of the methodological considerations raised by comparative historical research-ers. I discuss event sequencing, network analysis, and diversity indexing as three such advances that have diminished the methodological division between comparative historical analysis and statistically informed research.

That 70s Method: Comparative Historical Analysis and the SPSS Revolution

Comparative historical sociology—or comparative historical analysis, as it was subsequently called (Mahoney and Rueschemeyer 2003)—was a reaction to the introduction of SPSS, the Statistical Package for the Social Sciences. According to Barry Wellman (1998), this easily accessible computer software caused a rev-olution in the social sciences. Wellman considers Norman Nie, Dale Bent, and Hadlai Hull's SPSS manual, initially issued in 1970, and revised and enlarged in 1975, to be one of the most influential sociological publications in the last decades of the twentieth century. Although not the only statistical software available at the time, SPSS was the first easy-to-use and reasonably comprehen-sive statistical package available for personal computers (PCs), which entered the market during the same period (Ceruzzi 1998). As Wellman (1998, 71–73) states, "[It] was the SPSS statistical package that in the early 1970s revolution-ized how sociology was done. . . . Such packages have enabled us to do our own computer-based statistical analysis instead of being forced to rely upon high priests of the Great Machine. . . . In those precomputer days, most people could do only limited analyses using counter-sorters and other IBM machines. Now, we do not have to be giants. We can be ordinary people, using statistical pack-ages to play with data and examine hundreds of analytical possibilities."

SPSS tilted the playing field so much toward statistical analysis that other modes of inquiry fell by the wayside. Computer-assisted statistical analysis of survey data became the prevailing orthodoxy in almost all major research universities. Yet the software itself was only the first step in the process. It was followed by the inauguration of the General Social Survey (GSS) in 1972, one of the main sources of data to be analyzed with the new software. The survey was administered by the National Opinion Research Center (NORC), the very institution where Nie and his collaborators had developed their statistical package (Davis and Smith 1991). It was this triumvirate of new technology (PC), new statistical software (SPSS), and a new dataset (GSS), rather than any grand social theory or philosophy of science, that established a new way of studying social life, one that had true momentum and began to dominate the social sciences at large. (On the introduction of 2 × 2 tables as comparative tools during the precomputer days referred to by Wellman, see Bargheer 2021.)

Yet SPSS and the statistical models that it assembled were anything but neutral tools. As Andrew Abbott (1988) has pointed out, the software incorporated primarily statistical tools based on the general linear model, with regression analysis as the most influential example. The general linear model makes an outcome variable dependent on a set of antecedent variables, up to an error term. In its most basic form, this model can be written as $Y = Xb + U$. To use such a model to represent social reality, one must map the processes of social life onto the algebra of linear transformations. The use of the model accordingly facilitates a particular way of seeing the social world.

The dominance of the general linear model has led many sociologists to construe the social world in terms of what Abbott calls "general linear reality," a set of assumptions about social life and about how the social world works, which contradicts major previous traditions within sociology. The model assumes (1) a social world that consists of fixed entities with variable attributes, (2) the existence of a monotonic causal flow in the sense that a cause is equally relevant at all times, (3) an univocal meaning of each effect so that an attribute has only one effect on another attribute, (4) an absence of sequence effects so that the temporal order in which attributes change does not influence the outcome, and (5) an independence of context in terms of both space and time.

The rise of this way of thinking about the social world was not restricted to scholars who used SPSS. Due to the newfound dominant position of regression analysis within the discipline, it was not merely that SPSS shifted the balance of forces toward using this particular research tool, but also that it had a spillover effect that influenced how scholars working in other fields began to think about the social world.

Defining Comparative Historical Analysis

The rise of regression analysis as the dominant research method put other fields of research on the defensive. Qualitative researchers, including those who worked with historical data, were increasingly faced with the stigma of not being sufficiently scientific. There were two main lines of reaction to this encroaching marginalization, which can be traced through the emerging genre of methods textbooks on comparative historical analysis. One group of researchers simply rejected the claim that their work was methodologically different in any significant way. Neil Smelser (1976), for instance, argued that all scientific research is comparative and that the use of macro-historical data is accordingly as scientific as the use of survey data. The only difference was to be found in the fact that what he called the method of "systematic comparative illustration" must be used whenever the number of relevant cases is small. According to this line of argument, there is one unified logic of scientific reasoning that can be applied to different sources of data. When the case number is large, quantitative tools can be applied; when the case number is small, a qualitative version of this logic has to be applied. Qualitative comparative analysis was thus simply a form of regression analysis for small Ns, that is, small case numbers. Because macro-historical researchers were usually interested in rare cases such as processes of state formation, the emergence of working-class movements, and social revolutions, the statistical tools made available by SPSS could not be applied.

This argument was eventually made famous by the introductory chapter in Theda Skocpol's *States and Social Revolutions* (1979) and by subsequent methodological elaborations by the same author and a group of coauthors and collaborators. According to Skocpol and Somers, the "logic involved in the use of comparative history for Macro-causal analysis resembles that of statistical analysis, which manipulates groups of cases to control sources of variation in order to make causal inferences when quantitative data are available about a large number of cases" (1980, 182). Comparing between cases, then, was the equivalent of using SPSS to control variables in a regression analysis based on survey data. According to this line of argument, the use of qualitative historical data becomes scientifically rigorous through the comparison of cases. While *States and Social Revolutions* served as a role model that showed how such research was to be carried out, it was Skocpol's (1984) contribution to a conference volume titled *Vision and Method in Historical Sociology* that gave further credibility to comparative historical analysis as a research method.

These publications resulted in a heated debate about the methodological status of comparative historical analysis. Critics pointed out that the small case numbers employed in historical research and the lack of independence between cases are among the main reasons why comparative historical research could not approximate the controlled experiment in a laboratory setting, which researchers using SPSS tried to emulate (Burawoy 1989). For Skocpol, there was only one form of scientific reasoning that could be applied across methods, while her critics pointed out that the strength of comparative historical analysis was to be found precisely in the fact that it corrected for some of the shortcomings of regression analysis.

Charles Ragin's *The Comparative Method* (1987), together with previous methodological considerations along the same lines (Ragin and Zaret 1983), provided one of the most influential examples for this point of view. Distinguishing between case-oriented analysis and variable-oriented analysis, Ragin argued that "the comparative method is not a bastard cousin of the statistical method. It is qualitatively different from the statistical method, and it is uniquely suited to the kinds of questions that many comparativists ask. . . . The focus is on comparing cases, and cases are examined as wholes—as combinations of characteristics" (1987, 16). Central to Ragin's methodological distinction was the identification of case-oriented research with qualitative data and variable-oriented research with quantitative data.

According to Ragin, qualitative comparative analysis was not a method of last resort to be applied whenever the case number was too small to apply SPSS; instead, it was a method ideally suited to study larger social constellations. Statistical tools such as those offered by SPSS were simply not suited for this kind of analysis. As Ragin states, "The most distinctive aspect of comparative social science is the wide gulf between qualitative and quantitative work. . . . More fundamentally to the gulf, however, is the fact that several other divisions coincide with the qualitative/quantitative split in comparative science and reinforce it. Qualitative researchers tend to look at cases as wholes, and they compare whole cases with each other. . . . Because the comparative method has this character, statistical criteria are less important to this approach" (1987, 2–3, 15).

Ragin thus turned Smelser's (and subsequently Skocpol's) argument on its head. Rather than arguing that the availability of only a small number of cases is the reason that the comparative method is employed, he argued that the selection of only a small number of cases is the effect of the use of a holistic comparative method that focuses on large social constellations. (On more recent versions of Ragin's and Skocpol's arguments, see chapter 10 in this volume.)

Comparative Historical Analysis and the Qualitative-Quantitative Divide

The differences between Ragin's and Skocpol's arguments are as crucial as the assumptions that they have in common. While they differed in their assessment of whether the comparative method represents an emulation of regression analysis or an alternative to it, both agree that the dividing line between comparative historical research and regression analysis is identical to the contrast between qualitative and quantitative research methods more broadly.

This chapter shows that this association of, on the one hand, the comparative method with qualitative analysis and, on the other, quantitative research with regression analysis is a result of the peculiarities of the historical moment and not of any intrinsic or necessary link between them. The way the lines of division between methods were drawn in the 1970s and 1980s is the consequence of the rise to dominance of the general linear model by means of computer programs such as SPSS. Skocpol's and Ragin's arguments do not tell us anything universally valid about research methods; they simply show us how scholars at that time positioned themselves vis-à-vis the new center of their discipline.

Nothing indicates the conjectural character of this methodological debate better than the fact that methods textbooks before the rise of SPSS did not draw boundaries between research methods in the same way. As Jennifer Platt (1996) has shown, the categories that are used to describe different research methods at the present are not identical with those used in the 1920s and 1930s, when the first methods textbooks in sociology were published, although some of the empirical studies then carried out have later been subsumed under contemporary methodological labels. She shows, for instance, that the notion of participant observation as a distinct method did not exist at the time. The same holds true for comparative historical analysis.

The most telling example is the survey method, which, by the 1970s, had become identified with regression analysis. Yet half a century earlier, the label was still used in a way that cuts across contemporary methodological categories. The term *social survey* initially addressed every form of data collection that was carried out in a systematic manner, regardless of the source of data that was used (Bulmer, Bales, and Sklar 1991). For instance, Robert Lynd and Helen Lynd's *Middletown* (1929), the most famous example of the social survey tradition, employed and distinguished between five sources of data: (1) participation in local life; (2) existing documentary material such as census data, court files, and school records, together with personal diaries and local histories; (3) the authors' own compilation of statistical data based on organizational records; (4) interviews ranging from casual encounters to carefully planned conversations; and finally, (5) questionnaires (505–10). Only with the subsequent introduction of nationwide opinion and attitude polling and the development of representative sampling techniques in the mid-1930s did the social survey attain the meaning that it has today, epitomized by the GSS, and associated with SPSS analysis (Converse 1987; Didier 2020). The name *social survey* stands today for the methodologically controlled collection of quantitative data and is accordingly juxtaposed with qualitative research.

Until the 1930s, however, one of the dominant methodological lines of demarcation was the distinction between experimental research (e.g., research based on data produced by the active intervention into social life) and observational research (e.g., research based on data produced by the observation of social life without active intervention), not the line between qualitative and quantitative research. The scientific ideal of the vast majority of sociologists in the 1920s and 1930s was the laboratory experiment, yet it was recognized that social life did not always allow for the controlled intervention that made the analogy meaningful (e.g., Ellwood 1933a, 1933b; on the use of the laboratory metaphor in sociology, see Owens 2014). Where intervention was impossible, observational data had to be used, which was by definition the case for the study of historical processes. Sources of observational historical data were both qualitative and quantitative.

It was only in the 1930s, when sociologists began to discuss regression analysis in their research methods textbooks, that the champions of this statistical tool likened its use to the controlled laboratory experiment, albeit relying on observational data. The initial response to this argument was overwhelmingly negative, as Stuart Chapin, one of the pioneers of the use of regression analysis in sociology, had to concede (Chapin 1947; Chapin 1955; Chapin and Queen 1937).

The critique of the analogy formulated by Pitirim Sorokin (1943) is apt to remind comparative historical sociologists of debates in their field that took place several decades later: "Virtually all so-called 'experimental' studies in the social sciences are pseudoexperimental: they hardly ever exhibit the 'constancy of all other conditions'; they can seldom vary their variable as it needs to be varied; their 'constancy' actually amounts merely to keeping all the variables constant on paper; their 'control groups' are not control groups in the real inductive sense. In short, I know of scarcely any really inductive and experimental study in the social sciences" (47).

Ernest Greenwood (1945) presented the foregoing argument in a somewhat less agitated way in a textbook on experimental research methods, where he referred to such paper experiments as ex post designs, and considered them to be insufficient applications of the inductive method. The main methodological debate at that time, then, was not one of statistics versus qualitative case studies, but rather one of controlled experiment versus observation. By the 1970s, however, this once-crucial distinction between experimental and observational methods was entirely forgotten. The claim of scholars using regression analysis to meet the standards of the experimental method was now taken at face value. It was at this point in time that the methodological debates on comparative historical analysis described earlier set in.

In the next section, I will focus on advances in quantitative research methods used in historical analysis over the past four decades that have made this association questionable. My analysis shows that the dividing lines drawn in the late 1970s and early 1980s no longer represent the current state of the discipline. I argue that quantitative methods have qualitative doubles and vice versa. The quantitative models that are in use in the social sciences today have expanded beyond general linear models. Justifications for comparative historical analysis as a research method, however, are at times articulated as though regression analysis is still the only method employed by quantitative researchers.

Transcending the Qualitative-Quantitative Divide

Abbott's critique of regression analysis already pointed to alternative approaches in quantitative analysis that transcend the assumptions of general linear models. In this section, I look at three such developments in quantitative analysis that depart from the assumptions of this model. The analysis shows that the dividing line between general linear models and models that transcend these assumptions is not identical to the distinction between qualitative and quantitative research methods. There are both qualitative and quantitative versions of ways of thinking that transcend the general linear model. I look at event sequencing, network analysis, and diversity indexing as three crucial departures from the model.

Event Sequencing

The study of event sequences transcends assumptions of linear time. In general linear models, time is conceptualized as a homogenous entity. These models employ what William Sewell (2005, 95) calls "experimental time," a form of time in which historical temporality is viewed as an ahistorical congealed block, which is then sliced into interchangeable units suitable for causal analysis. This is the approach employed by Skocpol. An alternative model of "eventful time" proposed by Sewell, by contrast, looks at social processes as unfolding over time.

Special attention is paid to those moments in time that transform social institutions and thus change the direction of social processes. Events, as identified by Sewell, are those sequences of time in which a given structure is transformed. As such, they are different from mere happenings—that is, temporal episodes that have no transformative effects. The significance of studying history from this perspective is to be found in the fact that unique constellations of factors can bring structural transformations about that have long-term effects, although these constellations are themselves only short-lived. (On an alternative way to take causal sequences into account in historical analysis, see chapter 11 in this volume.)

Abbott (1997) used the term *turning point* to describe such changes in the direction of a social process. Studying typical or general constellations of variables, as general linear models do, misses the importance of these unique and historically contingent constellations, which produce turning points. What distinguishes eventful temporality from the "one damn thing after another" account of history is that time is not assumed to be a simple succession of unique events each of which could be described as a turning point. Past events can instead constrain future developments, a phenomenon that is known as path dependency (Aminzade 1992; Mahoney 2000).

Although sociologists commonly use the term *event* to account for such moments in time that produce turning points, political scientists more often choose the term *critical juncture* (Berins Collier and Collier 1991). An early influential use of the idea can be found in Seymour Lipset and Stein Rokkan's work titled *Party Systems and Voter Alignments* (1967), which traces the origins of Western European party systems to three "crucial junctures," which are located much earlier in the history of each nation and shaped mass politics in the region for decades to come (37–38).

The role played by human agency in bringing about such events or critical junctures has received a substantial amount of attention. Giovanni Capoccia, for instance, has argued that critical junctures are best perceived as relatively short periods of time during which there is a substantially heightened probability that agents' choices will affect the outcome of interest (Capoccia 2015; Capoccia and Kelemen 2007). Elisabeth Clemens's (2015) study of economic crises sheds additional light on this topic. Pointing out that those sequences of time that we identify subsequently as events have a temporal duration, she suggests that we take into account that actors respond differently to critical situations. The argument has the benefit of taking into account that actors learn from past experience; that is, one of the reasons why history does not simply repeat itself, but is marked by turning points, is that actors react differently to similar situations, based on past experiences.

While this recent debate gives us a more nuanced picture of how to conceptualize and study events than some of the earlier evocations of the concept, the major insight has remained the same. Big structures and enduring processes can be produced by unique conjunctures of the situation. Methodological tools such as regression analysis, which can only study general regularities, are accordingly not well suited to capturing the causal forces that bring these structures and processes about.

Scholars who highlight the importance of turning points use different methodological tools to study temporality. Historical narratives, for instance, as used by historians to study historical processes, have been introduced to the social sciences as "process tracing" (Bennett and George 2001; Büthe 2002; George and Bennett 2005).

Event-structure analysis, by contrast, provides a more formal analytical procedure that is designed to analyze and interpret text, in particular the temporal sequences that constitute the narrative of an event. It was introduced by David

Heise (Corsaro and Heise 1990; Heise 1989), and further developed by Larry Griffin (1993, 2007). Its basic purpose is to aid the analyst in "unpacking" an event, that is, in breaking it into its constituent parts, and analytically reconstituting it as a causal interpretation of what happened, and why it happened as it did. Unlike most other formal analytical techniques, event-structure analysis is completely nonnumeric and nonstatistical.

Abbott, by contrast, has advanced a quantitative tool to study eventful temporality. Following considerations on the importance of time and narrative (Abbott 1990), he and Alexandra Hrycak (Abbott and Hrycak 1990) put some of these ideas to work by adapting optimal matching analysis—a statistical procedure designed to analyze sequence data—to social inquiry. The crucial insight here is that studying social processes either with models of experimental time or eventful time does not fall in line with the distinction between qualitative and quantitative research methods.

The general linear model epitomized by regression analysis has also been called into question from yet another direction. The methodological tools advanced by Abbott and Griffin analyze relations between events; that is, sequences of events are matched in order to discern typical patterns. In recent years, scholars have, in addition, looked at power law distributions as models to understand the unfolding of social processes. Here the focus is on the size of events in order to make inferences about the underlying generative process. Events such as strikes, warfare, and revolutions, that is, the kinds of empirical phenomena that are the bread-and-butter business of historical analysis, display size distributions that are not well captured by either linear or log-linear equations. Instead, they resemble power law distributions known from the study of wildfires, avalanches, and epidemics (Biggs 2005; Braha 2012; Roberts and Turcotte 1998). A power law entails a skewed distribution, with many more small events than large ones. The steeper the slope, the more pronounced is the skew, that is, the greater the preponderance of small events relative to large ones. This makes it incorrect to apply statistics that are based on measures of variance and standard variation, such as regression analysis.

The same caveat applies to the causal interpretation of this distribution, as Lars-Erik Cederman (2003) has pointed out. The causal model of regression analysis is frequently captured by the analogy of a table full of billiard balls that are hitting each other. Power law distributions, by contrast, are better captured by the causal analogy of sand slowly trickling onto a pile, which from time to time produces avalanches. In this analogy, a steady, linear input generates tensions inside a system, which in turn lead to nonlinear and delayed output, ranging from small events to huge ones. Cederman adopts a model of self-organized criticality to provide a causal mechanism for these avalanche-like events described by power law distributions. Self-organized criticality is an umbrella term that connotes slowly-driven threshold systems that exhibit a series of meta-stable equilibria interrupted by disturbances whose scales are described by power law distributions (Zhukov, Kanishchev, and Lyamin 2016).

Biggs applied this insight to historical data on the outbreaks of class conflict (Biggs 2003; Biggs 2005). For strikes and strike waves, he finds that the size distribution follows a power law that spans two or three orders of magnitude. When analyzed quantitatively, exogenous variables are unable to predict the magnitude of such waves. Instead, the threshold model of collective action advanced by Mark Granovetter (Granovetter 1978; Granovetter and Soong 1983) illustrates how a slight shift in individual proclivities can lead to a large jump in participation. In this model, the event is the number of individuals who shift from nonparticipation to participation when the distribution of thresholds is perturbed.

The classic application of power law distributions to historical data was provided by Lewis Richardson's (1948) analysis of warfare events from 1820 to 1945, and has been confirmed subsequently (Bohorquez et al. 2009; Clauset, Young, and Gleditsch 2007; Johnson et al. 2011). A number of social scientists had made similar observations previously, albeit without using statistical tools. Biggs shows that epidemics and wildfires were frequently evoked analogies used to describe nineteenth-century mass events associated with working-class politics. When American workers organized and struck en masse in 1886, Friedrich Engels, for instance, described how the movement "spread with the rapidity of a prairie fire" (Biggs 2005, 1690). Although such analogies could be found well before statistical tools were employed, statistical analysis nevertheless has advantages. Distributions that describe power laws often go against our intuition because they involve, by definition, nonlinear discrepancies in scale.

This insight also applies to our understanding of events and critical junctures. Comparative historical researchers frequently study social processes in the *longue durée*, yet what qualifies as a sufficiently long time scale crucially depends on whether one is dealing with a linear process or one that is better described by a power law distribution. Aaron Clauset (2018), for instance, has shown that the common assumption that World War II was followed by an unusually long period of peace crucially depends on linear thinking. If warfare takes place as series of events that describe a power law, another 100 to 140 years would be needed to speak statistically of an unusually long period of peace. Whether scholars should try to explain the seventy years of peace since the war as a continuation of a normal pattern or as a change in direction, and thus as an event or critical juncture in the sense described earlier, crucially depends on whether the data are interpreted in a linear or nonlinear way.

Biggs (2018) has pointed out that this insight also has implications for data collection: from a power law perspective, it is as important to have exact data on the size of big events as to have exact data on the frequency of small events. Counting the number of all protest events over a certain period, without having equally reliable data on the size of these events, will not allow the researcher to detect differences in scale that describe power law distributions. The tendency of comparative historical analysis to translate continuous variables into dichotomous variables (e.g., in distinguishing between high or low unemployment rates, early or late industrialization, or weak or strong states) can make it more difficult, if not entirely impossible, to observe relevant scale discrepancies.

Network Analysis

Power law distributions do not only contradict the general linear model on a descriptive level but also point to the existence of causal mechanisms that go against its core assumptions. The strike waves analyzed by Biggs, for instance, are driven by a diffusion process. General linear models, however, are built on the assumption that there is no interaction effect between variables (i.e., the assumption that variables are independent).

Diffusion processes can also be found to be at work in the social revolutions described by Skocpol, with the underlying causal mechanism ranging from demonstration effects (Beissinger 2002, 2007) to imposition from the outside (Halliday 1999; Katz 1997). Although Skocpol did not ignore interstate competition in the form of warfare in her account of social revolutions, she did not pay attention to diffusion processes. One of the criticisms of her theory is her failure to take into account that prior revolutions provide examples or historical lessons (whether positive or negative) for subsequent revolutions. The leading actors behind the Russian revolution, for instance, drew central lessons from previous failed socialist revolutions (Burawoy 1989).

This insight extends beyond revolutions. Processes of transition toward democracy have been shown to follow a model of diffusion that is marked by spatial association, where states' geographical proximity accounts for the spread of democracy (O'Loughlin et al. 1998; Starr 1991). Building on the growing literature on this topic, Barbara Wejnert (2005) has systematically compared endogenous and exogenous factors that have influenced democratization across the globe over the past two hundred years and came to the conclusion that, when assessed alone, endogenous development indicators (i.e., socioeconomic development factors) are robust predictors of democracy, but that their predictive power fades with the inclusion of exogenous diffusion variables (i.e., spatial factors, networks, and media communication).

The study of events as turning points discussed in the previous section is one way to take the importance of diffusion into account. If actors learn from experience, then the temporal order of events matters, and events cannot be modeled as independent cases. Yet in order to say something more specific about how, when, and why such effects take place, one has to study the actual structure of relations between cases, which is the raison d'être of network analysis.

This approach represents one of the alternatives to general linear models that Abbott (1988) already highlighted.

As Roger Gould (1991, 1995) has pointed out, network analysis is based on assumptions about the empirical world that are fundamentally different than those of the variable-based approach of regression analysis. The notion of variables as self-contained entities with attributes that inform models of general linear reality is replaced by the assumption that relations come first and entities or variables second. Regression analysis is accordingly not the tool of choice for network analysis, although there are studies that enter data on the number of network ties as variables into regression models. A statistical tool genuinely designed for the assumptions underlying network analysis is blockmodeling, which identifies entities that have similar patterns of ties to other entities in a network. Blockmodeling thus looks for similarities or structural equivalence, which allows for the representation of a block as a single entity. It is thus a data reduction tool, just as is the mean, the median, or the variance used in regression analysis.

Network analysis has been applied to historical data and contributes innovative insights to longstanding debates. Using blockmodel analysis, Peter Bearman (1993), for instance, shows that patronage ties, rather than religious identities, account for the outbreak of the English Civil War in the seventeenth century; John Padgett and Christopher Ansell (1993) account for the birth of the state in renaissance Italy through the unique position of the Medici as brokers in marriage and business networks, rather than through a conflict between group interests; and Gould (1991, 1995) shows that neighborhood ties, rather than class interest, account for the uprising of the Paris commune in 1871.

There are, of course, also qualitative approaches that parallel network analysis in focusing on the structure of relations between entities, rather than on the individual attributes of these entities. World systems theory and its predecessor, dependency theory, are the most influential examples (Hopkins and Wallerstein 1981; Wallerstein 1974). These approaches depart from the assumption of modernization theory, which treats nation-states as variable-like self-contained entities that exist prior to the relations between them. Instead, world systems theory gives priority to the relationships between countries and their position either at the center, periphery, or semi-periphery of this system, rather than to any attributes of individual countries. An attempt to determine the structural position of countries in the core, semi-periphery, or periphery of the world system by using network analysis has been advanced by David Snyder and Edward Kick (1979). Using blockmodeling, they show that the effects of structural position on the economic growth of nations from 1955 to 1970 are highly consistent with world systems theory.

Yet as Julian Go and George Lawson (2017) have pointed out, world systems theory has a tendency to slip back into a variable-like analysis, because it treats the world system as a single entity with a fixed set of attributes. As such, it has more in common with the theory of social systems that informed modernization theory than it acknowledges. In contrast to this systems approach, Go and Lawson advance a relational approach to historical sociology, called global historical sociology, which takes various constellations of international ties and transnational institutions into account. Network analysis is among the tools that they associate with this "methodological relationalism" (Go and Lawson 2017, 26).

The qualitative studies assembled by Go and Lawson make innovative contributions to some of the defining empirical cases of comparative historical analysis. The work of John Hobson (2004, 2017), for instance, challenges the ethnocentric bias of mainstream accounts of the development of capitalism in the West, which assume that Europeans have pioneered their own development and that the East has been a passive bystander. In describing the rise of what he calls the "Oriental West," Hobson argues that Europe first assimilated many Eastern inventions and then appropriated Eastern resources through imperialism. This analysis echoes the work of historians who, in more recent years, have made efforts to develop global histories of the development of the West to counter Eurocentric biases (Frank 1998; Goody 1996; Pomeranz 2000). Not the comparison of states as independent variables but, instead, a study of the constitutive relationships between them stands in the foreground of these works.

Although network analysis has many points in common with the critiques of general linear models described in the previous section, there are also differences. The model of eventful temporality advanced by Sewell has been challenged from a network perspective (Erikson 2018). While Sewell has treated events as conceptually different from social structures (hence the identification of events as brief but significant moments that produce large-scale and lasting structural transformations), network analysis can be used to conceptualize events as part of a network structure. Martin (2018) argues that a network structure of relations is not only a cross-sectional but also a longitudinal phenomenon that can contain transformative dynamics. The notion that structures are "stable" and that there must be some other explanatory approach when things "happen," such as "events," flies in the face of the core insights of a structural approach. Many things that strike us as events that take place in network structures, such as the formation or dissolution of relations, are best understood as parts of these very structures.

Diversity Measures

Network analysis focuses on the connections or ties within a population. When it comes to causal explanation, the ties between these entities, rather than the entities themselves, are what matter. As such, network analysis differs from scholarship that has focused on diversity as an explanatory factor. Here, it is the range of variation between individual entities, rather than their ties, that is of prime interest.

A stronghold of research on diversity is the field of ecology. Biologists have developed a number of different measures or indices to assess the composition of ecosystems. A diversity index is a quantitative measure that reflects how many different species there are in a community and simultaneously takes into account how evenly the basic entities (i.e., individuals) are distributed among those species. One of the most prominent of these measures is the Simpson index, named after its creator, the statistician Edward H. Simpson (1949). The measure equals the probability that two individuals taken at random from the dataset of interest represent the same type. It was later applied to language diversity and is known in linguistics as the Greenberg index (Greenberg 1956). A revised version of this index was introduced to the social sciences by Stanley Lieberson (1964, 1969). The index allows for measuring diversity in categorical data for which measures of dispersion do not apply (Agresti and Agresti 1978; Teachman 1980).

One of the most prominent fields of application of Lieberson's index is the study of the relation between religious pluralism and religious participation. The classic argument on the relation between the two can be found in the work of Peter Berger and Thomas Luckmann (Berger 1967; Berger and Luckmann 1966), who argued that religious pluralism (i.e., exposure to different belief systems) reduces the plausibility of religion as an objective reality, and in consequence leads to a decline in religious activity.

Kevin Christiano (1987) was the first to use Lieberson's index to study this argument. The index was subsequently used by Roger Finke and Rodney Stark (1988), who argue in opposition to Berger that "religious practice is strongly and positively associated with pluralism" (762). They hold that more diversity of religious organizations implies that the menu of religious services available in a heterogeneous community better matches the tastes of potential adherents.

Finke and Stark's contribution has turned into the central point of reference in the debate on religious pluralism. To test their hypothesis, Mark Chaves and Philip Gorski (2001) conducted a meta-analysis of twenty-six studies that reports 193 correlations. They concluded that a positive relationship between religious pluralism and religious participation can be found in only a limited number of contexts (Chaves and Gorski 2001, 264).

The study of diversity is not limited to the topic of religion. In his own work, Lieberson (1980) looked at the field of race relations in the United States since the late nineteenth century and argued that antagonism and dispositions in multiethnic or multiracial settings change in accordance with the diversity of the population at large. More specifically, the ambitions for personal achievement of white immigrants to America in the late nineteenth and early twentieth centuries were assisted by the arrival of southern Blacks in northern cities. In an environment that was newly diversified from the standpoint of race, the foreign-born no longer occupied the lowest rank in an imaginary queue symbolizing the relative desirability of different social groups. Because the European immigrants were at least the same race as white Americans, negative dispositions toward them were muffled and modified; that is, the presence of Blacks made it harder to discriminate against the new Europeans because the alternative was viewed even less favorably (Lieberson 1980, 380–81).

In line with this empirical finding, yet initially without considering diversity as an independent explanatory factor, racism has been used to account for the peculiarities of the welfare state in the United States. Robert Lieberman (1988), for instance, has shown that unwillingness to spend tax money for the benefit of Black Americans was among the main reasons why welfare state programs faltered or failed to come into being in the first place. The literature on this topic has grown substantially over time. By 2000, Jeff Manza could speak of an explosion of research in this field. It should be noted, however, that these studies are, with the exception of the initial contribution by Lieberson, first and foremost studies of racism, not studies of racial diversity.

Comparative research on welfare state regimes, by contrast, has put the diversity aspect into the foreground. Alberto Alesina, Edward Glaeser, and Bruce Sacerdote (2001, 48), for instance, use a fractionalization measure that includes racial, ethnic, and linguistic diversity. The measure was developed by William Easterly and Ross Levine (1997) to test whether racial diversity affects opinions on welfare state provisions across countries. Similar to the original Simpson index, their measure is computed as the probability of randomly drawing out of the country's population two individuals who do not belong to the same group. The analysis confirms that in the case of the United States, racial diversity increases the unwillingness to pay for welfare state provisions. In European countries, it is predominantly ethnic diversity that makes a difference.

These findings resonate with previous research on the welfare state in Europe. The fact that the inauguration or expansion of welfare state programs finds a limit when an attempt is made to extend them beyond the confines of the ethnically semi-homogenous nation-state of the postwar era is shown by the inability of welfare state provisions in the European Union to move beyond mere regulative provisions and to also include redistributive measures (Leibfried and Pierson 1995). The social solidarity necessary for the advance of redistributive welfare state provisions was historically contingent on the emergence of the ethnically homogenous nation-state and, as some scholars fear, also finds its limits at the borders of these states (Offe 2000, 2003).

While these studies have been used to reassess accounts of American exceptionalism, diversity has also been employed to study the phenomenon of European exceptionalism, that is, the question of why Enlightenment science, industrial capitalism, and parliamentary democracy developed on the European continent rather than elsewhere in the world. Rather than attributing the difference to a shared European cultural heritage, either in the form of Greek democracy, Roman law, or Christian religion, scholars have paid attention to the political fragmentation of Europe as a geographic area. Eric Jones's now-classic book *The European Miracle* (1981) is a central point of reference in this debate. He argues that one of the central explanatory factors in the rise of Europe was the small size of the continent and the absence of a central power. European states were constantly surrounded by competitors. If the government of one was lax, it impaired its own prestige and military security. Competition between states was thus a major driver of the development.

Joel Moykr (2017), among others, has taken up the argument and used it to account for the rise of technologically driven economic progress in Europe. The fact that the continent was politically fragmented made it impossible for local rulers to fully eradicate dissenting opinions and free scientific inquiry. A person persecuted in one place could find shelter in another. It was thus Europe's political fragmentation, rather than its cultural unity, that facilitated some of its most cherished features. The argument that political fragmentation accounts for Europe's uniqueness has also been applied to the phenomena of international trade (Gelderblom 2005), state building (Hont 2005), and representative government (Dincecco and Wang 2018; Stasavage 2016).

The proponents of a global historical sociology discussed in the previous section may find wanting such accounts of European development that ignore the interactions between Europe and the rest of the world. In its initial formulation by Jones, the argument did indeed display the same degree of Eurocentrism as the work of scholars who highlight the importance of cultural factors to account for the peculiarities of Europe's history. There have, however, been efforts to combine these two perspectives. Alexander Anievas and Kerem Nişancıoğlu (2007), for instance, reintroduce external conditions to show that Britain's colonization of India was a critical conjunctural factor that, together with geographic fragmentation, explains Europe's subsequent development.

Whether combined with a postcolonial perspective or not, it should be noted that these studies of political diversity pose an equally great challenge to the Skocpolian design of comparative historical analysis as the approaches described in the preceding sections. Comparativists frequently choose a small number of nation-states as their units of analysis. The studies of Jones and others, however, point to the fact that this research design omits from analysis the very factor that is causally most relevant, that is, the overall diversity of the entire population.

It is in fact the research design of 1970s-style comparative historical analysis, and not the available number of cases, that accounts for this practice of case

selection. The so-called small N problem is in many cases a house-made problem. In his influential study of state formation in Europe, for instance, Thomas
Ertman (1997) estimated that in addition to a comparatively small number of
territorial states, there were as many as fifteen hundred autonomous territories
and two hundred midget states in eighteenth-century Europe, together with a
smaller number of city republics and city-states. Yet following the Skocpolian
version of the comparative historical method, only about thirty territorial states
entered his analysis. Outside of the strictures of this method, however, there
is no reason why scholars who want to study macro-historical configurations
should not be able to take diversity into account.

Where to Go from Here?

When comparative historical sociology was established as an independent section of the ASA, it was positioned in relation to the then-emerging orthodoxy
of regression analysis powered by SPSS. Methodological debates centered on
the question of whether historical researchers should emulate the logic of this
specific form of statistical analysis or provide an alternative to it. Both sides of
the debate agreed that it was the comparison between cases that made historical analysis scientific. Whether emulating regression analysis (e.g., Skocpol) or
rejecting it as a role model (e.g., Ragin), methodological debates in this field
have converged on the assumption that comparative historical analysis is a
qualitative research method.

The ambitions to demarcate comparative historical analysis as a unique
qualitative alternative to quantitative research methods, as done in the late
1970s and early 1980s, increasingly lost their plausibility. Tellingly, in a recent
update on comparative historical analysis as a field of inquiry, Kathleen Thelen
and James Mahoney (2016, 19) concluded that "CHA [comparative historical
analysis] does not define itself primarily in terms of a single metatheory, a
specific method, or a particular type of data. Scholars in this camp are typically
quite pragmatic, even opportunistic, in these respects." Given that the authors
continue to outline what they consider to be the methodological peculiarities
of comparative historical analysis, the statement that it is not a specific method
reads almost like a slip of the tongue, yet it is a slip that can be endorsed in light
of the preceding analysis.

The methodological developments within the social sciences over the past
forty years have not only decentered the role of regression analysis in statistical
analysis but, in consequence, also dissolved the plausibility of the close connection or almost identity of historical research using comparative analysis. This
is not merely indicated by the fact that many of the most prominent works in
this field are either historical or comparative (with comparison understood as

cross-country comparison), rather than both, but it is also reflected in the application of quantitative tools to historical data. As shown throughout this chapter, event sequencing, network analysis, and diversity indexing are three main examples for such applications. This is not to make a claim for the superiority of statistical analysis. All three nonlinear quantitative alternatives to regression analysis have qualitative doubles; that is, the assumptions about social life that inform them can also be found in qualitative studies. In fact, the quantitative versions of the three approaches are based on the very same insights into the limits of regression analysis that are voiced by qualitative researchers.

The three lines of nonlinear quantitative analysis and their qualitative doubles do not, however, converge with each other; that is, they do not form a neatly bundled package or unit that can make claims to either methodological unity or distinctness. While event sequencing, network analysis, and diversity indexing can and have been advanced in combination with each other, they are not intrinsically related. Scholars who apply one of these approaches are at times ignoring or outright contradicting central assumptions of one or both of the other two approaches.

The central aim of this chapter is to show that the attempt to uphold the view that comparative historical analysis is a unique method produces more problems than it solves. Upholding this view condemns historical scholarship in sociology to fighting methodological battles that made sense in the late 1970s and early 1980s but are gradually running out of people who can at least remember what the argument against mainstream sociology was actually about, given that the methods that are mainstream today have moved into a different direction.

Yet what is the place of comparative analysis in historical research if the initial assumptions about methodological unity and uniqueness are not upheld? In this volume, Damon Mayrl (chapter 2) and Xiaohong Xu (chapter 3) present evidence that macro-historical comparison as practiced in the 1970s and 1980s is still relevant, albeit for different reasons than initially envisioned. Among other points, Mayrl argues that comparison facilitates analogical reasoning that enables us to gain explanatory cues from other cases, while Xu holds that comparison allows us to break up taken-for-granted assumptions about causal relationships in the case under investigation.

The analysis of the methodological developments described in this chapter likewise does not imply that comparison no longer has a place in historical research. The relevant question is not "whether" to compare but "how" to compare. Comparison, whether paired with historical analysis or not, is part of every scientific inquiry. This includes regression analysis, which compares the attributes of variables. The three nonlinear approaches discussed in this chapter are likewise comparative. Event sequencing compares different orders of events as they unfold over time, network analysis compares the equivalence of structural patterns across cases, and diversity indices compare individual cases in a population to determine their range of variation. None of these approaches is limited to a single case in a way that would make it noncomparative.

What is at stake is thus not the question of whether comparative research is relevant but whether there is something unique about qualitative comparative analysis that would make the assumption that this field of inquiry belongs in a separate methodological camp meaningful. This analysis suggests that this is not a meaningful assumption. Put differently, sociologists should continue to engage in research that is comparative, historical, and qualitative, yet they are well advised to give up the assumption that these three things are intrinsically connected to each other.

Note

This chapter has received funding from the European Union's Horizon 2020 research and innovation program under the Marie Skłodowska-Curie grant agreement No. 754513 and the Aarhus University Research Foundation.

References

Abbott, Andrew. 1988. "Transcending General Linear Reality." *Sociological Theory* 6(2):169–86.
——. 1990. "Conceptions of Time and Events in Social Science Methods: Causal and Narrative Approaches." *Historical Methods* 23(4):140–50.
——. 1991. "History and Sociology: The Lost Synthesis." *Social Science History* 15(2):201–38.
——. 1997. "On the Concept of Turning Point." *Comparative Social Research* 16:85–105.
Abbott, Andrew, and Alexandra Hrycak. 1990. "Measuring Resemblance in Sequence Data: An Optimal Matching Analysis of Musicians' Careers." *American Journal of Sociology* 96(1):144–85.
Agresti, Alan, and Barbara F. Agresti. 1978. "Statistical Analysis of Qualitative Variation." *Sociological Methodology* 9:204–37.
Alesina, Alberto, Edward Glaeser, and Bruce Sacerdote. 2001. "Why Doesn't the US Have a European-Style Welfare System? Working Paper 8524." Cambridge, MA: National Bureau of Economic Research.
Aminzade, Ronald. 1992. "Historical Sociology and Time." *Sociological Methods and Research* 20:456–80.
Anievas, Alexander, and Kerem Nişancioğlu. 2007. "How Did the West Usurp the Rest? Origins of the Great Divergence Over the Longue Durée." *Comparative Studies in Society and History* 59(1):34–67.
Baldwin, Peter. 2004. "Comparing and Generalizing: Why All History Is Comparative, Yet No History Is Sociology." In *Comparison and History: Europe in Cross-National Perspective,* edited by Deborah Cohen and Maura O'Connor, 1–22. London: Routledge.
Bargheer, Stefan. 2021. "Paper Tools and the Sociological Imagination: How 2x2 Tables Shaped the Work of Mills, Lazarsfeld, and Parsons." *American Sociologist* 52(2): 254–75.
Bearman, Peter S. 1993. *Relations Into Rhetorics: Local Elite Social Structure in Norfolk, England, 1540–1640.* New Brunswick, NJ: Rutgers University Press.

Beissinger, Mark R. 2002. *Nationalist Mobilization and the Collapse of the Soviet State*. Cambridge: Cambridge University Press.

——. 2007. "Structure and Example in Modular Political Phenomena: The Diffusion of Bulldozer/Rose/Orange/Tulip Revolutions." *Perspectives on Politics* 5(2):259–76.

Bennett, Andrew, and Alexander L. George. 2001. "Case Studies and Process Tracing in History and Political Science: Similar Strokes for Different Foci." In *Bridges and Boundaries: Historians, Political Scientists, and the Study of International Relations*, edited by Colin Elman and Miriam Fendius Elman, 137–66. Cambridge, MA: MIT Press.

Berger, Peter L. 1967. *The Sacred Canopy: Elements of a Sociological Theory of Religion*. New York: Doubleday.

Berger, Peter L., and Thomas Luckmann. 1966. "Secularization and Pluralism." *International Yearbook for the Sociology of Religion* 2:73–86.

Berins Collier, Ruth, and David Collier. 1991. *Shaping the Political Arena: Critical Junctures, the Labor Movement, and Regime Dynamics in Latin America*. Princeton, NJ: Princeton University Press.

Biggs, Michael. 2003. "Positive Feedback in Collective Mobilization: The American Strike Wave of 1886." *Theory and Society* 32:217–54.

——. 2005. "Strikes as Forest Fires: Chicago and Paris in the Late Nineteenth Century." *American Journal of Sociology* 110(6):1684–714.

——. 2018. "Size Matters: Quantifying Protest by Counting Participants." *Sociological Methods and Research* 47(3):351–83.

Bohorquez, Juan Camilo, Sean Gourley, Alexander R. Dixon, Michael Spagat, and Neil F. Johnson. 2009. "Common Ecology Quantifies Human Insurgency." *Nature* 462:911–14.

Braha, Dan. 2012. "Global Civil Unrest: Contagion, Self-Organization, and Prediction." *PLOS One* 7(10):1–9.

Bulmer, Martin, Kevin Bales, and Kathryn Kish Sklar, eds. 1991. *The Social Survey in Historical Perspective, 1880–1940*. Cambridge: Cambridge University Press.

Burawoy, Michael. 1989. "Two Methods in Search of Science: Skocpol Versus Trotsky." *Theory and Society* 18(6):759–805.

Büthe, Tim. 2002. "Taking Temporality Seriously: Modeling History and the Use of Narratives as Evidence." *American Political Science Review* 96(3):481–93.

Capoccia, Giovanni. 2015. "Critical Junctures and Institutional Change." In *Advances in Comparative-Historical Analysis*, edited by James Mahoney and Kathleen Ann Thelen, 147–79. Cambridge: Cambridge University Press.

Capoccia, Giovanni, and R. Daniel Kelemen. 2007. "The Study of Critical Junctures: Theory, Narrative, and Counterfactuals in Institutional Analysis." *World Politics* 59(3):341–69.

Cederman, Lars-Erik. 2003. "Modeling the Size of Wars: From Billiard Balls to Sandpiles." *American Political Science Review* 97(1):135–50.

Ceruzzi, Paul E. 1998. *A History of Modern Computing*. Cambridge, MA: MIT Press.

Chapin, F. Stuart. 1947. *Experimental Designs in Sociological Research*. New York: Harper.

——. 1955. *Experimental Designs in Sociological Research*. Revised edition. New York: Harper.

Chapin, F. Stuart, and Stuart Alfred Queen. 1937. *Research Memorandum on Social Work in the Depression*. New York: Social Science Research Council.

Chaves, Mark, and Philip S. Gorski. 2001. "Religious Pluralism and Religious Participation." *Annual Review of Sociology* 27:261–81.

Christiano, Kevin J. 1987. *Religious Diversity and Social Change: American Cities, 1890–1906*. Cambridge: Cambridge University Press.

Clauset, Aaron. 2018. "Trends and Fluctuations in the Severity of Interstate Wars." *Science Advance* 4:1–9.

Clauset, Aaron, Maxwell Young, and Kristian Skrede Gleditsch. 2007. "On the Frequency of Severe Terrorist Events." *Journal of Conflict Resolution* 51(1):58–87.

Clemens, Elisabeth S. 2015. "Organizing Powers in Eventful Times." *Social Science History* 39:1–24.

Converse, Jean M. 1987. *Survey Research in the United States: Roots and Emergence, 1890–1960.* Berkeley: University of California Press.

Corsaro, William A., and David R. Heise. 1990. "Event Structure Models from Ethnographic Data." *Sociological Methodology* 20:1–57.

Davis, James A., and Tom W. Smith. 1991. *The NORC General Social Survey: A User's Guide.* Thousand Oaks, CA: Sage.

Didier, Emmanuel. 2020. "America by the Numbers: Quantification, Democracy, and the Birth of National Statistics." Cambridge, MA: MIT Press.

Dincecco, Mark, and Yuhua Wang. 2018. "Violent Conflict and Political Development Over the Long Run: China Versus Europe." *Annual Review of Political Science* 21:341–58.

Easterly, William, and Ross Levine. 1997. "Africa's Growth Tragedy: Policies and Ethnic Divisions." *Quarterly Journal of Economics* 112(4):1203–50.

Ellwood, Charles A. 1933a. *Methods in Sociology: A Critical Study.* Durham, NC: Duke University Press.

——. 1933b. "Observation and the Survey Method in Sociology." *Social Forces* 12(1):51–57.

Erikson, Emily. 2018. "Introduction to Events and Networks Symposium." *Sociological Theory* 36(2):185–86.

Ertman, Thomas. 1997. *Birth of the Leviathan: Building States and Regimes in Medieval and Early Modern Europe.* Cambridge: Cambridge University Press.

Finke, Roger, and Rodney Stark. 1988. "Religious Economies and Sacred Canopies: Religious Mobilization in American Cities, 1906." *American Sociological Review* 53(1):41–49.

——. 1998. "Reply to Olson: Religious Choice and Competition." *American Sociological Review* 63(1):761–66.

Frank, Andre Gunder. 1998. *ReOrient: Global Economy in the Asian Age.* Berkeley: University of California Press.

Gelderblom, Oscar. 2005. *Cities of Commerce: The Institutional Foundations of International Trade in the Low Countries, 1250–1650.* Princeton, NJ: Princeton University Press.

George, Alexander L., and Andrew Bennett. 2005. *Case Studies and Theory Development in the Social Sciences.* Cambridge, MA: MIT Press.

Gingrich, Andre. 2012. "Comparative Methods in Socio-cultural Anthropology Today." In *Sage Handbook of Social Anthropology, vol. 2*, edited by Oliva Harris Richard Fardon, Trevor H. J. Marchand, Mark Nuttall, Cris Shore, Veronica Strang, and Richard Wilson. Thousand Oaks: Sage.

Go, Julian, and George Lawson, eds. 2017. *Global Historical Sociology.* Cambridge: Cambridge University Press.

Goody, Jack. 1996. *The East in the West.* Cambridge: Cambridge University Press.

Gould, Roger V. 1991. "Multiple Networks and Mobilization in the Paris Commune, 1871." *American Sociological Review* 56(6):716–29.

——. 1995. *Insurgent Identities: Class, Community, and Protest in Paris from 1848 to the Commune.* Chicago: University of Chicago Press.

Granovetter, Mark. 1978. "Threshold Models of Collective Behavior." *American Journal of Sociology* 83(6):1420–43.

Granovetter, Mark, and Roland Soong. 1983. "Threshold Models of Diffusion and Collective Behavior." *Journal of Mathematical Sociology* 9(3):165–79.

Greenberg, Joseph H. 1956. "The Measurement of Linguistic Diversity." *Language* 32(1):109–15.

Greenwood, Ernest. 1945. *Experimental Sociology: A Study in Method.* New York: King's Crown.

Griffin, Larry J. 1993. "Narrative, Event-Structure Analysis and Causal Interpretation in Historical Sociology." *American Journal of Sociology* 98(5):1094–133.

——. 2007. "Historical Sociology, Narrative and Event-Structure Analysis: Fifteen Years Later." *Sociologica* 3:1–17.

Halliday, Fred. 1999. *Revolution and World Politics: The Rise and Fall of the Sixth Great Power.* Durham, NC: Duke University Press.

Heise, David R. 1989. "Modeling Event Structures." *Journal of Mathematical Sociology* 14(2–3):139–69.

Hobson, John M. 2004. *The Eastern Origins of Western Civilization.* Cambridge: Cambridge University Press.

——. 2017. "Worlding the Rise of Capitalism: The Multicivilizational Roots of Modernity." In *Global Historical Sociology*, edited by Julian Go and George Lawson, 221–40. Cambridge: Cambridge University Press.

Hont, Istvan. 2005. *Jealousy of Trade: International Competition and the Nation State in Historical Perspective.* Cambridge, MA: Belknap Press of Harvard University Press.

Hopkins, Terence K., and Immanuel Wallerstein. 1981. "Patterns of Development of the Modern World-System." In *World-Systems Analysis: Theory and Methodology*, edited by Terence K. Hopkins and Immanuel Wallerstein, 41–82. London: Sage.

Johnson, Neil, Spencer Carran, Joel Botner, Kyle Fontaine, Nathan Laxague, Philip Nuetzel, Jessica Turnley, and Brian Tivnan. 2011. "Pattern in Escalations in Insurgent and Terrorist Activity." *Science* 333:81–84.

Jones, Eric L. 1981. *The European Miracle: Environments, Economies, and Geopolitics in the History of Europe and Asia.* Cambridge: Cambridge University Press.

Katz, Mark N. 1997. *Revolutions and Revolutionary Waves.* New York: Palgrave Macmillan.

Leibfried, Stephan, and Paul Pierson, eds. 1995. *European Social Policy: Between Fragmentation and Integration.* Washington, DC: Brookings Institution.

Lieberman, Robert C. 1988. *Shifting the Color Line: Race and the American Welfare State* Cambridge, MA: Harvard University Press.

Lieberson, Stanley. 1964. "An Extension of Greenberg's Linguistic Diversity Measures." *Language* 40(4):526–31.

——. 1969. "Measuring Population Diversity." *American Sociological Review* 34(6):850–62.

——. 1980. *A Piece of the Pie: Blacks and White Immigrants Since 1880.* Berkeley: University of California Press.

Lipset, Seymour Martin, and Stein Rokkan, eds. 1967. *Party Systems and Voter Alignments: Cross-National Perspectives.* New York: Free Press.

Lynd, Robert S., and Helen M. Lynd. 1929. *Middletown: A Study in Contemporary American Culture.* New York: Harcourt, Brace.

Mahoney, James. 2000. "Path Dependence in Historical Sociology." *Theory and Society* 29(4):507–48.

——. 2004. "Comparative-Historical Methodology." *Annual Review of Sociology* 30:81–101.

Mahoney, James, and Dietrich Rueschemeyer, eds. 2003. *Comparative Historical Analysis in the Social Sciences.* Cambridge: Cambridge University Press.

Manza, Jeff. 2000. "Race and the Underdevelopment of the American Welfare State." *Theory and Society* 29(6):819–32.

Martin, John Levi. 2018. "Getting Off the Cartesian Clothesline." *Sociological Theory* 36(2):194–200.

Mokyr, Joel. 2017. *A Culture of Growth: The Origins of the Modern Economy.* Princeton, NJ: Princeton University Press.

Offe, Claus. 2000. "The Democratic Welfare State in an Integrating Europe." In *Democracy Beyond the State? The European Dilemma and the Emerging Global Order*, edited by Michael T. Greven and Louis W. Pauly, 63–89. Boston: Rowman and Littlefield.

———. 2003. "The European Model of 'Social' Capitalism: Can It Survive European Integration?" *Journal of Political Philosophy* 11(4):437–69.

O'Loughlin, John, Michael D. Ward, Corey L. Lofdahl, Jordin S. Cohen, David S. Brown, David Reilly, Kristian S. Gleditsch, and Michael Shin. 1998. "The Diffusion of Democracy, 1946–1994." *Annals of the Association of American Geographers* 88(4):545–74.

Owens, B. Robert. 2014. "'Laboratory Talk' in U.S. Sociology, 1890–1930: The Performance of Scientific Legitimacy." *Journal of the History of the Behavioral Sciences* 50(3):302–20.

Padgett, John F., and Christopher K. Ansell. 1993. "Robust Action and the Rise of the Medici, 1400–1434." *American Journal of Sociology* 98(6):1259–319.

Platt, Jennifer. 1996. *A History of Sociological Research Methods in America, 1920–1960*. Cambridge: Cambridge University Press.

Pomeranz, Kenneth. 2000. *The Great Divergence: China, Europe, and the Making of the Modern World Economy*. Princeton, NJ: Princeton University Press.

Ragin, Charles. 1987. *The Comparative Method: Moving Beyond Qualitative and Quantitative Strategies*. Berkeley: University of California Press.

Ragin, Charles, and David Zaret. 1983. "Theory and Method in Comparative Research: Two Strategies." *Social Forces* 61(3):731–54.

Richardson, Lewis F. 1948. "Variation of the Frequency of Fatal Quarrels with Magnitude." *Journal of the American Statistical Association* 43(244):523–46.

Roberts, D. C., and D. L. Turcotte. 1998. "Fractality and Self-Organized Criticality of Wars." *Fractals* 6(2):351–57.

Rosich, Katherine J. 2005. *History of the American Sociological Association: 1981–2004*. Washington, DC: American Sociological Association.

Sewell, William H. 2005. *Logics of History: Social Theory and Social Transformation*. Chicago: University of Chicago Press.

Simpson, Edward H. 1949. "Measurement of Diversity." *Nature* 163:688.

Skocpol, Theda. 1979. *States and Social Revolutions: A Comparative Analysis of France, Russia and China*. Cambridge: Cambridge University Press.

———. 1984. "Emerging Agendas and Recurrent Strategies in Historical Sociology." In *Vision and Method in Historical Sociology*, edited by Theda Skocpol, 356–91. Cambridge: Cambridge University Press.

Skocpol, Theda, and Margaret Somers. 1980. "The Uses of Comparative History in Macrosocial Inquiry." *Comparative Studies in Society and History* 22(2):174–97.

Smelser, Neil. 1976. *Comparative Methods in the Social Sciences*. Englewood Cliffs, NJ: Prentice-Hall.

Snyder, David, and Edward L. Kick. 1979. "Structural Position in the World System and Economic Growth, 1955–1970: A Multiple-Network Analysis of Transnational Interactions." *American Journal of Sociology* 84(5):1096–126.

Sorokin, Pitirim A. 1943. *Sociocultural Causality, Space, Time: A Study of Referential Principles of Sociology and Social Science*. Durham, NC: Duke University Press.

Starr, Harvey. 1991. "Democratic Dominoes: Diffusion Approaches to the Spread of Democracy in the International System." *Journal of Conflict Resolution* 35(2):356–81.

Stasavage, David. 2016. "Representation and Consent: Why They Arose in Europe and Not Elsewhere." *Annual Review of Political Science* 19:145–62.

Teachman, Jay D. 1980. "Analysis of Population Diversity: Measures of Qualitative Variation." *Sociological Methods and Research* 8(3):341–62.

Thelen, Kathleen Ann, and James Mahoney. 2016. "Comparative-Historical Analysis in Contemporary Political Science." In *Advances in Comparative-Historical Analysis*, edited by James Mahoney and Kathleen Ann Thelen, 1–36. Cambridge: Cambridge University Press.

Wallerstein, Immanuel. 1974. "The Rise and Future Demise of the World Capitalist System: Concepts for Comparative Analysis." *Comparative Studies in Society and History* 16(4):387–415.

Wejnert, Barbara. 2005. "Diffusion, Development, and Democracy, 1800–1999." *American Sociological Review* 70(1):53–81.

Wellman, Barry. 1998. "Doing It Ourselves." In *Required Reading: Sociology's Most Influential Books*, edited by Dan Clawson, 71–78. Amherst: University of Massachusetts Press.

Zhukov, Dmitry S., Valery V. Kanishchev, and Sergey K. Lyamin. 2016. "Application of the Theory of Self-Organized Criticality to the Investigation of Historical Processes." *SAGE Open*, 1–10.

CHAPTER 2

COMPARISON IN ACTION

Immersion and Recursion as Heuristics in Historical Sociology

DAMON MAYRL

Introduction

What is the role of comparison in historical research? For decades, if not centuries, the standard answer has been that it allows the researcher to infer causality. This is the basis of the received model of comparative social science, based on John Stuart Mill's methods of difference and agreement, and propounded a generation (or two) ago in the writings of Adam Przeworski and Henry Teune (1970), Arend Lijphart (1971, 1975), and Theda Skocpol (1979; Skocpol and Somers 1980). The comparative method promised to place historical and other case-based analyses on a rigorous scientific footing, following a quasi-experimental logic, that would allow them to withstand scrutiny in an era of positivist ascendance (Calhoun 1996; Steinmetz 2005; see also chapter 1 in this volume).

Over the years, the flaws and inconsistencies in the received, inferential model of comparison have been revealed (e.g., Goldthorpe 1991; Lieberson 1991, 1994; Sewell 2005). Many of these derive from the attempt to impose a quasi-experimental logic of control on an open system (Collier 1994). As a system that attempts to "control" for different variables through systematic comparison, it has been challenged on the grounds that any two historical cases will necessarily be overdetermined, and as such, there are too many variables to possibly control for. The variable logic of the received model also suffers from many of the more general flaws of methods assuming a model of "general linear reality" (Abbott 2001), problems that are especially acute for historical research where temporal processes and constantly shifting cultural meanings make it particularly difficult to assume a variable logic (Sewell 2005).

The positivist presentation of the inferential model also misrepresents the research process. By representing itself as a "controlled comparison" that "manipulates groups of cases to control sources of variation" (Skocpol and Somers 1980, 182), the received model suggests a research design where all relevant factors are identified up front and simply analyzed straightforwardly through cases. Yet this presentation—indebted to the classic distinction between the context of discovery and the context of justification (Popper 1934)—conceals the messy nature of historical research, where one rarely has awareness of all relevant factors up front and where the contexts of discovery and justification are substantially mixed (Abbott 2004; Feyerabend 1975; Somers 1998). If it is true, as Andrew Abbott (2004, 19) writes, that historians "hide their arduous research process under an elegant mantle of prose," it is equally true that the received comparative model allows sociologists—for better or (almost certainly) worse—to hide the messy reality of theorization under an elegant positivist design.

A second problem with Millian comparative methods is that, although they claim to "rule out" variables through the method of similarity or difference, the actual causal mechanisms at work may not in fact be ruled out through these procedures. This is because empirical regularities are distinct from the deeper causal mechanisms that power social phenomena (Aviles and Reed 2017; Bhaskar 1986; Gorski 2009; Gross 2009; Hedström and Ylikoski 2010; Steinmetz 1998, 2004; see also chapter 8 in this volume). Accordingly, "controlling" for empirical regularities does not actually control for these deeper processes and mechanisms. The well-known problem of equifinality—i.e., that there may be more than one causal pathway to the same outcome—is but one version of this broader problem (George and Bennett 2005). Accordingly, surface similarities or differences that may initially have been ruled out as causally relevant may actually be manifestations of important causal processes that are empirically realized in nonobvious ways through causal conjunctures (Ragin 1987).

For all of these reasons, many social scientists now acknowledge that comparative methods based on Millian methods, on their own, do not "offer a strong basis for most kinds of causal inference" (Goertz and Mahoney 2012, 89). Instead, they argue that they must be supplemented with within-case methods to bolster their inferential possibility (George and Bennett 2005; Goertz and Mahoney 2012; Lange 2013). This points to a final issue for the classic comparative method: it is by no means clear that comparison is a necessary feature of good historical sociology. It is evident that one may obtain great historical insights without comparison through single-case studies based on noncomparative methods such as sequence analysis (Abbott 1995) or process tracing (Bennett and Checkel 2014; Goldstone 2003).

Most of the criticisms lodged at the received comparative method center around its ability, or lack thereof, to compellingly generate causal inferences. If comparison—at least according to the received model—seems to be a poor means of inferring causality, and if historical sociology appears to be quite capable of producing compelling explanations without using comparison, is there any point in comparing? What leverage does comparison provide in contemporary historical sociology?

In this chapter, I argue that we may gain a better understanding of the utility of comparison by attending to how comparison works *in practice*. A close examination of how scholars compare reveals that the virtues of comparison inhere less in its ability to generate compelling causal inferences and more in its supporting role in generating theoretical cues and methodological leads for the narrative, sequence, and processual methods that do the heavy causal lifting. That is to say, comparison is helpful—perhaps essential—for its sensitizing, analogizing, contextualizing, and heuristic roles. In practice, this heuristic role for comparison is realized through the deep *immersion* in multiple cases required of the researcher, in combination with the essentially *recursive* nature of comparison as enacted, whereby the researcher repeatedly tacks back and forth between cases over the course of the research process. Together, immersion and recursion enhance both the stock of knowledge researchers develop about their cases and their ability to glean insights about potential mechanisms to be excavated. The "comparative method" must therefore be understood in dynamic terms as an ongoing process realized throughout the course of a research project.

Like other postpositivist scholars (e.g., Aviles and Reed 2017; Bhaskar 1986; Gorski 2009; Gross 2009; Hedström and Ylikoski 2010; Steinmetz 2004, 2014), I start from the premise that the goal of historical research is to uncover and elaborate causal mechanisms that inhere across multiple cases and that combine in historical conjunctures to produce outcomes of interest (Adams, Clemens, and Orloff 2005). Mechanisms are the core of causality; consequently, one theorizes by developing "concepts, images, models, or narratives that describe particular causal entities with specific intrinsic structures or powers" (i.e., mechanisms) (Steinmetz 2014, 423). Because the goal is to explain the underlying mechanisms, rather than the events themselves, attention to empirical regularities and discontinuities is essential. However, as Steinmetz (2014, 424) reminds us, empirical similarities may be deceiving, and "there may well be a completely different causal nexus in each case." For this reason, the use of comparison to identify empirical patterns is only ever the first step toward identifying the deeper mechanisms that produce those patterns.

To investigate and theorize the role of enacted comparison, I first draw on insights from cognitive psychology to lay out the optimal conditions for noticing things. I then explicate the immersive, recursive practice of historical research and show how that recursive, immersive practice helps sensitize the researcher to potential mechanisms throughout the research process. To illustrate my argument, I show how comparison acted as a heuristic in my own research on secularization. I conclude with implications of my argument for the practice of knowledge production in historical sociology.

Why Does Comparison Work?

In its classic formulation, the most-similar- and most-different-case comparisons rely on Mill's methods of difference and similarity to infer causality. By comparing two cases that have a different outcome of interest but that are otherwise similar in all aspects but one (or that vary maximally while converging on the same outcome), it is argued that one may infer causality from the factor that differs (or that holds across the varied cases) (Skocpol and Somers 1980). Critics have regularly remarked that Mill's methods of similarity and difference, and the classic comparative methods derived therefrom, make implausible claims about their inferential power. But they nearly as regularly note that, despite this problem, comparative studies can produce amazing insights: "It is remarkable, in view of the logical and empirical failure of Skocpol's program of experimental induction, that her analysis of social revolutions remains so powerful and convincing," remarks William Sewell (2005, 97) of Skocpol's (1979) classic *States and Social Revolutions*. It is therefore perhaps unsurprising that, despite the many blows it has suffered—including being disavowed by some of its earliest champions (Munck and Snyder 2007, 479)—the venerable "most-similar" and "most-different-case comparison" methods articulated by Przeworski and Teune (1970) continue to be discussed in methods books (e.g., George and Bennett 2005; Gerring 2007) and used as a methodological justification in journal articles (e.g., McCabe and Berman 2016).

If most-similar and most-different-case comparisons are logically incoherent, why do they work? In part, this is because much of the actual causal inference takes place in the within-case methods that often accompany them (Goertz and Mahoney 2012; Lange 2013). But it is also, I argue, because the most-similar comparative design actually does important analytic work. The most-similar-case design is a useful fiction that works, not because of its formal logic, but because it acts as a *heuristic*. Heuristics are methods or processes that enable us to discover or learn something for ourselves (Abbott 2004). Comparison, I argue, acts as a heuristic by sensitizing the researcher to puzzles and clues. These in turn orient the researcher toward the identification of causal mechanisms. The most-similar-case comparison works, then, not because it allows us to infer causality but because it improves our ability to notice things.

Why Do We Notice Things?

Sadly for social scientists, there is no magic formula we can use to improve our ability to notice things. We cannot predict in advance what we will notice or when a discovery will jump out at us. However, we can arrange our research practices in ways that prepare our minds and maximize the likelihood that we will have those moments of discovery. These arrangements—when done systematically, methods—are heuristics. While the workings of the creative mind remain shrouded in mystery, cognitive psychologists have made great strides in understanding the conditions that promote insight, creativity, and learning.

Cognitive psychologists have shown that comprehension and understanding emerge from our ability to draw connections between new things we encounter and our existing knowledge base. Both breadth and depth matter here. Broad knowledge can help us make more creative connections and draw unexpected analogies, meaning that in some respects "it is more crucial for knowledge to be broad than deep" (Simonton 2016, 232). But depth is also important. Relative to novices, for example, experts are more able to recognize meaningful patterns precisely because they are able to see the bigger picture and to draw more connections and contrasts among them (Ambrose et al. 2010). Simply knowing more about something also helps us identify those things that are genuinely surprising—surprises that an unprepared mind might be likely to miss. As Abbott (2004, 244) puts it, "You have to know the background before you can see that something doesn't fit into it." If this is the case, then it follows that one condition that fosters our ability to notice things is simply having developed a deep and exhaustive knowledge, both of the relevant subject matter and of other information that might at first seem entirely irrelevant.

A second condition that helps us notice things is to come back to them on a periodic basis. As Thomas Kuhn (1962, 111) noted, often all that was needed for a scientific revolution was for scientists to revisit familiar locales with new knowledge in mind. As a result, they were able to "see new and different things when looking with familiar instruments in places they have looked before." In the course of revisiting an object, we are shaped by the other experiences we have had and the things we have been working on in the interim; this may prime us to see new things, related to our more recent encounters, in otherwise familiar material (Kahneman 2011). Armed with this novel mental background, aspects of that material crucial to understanding may become newly foregrounded and appear in higher relief (Zerubavel 2015). Repeatedly revisiting familiar material, therefore, may help us see new things and draw new connections.

Finally, we may be more likely to experience moments of insight when we allow time to step away from a problem and let it "percolate" in the background (Carey 2014). Although often experienced as a sudden flash, insight generally is the product of a protracted period of "incubation" that takes place over time (Runco 2014). The mental processing that occurs during incubation largely takes place in our subconscious, where the brain continually scans the environment and is receptive to new clues and associations it picks up during that time (Simonton 2004). Temporarily setting aside a task before finishing it ironically helps to keep those ideas at the forefront of our mind. It creates "heightened awareness" and a "tuned, scavenging mind" that seeks out ideas and materials relevant to the unfinished questions we have placed on the back burner (Carey 2014, 142, 146). By allowing downtime for projects to percolate in the background, we increase the likelihood that the encounters with facts and ideas that we have in the interim will spark an unexpected association or creative insight that pushes our thinking forward (Simonton 2004).

In short, we are more likely to notice things when we have a broad and deep set of knowledge, when we regularly revisit existing sources of information, and when we leave time for subconscious associational processes to work. Adopting a method that maximizes these structural conditions acts as a facilitating heuristic. Comparison, I argue, does precisely this.

The Practice of Comparison

Comparison's heuristic ability derives from core practical aspects of the comparative method. The comparative method first requires scholars to become familiar with two or more cases—their histories and the broad contours of their points of convergence and divergence. Once this baseline familiarity has been achieved, the researcher dives into deeper analyses on particular topics, first in one case, then the other. In this way, comparison adopts an iterative, recursive form in which the researcher tacks back and forth from case to case, investigating new or revisiting familiar aspects of each case history as needed to identify and analyze relevant causal processes and mechanisms. Thus, comparison requires both ongoing *immersion* in multiple cases simultaneously and a *recursive* form where the researcher moves from case to case. As research practices, both immersion and recursion help maximize the heuristic potential of the comparative method.

A Warrant for Immersion

Existing methodological statements on historical comparison emphasize the importance of acquiring an in-depth understanding of the cases being studied. As Ragin (1987, 51–52) puts it, the comparative method "forces investigators to get very close to their data and become familiar with their cases as they try to pinpoint key differences between cases." The depth of the analysis is crucial. Because historical outcomes are subject to conjunctural causation, the ultimate causal mechanisms historical sociologists seek to illuminate are often not immediately apparent, and apparent surface similarities can be deceiving. Because a superficial understanding of any case can easily lead to incorrect conclusions, comparison requires scholars to develop intimate knowledge about their cases. It is only by "examining differences and similarities *in context* [that] it is possible to determine how different combinations of conditions have the same causal significance and how similar causal factors can operate in opposite directions" (Ragin 1987, 49, emphasis original). For this reason, the compiling of detailed explanatory case histories is recognized as an important initial step in historical comparative research (e.g., Steinmetz 2004).

The ability to deploy this contextualized knowledge of each case is not simply a matter of deep knowledge about the relatively narrow topic of interest, however. Instead, the "intimacy of analysis" in a small N comparison "draws on—and indeed insists on—deep background knowledge of the [cases] being examined" (Tarrow 2010, 243). Having a broad understanding of the history of each case not only enhances the researcher's ability to contextualize the similarities and differences that they find but also can serve as a healthy prophylactic against any potential distortions in the secondary historiography of the cases (Mahoney and Rueschemeyer 2003)—that is, breadth can act as a check against "bad history" entering into the analysis. The ability to contextualize case history in this broader sense, therefore, and to appreciate its possible similarities and differences, requires knowledge of the case that is broad as well as deep.

Thus, in practice, the comparative method requires researchers to undertake exhaustive research into the histories of their cases that are both broad and deep. Abbott (2014, 30), recalling his own research into the history of library research infrastructure, credits the insights at the core of that project to his "complete immersion" in the case, which enabled him to contextualize and recognize the importance of what he saw: "Only by immersion could I understand which of the many things staring me in the face were the important ones. Indeed, even the underlying puzzle . . . had emerged only gradually over the history of the research." Thus, a first practical dimension to comparison is its warrant—its directive—to make the researcher develop this intimate familiarity, broadly and deeply, through complete immersion in each case.

Recursion as Comparative Practice

In published works, comparative case studies are often presented as independent cases juxtaposed against one another, with relevant factors highlighted and traced through individual case studies. Yet this presentation belies the actual practice of comparative research that allows researchers to identify salient similarities and differences and to uncover and trace essential causal mechanisms. In practice, comparative research is *recursive*, involving the iterative revisiting of cases with different theoretical and empirical questions in mind. In comparison as practiced, the researcher repeatedly and relentlessly draws comparisons across cases, and between theory and data, in an ongoing cycle throughout the research process. The comparisons vary as needed to answer questions raised by the research process itself; consequently, researchers compare cases not only in terms of an initial set of theoretical explanations but also in terms of emergent puzzles, reading the cases off of one another to uncover salient points of convergence and divergence. It is through recursive comparison with alternative cases, theories, narratives, and evidence that underlying mechanisms are identified, excavated, and theorized.

Historical sociologists have not traditionally been encouraged to think of comparison in these terms. Indeed, the recursive nature of comparison-in-practice rejects one of the dominant presuppositions of the most-similar-case comparison model—that is, the distinction between the context of discovery and the context of justification. Karl Popper (1934), among others, characterized the research process as being divided into two distinct moments: a context of discovery, where hypotheses were generated, and a context of justification, where those hypotheses were tested, verified, and falsified. Whereas Popper viewed these as separate moments, it is increasingly recognized that this is an inaccurate model of how the research process actually unfolds. Science studies scholars have shown that scientific research is not divided into discreet phases but is instead "a complicated *mixture* of procedures" that combine into "a uniform practice" (Feyerabend 1975, 149, emphasis original; see also Abbott 2004, 2014). Discovery and justification thus occur simultaneously throughout the research process, as new ideas emerge and new evidence is gathered. As Tavory and Timmermans (2014, 6) put it, "researchers theorize on the go."

Historical sociology is not immune to this dynamic. In fact, some recent analyses of classics of comparative historical sociology have pointed to an apparent actual practice of historical work that closely adheres to a recursive model. This is clear in revisionist readings of Skocpol's *States and Social Revolutions* by Philip Gorski (2004) and William Sewell (2005). According to Gorski (2004, 23), Skocpol "portrays the 'comparative method' as a sort of dialogue between theory and observation, an interpretive reasoning process in which an explanatory model is gradually fine-tuned to fit a set of historical cases." Sewell's (2005) reconstruction of Skocpol's apparent research practice (speculatively derived from hints dropped in the preface of her book [Skocpol 1979]) also depicts a recursive model at work:

She began, she tells us, with the history of the Chinese Revolution, then found the Chinese development suggested unsuspected analogies with the French case and finally used an analytic scheme worked out from the Chinese and French cases to interpret Russian history. *One suspects that this mutual reading of each of the cases in terms of the others continued and kept spiraling back*: that, for example, Trotsky's emphasis on backward Russia's unsuccessful military competition with the European powers must have suggested parallels in the crisis of the French Old Regime or that Georges Lefebvre's analyses of the crucial contribution of aristocratic resistance and peasant revolts to the French Revolution must have thrown a sharp light on the roles of landlords and peasants in Russia and China.

I suspect that Skocpol formulated and deepened her interpretations of key revolutionary events by just such a process of critically extending narratives from each of the cases to each of the others. A rough causal logic certainly guided such analogical extensions: if attempts to reform the sprawling agrarian state of imperial Russia arose in response to the threat of German military prowess, is it not likely that comparable attempts to reform a roughly similar French state might have arisen from repeated defeats at the hands of England? But Skocpol's presentation of comparative method as a means of testing already formulated general propositions gets it the wrong way round. *It would be more accurate to say that comparison generated propositions whose potential generality was tested by their ability to illuminate the conjunctural unfolding of analogous causal processes in the three cases.* . . . The true payoff of Skocpol's comparative history, then, is not the rigorous testing of abstract generalizations but the discovery of analogies on which new and convincing narratives of eventful sequences can be constructed. (Sewell 2005, 99–100, emphasis added)

In practice, then, comparison is essentially a recursive enterprise, built around critical extensions, analogies, and continuous rereading of cases.

The Heuristic Benefits of Immersion and Recursion

The practical aspects of comparison—immersion and recursion—are closely aligned with the conditions necessary to maximize novel insights. As such, they facilitate the processes at the core of knowledge generation: abduction and analogy.

Abduction is the core form of reasoning in historical sociology, and we compare recursively to improve our ability to abduct. Abduction is one of Charles Sanders Peirce's three forms of reasoning (alongside induction and deduction) and is "the process of forming an explanatory hypothesis" for an unexpected puzzle through creative inference. Abduction "starts with consequences and then constructs reasons" (Timmermans and Tavory 2012, 171) by "ask[ing] what has to be true about the world in order to explain the empirical event under investigation" (Decoteau 2017:72).[1]

According to Timmermans and Tavory (2012, 173), the ability to come up with creative hypotheses depends in large part on "the researcher's cultivated position" and "rests for a large part on the scope and sophistication of the theoretical background a researcher brings to research." By having a larger stock of theories and concepts available to draw on, a researcher will be able to come up with more and better hypotheses to explain an unexpected phenomenon. In historical research, however, abduction and the generation of novel explanations depend not only on the researcher's background knowledge of theories and concepts but also on knowledge of historical features of one's case(s) (and others besides). In this regard, in addition to having a sophisticated and broad understanding of theories and concepts, abduction is facilitated when a researcher has a large amount of what Stefan Bargheer (2014, 15) calls "junk knowledge," or "knowledge which has no direct payoff or use for the empirical case a researcher is working on at the moment." According to Bargheer, junk knowledge is useful because "it assists the formulation of original ideas in the encounter with empirical evidence." As such, it "facilitates the process of making sense of new data, of translating this data into equally new arguments" (2014, 15).

Junk knowledge is an inevitable by-product of immersion. The deep reading of historical material and cases essential to historical research inevitably leads to the accretion of junk knowledge as a by-product of theorizing and analysis. This junk knowledge can then become important during the process of recursive comparison, as historical details previously viewed as unimportant "junk" may assume new significance in light of new data or theoretical leads uncovered later in the process. Hence, both a range of theories and concepts and a range of empirical knowledge are both crucial to successful abduction in historical research. Immersion in a case—knowing it inside and out—enables the drawing of connections in innovative ways, thereby facilitating abduction.

Immersion and recursion also both facilitate and rely upon *analogy*—an explicitly comparative reasoning process consisting of "structural alignment and mapping between separate, distinctive domains and their parts" (Vaughan 2014, 61). Analogy is an important, yet largely undertheorized, aspect of theorization (Abbott 2004; Stinchcombe 1978; Swedberg 2012; Vaughan 2014). Analogy provides the building blocks for abduction by identifying comparable features in other cases or domains whose concepts and theories may form the basis for alternative explanations. The point of analogy is thus to identify parallel examples that may provide alternative explanations (see also chapter 3 in this volume).

Analogy plays at least three roles in comparison. First, it can be a source of theories, concepts, and mechanisms. Analogy may be particularly useful when it helps to identify concepts that might be used to unearth mechanisms. Concepts, as Gorski (2009) notes, are the instruments through which social scientists can access empirically unobservable mechanisms. Concepts can be generated or borrowed via analogous reasoning and used to uncover and theorize mechanisms by testing them against the data. Second, analogies can also act as maps or guides to the gathering of additional data sources. Identifying an analogy between two or more cases can suggest the need to gather further information in an area that may previously not have seemed important. Finally, analogy may be theoretically fruitful even when it fails. Attempts to draw analogies between cases may ultimately reveal them not to analogize properly. In attempting to understand the reasons why two cases do not analogize, there may be clues to the presence of important factors or mechanisms that need to be incorporated into an explanation.

Our ability to draw these analogies is affected by both the content of what we have in our minds and our ability to forge unexpected connections across our cases. While immersion facilitates this, recursion is also essential, as it allows the researcher regularly to see new things, even in data that may have been previously visited. As discussed earlier, our ability to notice and evaluate evidence depends in part upon what else we are thinking about at a particular moment in time. In other words, the theories and concepts foremost in our minds—as well as the historical evidence we uncover—affect what we see at any given point in time, so our knowledge and analysis, and the analogies that may occur to us, change as we proceed. The mental breaks produced as we shift from case to case also provide an occasion for problems and their solutions to percolate in our subconscious minds. As we iteratively move from case to case, we maximize the opportunity for our minds to produce new connections that can unlock novel insights into our research questions.

Recursion is therefore essential to identifying and theorizing mechanisms: repeatedly revisiting aspects of our case through successive approximations means that we will be sensitized to different things at different points in time. The iterative nature of the comparative method thus improves our ability to identify and analyze causal mechanisms in their complexity.

* * *

Comparison, in short, works because it (1) increases our knowledge of relevant theories, concepts, and empirical data in ways that (2) allow us to see things differently and draw better analogies, thereby (3) improving our ability to accurately abduct and thus theorize real causal mechanisms. Its role is essentially heuristic, a role it can play due to how the comparative method works in practice.

Comparison in Action: A Case Study

To illustrate how comparison works as a heuristic in practice, I draw upon my own research for my recent book, *Secular Conversions* (Mayrl 2016). My book explains an empirical puzzle: why the United States and Australia developed divergent policies governing religious education in the 1960s, after maintaining nearly identical such policies throughout the late nineteenth and early twentieth centuries. This empirical puzzle was also a theoretical puzzle because existing theories of secularization could not account for it. I argue that the divergence has its roots in three kinds of political conflict, each fought over different stakes, but that the policy differences between the countries reflected how those mechanisms interacted with the structure of the state in each country. Based on this analysis, I abstract to a more general theory of religious change that explains secularization as the outcome of the interaction of generalizable political processes and the specific institutional contexts of given countries.

The research I conducted for this book began as a classic "most-similar-case" design. The United States and Australia made for a great comparison because both are religiously diverse countries with common constitutional provisions disestablishing religion, shared colonial legacies as British settler societies, and parallel histories in managing religious education. Despite these similarities, however, the two countries nevertheless developed divergent religious education policies. The ultimate argument I make in the book does not reflect the working out of Millian methods, however. Instead, it is the end product of a winding comparative journey. Indeed, the identification and analysis of mechanisms emerged over the course of the research process, largely thanks to the benefits of ongoing comparison. And in important ways, a factor I thought I had "controlled for" at the beginning ended up playing an important role in the end.

Immersion, Recursion, and Preliminary Case Histories

My analysis began with immersion, in the form of writing parallel case histories. Existing theories of secularization, though inadequate for explaining my empirical puzzle, nevertheless pointed me to the importance of politics, for example, and as a result, I initially structured my research design to examine the politics surrounding a number of "critical junctures" (Thelen 1999) in each country in the postwar era. I supplemented this focus with intuitions drawn from other theories in the sociology of public policy, which suggested the importance of looking at the motives and actions of state actors. As a result, my initial research design focused on how state agencies intersected with activist campaigns in the immediate postwar period.

As I began work on the project, I created and filled in a comparative chart noting potentially salient "variables" suggested by the literature, as well as other interesting features of each case suggested by my reading of the broader literature in American and Australian history. Compiling this chart required me to familiarize myself with my two cases in great depth. More importantly, it also gave me some first leads into what would ultimately end up being theoretically important attributes. These leads, importantly, derived not from theory, but from the historical reading I was doing as part of my immersion process.

For example, one core lead that emerged relatively quickly from my reading in the history of American law was that the American Supreme Court's interpretation of the First Amendment's religion clauses was quite different from how the Australian High Court had interpreted its very similar constitutional provision (section 116). What at first appeared to be a straightforward similarity between the two countries (similar constitutional restrictions on church-state interaction) now presented as a puzzle: Why did the two courts' constitutional interpretations develop in such different ways? Although I did not pursue a solution to this puzzle immediately, I made note of it as a potentially salient feature worth further investigation.

As George Steinmetz (2004) suggests, the writing of parallel case studies is an essential step in historical research. However, rather than writing these case studies in a discrete fashion, I wrote them in light of one another, tacking back and forth to identify the broad thematic contours of each policy history and filling in gaps in particular countries by searching out additional materials, so as to have fully comparable studies. The gathering of data for each country was influenced by the data I collected in the other, so that particularly interesting or noteworthy aspects of the American case history led me to seek out parallel historical information on the Australian case, and vice versa.

This basic history writing, done through this recursive process, served a dual purpose. First, it allowed me to identify patterns that inhered across both cases—that is, relevant points of similarity that suggested the possibility that common causal mechanisms were at play. Both histories featured strong and recurrent conflicts between Catholics and Protestants, for instance; and both histories revealed moments when educators and religious leaders came into conflict over the curriculum—although these latter conflicts appeared to be far more frequent and longstanding in the United States. From these, I used abduction to construct an account of two different kinds of political conflict—religious conflict and professional conflict—which became two of the three core causal processes I focused on in the book.

Second, it shed light on curious discrepancies between the cases, where the histories seemed fundamentally different, which required me to expand the project's scope. For instance, a reading of my cases against one another drew my attention to the starkly secular education policies that emerged in nineteenth-century Victoria—an apparently anomalous finding that seemingly went against the experience of other jurisdictions. This was an important discovery that hinted to me that a third form of political conflict, state-building, might be at play. As a result, I extended the scope of my project back in time to the early nineteenth century to explore the nature of the state-building process in each country—a step that also enabled me to examine the development of professional conflict in greater detail. My recursive comparison also revealed the relative quiescence of Australian teachers, the relative absence of legal activism around religion in Australia, and the divergent campaign strategies of Catholics around public aid in each country. These discrepancies in turn became points of departure for my analysis of how institutional factors led the processes to play out differently in the two countries.

In short, as my research process progressed, the temporal and analytic scope of the comparison expanded, even as I narrowed in on a smaller set of causal processes. This would have been impossible had I conducted the case analyses completely independently, as it was only in recursively reading them off of one another that the patterns and discrepancies became clear in ways that led me to restructure my empirical and analytic focus.

From Junk Knowledge to Useful Analogy: Recursion and the Elaboration of the Argument

Once I had identified a tentatively plausible set of causal processes, I revisited my historical data with those processes specifically in mind. In tracing them out across my two case histories, to determine the conditions under which they became actualized and how they intersected with other social phenomena to produce contingent outcomes. My goal here was to better understand the inner logic of the processes themselves. In this stage of the research process, I benefited from my earlier construction of case narratives, but in performing a systematic comparison, I was forced to seek out additional data—about moments of religious conflict over education, about professional educators' ideas about religion, and about the process of constructing public education in each country. Tracing my processes back through Australian and American history alerted me to variation in both the dynamics and strength of each process. These observations, gleaned through comparison, raised a number of important questions. Why, for example, did state-building seem to be so much less conflictual in the United States? Why were Australian educators seemingly less interested in challenging or transforming religious education policy than American educators? And why did Australian religious minorities not take their cases into the courts, as their American counterparts did?

Answering these questions was only possible through additional recursive comparisons that both forced me to gather new data and also inspired me to revisit material that I had previously not seen as particularly important. These recursive revisitations themselves ended up providing key insights. For instance, early on in the project, I had read two works about the development of American church-state jurisprudence. One of them, Gregg Ivers's (1995) *To Build a Wall*, devoted a chapter to the American Jewish Congress's successful attempt to carve out an exception to restrictive standing rules for First Amendment issues.[2] Another, Richard Morgan's (1968) *The Politics of Religious Conflict*, had a discussion of the problems that many litigants faced in gaining standing before the Supreme Court. In my initial reading, I made note of this information but did not truly absorb its impact—to me, it was junk knowledge.

It was only once I returned to reading more deeply about those groups in Australia who did try to use litigation that the importance of these discussions became clear to me. In the course of my work, I stumbled across a short piece in the 1964 issue of the *Australian Law Journal* that discussed the potential barrier that standing rules might present to Australians who might want to litigate church-state matters (Anonymous 1964). M. J. Ely's (1981) *Erosion of the Judicial Process* confirmed the prescience of this statement, clearly demonstrating the important role that standing rules played in frustrating a legal challenge to state aid by a Protestant group. These readings called to mind the "junk knowledge" I had gleaned from Ivers's and Morgan's books, suggesting an important parallel might be at work. Thus alerted to the importance of standing rules in the Australian context, Ivers's and Morgan's work took on a different appearance. I returned to the American case to try to deepen my understanding both of standing rules and how they had shaped judicial activism in the United States, drawing on the legal literature on standing rules and court procedures. Armed with that additional information, I returned again to the Australian case and explored the legal literature there on standing rules and court procedures. Ultimately, I uncovered a consistent pattern in how standing rules shaped political contests in the legal sphere across the two countries, affecting how and where religious conflict could be expressed, and how policies could be altered.

Abduction and the Crystallization of the Argument

These kinds of recursive comparisons across all three processes eventually revealed an important pattern, of which standing rules were only a part: institutional contexts played a key role in determining how the mechanisms I identified were expressed and whether they led to policy change. Reasoning by analogy, I sought to see whether the rules and procedures so important in the courts had also mattered in other settings where religious education had been debated—and I found that they had. Indeed, this pattern was visible across a range of institutions and affected all three kinds of political conflict, not just during the 1960s, but in a recurrent pattern stretching back to the nineteenth century. Examining why the processes did not seem to play out the same in both places revealed the importance of these institutional factors as important conjunctural forces shaping the two countries' outcomes. Here was a generalizable argument that also provided a superior explanation to my initial puzzle.

It is worth emphasizing that this argument took me far afield from my initial comparative design. Indeed, what I had initially seen as similarities (the shared common-law legal system and constitutional language) ended up concealing an important explanatory factor (standing rules, which shaped how political actors could or could not access the legal system). Although the "most-similar-cases" design provided an excellent starting point, the most important factors emerged only after immersion in the cases and recursive revisiting and elaboration of each case history in light of the other.

* * *

There are a few summary lessons to be gleaned from this brief history of a research process. First, the most-similar comparison that I began with did not structure my project according to a variable logic in any sense. The actual twists and turns of the research process made use of comparison, but in a much more ongoing, contingent, and serendipitous fashion. Moreover, comparison worked as a heuristic throughout the project. That is to say, comparison mattered because it enabled me to identify (and ultimately explain) an empirical puzzle *and* to identify generalizable mechanisms that led to that puzzling outcome. It was not a means of making inferences. It was a guide to organizing my within-case methods.

Second, comparison is integrated into, and integral to, the research process at all points in time. There is no distinction between a context of discovery and a context of justification. Data collection and interpretation work in tandem, in a winding and (often) lengthy process of testing ideas, claims, and evidence in one setting in light of another. The goal is the identification of plausible mechanisms and the generation of a compelling explanatory account of how those mechanisms work in practice to produce particular outcomes. Comparison is the handmaiden to the realization of this goal.

Implications

In this chapter, I have argued that there is value in thinking about comparison, not as a formal method for assessing causal inference, but instead as a practice with heuristic benefits for the development of historical explanations. As a practice, comparison requires scholars to immerse themselves in their cases in ways that build up an expansive bank of junk knowledge and to move recursively between cases in ways that allow them to revisit data repeatedly with different purposes or contextual factors in mind. Importantly, this recursive process involves not only tacking between data and theory, as is sometimes recognized (e.g., George and Bennett 2005; Tavory and Timmermans 2014), but also between cases and even within the pool of historical evidence for each case. By enabling constant recontextualization of data, this iterative approach maximizes the likelihood of drawing creative connections. In this sense, the *process of comparison itself* is essential for the production of historical sociological knowledge. In sum, comparison "works" because comparative designs, diligently pursued, saturate our minds with empirical knowledge while allowing us to repeatedly see things differently, thereby helping us to attend, abduct, and identify causal mechanisms more effectively.

Thinking of comparison as being warranted not on the basis of causal inference, but for its heuristic and abductive power instead, has implications for case selection, methods training, and peer review. In terms of case selection, this understanding implies important differences in the logic of research design. The most-similar-case comparison is based on a variable logic of control—that is, one compares cases across a series of "variables" in order to "control" for possible intervening factors, with the goal of determining whether a factor is "necessary" or "sufficient" for the outcome in question (Mahoney 2003). By contrast, I have argued that we compare instead to sensitize us to points of (potentially) salient difference that can provide entry points to the investigation of mechanisms. The important factors in a comparison are not the "variables" actually suggested by previous theories, but instead the puzzles that emerge from thinking about why existing explanations do not work (or work incompletely) in a given case. It is these puzzles that produce the suspicions and leads that can set us off on the pursuit of the deeper causal mechanisms. In this respect, our "suspicions" that there may be causal mechanisms to be uncovered emerge out of the puzzles that comparison attunes us to.

This insight suggests that comparison *in and of itself* may be useful, apart from "controlling" for any particular attributes. It suggests a shift in how we judge the grounds for comparison from a logic of *control* to a *probing* logic, from controlling *variables* to comparing *attributes*. Because there is no assumption that the comparison itself is necessary for inferring causality, there is a less stringent demand for cases to be *most* similar. Instead, they can be *sufficiently* similar, following a satisficing rather than a maximizing logic. Having cases with *some* similarities increases the confidence that one has identified instances of a "type" worth investigating further, but the number of differences can be multiple because one discards the variable logic that would lead us to search for a single causal factor at work in one case but not the other. We may also consider additional grounds as adequate justification for comparison. Cases may also be selected based on an empirical puzzle to be solved—for the puzzle to exist, the cases must *prima facie* be sufficiently similar. Cases may also be selected, as Steinmetz (2004) argues, based on a suspected shared mechanism.

In short, when it comes to case selection, the practice of research can still begin with something approximating a "most-similar-case" design, as doing so can still lead to productive analyses. But the comparison should not be understood as "controlling" for various causal factors. Instead, it should be driven by theoretical puzzles, where the comparison reveals weaknesses, inconsistencies, or lacunae in existing theories; in addition, other kinds of comparisons, such as realist comparisons of mechanisms, are also permissible. In sum, the options available for case selection should be relaxed, while at the same time, authors should be clear about which of the various possible motivations for their case selection has led them to select those cases.

One objection to this approach to case selection might be that we could get different results if we choose different cases against which to compare one case. Since comparison largely works by sensitizing us to differences and facilitating abduction and analogy, different foils may lead us to notice different things.[3] This is an unavoidable issue, but also one that the received model does not really allow us to overcome, either. The good news is that over the long haul, the broader community of scholars is able to revisit cases through additional sets of comparisons, which means that any idiosyncratic findings will be corrected or contextualized in the course of ongoing collective work (see also Pierson and Skocpol 2002). Recursion is not only a feature of individual studies, in other words, but also of the larger scholarly community, since repeated revisitations and comparisons of cases are necessary for knowledge accumulation (Beck 2018).

Another implication has to do with graduate methods training. Because, as indicated earlier, there is no need to abandon the most-similar-case structure, that method may fruitfully continue to be taught. But graduate training ought to alert students to the true logic undergirding comparison and to reemphasize both within-case methods such as process tracing and sequence analysis and to spend more time on matters of presentation and framing.

Finally, this practical approach to comparison has implications for peer review. After a half-century of inference-driven comparison, it is not surprising that reviewers reflexively reach for the language of control in evaluating manuscripts structured around a comparison. Rather than criticizing case selection based on "omitted variables," reviewers ought to pay closer attention to the within-case methods used in a given study and to relate them to the identification and explication of mechanisms. Journals ought to consider providing guidance to reviewers to facilitate this process.

Acknowledgments

I thank Carly Knight, Josh Pacewicz, Nick Wilson, Xiaohong Xu, and the other members of the postpositivist comparative methods working group for their help workshopping earlier drafts of this chapter; and Ruth Braunstein, Christel Kesler, Erin McDonnell, Lynette Shaw, and audiences at NYU-Abu Dhabi and the 2017 annual meeting of the Social Science History Association for valuable feedback.

Notes

1. Following the critical realist tradition (e.g., Bhaskar 1986; Steinmetz 2014), Decoteau (2017) characterizes this as "retroduction," while noting that Peirce himself used "abduction" and "retroduction" fairly indiscriminately.
2. Standing rules govern whether a petitioning party is recognized as having sufficient interest in a case to be allowed to file suit before the court. Parties unable to claim standing cannot pursue judicial redress (Jaffe 1968).
3. For example, the fact that I compared American religious education policy against Australia, whereas Ahmet Kuru compared it against France and Turkey, led us to highlight different factors contributing to secularization (cf. Kuru 2009; Mayrl 2016). In the end, the argument that I make is broad enough to incorporate the insights Kuru gleaned from his study, if under slightly different terms (Kuru emphasizes the role of secularist ideologies produced in the course of struggling or not against an *ancien régime*; I interpret these findings as a special case of a broader constitutive effect of institutions that extends beyond *ancien régimes*).

References

Abbott, Andrew. 1995. "Sequence Analysis: New Methods for Old Ideas." *Annual Review of Sociology* 21:93–113.

——. 2001. *Time Matters: On Theory and Method.* Chicago: University of Chicago Press.

——. 2004. *Methods of Discovery: Heuristics for the Social Sciences.* New York: Norton.

——. 2014. *Digital Paper: A Manual for Research and Writing with Library and Internet Materials.* Chicago: University of Chicago Press.

Adams, Julia, Elisabeth S. Clemens, and Ann Shola Orloff. 2005. "Introduction: Social Theory, Modernity, and the Three Waves of Historical Sociology." In *Remaking Modernity: Politics, History, and Sociology*, edited by Julia Adams, Elisabeth S. Clemens, and Ann Shola Orloff, 1–72. Durham, NC: Duke University Press.

Ambrose, Susan A., Michael W. Bridges, Michele DiPietro, Marsha C. Lovett, and Marie K. Norman. 2010. *How Learning Works: Seven Research-Based Principles for Smart Teaching.* San Francisco: Jossey-Bass.

Anonymous. 1964. "Current Topics." *Australian Law Journal* 38:145–46.

Aviles, Natalie B., and Isaac Reed. 2017. "*Ratio via Machina*: Three Standards of Mechanistic Explanation in Sociology." *Sociological Methods and Research* 46(4):715–38.

Bargheer, Stefan. 2014. "The Use(fulness) of Theory." *Perspectives* 36(2):13–15.

Beck, Colin J. 2018. "The Structure of Comparison in the Study of Revolution." *Sociological Theory* 36(2):134–61.

Bennett, Andrew, and Jeffrey T. Checkel. 2014. "Process Tracing: From Philosophical Roots to Best Practices." In *Process Tracing: From Metaphor to Analytic Tool*, edited by Andrew Bennett and Jeffrey T. Checkel, 3–37. New York: Cambridge University Press.

Bhaskar, Roy. 1986. *Scientific Realism and Human Emancipation*. London: Verso.

Calhoun, Craig. 1996. "The Rise and Domestication of Historical Sociology." In *The Historic Turn in the Human Sciences*, edited by Terrence J. McDonald, 305–37. Ann Arbor: University of Michigan Press.

Carey, Benedict. 2014. *How We Learn: The Surprising Truth About When, Where, and Why It Happens*. New York: Random House.

Collier, Andrew. 1994. *Critical Realism: An Introduction to Roy Bhaskar's Philosophy*. New York: Verso.

Decoteau, Claire. 2017. "The AART of Ethnography: A Critical Realist Explanatory Research Model." *Journal for the Theory of Social Behaviour* 47(1):58–82.

Ely, M. J. 1981. *Erosion of the Judicial Process: An Aspect of Church-State Entanglement in Australia, 1956–1980*. Melbourne: Defence of Government Schools, Victoria.

Feyerabend, Paul. 1975. *Against Method*. London: Verso.

George, Alexander, and Andrew Bennett. 2005. *Case Studies and Theory Development in the Social Sciences*. Cambridge, MA: MIT Press.

Gerring, John. 2007. *Case Study Research: Principles and Practices*. New York: Cambridge University Press.

Goertz, Gary, and James Mahoney. 2012. *A Tale of Two Cultures: Qualitative and Quantitative Research in the Social Sciences*. Princeton, NJ: Princeton University Press.

Goldstone, Jack A. 2003. "Comparative Historical Analysis and Knowledge Accumulation in the Study of Revolutions." In *Comparative Historical Analysis in the Social Sciences*, edited by James Mahoney and Dietrich Rueschemeyer, 41–90. New York: Cambridge University Press.

Goldthorpe, John H. 1991. "The Uses of History in Sociology: Reflections on Some Recent Tendencies." *British Journal of Sociology* 42(2):211–30.

Gorski, Philip S. 2004. "The Poverty of Deductivism: A Constructive Realist Approach to Sociological Explanation." *Sociological Methodology* 34(1):1–33.

——. 2009. "Social 'Mechanisms' and Comparative-Historical Sociology: A Critical Realist Proposal." In *Frontiers of Sociology*, edited by Peter Hedström and Björn Wittrock, 147–94. Leiden, Netherlands: Brill.

Gross, Neil. 2009. "A Pragmatist Theory of Social Mechanisms." *American Sociological Review* 74:358–79.

Hedström, Peter, and Petri Ylikoski. 2010. "Causal Mechanisms in the Social Sciences." *Annual Review of Sociology* 36:49–67.

Ivers, Gregg. 1995. *To Build a Wall: American Jews and the Separation of Church and State*. Charlottesville: University Press of Virginia.

Jaffe, Louis L. 1968. "The Citizen as Litigant in Public Actions: The Non-Hohfeldian or Ideological Plaintiff." *University of Pennsylvania Law Review* 116:1033–47.

Kahneman, Daniel. 2011. *Thinking, Fast and Slow*. New York: Farrar, Straus and Giroux.

Kuhn, Thomas. 1962. *The Structure of Scientific Revolutions*. Chicago: University of Chicago Press.

Kuru, Ahmet T. 2009. *Secularism and State Policies Toward Religion in the United States, France, and Turkey*. New York: Cambridge University Press.

Lange, Matthew. 2013. *Comparative-Historical Methods*. Thousand Oaks, CA: Sage.

Lieberson, Stanley. 1991. "Small N's and Big Conclusions: An Examination of the Reasoning in Comparative Studies Based on a Small Number of Cases." *Social Forces* 70(2):307–20.

——. 1994. "More on the Uneasy Case for Using Mill-Type Methods in Small-*N* Comparative Studies." *Social Forces* 72(4):1225–37.

Lijphart, Arend. 1971. "Comparative Politics and the Comparative Method." *American Political Science Review* 65:682–93.

——. 1975. "The Comparable-Cases Strategy in Comparative Research." *Comparative Political Studies* 8(2):158–77.

Mahoney, James. 2003. "Strategies of Causal Assessment in Comparative Historical Analysis." In *Comparative Historical Analysis in the Social Sciences*, edited by James Mahoney and Dietrich Rueschemeyer, 337–72. New York: Cambridge University Press.

Mahoney, James, and Dietrich Rueschemeyer. 2003. "Comparative Historical Analysis: Achievements and Agendas." In *Comparative Historical Analysis in the Social Sciences*, edited by James Mahoney and Dietrich Rueschemeyer, 3–38. New York: Cambridge University Press.

Mayrl, Damon. 2016. *Secular Conversions: Political Institutions and Religious Education in the United States and Australia, 1800–2000*. New York: Cambridge University Press.

McCabe, Joshua T., and Elizabeth Popp Berman. 2016. "American Exceptionalism Revisited: Tax Relief, Poverty Reduction, and the Politics of Child Tax Credits." *Sociological Science* 3:540–67.

Morgan, Richard E. 1968. *The Politics of Religious Conflict: Church and State in America*. 2nd edition. Washington, DC: University Press of America.

Munck, Gerardo L., and Richard Snyder. 2007. *Passion, Craft, and Method in Comparative Politics*. Baltimore, MD: Johns Hopkins University Press.

Pierson, Paul, and Theda Skocpol. 2002. "Historical Institutionalism in Contemporary Political Science." In *Political Science: The State of the Discipline*, edited by Ira Katznelson and Helen V. Milner, 693–721. New York: Norton.

Popper, Karl. 1934. *The Logic of Scientific Discovery*. New York: Basic Books.

Przeworski, Adam, and Henry Teune. 1970. *The Logic of Comparative Social Inquiry*. New York: Wiley.

Ragin, Charles. 1987. *The Comparative Method: Moving Beyond Qualitative and Quantitative Strategies*. Berkeley: University of California Press.

Runco, Mark A. 2014. *Creativity: Theories and Themes: Research, Development, and Practice*. 2nd edition. Waltham, MA: Elsevier.

Sewell, William H., Jr. 2005. *Logics of History: Social Theory and Social Transformation*. Chicago: University of Chicago Press.

Simonton, Dean Keith. 2004. *Creativity in Science: Change, Logic, Genius, and Zeitgeist*. New York: Cambridge University Press.

——. 2016. "Creative Genius, Knowledge, and Reason: The Lives and Works of Eminent Creators." In *Creativity and Reason in Cognitive Development*, edited by James C. Kaufman, 226–45. New York: Cambridge University Press.

Skocpol, Theda. 1979. *States and Social Revolutions: A Comparative Analysis of France, Russia, and China*. Cambridge: Cambridge University Press.

Skocpol, Theda, and Margaret Somers. 1980. "The Uses of Comparative History in Macrosocial Inquiry." *Comparative Studies in Society and History* 22:174–97.

Somers, Margaret R. 1998. " 'We're No Angels': Realism, Rational Choice, and Relationality in Social Science." *American Journal of Sociology* 104:722–84.

Steinmetz, George. 1998. "Critical Realism and Historical Sociology: A Review Article." *Comparative Studies in Society and History* 40:170–86.

——. 2004. "Odious Comparisons: Incommensurability, the Case Study, and 'Small N's' in Sociology." *Sociological Theory* 22(3):371–400.

——, ed. 2005. *The Politics of Method in the Human Sciences: Positivism and Its Epistemological Others*. Durham, NC: Duke University Press.

——. 2014. "Comparative History and Its Critics: A Genealogy and a Possible Solution." In *A Companion to Global Historical Thought*, edited by Prasenjit Duara, Viren Murthy, and Andrew Sartori, 412–36. Malden, MA: Wiley Blackwell.

Stinchcombe, Arthur L. 1978. *Theoretical Methods in Social History*. New York: Academic Press.

Swedberg, Richard. 2012. "Theorizing in Sociology and Social Science: Turning to the Context of Discovery." *Theory and Society* 41:1–40.

Tarrow, Sidney. 2010. "The Strategy of Paired Comparison: Toward a Theory of Practice." *Comparative Political Studies* 43(2):230–59.

Tavory, Iddo, and Stefan Timmermans. 2014. *Abductive Analysis: Theorizing Qualitative Research*. Chicago: University of Chicago Press.

Thelen, Kathleen. 1999. "Historical Institutionalism in Comparative Politics." *Annual Review of Political Science* 2:369–404.

Timmermans, Stefan, and Iddo Tavory. 2012. "Theory Construction in Qualitative Research: From Grounded Theory to Abductive Analysis." *Sociological Theory* 30(3):167–86.

Vaughan, Diane. 2014. "Analogy, Cases, and Comparative Social Organization." In *Theorizing in Social Science: The Context of Discovery*, edited by Richard Swedberg, 61–84. Palo Alto, CA: Stanford University Press.

Zerubavel, Eviatar. 2015. *Hidden in Plain Sight: The Social Structure of Irrelevance*. New York: Oxford University Press.

CHAPTER 3

THE MEANINGFULNESS OF COMPARISON

A Macro-Phenomenological Exploration

XIAOHONG XU

W hen historical sociology gathered momentum as a robust intellectual movement a few decades ago, comparative historical methods were advanced as one of its distinctive features (Skocpol and Somers 1980). Yet this methodological advocacy has since stimulated a series of debates challenging the logic of comparison that it invokes from John Stuart Mill. This chapter shifts the focus from methodological and philosophical deliberation on the rationality and justification of comparison to a phenomenological perspective that is intended to reveal how comparison, at levels of the consciousness, subconsciousness, and unconsciousness, indispensably frames and takes part in the construction of theories and meanings that individuals and community of scholars undertake. By clarifying the diverse roles that comparative methods play in different stages of the knowledge creation process, this chapter attempts to enhance the reflexivity of methodological pluralism in historical sociology and contextualize this enterprise in humanity's exploration of creativity and freedom.

The following analysis is divided into six sections. The first section deals with "how comparison is possible" and gives a brief review of the debates on the Skocpolian comparative historical methods and the epistemological crisis of comparison these debates have incurred in contemporary historical sociology. The second section explains why we need to shift the conversation from "whether to compare" to "why to compare" and why a macro-phenomenological approach is useful to understand comparison as vehicle of meaning creation and theory creation. The third and fourth sections then proceed to dissect various ways in which comparative methods actually consciously or uncon-sciously shape how scholars construct innovative social imaginaries, setting them apart from conventional thinking. I discuss more specifically two main categories of comparative strategies: comparison as deconstruction (in order to break away from conventional understanding) and comparison as reconstruc-tion (in order to establish new connections). The following fifth section then discusses the objects of analysis in comparison and argues that mechanism of determination and mechanism of creativity—that is, emergent meaningful mechanism—are interesting to historical sociologists for different reasons and makes a case for the comparison of dynamic transformational processes that synthesize these two aspects. Lastly, I contextualize comparison as an epistemo-logical exercise in modernity and discuss its duality as method of analysis and method of practice. I conclude, with an example from Marx, that much of our epistemological unease with comparison is due to the open-ended future that modernity has introduced. Thus, we need to confront this second-order ques-tion and self-consciously put comparison to use in identifying new problems and expanding toolkits in seeking solutions to them.

How Is Comparison Possible After Positivism?

Sociology was born as a discipline of comparative social morphology. Classical sociologists such as Auguste Comte, Alexis de Tocqueville, Karl Marx, Ferdi-nand Tönnies, Max Weber, Emile Durkheim, and W. E. B. du Bois all attempted to grasp the unprecedented changes that were unfolding in their time. While some of them—especially Tocqueville and Weber—were more invested in ana-lyzing different national trajectories than others, their big comparative question was the contrast of social morphologies ushered in modernity and the "laws" of historical changes therein that await to be discovered. Fast forward a few decades, in the heydays of structural functionalism, such impulse of comparing social morphologies became preponderant and turned into a linear comparison in the axis of modernization. In this mode of linear comparison, the essential question was the degree of integration and coordination of various institutions in different national societies in coping with the transition from traditional to modern social system, often with the structural integration of American individualistic values, free market order, and effective public institutions as the template for such a system. Comparison of uneven and diverse historical trajec-tories, which were important, although secondary, to classical sociologists, was hence suppressed. Events and changes in these trajectories, if they were consid-ered at all, were diagnosed as indicative of structural functional adjustments.

In the 1960s and 1970s, this suppressed impulse to compare uneven and diverse historical trajectories in modernity had burst out of the shackles of the

linear comparison of the modernization theory, in the form of a robust intellectual movement that is retrospectively known as the second wave of historical
sociology (Adams, Clemens, and Orloff 2005). Incorporating the experiences
of social upheavals in their time into their research, scholars like Charles Tilly,
Theda Skocpol, Perry Anderson, and E. P. Thompson, to name just a few, had
called for the revisiting of fundamental questions in the historical changes of
modernity, such as the rise of capitalism, state formation, revolutions, nationalism, and class formation. This had whetted up an ambition for comparative historical research, in search for some methodological guidelines to discipline the
emergent collective exploration of patterns of social change (Calhoun 1996).
Exemplary of this wave is Theda Skocpol, who developed a set of "comparative
historical methods" in completing her ambitious and provocative comparison
of the French, Russian, and Chinese Revolutions in *States and Social Revolutions* (Skocpol 1979).

The two pillars of Skocpol's comparative historical research are the structural
analytical perspective, which is to identify structural variables to explain major
social changes and events; and John Stuart Mill's logic, particularly method of
agreement and method of difference, which she believed can reveal regularities
in historical changes.

In her own explanation of social revolutions, she uses three structural variables: interstate competition, leverage between the landed class and state elites,
and autonomy and solidarity of the peasantry. She claimed to have extracted
these three structural variables, as she compared the three major revolutions
of China, Russia, and France and contrasted them with other "negative" cases
that have not experienced social revolutions (England/Britain, Prussia/Ger-
many, Russia before 1905, Japan, and even Turkey). Although she emphasized
that these were three variables, what in fact emerged in her account is her
abstraction of a chain of causal events. That is, an agrarian bureaucratic state,
in face of intense pressure from its international rival(s) who was rapidly mod-
ernizing, was forced to adopt and implement some reforms to enhance state
centralization in order to strengthen its economic and military might; yet,
these reforms impinged upon the vested interests of their traditional allies—the
landed classes (French and Russian aristocrats and Chinese gentry) and thus
triggered the resistance of this key group of stakeholders, who, in all these three
cases, happened to have sufficient leverage to put up their revolt and raise an
opposing set of reform ideas. This conflict between state elites and the landed
class then weakened machineries of social control, emboldening the peasantry,
who already had considerable autonomy and solidarity (with the exception of
Chinese peasants, which Skocpol claimed is the exception that proves the rule)
to organize a rebellion. A social revolutionary crisis thus ensued, setting the
stage for revolutionaries like Maximilien Robespierre, Vladimir Lenin, Sun Yat-
sen, and Mao Zedong. Providing this narrative of an event chain in which one

event follows another, Skocpol nevertheless claimed the causation is made of three additive structural variables and argued that they are extracted based on Mill's methods. She and her coauthor Margaret Somers further argued that this way of extracting structural variables using Mill's methods is particularly suitable for small N multivariate analysis, which is typical of historical sociology (Skocpol 1979; Skocpol and Somers 1980).

The case that Skocpol made for "comparative historical methods" has stimulated enormous interest but also provoked many criticisms for the Millian logic that it invokes. These criticisms can be divided into five categories. The first criticism takes issue with its logic of causal determinism. Stanley Lieberson (1991) contends that there are too many strong assumptions in the Millian logic that are impossible to meet in applying Mill's methods in social sciences, including deterministic causation, single cause, no interaction with other variables, and no measurement errors. He uses examples of drunk driving to show why using Mill's methods can be problematic: for example, if two drunk drivers are driving on the road and one driver turns right and has a car accident while the other driver does not turn right and does not have a car accident, the research may reach the wrong conclusion that it is the right turn, not drunk driving, that causes car accidents. To Craig Calhoun (1996), dressing up Mill's methods as scientific equivalent of statistical methods in historical sociology may backfire and compromise historical sociology's most critical thrust of historicizing social formations.

The second criticism is that the variable-based thinking underlying Skocpol's comparative historical methods is in contradiction with the eventfulness and heterogeneity of historical temporalities (Burawoy 1989; Sewell 1996). In his critique of Skocpol's comparative study of revolutions, Michael Burawoy pointed out that her variable-based comparison operates on "freezing time" and compresses ups and downs in actual events into simply data points.

The third criticism revolves around its inductionism. Burawoy (1989), for example, was particularly critical of the suggestion that theoretical arguments can be purely derived from applying Mill's methods in comparative historical research. Instead, he argues that comparing historical trajectories is always theory laden, with different "research programs" contending with each other to develop robust auxiliary hypotheses extending from their core premises (see also, Kiser and Hechter 1991).

The fourth criticism challenges the assumption of the equivalence of "cases" that are being compared and argues that the heterogeneity of cultures and meanings across different social contexts (e.g., an antitax event in China's Qing dynasty versus an antitax event in eighteenth-century France under the Bourbon monarchy) may render these cases incommensurable. In this regard, subaltern studies (which claim that the world of meanings inhabited by Indian subalterns is so radically different from the West that Western concepts would inevitably do violence to them), translation studies (which emphasize the untranslatability of meanings across languages and cultural constellations), and "unique event" scholarship (which emphasizes that some events, such as the Holocaust, are unique and beyond comparison) are particularly resistant to comparative agenda (Steinmetz 2004).

The fifth criticism challenges the assumption of the independence of cases that are being compared and instead underscores entangled, connected, and circulatory history between cases and events. For example, comparing economic development in India and Britain in the nineteenth century can be problematic because of the entangled history between these two countries; or comparing the French, Russian, and Chinese Revolutions as three independent cases, as Skocpol did, runs the risk of casting aside the circulatory history of revolutionary ideas that flowed from the French Revolution, through the Russian Revolution, to the Chinese Revolution (Steinmetz 2014).

These five major criticisms call into question how we think about comparative historical methods. Is comparison still justifiable? And how? George Steinmetz (2004) gives an affirmative answer. He argues that if our confidence in doing comparative research is shaken by these criticisms, it is largely because our conventional understanding of comparison is philosophically problematic. That is, the Millian conception of comparison is premised on positivist methodology and empiricist ontology. According to these assumptions, to do comparative research means to search for constant conjunction of events in the Humean sense. In contrast, drawing on the critical realist philosophy of science developed by Roy Bhaskar, Steinmetz espouses the notion of ontological stratification, for which the empirical, the actual, and the real are at different levels of social reality. From this perspective, social historical research is not merely about searching for the correlation between various observations at the empirical level, as Hume proposed. Rather, the same event/phenomenon may be caused by different underlying mechanisms at the real level. Conversely, the same mechanism may also cause different events and phenomena in different cases. Once we distinguish the level of empirical events and the level of structural mechanisms, we can break away from the conventional misconception of comparison in positivism and empiricism and explore how various causal mechanisms exert their power in different cases in myriad ways.

A Macro-Phenomenological Approach to Comparison

Steinmetz's ontological justification has opened up much space for the philosophical and practical reflections on comparative methods, as several chapters in this edited volume have testified to. The motivation of this chapter is different. My purpose is not to strengthen the justification for comparative methods or to suggest ways to substantively improve practice of comparison. Instead, my focus is to understand what makes comparative research more "interesting" than other research. By doing so, we may not only be able to design more interesting comparisons but also better appreciate how comparison works in creative knowledge production and practical life.

In his classical essay on what makes a social theory interesting, Murray Davis (1971) advances a phenomenological analysis of how great social theories break away from entrenched views and established perceptions by providing refreshing angles, drawing unseen links, and bringing to light surprising yet convincing paradoxes. Comparison should also be understood from this phenomenological perspective. Comparative horizon is integral in social imaginaries, whether comparison is deployed consciously or subconsciously in our cognitive construction of the social world. Hence, a certain comparative angle is also entrenched in commonsensical and conventional understandings that the "interesting" comparisons seek to challenge and debunk. The macro-phenomenology of comparison proposed here thus endeavors to understand what makes great comparisons in the scholarly literature interesting and meaningful and how they take part in theoretical innovations. I call it macro-phenomenological to signify its shift of focus from micro-level everyday situations, which is what phenomenology typically does, to macro-level social imaginaries and comparative horizons.[1]

This macro-phenomenology of comparative horizons operates on a set of different understandings than the existing assumptions about comparison. Like the previously mentioned criticisms of comparison, the macro-phenomenological approach acknowledges the messiness of the working comparative horizon that we typically adopt. It is based on the view that a given case's reference group is not self-apparent. Rather, it argues that what great comparative research accomplishes is to disrupt unexamined understanding of case-group relationship, with which theoretical conventions are bundled together, and refresh our perception of case-group relationships based on new barometers of comparison (Walton 1992, 122). The macro-phenomenology of comparison also recognizes the fact that the topology of the social world is uneven and heterogenous and that units such as nation-state, state, county, corporation, and organization may not self-evidently constitute clearly stratified levels of comparison. What makes a comparative study interesting is often that it unsettles familiar comparison and draws unseen comparison, in a similar way that a joke disrupts the "contrast space" in which a statement is customarily encoded and throws it into a new "contrast space" that makes people laugh and reflect (Tavory and Timmermans 2014, 113–14).

It is from this phenomenological perspective that this chapter aims to understand how comparative methods are deployed to generate new theories and insights. In the following section, I examine three facets: comparison as deconstruction; comparison as reconstruction; and comparison *of* meaning-making and comparison *as* meaning-making.

Comparison as Deconstruction

Scholars and thinkers use comparison in a variety of ways to debunk conventional wisdoms. We can discern and categorize five common forms of deconstructive comparison.

Defamiliarize the Familiar

As Pierre Bourdieu has pointed out, the task of the sociologist is to denaturalize and to defatalize the social world (Bourdieu and Wacquant 1992, 49). While Bourdieu is better known for championing historicization as a potent means to accomplish denaturalization (Gorski 2013, 353), comparative methods can also serve to defamiliarize the world we are familiar with, denaturalize our natural understandings, and, through othering one's background cultures, shed light on the hidden cultural cultures that one is embedded in and has taken for granted.

Contrary to the notion of cultural incommensurability, which has been raised to reject comparison (as we have mentioned earlier), comparativists make the case that cultural structures are rendered more comprehensible when they are subject to comparative scrutiny. For example, in his *Empire of Signs*, Roland Barthes argued that semiotic analysis of Japanese culture was a "disturbance" and "a shock of meaning" because it helped to put the cultural structures of France and Europe in perspective: "Someday we must write the history of our own obscurity—manifest the density of our own narcissism" (Barthes 1982, 4).

From this perspective, historicization is only one particular genre of comparison that compares across time, when we realize things can be different in the past and examine how the present social and cultural relationships have been whipped into shape. Michel Foucault's (1977) genealogical method is such a case in point too.

De-essentialize the Others

Essentialism is the tendency to view one's own culture as dynamic while regarding others' meaning systems as inherently static. This tendency is especially manifest in the orientalist writings, which are characterized by their search for stable correlations between cultural structures or institutions and historical events in their others. In this orientalist framework, the others have become "immobile empires" in which ossified cultural structures and institutions and historical events have cyclically reinforced and regenerated each other.

To de-essentialize the others means to render visible the internal dynamism, diversity, contradictions, and conflicts within the others and to recognize the isomorphism of the internal dynamism, diversity, contradictions, and conflicts between the others and one's own background culture. This de-essentializing thrust is especially pronounced in the postcolonial critique of orientalism. But it can also enrich comparative research in a different sense: this way, the researcher begins to explain the difference that is being compared, not so much as the stable reproduction of innate cultural traits or institutions, but as the contingent outcome of these dynamic contentions and struggle. This is also reflected in scholarly attempts to unearth "liberal traditions" in non-Western contexts (e.g., de Bary 1983; Sen 1997). While they may appear to be guilty of imposing "Western" concepts on non-Western contexts, a strong comparativist argument can be made for it: for both Bourdieu and Charles Tilly, it is sociologically meaningful to lay bare and understand the state of struggle and contention, instead of fatalizing the particular sociocultural structures and mystifying power relationships implicated in it (Emirbayer 2010).[2]

This use of comparison to de-essentialize the others often goes together with the attempt to defamiliarize the familiar and mirrors it. In both circumstances, comparison serves to bring to light the dynamic and contested sociocultural formations and the power relationships that come along with them. The critique of the Whig interpretation and the rise of the revisionist scholarship in the Anglo-European historiography (which de-essentializes and defamiliarizes the Anglo-European history), for example, has created favorable space for Wenkai He (2013) to ask new comparative questions about the success and failure of creating a modern fiscal state in the midst of credit crises in early modern England and nineteenth-century Japan and China and shed light on the contingent political processes leading to their divergent outcomes in institution building.

Shift Background Comparison Through Critical Case Studies

Although case studies do not foreground comparative research design, they usually imply background comparison. Theoretical conventions are usually bound to known cases (Walton 1992, 122). By identifying new cases, critical case studies can shift background comparison and refresh and challenge existing theories to discover causal processes that are hidden and unseen in the conventional account. As Dietrich Rueschemeyer (2003, 317, cited from Rueschemeyer,

Huber Stephens, and Stephens 1992, 38) put it, "the theoretical framework—when informed by previous thought and research—provides the background against which the picture of the cases studied yields more telling results."

The "negative case methodology" advocated by Rebecca Emigh (1997) adopts this strategy. Because the extant theories of the capitalist breakthrough, such as Robert Brenner's thesis of agrarian capitalism, were bound to the English case, Emigh identified the region of Tuscany as a critical negative case that had all the prerequisite conditions according to the extant theories but did not result in the capitalist breakthrough. According to her, a crucial mechanism that was missing in Tuscany was the conversion from agrarian to urban capital.

Unravel Inherent Sequentiality

When we focus on a single case, our understanding of its causation is shaped by our narrative of its chain of events. For example, A occurs, then B events occur, and C happens, which eventually leads to D. When we connect these events into a chain, we may falsely believe in their "inherent sequentiality" and the historical necessity of their interlocking causality and may overestimate the importance of some factors that are neither necessary nor sufficient in the chain of events (Mahoney 2000, 530). A great comparative study can help disentangle the chain of events by putting them in perspective. Comparative researchers commonly deal with the following three types of errors.

1. Teleology in historical narratives. Teleological thinking biases us toward searching for "origins" that seem to inevitably lead to the outcome we are interested in and makes us oblivious to the divergent pathways that are possible and the contingent turning points that transition from one stage to another. For example, the conventional narrative of the Chinese Cultural Revolution usually traces its origins to the line struggle between Mao and his lieutenants, which eventually led to Mao's mobilization of the masses to attack the party officialdom; that is, the conflict between charismatic leader and the routinizing bureaucracy. In my own research (Xu 2017), by comparing the Cultural Revolution with other mass campaigns (especially the anti-Rightists campaign in 1957), I found that the Cultural Revolution was not a linear development but involved a qualitative change in the summer of 1966 due to the contingent interactions between elite conflict and mass mobilization, thereby debunking the teleological explanation of the Cultural Revolution.

2. Selection bias. By selecting only positive cases and neglecting negative cases, one may exaggerate the importance of factors that are manifest in both positive and negative cases and underplay factors that actually explain the

difference. For example, in his study of the rise of Chinese Communism, historian Arif Dirlik (1989) traced its origins to the crisis of the May Fourth Movement (1917–1921), arguing that participants of the movement, sensing its crisis in 1920, joined the Communist movement in order to carry on the movement momentum that they found was evaporating in the May Fourth activism. Such an explanation has selection bias because many May Fourth activists did not join the Communist movement but actively opposed it. My own research thus looks for the missing mechanism that explains the elective affinities of group ethos between certain May Fourth activist organizations and the Communist organizational form (Xu 2013).

3. Irreciprocal comparison. Comparison based on an irreciprocal barometer across cases often results in a wrong conception of causality. For example, the classic question in economic history is why England had the capitalist breakthrough and industrial revolution, whereas China did not. Researchers have traced back through centuries to identify what makes England unique. Yet, as Kenneth Pomeranz has pointed out in *The Great Divergence* (2009), England and China are not a reciprocal comparison in terms of scale and economic geography. Instead, England should be compared to the lower Yangtze Delta region of China, with which it was actually on par with regard to market institutions, industriousness, and population-control techniques. He thus concluded that the preexisting theories in economic history that resort to cultural or institutional factors (e.g., the Protestant ethic, free market institutions) actually do not explain why the Industrial Revolution took place in England but not in China.

Unpack Family Resemblance

The fifth way in which comparison can be used to debunk and deconstruct a conventional wisdom is to break "family resemblance" in the words and concepts that are often liberally and unreflexively used, whose similar guise may gloss over different underlying causal mechanisms, like games that do not share a common quality (Wittgenstein 2009, 66). Rigorous comparison can help to reveal these different mechanisms and introduce new typologies.

For example, in comparing the aristocrats in France with those in Britain, Tocqueville (1983) concludes that although they appeared the same and obtained the same name, they diverged significantly in that the French aristocrats had degenerated into merely a status group of nobilities, with rigid social closure but no political leadership, while their British counterparts, by establishing good terms with the rising bourgeoise and being highly open to accept the latter, were able to maintain their aristocratic rule. A recent example is Richard Biernacki's (1995) trenchant analysis of divergent approaches to labor commodification in Germany and Britain. It is commonly known that according to Marx's labor theory of value, the exchange value of commodities was the "socially necessary labor time" invested in producing them. Biernacki shows that behind this universalistic formulation is hidden two starkly different approaches: the British commodification of labor took the form of appropriation of the worker's materialized labor via actual products, whereas in Germany, it manifested as timed appropriation of the worker's activity and labor power. They took these distinctive forms because, in Britain, free trade of manufactured goods existed long before labor also became a commodity (which hence became based on the assumption of independent producers), whereas in Germany, the creation of the commodities market and labor market was simultaneous, when the commodification of labor borrowed its form from feudal levies.

Comparison as Reconstruction

There are three common ways in which comparison is used to construct and advance a new theory.

Analogy

Historians are particularly known for being deft at historical analogies. Identifying and explicating unexpected analogies can often bring forth refreshing perspectives for the case at hand. Drawing analogies and thereby offering "history lessons" is also how history was practiced before modernity (Koselleck 2004). In the modern era, analogic reasoning is also widely used yet remains little pondered over. Typically, analogic reasoning involves stripping off features that seem relevant in single-case narratives (in sequentiality) and identifying what Arthur Stinchcombe (1978) calls "deep analogy" (i.e., equivalent structural forces and features across different cases) (see also, Vaughan 2006). Damon Mayrl's contribution to this volume in chapter 2 delves deeper in this process.

A great example of this analogic reasoning is Theda Skocpol's comparison of the nobility in France with the gentry in China. Despite the fact that the gentry was not hereditary as the European nobility was and its mode of social reproduction and relationship to the state differed markedly from the latter, Skocpol considers the source of their power to be equivalent, that is, land ownership in a predominantly agrarian society. She thus renders the gentry's relationship to the Chinese imperial state commensurable with the relationship between European nobility and their monarchs. Highlighting the common balance of power between socioeconomic power and political power, she is able to identify this tension as a major cause of social revolutions (Skocpol 1979, xiii).

Contrast

In opposition to analogy, which establishes structural similarity and equivalence between cases that seem different, contrast is used to identify and articulate structural differences between cases. Skocpol and Somers (1980, 178) consider "contrast of contexts" as a main approach in comparative history, through which the analyst focuses on "broad themes or orienting questions or ideal-type concepts" that are common across cases in order to "bring out the unique features of each particular cases included in their discussions, and to show how these unique features affect the working-out of putatively general social processes." They accurately capture the operation of contrasting. However, the end result of contrasting is not merely the description of the particularity of the cases, as they claim. It is true that faithfulness to case holism characterizes this kind of "case-oriented" comparison (Ragin 1987). The "working out" of the contrasts in the cases, however, does not necessarily mean, as Skocpol and Somers suggest, that contrast of contexts in case analysis is simply idiographic description and produces no constructive theoretical advances.

To take the aforementioned example from Biernacki's contrasting of labor commodification in Britain and Germany, the general patterns emerging from the contrast center on the timing and sequence of free trade of goods vis-à-vis labor commodification. These are social processes whose working out can be observed and analyzed in other contexts.

Both analogy and contrast endeavor to discover modular causal processes across cases, even though the components of the causal processes under comparison are equivalent in the analogous comparison and distinctive in the contrasting comparison (Knight and Reed 2019). These causal processes are modular in the sense that their components being compared are sufficiently independent of one other and are portable across cases, including cases beyond those being compared (Woodward 2003, 336; cf. Bengtsson and Hertting 2014). In both Skocpol's analogous comparison of social revolutions and Biernacki's contrasting comparison of labor commodification, components of their models do not rely on one another to obtain their causal impacts. If one component is found lacking, the comparative scholar looks for an explanation for that anomaly while temporarily bracketing out other components. For example, the Chinese Revolution was not preconditioned by a strong tradition of solidarity and community of peasant socioeconomic life, which their French and Russian counterparts had. To account for this anomaly, Skocpol held constant the other structural preconditions and only searched for an extra explanation by drawing upon Eric Hobsbawm's notion of "social banditry," which can supplant peasant solidary community while making sense of the particular pathway of the communist growth in rural areas (Skocpol 1979, 152–54).

The modularity of causal models in these two forms of reconstructive comparison is different from the third form, where modularity, if any at all, resides not so much in the components of causal models as in the "scenes" of collective problem-solving.

"Reiterated Problem-Solving"

Jeffrey Haydu (1998) proposed approaching comparison, especially comparison across time periods (which are not independent cases but interconnected through memories and institutional legacies), as situations of reiterated problem-solving. What makes the cases comparable is the analogousness of the problem that confronts the actors. The comparison then endeavors to tease out how actors come up with solutions to surmount the challenges and how the varying constraining and enabling forces that make their solutions succeed or fail. Haydu used recurrent dilemmas of American managerial control over workers and work practices in different time periods as an illustration of this comparative approach. A less methodical form often permeates in insinuating analogies that laypersons and sometimes professional historians make in order to derive certain "history lessons." A recent example is the widely suggested analogy to the Weimar Republic in the United States after the election of Donald Trump, which has led to many value-charged discussions about how to avert the "mistakes" that the Weimar politicians made (Bessner 2017).

For Haydu, the exact degree to which the problems that the actors in cases under comparison are confronting are analogous can be an open question. The key is to arrive at a judicious analytical judgment about their comparability based on the assessment of how the actors construct the problem as well as the solutions they realistically arrive at. Haydu even acknowledged that approaching comparison as reiterated problem-solving can accommodate contestations among the actors over the very definition of the problems they are poised to solve, not to mention their contestations over solutions. As he put it, "a problem-solving account should include other actors, with their own definitions of problems and proposed solutions. Practices at particular times will reflect the clash of rival solutions, and one group's initial remedies will be modified in the face of another's backlash. These dynamics will complicate interpretation but not alter the logic of reiterated problem solving" (Haydu 1998, 355–56).

By incorporating the actors' competing problem constructions and leaving the degree of analogousness of problems that actors confront as an open question, this mode of reconstructive comparison thus diverges even further from the modularity of causal models required in the first two modes of deep analogy and contrast, where causal models are decomposed into mutually independent causal chains or forces. In contrast, once we incorporate the meaning-making and agentic processes, which involve actors' negotiations, interactions, and contestations, if one component of the meaning-making processes is taken away, the meanings that other components obtain would also change—an analytical principle that the linguistic turn has made patently clear in the human sciences (Hirschman and Reed 2014). Of course, these interactions, negotiations, contentions, and alignments are not stochastic and often manifest patterns of structuration. Their patterns of structuration, however, are emergent properties and are contingently subject to dissolvement.

This means that we need not only to compare the structural forces as conventionally conceptualized in material, cultural, or institutional mechanisms but also, more importantly, to make sense—while taking into account those structural forces—of the crucial role that "meaning mechanisms" play in "formation stories" (Hirschman and Reed 2014; Norton 2014). That is to say, comparative research should not only compare how structural forces shape outcomes of our interest but also compare the creative processes where actors' individual and collective agency makes a difference. The phenomenologically "interesting" comparative studies often *make these two types of comparison enrich each other*. This expanded conception of comparison helps to zoom in on the emergent processes through which the outcomes to be explained are eventuated through dynamic interactions and contestations that are partially shaped by sociocultural structures and yet partially transform them.

Comparing Dynamic Transformational Processes

In the recent historical social sciences, two intellectual developments have sparked this type of comparison of dynamic transformational processes. The first is the emphasis on uncertainty and contingency. In this regard, Michel Foucault (1977) has provided the most radical articulation in his essay "Nietzsche, Genealogy, History," in which history manifests as an endless constellation of contingent processes. A less expansive but methodologically more rigorous demonstration in historical sociology is Ivan Ermakoff's (2008, 2015) theory of collective alignment in moments of historical indeterminacy. The second development is the proliferation of the revisionist history in national historiography, which challenges the conventional interpretation that often sugarcoats the perspective of winners in national politics with a rather essentialized sociocultural structural explanation (e.g., see *The Whig Interpretation of History* by Butterfield [1965]).

The confluence of these two developments generates new comparative imagination that departs from explanations based on modular causal forces and instead mobilizes dynamic transformational processes to explain divergent outcomes. Through this lens, the outcomes are not products of the natural actualization of structural forces but results of intrinsically contingent yet structuring social processes of interactions, contentions, and alignments, through which the causal weight of structural forces is rendered dynamically palpable. I offer two examples here.

The first example is Steven Pincus's (2009) new interpretation of the Glorious Revolution in his book *1688: The First Modern Revolution*. In it, he challenged the Whig interpretation that privileges the role of the English liberal tradition and pointed out that, for a long time before the Glorious Revolution, many English political elites admired and emulated the model of "Catholic modernity" that Louis XIV of France had conceived and inaugurated. James II was one of these admirers, according to Pincus. This model of modernity had provoked the opponents of its admirers in England to envision a different political program (especially in ideas about religion, foreign policy, and economy). The result of the Glorious Revolution came about through a protracted process of conflicts and alignments. Therefore, Pincus's interpretation of this process takes into account both structural forces and dynamic and contingent factors.

The second example is the role of ideas and ideologies in the great divergence question. Although Kenneth Pomeranz highlighted contingency emphatically, he did little to ground contingency in ideas, especially interactions and conflicts over ideas. Ho-fung Hung's (2008) intervention into the debate, however, opened up further room for us to explore this question. He argued that despite enormous commercial growth in Qing China, capital accumulation occurred on a limited scale because merchants were generally reluctant to expand production but instead invested their newly accumulated wealth in land estates and securing offspring's pathway to officialdom. The reason, he contended, is that the Qing state, although probusiness most of the time, was paternalistic toward the urban poor and always tended to suppress the merchants in favor of labor when conflicts between merchants and labor arose. This paternalistic policy thus increased the risk of merchants' capital expansion. Although the English state had a similar paternalistic policy before the eighteenth century, it began, after the mid-eighteenth century and under the influence of the Scottish Enlightenment and new political economy, to break away from this *relative* and *conditional* support for capital and instead lend *absolute* and *unconditional* support to capital, thus creating the condition for unprecedented capital expansion. While cogent, this explanation gives rise to further questions about why the English state adopted this new capital-centered economic thought and relinquished its paternalism; why the Chinese state failed to do so, even though a similar current of economic ideas and statecraft also emerged in China around the same time (Rowe 2002); and why Turgot's reform in France, which was based on this set of new economic ideas, miscarried. Raising these questions induces us to pay attention to many parallel historical processes (intellectual change, economic change, and political change) and examine how these changes played out through the conflicts and alignments of different social groups, leading eventually to the great divergence in the global economy.

In both cases, strategies of deconstructivist comparison are first mobilized to destabilize the conventional explanations that emphasize essentialized sociocultural and institutional conditions and the inherent sequentiality that connects their conditions to the outcomes. Contingent dynamic processes of conflicts and alignments are then introduced to reconstruct the comparison, particularly the comparison of critical junctures where actors' agentic dimension and structural forces shed light onto each other.

This brief illustration of the comparison of dynamic transformational processes clarifies two situations that shape our perception of certain comparisons as interesting. In the first and more common situation, interesting comparisons reveal mechanisms of causal determination that are hidden in conventional comparative accounts. A second and much less contemplated situation, however, is to unpack mechanisms of emergent creativity and transformations in "formation stories," whether they are a revolutionary rupture, great divergence, or institutional innovation (Hirschman and Reed 2014). Ideally, comparing dynamic transformational processes should deliver both mechanisms of determination and mechanisms of emergent creativity.

The Duality of Comparison: Method of Analysis and Method of Practice

This approach to comparison is not only more interesting but also more meaningful because comparison is not only a method of analysis but also a method of practice. As a method of analysis, comparative research endeavors to break the complicit relationship between our received wisdoms about the social world and the unreflexive comparative horizon we are given and to challenge the former by changing the latter. But, as a method of practice, comparison is part and parcel of our practical creativity, because our investigation of the concatenations of past structural forces and contingent agentic processes is deeply connected with the changeability of our current historical context and the openness of the future. As Reinhart Koselleck (2004, 29–40) incisively pointed out, the old *historie* before modernity was predicated on the notion that history is iterable and thus offers changeless history lessons, whereas in modernity, an empiricist commitment to understand the singularity of each historical event and process is precisely tied with the modern notion of the constructability of the present and the future. Insofar as comparative research in modern scholarship has diverged from traditional "history lessons," it is part and parcel of this practical creativity of history that we are embedded in. The macro-phenomenological perspective captures precisely this duality of comparison as both method of analysis and method of practice.

Our previous anxiety about the legitimacy of comparative methods in the postpositivist social sciences, which Steinmetz (2004) has convincingly addressed on the philosophical ground, is based on three assumptions that are problematic phenomenologically. First, the reference group or population, of which the cases under investigation are part, is self-evident. Second, what counts as a case is self-evident, with the casing process being taken for granted (Walton 1992). Third, the social world is clearly stratified into distinct levels of analysis, and the universe in which findings based on cases under investigation can be generalized is also self-evident. Yet, as John Walton (1992, 125–26) provocatively contended, we usually come to terms with cases not based on our prior knowledge of the properties of a universe. Instead, "the universe is inferred from the case" and not the other way around.

The macro-phenomenological perspective instead acknowledges the messiness of the comparative horizon that the average person operates with (and ontologically justifiably so) and argues that a good comparison is precisely to dislodge the received wisdom about the reference group and alter our comparative horizon through repositioning our angle and reconstructing the objects of our analysis. And it is precisely because comparison is as much a method of practice as a method of analysis, its function as a method of analysis gains its source of strength from its practical function because it is an essential skill in our knowledge set in confronting a changeable present and an open-ended future. In this regard, Marx's practice is worth unpacking.

Marx began *The Eighteenth Brumaire of Louis Bonaparte* by dispelling a misrecognized comparison. That is, the French revolutionaries of 1848 were constantly making analogies between the history they were making with the Great Revolution of 1789 to the extent that they took "Caussidière for Danton, Louis Blanc for Robespierre, the Montagne of 1848 to 1851 for the Montagne of 1793 to 1795, the nephew for the uncle" (Marx 1963, 15). This style of comparison, however, is a form of misrecognition because the structural context has already shifted. And this misrecognized comparison is itself a contributing factor to the failure of the 1848 revolution due to the incapacitation of the revolutionaries to Louis Bonaparte's counterrevolutionary assault and dictatorial ambition. What Marx sought to accomplish through his comparison is to spell out the rather different structural forces that shaped these two revolutions (e.g., composition and structure of social classes, competition and alignments of political forces, changes in modes of production, and evolution of political institutions) as well as the interactive contingencies that actors brought about (including their misrecognized comparison, such as the 1789 revolutionaries' emulation of ancient Romans and the 1848 revolutionaries' emulation of the 1789 revolutionaries). The creative practice of his comparison was ultimately dedicated to opening up new possibilities for the present and future history because these possibilities would only be free from being haunted by the ghosts of the past after we have critically examined the comparative history of the past. As Marx eloquently put it, "The social revolution of the nineteenth century cannot take its poetry from the past but only from the future. It cannot begin with itself before it has stripped away all superstition about the past. The former revolutions required recollections of past world history in order to smother their own content. The revolution of the nineteenth century must let the dead bury their dead in order to arrive at its own content" (1963, 18).

In this sense, the burial of the past is not to forget it. Drawing from a distinction that Walter Benjamin once made, the "transmissibility" of the past has been replaced by its "citability" (Arendt 1968, 38; see also, Koselleck 2004, 39). As mode of practice, comparison helps to transform the transmissibility of the past into its citability and create conditions for new possibilities of the future. Comparison of dynamic transformational processes is hence an essential part of practical creativity.

Notes

1. I appreciate Nicholas Wilson's suggestion of this terminology.
2. This focus on contention and struggle is related to the shift in historical sociology from explaining social change as anomalous, which was the default position in structural functionalism, to taking social change as the normal state of affairs and approaching stability and persistence as the result of power struggle and contention (Abbott 2004, 7–8).

References

Abbott, Andrew. 2004. *Methods of Discovery: Heuristics for the Social Sciences*. New York: Norton.

Adams, Julia, Elisabeth Clemens, and Ann Shola Orloff. 2005. "Introduction: Social Theory, Modernity, and the Three Waves of Historical Sociology." In *Remaking Modernity: Politics, History, and Sociology*, edited by Julia Adams, Elisabeth Clemens, and Ann Shola Orloff, 1–72. Durham, NC: Duke University Press.

Arendt, Hannah. 1968. "Introduction: Walter Benjamin (1892–1940)." In *Illuminations: Essays and Reflections*, edited by Walter Benjamin, 1–58. New York: Schocken.

Barthes, Roland. 1982. *Empire of Signs*. New York: Hill and Wang.

Bengtsson, Bo, and Nils Hertting. 2014. "Generalization by Mechanism: Thin Rationality and Ideal-Type Analysis in Case Study Research." *Philosophy of the Social Sciences* 44(6):707–32.

Bessner, Daniel. 2017. "The Ghosts of Weimar: The Weimar Analogy in American Thought." *Social Research: An International Quarterly* 84(4):831–55.

Biernacki, Richard. 1995. *The Fabrication of Labor: Germany and Britain, 1640–1914.* Berkeley: University of California Press.

Bourdieu, Pierre, and Loïc J. D. Wacquant. 1992. *An Invitation to Reflexive Sociology.* Chicago: University of Chicago Press.

Burawoy, Michael. 1989. "Two Methods in Search of Science." *Theory and Society* 18(6):759–805.

Butterfield, Herbert. 1965. *The Whig Interpretation of History.* New York: Norton.

Calhoun, Craig. 1996. "The Rise and Domestication of Historical Sociology." In *The Historic Turn in the Human Sciences,* edited by Terrence J. McDonald, 305–37. Ann Arbor: University of Michigan Press.

Davis, Murray S. 1971. "That's Interesting: Towards a Phenomenology of Sociology and a Sociology of Phenomenology." *Philosophy of the Social Sciences* 1(4):309–44.

De Bary, William Theodore. 1983. *The Liberal Tradition in China.* New York: Columbia University Press.

Dirlik, Arif. 1989. *The Origins of Chinese Communism.* New York: Oxford University Press.

Emigh, Rebecca Jean. 1997. "The Power of Negative Thinking: The Use of Negative Case Methodology in the Development of Sociological Theory." *Theory and Society* 26(5):649–84.

Emirbayer, Mustafa. 2010. "Tilly and Bourdieu." *American Sociologist* 41(4):400–22.

Ermakoff, Ivan. 2008. *Ruling Oneself Out: A Theory of Collective Abdications.* Durham, NC: Duke University Press.

——. 2015. "The Structure of Contingency." *American Journal of Sociology* 121(1):64–125.

Foucault, Michel. 1977. "Nietzsche, Genealogy, History." In *Language, Counter-Memory, Practice: Selected Essays and Interviews,* edited by Donald F. Bouchard, 139–64. Ithaca, NY: Cornell University Press.

Gorski, Philip S. 2013. "Bourdieusian Theory and Historical Analysis: Maps, Mechanisms, and Methods." In *Bourdieu and Historical Analysis,* edited by Philip Gorski, 327–67. Durham, NC: Duke University Press.

Haydu, Jeffrey. 1998. "Making Use of the Past: Time Periods as Cases to Compare and as Sequences of Problem Solving." *American Journal of Sociology* 104(2):339–71.

He, Wenkai. 2013. *Paths Toward the Modern Fiscal State, England, Japan, and China.* Cambridge, MA: Harvard University Press.

Hirschman, Daniel, and Isaac Ariail Reed. 2014. "Formation Stories and Causality in Sociology." *Sociological Theory* 32(4):259–82.

Hung, Ho-fung. 2008. "Agricultural Revolution and Elite Reproduction in Qing China: The Transition to Capitalism Debate Revisited." *American Sociological Review* 73(4):569–88.

Kiser, Edgar, and Michael Hechter. 1991. "The Role of General Theory in Comparative-Historical Sociology." *American Journal of Sociology* 97(1):1–30.

Knight, Carly R., and Isaac Ariail Reed. 2019. "Meaning and Modularity: The Multivalence of 'Mechanism' in Sociological Explanation." *Sociological Theory* 37(3):234–56.

Koselleck, Reinhart. 2004. *Futures Past: On the Semantics of Historical Time.* Cambridge, MA: MIT Press.

Lieberson, Stanley. 1991. "Small N's and Big Conclusions: An Examination of the Reasoning in Comparative Studies Based on a Small Number of Cases." *Social Forces* 70(2):307–20.

Mahoney, James. 2000. "Path Dependence in Historical Sociology." *Theory and Society* 29(4):507–48.

Marx, Karl. 1963. *The 18th Brumaire of Louis Bonaparte.* New York: International Publishers.

Norton, Matthew. 2014. "Mechanisms and Meaning Structures." *Sociological Theory* 32(2): 162–87.

Pincus, Steven. 2009. *1688: The First Modern Revolution*. New Haven, CT: Yale University Press.

Pomeranz, Kenneth. 2009. *The Great Divergence: China, Europe, and the Making of the Modern World Economy*. Princeton, NJ: Princeton University Press.

Ragin, Charles C. 1987. *The Comparative Method: Moving Beyond Qualitative and Quantitative Strategies*. Berkeley: University of California Press.

Rowe, William T. 2002. *Saving the World: Chen Hongmou and Elite Consciousness in Eighteenth-Century China*. Stanford, CA: Stanford University Press.

Rueschemeyer, Dietrich. 2003. "Can One or a Few Cases Yield Theoretical Gains?" In *Comparative Historical Analysis in the Social Sciences*, edited by James Mahoney and Dietrich Rueschemeyer, 305–36. Cambridge: Cambridge University Press.

Rueschemeyer, Dietrich, Evelyne Huber Stephens, and John D. Stephens. 1992. *Capitalist Development and Democracy*. Chicago: University of Chicago Press.

Sen, Amartya. 1997. "Human Rights and Asian Values." *New Republic* 217(2–3):33–40.

Sewell, William H., Jr. 1996. "Three Temporalities: Toward an Eventful Sociology." In *The Historic Turn in the Human Sciences*, edited by Terrence J. McDonald, 245–80. Ann Arbor: University of Michigan Press.

Skocpol, Theda. 1979. *States and Social Revolutions: A Comparative Analysis of France, Russia, and China*. New York: Cambridge University Press.

Skocpol, Theda, and Margaret Somers. 1980. "The Uses of Comparative History in Macrosocial Inquiry." *Comparative Studies in Society and History* 22(2):174–97.

Steinmetz, George. 2004. "Odious Comparisons: Incommensurability, the Case Study, and 'Small N's' in Sociology." *Sociological Theory* 22(3):371–400.

——. 2014. "Comparative History and Its Critics." In *A Companion to Global Historical Thought*, edited by Prasenjit Duara, Viren Murthy, and Andrew Sartori, 412–36. Malden, MA: Wiley Blackwell.

Stinchcombe, Arthur L. 1978. *Theoretical Methods in Social History*. New York: Academic Press.

Tavory, Iddo, and Stefan Timmermans. 2014. *Abductive Analysis: Theorizing Qualitative Research*. Chicago: University of Chicago Press.

Tocqueville, Alexis de. 1983. *The Old Régime and the French Revolution*. New York: Anchor, Doubleday.

Vaughan, Diane. 2006. "NASA Revisited: Theory, Analogy, and Public Sociology." *American Journal of Sociology* 112(2):353–93.

Walton, John. 1992. "Making the Theoretical Case." In *What Is a Case? Exploring the Foundations of Social Inquiry*, edited by Charles C. Ragin and Howard S. Becker, 121–37. Cambridge: Cambridge University Press.

Wittgenstein, Ludwig. 2009. *Philosophical Investigations*. Edited and translated by P. M. S. Hacker and Joachim Schulte. 4th edition. Oxford: Wiley-Blackwell.

Woodward, James. 2003. *Making Things Happen: A Theory of Causal Explanation*. New York: Oxford University Press.

Xu, Xiaohong. 2013. "Belonging Before Believing: Group Ethos and Bloc Recruitment in the Making of Chinese Communism." *American Sociological Review* 78(5):773–96.

——. 2017. "Dialogic Struggle in the Becoming of the Cultural Revolution: Between Elite Conflict and Mass Mobilization." *Critical Historical Studies* 4(2):209–42.

CHAPTER 4

FROM CAUSALITY TO CONSTITUTION

Why Good Historical Comparisons Are the Same as Good
Ethnographic Case Studies, Deep Down

JOSH PACEWICZ

What can one conclude based on study of a single case? The question is deceptively simple, and methodological writings more commonly focuses on the seemingly thornier question of comparison. But in some ways, scholars' treatment of single cases is not that different from how they conduct comparisons, because single cases typically entail an implicit comparison between empirical observation and the academic knowledge on a given topic (Burawoy 1998; Emigh 1997). In conducting a case study, a scholar usually makes a pretense at using their observations to say something that is universally, or at least more broadly, valid.

My chapter advances an argument about the utility of case studies under the guise of disambiguating debates in a subfield that is adjacent to historical comparative sociology: debates among ethnographers about how to draw conclusions from observation of a single ethnographic case. But although the ostensible topic of the chapter is the single-case study, I undertake the exercise primarily for the sake of comparison. At base, debates about comparison among historical sociologists and those about single-case studies among ethnographers boil down to why we should conduct in-depth qualitative research in the first place. In this light, my first task is distilling many of the insights from this volume to see if, beyond the ideocracies of each author, there is a coherent overarching prescription about the utility of comparison. And second, I delve into several exemplary ethnographies to see whether insights from historical sociology can provide prescriptions for how good ethnographies already employ case studies. My takeaway is conventionalist in the main. To quote this book's introduction, the tricky methodological questions have already been solved—sometimes implicitly—by "actually practicing social scientists, in muddling through the difficult research process and its dialog with data." But what exemplary scholars do is often out of step with methodological prescriptions, and in this respect, ethnography and historical sociology are in a similar boat. In both cases, the methods literature has concerned itself with largely causality, but much of the groundbreaking empirical work advances a style of argumentation that I detail as constitutive arguments.

A constitutive argument is a context-independent description that concerns the makeup of a social phenomenon and commonly focuses on existence, categorization, or casing. In formal terms, a well-formulated constitutive argument pinpoints the features of a situation that are equivalent to a social phenomenon taking place (Dasgupta 2017). As such, constitutive arguments generally blend observations of empirical events, trends, or facts with theoretical arguments that may lend themselves to empirical predictions but are not themselves empirically observable. For the latter reason, constitutive arguments are often read by an academic audience as causal, but I will argue that they are better understood as incidentally causal in the sense that any empirical predictions derived from them merely lend plausibility to their central theoretical postulates.

Examples of constitutive arguments abound in everyday speech. Sarah suffered a heart attack due to a blockage in one of her coronary arteries. Will committed fraud when he acted on an insider stock tip that he learned during his college reunion. Both statements make context-independent claims about the nature of a phenomenon or social relationship. And since American sociologists generally associate analysis with causality (Abend, Petre, and Sauder 2013), one is tempted to read both statements as causal (i.e., as the blockage of an artery causing a heart attack or trades based on insider information causing a fraud). But note that neither statement concerns a relationship between two independent factors or variables. Rather, both statements restate the outcome of interest, whether the heart attack or fraud, in terms that strip away epiphenomenal characteristics of the situation and isolate a phenomenon's defining features. Placing a trade based on nonpublic information does not cause a fraud to take place—those activities are the fraud and always constitute fraud regardless of why a person undertakes them. Blockage of the coronary artery is the heart attack, not its cause; the cause might be stress, use of illicit drugs, or a lifetime of poor diet and little exercise. One can easily extend the distinction to more complex social processes. The claim that Donald Trump won the 2016 election by amassing over 270 electoral votes is likewise a constitutive rather than causal argument; it does not explain why Trump won, but rather specifies conditions of victory within the American electoral system.

If the argument seems pedantic, consider that confusion between causality and constitution belies many methodological prescriptions on the utility of ethnographic case studies. American sociologists have historically equated causality with the discipline's most scientific aspects (Abbott 1992; Becker 2008, 17), and in the matter of case selection, ethnographers are "more royalist than the king"—that is, even more likely than other social scientists to emphasize their own ability to make causal claims, especially when publishing in general sociology journals (Abend et al. 2013, 615). Defenders of ethnography often point to the ability of the methd to get to the internal conditions of cases and therefore produce fuller or more satisfactory causal accounts than qualitative sociology (Hirschman and Reed 2014; Lichterman and Reed 2015; Martin 2011; Reed 2011). Following Gross (2009), ethnographies can illuminate the "gears" that form the links of mechanistic explanations.

Yet it does not follow from this that ethnographers' ability to see the internal conditions of cases is the primary way in which ethnographies inform the audience's understanding of the social world. Ethnographers usually make a combination of causal and constitutive claims, which become decoupled in the course of disciplinary debate and inquiry—and it is the latter claims that tend to carry. One can easily list ethnographies that reshaped the field with constitutive arguments. Household gender relations are built on an implicit economy of exchange (Hochschild 1989). Becoming a habitual user of some intoxicants involves redefining their physiologically ambiguous effects as pleasurable (Becker 1953). Financial markets contain subcultures consisting of traders who adhere to common norms of opportunism (Abolafia 2001). The presentation of lessons in schools is shaped by a hidden curriculum that presupposes different personality traits in students (Anyon 1980). Other sociologists are often less interested in what the gears of the machine produce than in a deeper understanding of what is inside the box in the first place—whether or not it is actually machine-like at all.

But why do such arguments carry so effectively, and how should one select cases to formulate those that do? I argue that ethnographers and historical sociologists can learn from each other by examining what successful exemplars already do. Two historical approaches offer particularly useful models for ethnography: the formation story approach (Hirschman and Reed 2014) and negative case analysis (Emigh 1997).

This chapter proceeds in three parts. The first section reviews debate over comparison in historical sociology, which I argue can be read as a broad move from strategies that facilitate causal arguments to those that facilitate constitutive arguments. The second section shows how such attention to the constitution of social phenomena disambiguates ethnographic debates about case selection. Current debates are muddled by a tendency among ethnographers to distinguish between empirically and theoretically oriented ethnography— between studies that allow one to "speak to empirical conditions in other cases (not observed)" (Small 2009, 5; see also Elman, Gerring, and Mahoney 2016;

King, Keohane, and Verba 1994) and those that allow one to formulate "theoretical generalizations" (see, e.g., Small 2009, Spillman 2014). Via engagement with Small's (2009) agenda-setting article on case selection, I show this distinction to be logically and practically untenable. Both empirically and theoretically oriented ethnographers are ultimately interested in making claims that other scholars will accept as informative about the world outside of their field site—as provisionally externally valid. Greater attention to constitutive arguments disambiguates this distinction and points to strategies for successfully utilizing cases.

The third and final section examines recent exemplars to determine how ethnographers actually use cases to make constitutive claims that others accept as informative about the world outside of their cases. Ethnographers do so by establishing a warrant for thinking that similar social formations are consequential elsewhere. The common distinction between empirically and theoretically oriented ethnography is actually about different conventions for how one makes such claims. Empirically oriented ethnographers follow the prescriptions of Small (2009) and make external validity claims inductively via "pointy" cases wherein the phenomenon of interest is large or bifurcated or otherwise suggest causal or logical relations to other variables of interest. Theoretically oriented ethnographers make constitutive claims abductively vis-à-vis existing theory (Timmermans and Tavory 2012). They are best served by resolutive cases, wherein analysis resolves a contradiction in the literature, or negative cases (Emigh 1997), wherein empirical regularities predicted by theory do not occur.

Historical Comparison: From Causal to Constitutive Argument

Many of the chapters in this volume detail a shift in historical sociology away from approaches that mobilize case studies to make causal arguments toward those that utilize comparison toward other ends. Theda Skocpol's use of John Stuart Mill's method is particularly instructive, since many authors show convincingly that her use of comparison to explain revolutions is not very causally convincing and yet very theoretically generative (see many chapters in this volume and also Mahoney 2000; Mayrl 2018; Sewell 2005; Steinmetz 2004). For this reason, many scholars argue that one should utilize comparison to instead achieve ends of the sort that Skocpol arrived at perhaps unwittingly. Following, Xiaohong Xu (chapter 3 in this volume), for instance, comparison is useful in both theoretical construction and deconstruction. Or following Damon Mayrl (chapter 2 in this volume), comparison allows a scholar to build up junk knowledge and recursively revisit data in order to facilitate the sort of analogical reasoning that allows for theorizing. My aim here is merely to identify what we mean by theorization, which, in the specific instance of methodological writings on comparison, I think it useful to equate narrowly with constitutive argument and separate clearly from causal argument. Likewise, a superordinate concern with the constitutive properties of social phenomenon is central to other recent methodological papers in historical sociology. Here, I consider two much-read recent prescriptions on constructing historical arguments: formation stories and negative case analysis.

Following Hirschman and Reed (2014), many contemporary historical sociologists produce formation stories, which provide narrative accounts of the emergence of new social types—actors, organizational forms, concepts, and the like. For example, scholars explain how think tanks became separate from lobby firms and universities (Medvetz 2012), autism became a common diagnosis (Eyal 2013), nonprofits became a stable organizational form (Barman 2013), and impersonal political authority emerged from cliental relations (Padgett and Ansell 1993). Consistent with sociologists' forementioned proclivities for fighting academic conflicts on the terrain of causality, Hirschman and Reed (2014) argue that formation stories lead to better causal explanations and are generally a useful corrective to epistemically naïve "forcing-cause accounts." Following Andrew Abbott (1988), such forcing-cause accounts presuppose a world of fixed entities with historically and contextually independent causal powers, which—like machines—reliably turn Xs into Ys. But history shows that the causal powers of Xs change. For example, the effects of a nobility title are different in feudal and contemporary times (Gorski 2009, 162). Hirschman and Reed (2014, 259–60) therefore see formation stories as a necessary component of satisfactory causal accounts because they "provide the historical and empirical boundaries for the functioning of forcing-cause accounts" that explain how a phenomenon became "stable enough to force or be forced." For this reason, Hirschman and Reed (2014, 260) see formation stories as "fundamentally causal"—although perhaps this is because they worry that others have traditionally "written [them] off as merely descriptive rather than explanatory claims."

The formation story is attractive in that it focuses our attention on what exemplary works of historical sociology do well, and my quibble is only with the claim that formation stories are fundamentally causal. In fact, I think it more correct to say that formation stories are fundamentally constitutive and incidentally causal. And these two types of claims often become decoupled in the course of disciplinary debate, with the former generally more influential.

Consider one influential formation story: Greta Krippner's account of financialization. Krippner popularized the financialization concept in an earlier article, which contains no causal argument (and remains more cited than her book). The article aims to determine "how to conceptualize most usefully long-term structural changes in the US economy" (Krippner 2005, 174). The argument is definitional or constitutive: Krippner argues that financialization is best understood as corporations' growing dependence on profits derived via financial mechanisms and defends this claim by considering and rejecting alternate ways of defining financialization. For example, she rejects measuring the growing importance of finance via employment numbers because financial firms employ few workers but impact the behavior of nonfinancial firms. At base then, the argument is really about what the contemporary American economy is all about, and the account blends elements that Philip Gorski (see the afterword in this volume) distinguishes as actual and real—that is, empirically observable and not empirically observable. On the one hand, the account subsumes empirical trends such as the growing share of corporate profits derived from their financial divisions as constitutive of financialization. On the other hand, the argument pinpoints an incentive structure that rewards corporations for maximizing profit through financial channels as a driver of financialization. The latter argument has numerous empirical implications but is not itself empirically observable. One could find good evidence of corporations responding to different incentives in lots of different ways (by interviewing managers and getting their rationalizations, by juxtaposing historical cases when pre- and postfinancialization managers responded to a similar situation similarly, and so on). But the incentive structure itself is a conceptual construct that one cannot directly observe.

It is for this reason that I see Krippner's financialization narrative as primarily constitutive and only incidentally causal, although the two styles of argument are logically linked. The account is incidentally causal, first, because it goes hand in hand with what one might classify as an account of formation that describes where financialization comes from. In *Capitalizing on Crisis*, Krippner (2011) provides this sort of account of where financialization came from, but we can discount this as the primary contribution based solely on the fact that most readers who have heard of financialization but have no particular interest in late twentieth-century American political development will have forgotten it.[1] And second, Krippner's argument and especially work inspired by it contain causal arguments that follow naturally from the constitutive argument about financialization. That is, the account points to empirical predictions that lend plausibility to the constitutive account rather than feature as the main event. For instance, Krippner's account suggests that financialization impacts inequality by changing workplace management in firms with financial investments—a causal argument substantiated by Ken-Hou Lin and Donald Tomaskovic-Devey (2013), who find that changes in renumeration within such firms account for half of labor's declining share of income vis-à-vis capital since the 1970s.

Constitutive arguments are likewise central to analysis of exceptional or negative cases, another common research strategy in historical sociology. Scholars have traditionally identified deviant cases as useful for generating or extending theory (Burawoy 1998; Emigh 1997; Ermakoff 2014), and contemporary historical sociologists frequently identify negative case analysis as consonant with Kuhnian (Kuhn 1961) and Lakatosian (Lakatos 1978) theories of science. These theories hold that knowledge does not advance through falsification since all theories cannot account for some anomalies (Emigh 1997; Ermakoff 2014). In this light, Rebecca Emigh (1997) argues that scientists' approach to anomalous cases is key to progressive science: scholars in a regressive regime simply ignore anomalies, whereas scholars in a progressive one incorporate them into existing theory by creating subtheories, identifying previously unnoticed countervailing mechanisms, and specifying scope conditions. Emigh (1997) therefore suggests that historical sociologists study negative cases, wherein an outcome predicted by theory should have occurred but did not. Although negative case analysis focuses attention on a surprisingly inactive causal mechanism, Emigh (1997, 649) argues that the aim is primarily to "expand a theory's range of explanation" by clarifying the conceptual model of a phenomenon.

For instance, Emigh (1997) illustrates negative case analysis via investigation of early modern Tuscany, which did not transition to capitalism despite having characteristics commonly associated with capitalist development, such as an efficient agricultural sector, declining feudal ties, a large urban economy, and a commercial manufacturing sector. Emigh (1997, 669) finds that this was due to preunification Italy's political geography. Cities were tied to their immediate countryside, which first stimulated development but later retarded it as markets had limited ties to other regions. Thus formulated, the account sounds as though it is motivated by a deterministic logic akin to Mill's method of difference, but Emigh argues otherwise. As others have argued, mechanisms are contextually and historically embedded (Hirschman and Reed 2014), and many incidental events or typically inconsequential mechanisms could prevent transition to capitalism, even if all theoretically consequential factors are present (Gorski 2009; Steinmetz 1998). For instance, one can easily imagine a state that has its transition to capitalism arrested by a plague or conquest. Rather, Emigh's account extends the range of theory by altering understanding of what capitalist transition consists of, both in the case of Tuscany *and in previously examined historical cases.* The analysis shows that political arrangements that allow for geographically extensive markets are a component of capitalist development, even in larger European states wherein this went unnoticed by virtue of many states having similar political geographies in common. Here again, the constitutive argument facilitates causal analysis but is separate from it.

There's No Such Thing as Empirical and Theoretical Generalizations

Historical sociologists' approaches to formulating constitutive arguments can disambiguate debates among ethnographers for how to select cases and utilize them to make claims. Generally, the issue of casing is not as central to debates about ethnographic methods, and there is hardly consensus among ethnographers about appropriate strategies of case selection. Nevertheless, one can identify two general approaches. Ethnographers discuss case selection, first, in the context of establishing external validity. Mario Small (2009) offers one widely applied set of guidelines, which is standard reading in graduate courses and offers advice that is consistent with the guidelines of funding entities like the National Science Foundation (Lamont and White 2005). But other ethnographers select and mobilize cases to "build theory," an ill-defined enterprise that ethnographers nevertheless widely take to be different from efforts to establish external validity.

In what follows, I argue that the distinction between empirically and theoretically oriented ethnography does reflect a different approach to case selection, but not for the reasons commonly provided in the literature. That is, ethnographic methods articles portray ethnographers in the two camps as interested in making different kinds of claims—most commonly, (externally valid) empirical generalizations versus theoretical generalizations of questionable or unclear external validity (Small 2009; Spillman 2014). Below, I first show that the distinction between empirical and theoretical generalization is logically and practically untenable. Then, via engagement with exemplars, I illustrate that empirically and theoretically oriented ethnographers routinely make similar types of context-independent constitutive claims, but according to different conventions for what makes such claims provisionally externally valid.

The distinction between empirical and theoretical generalization was popularized by Small's (2009) influential article, which is centrally concerned with how to make ethnographic findings legible to survey researchers. Small (2009, 10) presents the problem as one of external validity: scholars in many subfields look to ethnographers to produce "case studies that somehow . . . 'speak' to empirical conditions in other cases (not observed)." But case selection strategies like random sampling, selection of "average" cases, and others that bear superficial resemblance to survey methodology fail. Just as one cannot draw valid inferences about a population by interviewing one person—even an entirely average person chosen at random—no selection criteria for field sites will get ethnographers any closer to statistical generalizability.

Given the nonexistence of "representative cases," Small argues that ethnographers should instead select cases deliberately to maximize their ability to make two types of inductive arguments: existence proofs and logical hypotheses that are compelling by virtue of direct observation of a causal mechanism.[2] I will argue that Small's formulation nicely spells out how some ethnographers make external validity claims, particularly those working in subfields populated by survey methodologists. But Small also falls short of universal rules for ethnographic casing because many ethnographers are interested in theory building instead, which does not fit easily into the existence proof or compelling hypothesis categories. Stefan Timmermans and Iddo Tavory (2012, 168), for instance, identify the core aim of their method as "construction of theoretical ideas on the basis of data" and "creative attempts to generalize mechanisms, particular cases, or links between causal statements."

Small allows that ethnographies can produce theory but argues that this is distinct from empirical generalizations. Small makes the distinction via his critical engagement with Michael Burawoy (1998), which Small illustrates via a reexamination of Clifford Geertz's account of the Balinease cockfight (1973). Small's (2009, 9) key claim is that Geertz was unconcerned with the empirical features of cockfights outside of his field site: Geertz expected his theory of games to "be applicable to other sites, [but not] the *empirical findings* to be so applicable—that is, for cockfights to look similar or to follow the same rules in other villages throughout or outside of Indonesia."[3] For Small (2009, 9), building theory is fine, but it is distinct from "some logical justification, some basis for feeling confident" that one has attained "empirical knowledge about how other cases work." Many sociologists ultimately want ethnographers to produce the latter sort of knowledge. For instance, Small (2009, 9) argues that ethnographers should study "one St. Louis neighborhood" that speaks to "conditions in black neighborhoods in general—in Boston, Los Angeles, New York, and perhaps even London and Rio de Janeiro."

There are two problems with Small's formulation. First, Small sets an impossibly high standard for social science—not just ethnography, but survey methods too. No social scientific method provides insight into empirical reality in general, if by this we mean something that allows one to make deterministic statements about unobserved cases. Presumably, the formulation unwittingly conflates reality "in general" with a representative sample. But representative samples—or, for that matter, knowledge about averages within an entire population—only allow one to make probabilistic statements about unobserved cases, not acquire "empirical knowledge" about them. The only way to know what Rio de Janeiro is really like is to go to Rio.

Second, if external validity means simply "some logical justification [or] basis for feeling confident" about probabilistic empirical statements, then Geertz's theory of games certainly does that (Small 2009, 9). For one, Geertz states his aim as developing "a less purely economic idea of what 'depth' in gaming amounts to" (1973, 432)—that is, to develop a theory of "deep gaming" or deep games in general. Geertz also develops the theory by engaging with Jeremy Bentham's account of deep play, which was presumably formulated based on observations in Britain, and this engagement concerns empirically observable features of games and is therefore not "purely theoretical." Geertz's analysis even facilitates prediction. For example, deep play often involves betting, but there are reasons to think that betting in deep games—wherever they occur—is not about the money but about public participation in a form of collective storytelling (Geertz 1973, 432–36). In sum, Geertz's "theory building" is just a vague label for an essentially constitutive argument: an analytical description of deep games, which identifies their key features and how they fit together. Just as in Krippner' account of financialization, Geertz's constitutive account leads to lots of empirical expectations that lead one to imagine that certain empirical features of deep games probably cluster together in other unobserved cases.

Small's (2009) position on Geertz is commonly interpreted ecumenically to imply a division of labor between ethnographers who make "empirical generalizations" and those who make "theoretical generalizations." Lyn Spillman (2014), for example, revisits the Balinese cockfight example and argues that some ethnographers are interested in gaining empirical knowledge about other cockfights, just as a survey methodologist would, whereas theoretically inclined ethnographers are interested in general insights that apply to other situations of gaming, but not necessarily other cockfights. That distinction also suffers under closer scrutiny. First, one can easily imagine a survey that samples cockfights as cases drawn from different kinds of populations—of deep games, holiday rituals, or masculine displays—and speaks to empirical regularities in the latter rather than cockfights as such (conversely, nothing prevents one from developing a theory that applies only to cockfights). Second, and more to the point, both the survey method and Geertz's approach employ theoretical constructs to explain empirical regularities—if by theoretical construct we mean an abstract entity that may be unobservable (Steinmetz 2004). Survey methodologists explain regularities by treating cases as members of a population in the statistical sense, an abstraction that cannot be empirically observed. Theoretically inclined ethnographers explain regularities via recourse to constitutive properties and mechanisms, which can similarly defy empirical observation and are sometimes only inferable from empirical patterns (Gorski 2009; Steinmetz 2004). Both explain empirical reality with theory, albeit in different ways. There is only generalization and no basis for distinguishing between empirical and theoretical generalization.

As final illustration of this point, consider a scenario in which a survey methodologist and historical sociologist are invited to make a prediction about whether Donald Trump's presidency and the events of January 6 are a harbinger of democratic decline and authoritarianism in the United States. The survey methodologist might collect a dataset of stable and failed democracies, however defined, code their characteristics into variables, and run a regression. The historical sociologist might construct a theory of democratic failure by analyzing a few cases to identify the typical path that nations follow as they acquire the characteristics of authoritarianism, and then assess the degree to which the United States has or likely will take each step. It should be evident that both arguments are about external validity, but neither guarantees empirical certainty about an unobserved and uncertain future. One can argue that one approach is preferable to the other in various ways (e.g., in the precision of uncertainty about predictions). But the approaches are, at base, similar. Both rely on different theoretical conventions for explaining and anticipating the same empirical regularities. By the same token, empirically and theoretically oriented ethnographers make similar types of external validity claims, but according to different conventions.

How to Think About Ethnographic Case Selection Like an Historical Sociologist

In this section, I argue that the primary difference between empirically and theoretically oriented ethnographies revolves around different conventions for making constitutive claims that others treat as provisionally externally valid. The claim that ethnographies produce analytically useful constitutive arguments is not new; many identify arguments like Geertz's as central to ethnography. Howard Becker (2008, 10), for example, argues that ethnographers contribute to knowledge by supplying underlying images of the world, which impact "selection and formulation of problems, the determination of what data are, the means to be used in getting the data, and the forms in which propositions are cast." Vaughan (2004, 323) argues that historical ethnography facilitates "analogical theorizing . . . a method that compares similar events or activities across different social settings and leads to more refined and generalizable theoretical expectations." Such aims are also implicit in pragmatic methods (Gross 2009) and those that emphasize abduction, wherein the goal is analysis that "abstracts . . . the phenomenon . . . turning it into a generalization than can be linked to other fields" (Timmermans and Tavory 2012, 177).

But prescriptions on how to select cases that facilitate such analogical reasoning are thin, and many unhelpfully recommend looking for theoretically generative cases (Burawoy 1998) or focus on the subjective experience of surprise (Timmermans and Tavory 2012). Here, the analogy to how contemporary historical sociologists make comparisons is useful because it focuses attention on what analogical reasoning gets us: that is, generative constitutive arguments.

Following Hirschman and Reed (2014), constitutive arguments are accounts of formation, which concern both the building blocks of the social world and how best to categorize them. As such, constitutive arguments take one of two general forms. The simpler form is an *existence proof*, which simply asserts that "X exists." More complex constitutive arguments concern the correct casing or categorization of social phenomena or relationships between their properties—commonly, arguments take the form "X is really a case of Y" or "A, B, and C are key features of X" (or incidental to X). But a constitutive argument about one case is typically not enough. Successful ethnographies require some warrant for convincing the audience that the constitutive properties of observed cases somehow inform accounts of other unobserved cases, and the conventional distinction between empirically and theoretically oriented ethnography is rooted in different conventions for making such provisional validity claims. In the two sections that follow, I illustrate differences in how empirically and theoretically oriented ethnographers make such claims via engagement with recent ethnographies that exemplify the strategy.

The Existence Proof

Many scholars argue that the simplest ethnographic finding is often the most theoretically generative: that a phenomenon exists. Following Small (2009), arguing that a phenomenon exists is also the only empirical claim that one can make with absolute certainty based on analysis of a single case. But in practice, existence proofs require more than simple observation of a phenomenon because social scientists chose to focus on only a small subset of all phenomena (Abbott 2014). To convince the audience that the phenomenon "matters," ethnographers must provide some warrant for thinking that it is consequential in other cases. In sum, a successful existence proof is simultaneously an importance proof. Successful ethnographies establish this warrant in one of two ways: following Small (2009), some do so inductively, whereas theoretically oriented ethnographies do so abductively.

One exemplar of the inductive strategy is Alexes Harris, Heather Evans, and Katherine Beckett's (2010) account of legal monetary sanctions. The authors engage primarily with criminologists in an effort to convince them that legal fees and fines are an important component of the criminal justice system. They do so via an analysis of such sanctions in Washington State, and the central claim is, effectively, that legal monetary sanctions are a thing that you should pay attention to. The article is noteworthy for its relative lack of theory building in the conventional sense. For instance, the authors treat what monetary sanctions are a "case of" as self-evident (Ragin 1992) and present their argument as consistent with existing disciplinary narratives:

Research shows that people who are convicted of crimes are . . . highly disadvantaged [and] criminal justice involvement . . . is both consequence and cause of poverty. [Because] the prevalence and consequences of monetary sanctions have not been systematically explored, the extent to which penal expansion contributes to inequality, and the full array of mechanisms by which it does so, has not been fully recognized. (Harris et al. 2010, 1756)

Harris et al. (2010) are not convincing the reader to rethink the nature of criminal justice involvement and instead illustrate another way in which the criminal justice system does what it does—that is, disadvantage the already disadvantaged. Their aim is to provide plausible reasons why monetary sanctions are independently burdensome for those who incur them and intertwined with other mechanisms that link criminal justice involvement and inequality. The authors support the argument with two types of data: data about the size and scope of monetary sanctions and data about the relationship between legal debt and behaviors that produce disadvantage. When talking about the size of monetary sanctions, for instance, they contextualize median debt burdens vis-à-vis expected annual earnings in Washington: 100 percent of whites' annual income, 69 percent of that of Hispanics, and 222 percent of that of African Americans. They also reproduce informants' accounts of rearrest, suffering further sanctions, avoiding the legal economy, returning to crime, and even giving up on life. Strictly speaking, these findings apply only to Washington State, and the logic of the warrant is inductive: the authors show that monetary sanctions are so surprisingly large and impactful in Washington that they *probably* matter, at least a little, elsewhere. And their argument succeeded, wildly. It inspired a multistate research project, which substantiated that legal monetary sanctions are a central and growing component of many states' criminal justice systems (Harris et al. 2017).

In contrast to this inductive strategy, other ethnographers rely on what might be termed *resolutive cases*, which resolve a contradiction or tension within the literature. A similar strategy is common in historical formation stories, wherein the usual result is reformulation of taken-for-granted historical categories. For example, Monica Prasad's (2012) *The Land of Too Much* begins by highlighting a contradiction within welfare state scholarship. Most scholars identify the American welfare state as extremely liberal in its deference to the market (Esping-Anderson 1991), but the American state was once also surprisingly interventionist. Until the 1970s, American income taxes were the most progressive in the world and federal agencies were unusually aggressive in policing monopolies. Prasad resolves this contradiction by showing that architects of the American state were uniquely focused on stimulating consumer demand to combat the Great Depression's deflationary spiral. This leads Prasad to a new theoretical distinction. European governments, which fixated on catching up to a wildly productive United States, developed "supply-side" states that won over workers with government benefits in exchange for policies that dampened consumption (e.g., wage controls, consumption taxes). American policymakers developed a "demand-side" state focused on substituting consumption and privatized welfare for state programs (i.e., traditionally via cheap credit, progressive income taxes, policies that encourage home ownership, and regulating and breaking up monopolies). The argument works because the American welfare state is something scholars care about on its own terms, but note that Prasad (2012) also resolves a theoretical contradiction and thereby provides insight into unobserved cases. By observing European welfare states alone, as Gosta Esping-Anderson (1991) did, one might conclude that they fall into liberal, conservative, and social democratic categories. But Prasad shows that they are also all supply-side welfare states.

One ethnographic example of a similarly resolutive case is Matthew Desmond's (2012) analysis of "disposable ties" in Milwaukee—or, strictly speaking, among residents of a trailer park and Black neighborhood therein. Desmond's argument is superficially similar to Harris et al.'s (2010): disposable ties exist and matter for accounts of urban poverty. But unlike Harris et al. (2010), Desmond spends little time on inductive arguments. For example, he makes no effort to contextualize the size or scope of wealth transfers via disposable ties, document how disposable ties impact poverty, and so on. Instead, the article goes straight to theory, shows that it is *already* muddled, and argues that the existence of disposable ties unmuddles it. Desmond's primary point of engagement is Carol Stack's (1975) *All Our Kin*, which argues that minority populations, although impoverished, rely on extensive kin networks for economic and social support. Desmond then marshals findings from other studies, survey measures, and logical extrapolation to convince the reader that Stack's narrative no longer fits the facts. The General Social Survey (GSS) shows that African Americans do not have more extensive social networks than whites, and even if they did, welfare state retrenchment makes the needs of impoverished Blacks larger than what kin networks could plausibly handle. The warrant, then, is a logical contradiction in the literature:

> If conditions have become decidedly worse for the urban poor since midcentury, how do they endure conditions of severe economic deprivation if doing so single-handedly is virtually impossible and if their kin are no longer a sufficient source of support? (Desmond 2012, 1299)

In sum, Desmond's discovery of disposable ties is significant because it fixes established disciplinary narratives.[4] Given historical developments, it is no longer clear what coherent underlying image of urban survival strategies might fit all the facts, and Desmond shows that such survival strategies consist of forming and breaking disposable ties. Technically, this finding is provisional until further study, since it is possible that people outside Milwaukee never form disposable ties. But this is equally true of Harris et al.'s case study (2010). The two articles merely employ a different sort of warrant to convince the reader that their newly discovered phenomenon is worth treating as provisionally externally valid in future studies.

Complex Constitutive Arguments: Casing and Categorization

Ethnographers also use competing conventions to facilitate complex constitutive arguments. Here again, one strategy is inductive and mirrors Small's (2009) advice for formulating plausible hypotheses. The other is more common among theoretically oriented ethnographers and mirrors negative case analysis in historical sociology.

Following Small (2009), case studies are useful for direct observation of causal mechanisms, which can give readers a plausible or logically compelling reason for thinking that causal relationships operate similarly in other cases.[5] To this end, Small (2009, 18) recommends looking to what might be described as "pointy" cases that are extreme in ways that point to causal mechanisms. For instance, he suggests studying marriage among the poor via analysis of an impoverished city wherein the mayor gives rent subsidies to unwed mothers who marry before the birth of their second child. Note that the logic is similar to that of instrumental variables in quantitative analysis. Presumably, marriage rates in impoverished cities are correlated with many factors that impact life outcomes (e.g., employment status, criminal justice involvement, household wealth). But in Small's imaginary city, the mayor's program creates single mothers who marry just for the incentive, a scenario that allows one to formulate an extremely plausible hypothesis about how marriage status alone impacts other life outcomes (or not). The extent to which this procedure truly concerns causal or constitutive relationships is debatable—Small (2009) argues that it concerns the former. But as I have argued, causal arguments are often informative by virtue of lending plausibility to unobservable aspects of constitutive arguments. Plausible hypotheses also inform scholars' implicit understanding of the "contrast space" for a causal argument, or the universe of relevant variables, which may or may not bear out in variable analyses (Lichterman and Reed 2015). For example, marriage may impact poverty in Small's imaginary case, but may also be so interrelated with other variables in other cases as to produce no observable causal effect. But even then, Small's hypothetical findings are noteworthy because they inform others' understanding of marriage as a phenomenon and its causal powers (whether realized or not).

One actual example of the plausible hypothesis approach is Robert Vargas's *Wounded City* (2016), which focuses on the relationship between political efficacy and neighborhood violence in Chicago's Little Village. In some respects, *Wounded City* is more than an effort to formulate a plausible hypothesis. For example, Vargas combines aspects of neighborhood ecology and political economy into a new theory of political fields. Nevertheless, the work is centrally motivated by a desire to convince criminologists to include political variables in future analyses.[6] To this end, Vargas mobilizes the peculiarities of Little Village, which consists of two gerrymandered areas with different relationships to Chicago's political structure. The west side is in a single alderman's district, who views it as an important constituency. It witnessed a decline of violent crime, much like other American neighborhoods in recent decades. The east side is gerrymandered into three aldermanic districts, none of which are important to their alderman. It witnessed an anomalous rise in violent hotspots. The case is "pointy" because the Little Village's two halves are similar in all the ways that matter, except for their gerrymandering. This contrast allows Vargas to pinpoint and enumerate how political efficacy matters: by allowing residents to get violence prevention, job, and surveillance programs via relations with ward officials and nonprofits. Here again, the analysis does not prove that political efficacy matters in other neighborhoods but shows how it is a central constituent of crime prevention strategies in Little Village, thereby giving the reader a logical reason to expect a causal effect elsewhere.

By contrast, other ethnographers formulate complex constitutive arguments via strategies that mirror negative case analysis in historical sociology. Following Emigh (1997), negative case analysis is useful when (a) the gap between empirical reality and a theoretically expected outcome is large and (b) examination of the case leads to a theoretical reformulation of the phenomenon. Ethnographers make such arguments in two ways, which might be further subdivided as negative outcome and negative cause analysis. In negative outcome analysis, a cause is present but its theoretically expected outcome is absent. In negative cause analysis, a common outcome is present but the cause usually associated with the outcome is absent.

One example of negative outcome analysis is Hana Brown's (2011) study of immigrant Liberians' relationship with the American state. Brown engages with theories of immigrant incorporation, which identify labor market participation as key to political incorporation: the documented and undocumented alike equate good citizenship with individual work and responsibility, which leads undocumented immigrants to question their own political legitimacy (Menjívar 2006). One would therefore expect the Liberians in Brown's study to question their own political legitimacy because most are displaced, illiterate refugees from the countryside, who are unemployed and likely unemployable (e.g., grandparents raising grandchildren). But Brown finds a negative outcome: Liberians feel entitled to a nurturing and personal relationship with the state. Brown shows that Liberians' disposition is due to their particular relationship with the United States, which they see as complicit in Liberia's civil war. Because many lost family in the war, they feel entitled to replacement personal-like ties with the state, a disposition reinforced by frequent and positive interaction with resettlement services.

As prescribed by Emigh (1997), Brown's analysis both explains the anomalous case and offers general insight into the constitutive properties of immigrant incorporation. Brown (2011, 161) argues that the immigrant incorporation is not purely about labor markets and the documented-undocumented distinction, as prior studies have assumed, but can also occur through political channels. This conclusion gives one a reason to expect refugee's political positionality vis-à-vis the United States to matter causally for experiences of immigration. It also expands understanding of what political incorporation is about, which points to counterfactuals that are informative even if not currently reflected in actually existing causal relationships. For instance, Liberians' relationship with the American state appears relatively unique, but one imagines that if other immigrants expected personalized ties to the state, their experience of incorporation would be comparable to those of Liberians. In sum, the analysis changes one's underlying image of what immigrant incorporation is in practice, which leads one to expect empirical regularities in other cases, including actual and hypothetical causal relations.

One example of negative cause analysis is my own study of partisan politics in a Rust Belt city (Pacewicz 2015). I engage with accounts of grassroots party politics, which identify community leaders and other local elites' exit from local party-building efforts as a key turning point in American politics (McAdam and Kloos 2014; Skocpol 2003). Scholars argue that community elites' exit allowed ideologically motivated activists to take over local branches of the two parties and—via control over primaries and other aspects of grassroots politicking—shift party priorities toward the extreme and reactionary, especially on the Republican side. Skocpol (2003) argues that this shift in grassroots politics occurred due to changes in the field of national political advocacy, which cut institutional ties between Washington, DC, and grassroots community institutions, leaving community elites and other locals parochial in outlook. In my study, I found that the outcome predicted by this theory is present, but the cause is absent. Since the 1970s, community elites had withdrawn from Democratic and especially Republican politics, leaving party affairs in the hands of ideologically polarized activists. But the theoretically expected cause was missing: community leaders were not more parochial in outlook. On the contrary, and consistent with scholarship in urban sociology, community elites had become much more outward looking and specifically preoccupied with entrepreneurial efforts to bring in investment and attract state and federal funding (Harvey 1989; Molotch 1976). Thus, the puzzle became why community elites—who became generally more interested and engaged in the world outside of city limits—withdrew from party politics in particular.

I resolved this puzzle by showing how changes in urban governance made party politics a local liability for community elites. Community notables became increasingly focused on economic development efforts centered on wooing outside employers, which they organize around broad-based partnerships that flexibly market the city to outsiders. In this context, engagement in party politics polarizes community initiatives, practically complicating both collective efforts to market the city and individual leaders' ability to rise within the local pecking order. In other words, party polarization at the grassroots is not just a case of rising extremism within political party networks, but rather a "disembedding of party politics from community governance," which allows for and encourages polarization among party activists. As such, the argument gives one a logical reason to expect both constitutive and causal regularities in other unobserved cases. One expects that in cities with similar economic histories, grassroots political parties now operate independently of local elite networks and are especially prone to capture by partisan activists—a significant shift from when the Democratic party and GOP were effectively an organizational extension of, respectively, the local labor movement and chamber of commerce (it later turned out that support for Donald Trump was particularly strong in the sorts of small Rust Belt towns I studied, and their shift toward the GOP in 2016 accounts for much of Trump's margin over Romney in 2012). One also expects that in communities in other regions wherein local elites are more fixated on economic development, they are extra avoidant of party politics—a scenario that promotes extremism among party activists who are maximally disembedded from moderating community institutions.

Discussion and Conclusions: Learning to Ask "What" Before "Why"

What can one conclude about the world based on ethnographic study of a single case? Or for that matter, what does juxtaposition of several historical cases actually get us? The other chapters in this volume suggest that historical sociologists have traditionally answered these questions in ways that are disconnected from how others interpret and utilize empirical research. In this chapter, I have argued that the same thing happens in ethnography and for the same reason: scholars have traditionally focused unduly on causal over constitutive arguments.

In the case of ethnography, a genre of methods papers, often written by those who do not themselves conduct case studies, offers blueprints for ethnographic "airplanes that will never fly" (Small 2009, 28): studies that copy the form but not function of survey methods research (e.g., Elman et al. 2016; King et al. 1994). Although of questionable practical utility for ethnographers, such articles do focus attention on ethnographers' capacity for making claims that speak to empirical reality outside their cases. Ethnographers themselves are partly to blame for mudding the water on this issue, especially by positing a distinction between empirically and theoretically oriented research (e.g., Small 2009; Spillman 2014). This distinction is perhaps functional in protecting a sanctum of theoretical ethnography from the usual disciplinary critiques, but it is logically and practically untenable. I have argued that disambiguating how ethnographers make external validity claims requires attention to noncausal arguments.

Meanwhile, outside the world of methods debates, ethnographic arguments routinely carry and inform others' understanding of the larger world, but those that do are neither causal arguments nor context-dependent "pure description." Rather, they fall into a third category that I identified as *constitutive arguments*: context-independent claims about the makeup and correct categorization of social phenomena, which inform others' understanding of empirical reality in unobserved cases. Contrary to the conventional division between empirical and theoretical ethnography, constitutive arguments usually combine empirical claims about unobserved cases with novel theoretical insights: poor urbanites' survival strategies consist of forming and breaking disposable ties (Desmond 2012), local GOP chapters have become disembedded from networks of corporate and urban governance (Pacewicz 2015), and positive interactions with the state are a form of immigrant incorporation (Brown 2011).

Greater clarity about the conventions that scholars use to make claims can help one better identify generative cases within the messy and open-ended stage of initial fieldwork—to see which among many possible cases is usefully "surprising" (Timmermans and Tavory 2012) or otherwise informative for others. I identified two such conventions, which revolve around different warrant for establishing that a phenomenon is relevant to other unobserved cases. Those ethnographies conventionally understood as empirically oriented follow the advice of Small (2009) and establish this warrant inductively. Ethnographers in this tradition examine "pointy" cases, wherein the phenomenon of interest is unusually large, bifurcated, or causally related to other issues of disciplinary interest. Theoretically oriented ethnographers make claims of external validity similarly to historical sociologists who examine single cases (Emigh 1997; Hirschman and Reed 2014). They proceed abductively and use existing theory to suggest that observed phenomena are of wider significance. They commonly look to resolutive cases, wherein analysis resolves what is otherwise a contradiction in the literature, or negative cases, wherein prior theory leads one to expect empirical regularities different from those that actually occur.

In sum, qualitative sociologists confronted by the messy reality of the social work are best served by asking how they can make a convincing argument about its makeup—whether they are ethnographers just entering the field of historical sociologists just entering the archives. Ethnographers who hope to study a single case can proceed most productively by plucking two types of cases from the many possibilities before them. They may proceed by looking for phenomena that are unusually large, bifurcated, or related to other phenomena of interest. Or they may proceed like historical sociologists by looking for cases that appear to resolve a preexisting debate with the literature or cases wherein a common causal sequence fails to manifest—either because a cause is present but result is absent or because a cause is absent but result is present.

At issue in this discussion are not merely practical concerns like arriving at interesting findings that warrant publication, but also assumptions about the nature of the social world. American sociologists tend to see causal arguments as most scientific, and this view is implicitly premised on the view that the social world is easily knowable and the proper categories of analysis self-evident. But following Becker (2008), the world only seems easily knowable because we tend to operate with common images of it, which are drawn from the common stock of popular media, fiction, or stereotype. These assumptions often misrepresent the social world. Moreover, it is especially important for social scientists to update their conceptual models because objects of social inquiry are notably changeable vis-à-vis phenomena in the natural sciences (Hirschman and Reed 2014). To return to one example from this chapter's introduction, consider that the causes of heart attacks have probably changed plenty since 1700, but their physiological basis in blocked coronary arteries has not. The same cannot be said of what social scientists mean by terms like *upward mobility, romantic relationships*, and *social movements*, which vary over time, by social context, and according to the positionality of participants. There is constant need for ethnographers and historical sociologists to remind the rest of us what it is that we are actually talking about. In this sense, good ethnography and good historical sociology both advance primarily through constitutive arguments.

Notes

1. Krippner (2011) argues that policy makers turned to financial markets to avoid having to pick sides in fierce distributional conflicts.
2. Small (2009) is also concerned with how to make claims about the different varieties or categories of a given phenomenon via saturation sampling. I do not discuss this here as my interest is in analysis of single cases.
3. Citing Garfinkel (1967), Small (2009, 17) adds that an ethnographer's theoretical perspectives may "render irrelevant whether a case study provides empirical information

on other cases" if, for instance, they believe reality to be radically situational. This is certainly true, but most academic ethnographers are not radical situationalists.

4. Ethnographers often employ this strategy via what might be termed defamiliarizing cases, which first reveals and problematizes taken-for-granted features of social phenomena and then resolves these contradictions—hence ethnographers' traditional interest in native tribes and later hobos, shopping clerks, townies, and other populations that were socially distant from academic researchers. One recent example of this strategy is Tavory's (2016) account of Orthodox Jews in Los Angeles. In Tavory's account (2016, 164), this unusual case led naturally to "focused empirical puzzles"—for instance, "Why do some orthodox Jews avoid hotdog sellers outright while others readily engage them?" Such focused puzzles accumulated into general empirical and theoretical puzzles that contradicted existing accounts of group formation and led Tavory to new insights about social boundaries: boundary maintenance consists less of prohibitions and spatial separation than frequent and meaningful interpellation by others.

5. This is a debatable and point. Some argue that the strength of ethnography is precisely ethnographers' ability to observe causal mechanisms directly (Jerolmack and Khan 2014), while others argue that most social mechanisms are theoretical abstractions that cannot be directly observed (Steinmetz 2004, 375). I take a middle position: some mechanisms and constitutive properties are abstractions that are not directly observable. One cannot "see" structural racism, an economic depression, or even many meaningful aspects of everyday interactions (e.g., resentments, prejudice, romantic attraction)— one infers these things from observable regularities. But ethnography does allow one to observe more empirical regularities than other methods.

6. Vargas (2016, 172–74) even argues for a "political econometrics" that would allow researchers to consider that "turf wars . . . and political power can . . . amplify or weaken a neighborhood effect."

References

Abbott, Andrew. 1988. "Transcending General Linear Reality." *Sociological Theory* 1:169–86.

——. 1992. "From Causes to Events: Notes on Narrative Positivism." *Sociological Methods and Research* 20(4):428–55.

——. 2014. "The Problem of Excess." *Sociological Theory* 32(1):1–26.

Abend, Gabriel, Caitlin Petre, and Michael Sauder. 2013. "Styles of Causal Thought: An Empirical Investigation." *American Journal of Sociology* 119(3):602–54.

Abolafia, Mitchel. 2001. *Making Markets: Opportunism and Restraint on Wall Street*. Cambridge, MA: Harvard University Press.

Anyon, Jean. 1980. "Social Class and the Hidden Curriculum of Work." *Journal of Education* 162:67–92.

Barman, Emily. 2013. "Classificatory Struggles in the Nonprofit Sector: The Formation of the National Taxonomy of Exempt Entities, 1969–1987." *Social Science History* 37(1):103–41.

Becker, Howard. 1953. "Becoming a Marihuana User." *American Journal of Sociology* 59:235–42.

——. 2008. *Tricks of the Trade: How to Think About Your Research While You're Doing It*. Chicago: University of Chicago Press.

Brown, Hana. 2011. "Refugees, Rights, and Race: How Legal Status Shapes Liberian Immigrants' Relationship with the State." *Social Problems* 58(1):144–63.

Burawoy, Michael. 1998. "The Extended Case Method." *Sociological Theory* 16:4–33.

Dasgupta, Shamik. 2017. "Constitutive Explanation." *Philosophical Issues* 27:74–97.

Desmond, Matthew. 2012. "Disposable Ties and the Urban Poor." *American Journal of Sociology* 117(5):1295–335.

Elman, Colin, John Gerring, and James Mahoney. 2016. "Case Study Research: Putting the Quant Into the Qual." *Sociological Methods and Research* 45(3):375–91.

Emigh, Rebecca Jean. 1997. "The Power of Negative Thinking: The Use of Negative Case Methodology in the Development of Sociological Theory." *Theory and Society* 26(5):649–84.

Ermakoff, Ivan. 2014. "Exceptional Cases: Epistemic Contributions and Normative Expectations." *European Journal of Sociology* 55(2):223–43.

Esping-Andersen, Gosta. 1991. *The Three Worlds of Welfare Capitalism.* New York: John Wiley.

Eyal, Gil. 2013. "For a Sociology of Expertise: The Social Origins of the Autism Epidemic." *American Journal of Sociology* 118(4):863–907.

Garfinkel, Harold. 1967. *Studies in Ethnomethodology.* Englewood Cliffs, NJ: Prentice-Hall.

Geertz, Clifford. 1973. *The Interpretation of Cultures.* New York: Basic Books.

Gorski, Philip. 2009. "Social 'Mechanisms' and Comparative-Historical Sociology: A Critical Realist Proposal." In *Frontiers of Sociology*, edited by Peter Hedström and Björn Wittrock, 147–94. Leiden, Netherlands: Brill.

Gross, Neil. 2009. "A Pragmatist Theory of Social Mechanisms." *American Sociological Review* 74(3):358–79.

Harris, Alexes, Heather Evans, and Katherine Beckett. 2010. "Drawing Blood from Stones: Legal Debt and Social Inequality in the Contemporary United States." *American Journal of Sociology* 115(6):1753–99.

Harris, Alexes, Beth Huebner, Karin Martin, Mary Pattillo, Becky Pettit, Sarah Shannon, Bryan Sykes, Chris Uggen, and April Fernandes. 2017. "Monetary Sanctions in the Criminal Justice System." Laura and John Arnold Foundation Report. http://www.monetarysanctions .org/wp-content/uploads/2017/04/Monetary-Sanctions-Legal-Review-Final.pdf.

Harvey, David. 1989. "From Managerialism to Entrepreneurialism: The Transformation in Urban Governance in Late Capitalism." *Geografiska Annaler B* 71:3–17.

Hirschman, Daniel, and Isaac Ariail Reed. 2014. "Formation Stories and Causality in Sociology." *Sociological Theory* 32(4):259–82.

Hochschild, Arlie Russell. 1989. *The Second Shift: Working Parents and the Revolution at Home.* New York: Avon.

Jerolmack, Colin, and Shamus Khan. 2014. "Talk Is Cheap: Ethnography and the Attitudinal Fallacy." *Sociological Methods and Research* 43(3):178–209.

King, Gary, Robert O. Keohane, and Sidney Verba. 1994. *Designing Social Inquiry: Scientific Inference in Qualitative Research.* Princeton, NJ: Princeton University Press.

Krippner, Greta. 2005. "The Financialization of the American Economy." *Socio-Economic Review* 3(2):173–208.

——. 2011. *Capitalizing on Crisis.* Cambridge, MA: Harvard University Press.

Kuhn, Thomas. 1962. *The Structure of Scientific Revolutions.* Chicago: University of Chicago Press.

Lakatos, Irme. 1978. *Philosophical Papers.* New York: Cambridge University Press.

Lamont, Michele, and Patricia White. 2005. "Workshop on Interdisciplinary Standards for Systematic Qualitative Research." National Science Foundation Workshop.

Lichterman, Paul, and Isaac Reed. 2015. "Theory and Contrastive Explanation in Ethnography." *Sociological Methods and Research* 44(4):585–635.

Lin, Ken-Hou, and Donald Tomaskovic-Devey. 2013. "Financialization and US Income Inequality, 1970–2008." *American Journal of Sociology* 118(5):1284–329.

Mahoney, James. 2000. "Strategies of Causal Inference in Small-N Analysis." *Sociological Methods and Research* 28(4):387–424.

Martin, John Levi. 2011. *The Explanation of Social Action*. Oxford: Oxford University Press.

Mayrl, Damon. 2018. "Heuristic and Recursive Comparison in Sociology." Unpublished Paper.

McAdam, Doug, and Karina Kloos. 2014. *Deeply Divided: Racial Politics and Social Movements in Post-War America*. Oxford: Oxford University Press.

Medvetz, Thomas. 2012. *Think Tanks in America*. Chicago: University of Chicago Press.

Menjívar, Cecilia. 2006. "Liminal Legality: Salvadoran and Guatemalan Immigrants' Lives in the United States." *American Journal of Sociology* 111(4):999–1037.

Molotch, Harvey. 1976. "The City as a Growth Machine: Toward a Political Economy of Place." *American Journal of Sociology* 82(2):309–32.

Pacewicz, Josh. 2015. "Playing the Neoliberal Game: Why Community Leaders Left Party Politics to Partisan Activists." *American Journal of Sociology* 121(3):826–81.

Padgett, John, and Christopher Ansell. 1993. "Robust Action and the Rise of the Medici, 1400–1434." *American Journal of Sociology* 98(6):1259–319.

Prasad, Monica. 2012. *The Land of Too Much: American Abundance and the Paradox of Poverty*. Cambridge, MA: Harvard University Press.

Ragin, Charles. 1992. "Introduction: Cases of 'What Is a Case?'" In *What Is a Case? Exploring the Foundations of Social Inquiry*, edited by Charles C. Ragin and Howard Saul Becker, 1–14. Cambridge: Cambridge University Press.

Reed, Isaac. 2011. *Interpretation and Social Knowledge: On the Use of Theory in the Social Sciences*. Chicago: University of Chicago Press.

Sewell, William H., Jr. 2005. *Logics of History: Social Theory and Social Transformation*. Chicago: University of Chicago Press.

Skocpol, Theda. 2003. *Diminished Democracy: From Membership to Management in American Civic Life*. Norman: University of Oklahoma Press.

Small, Mario Luis. 2009. "'How Many Cases Do I Need?' On Science and the Logic of Case Selection in Field-Based Research." *Ethnography* 10(1):5–38.

Spillman, Lyn. 2014. "Mixed Methods and the Logic of Qualitative Inference." *Qualitative Sociology* 37(2):189–205.

Stack, Carol. 1975. *All Our Kin: Strategies for Survival in a Black Community*. New York: Basic Books.

Steinmetz, George. 1998. "Critical Realism and Historical Sociology: A Review Article." *Comparative Studies in Society and History* 40:170–86.

——. 2004. "Odious Comparisons: Incommensurability, the Case Study, and 'Small N's' in Sociology." *Sociological Theory* 22(3):371–400.

Tavory, Iddo. 2016. *Summoned: Identification and Religious Life in a Jewish Neighborhood*. Chicago: University of Chicago Press.

Timmermans, Stefan, and Iddo Tavory. 2012. "Theory Construction in Qualitative Research: From Grounded Theory to Abductive Analysis." *Sociological Theory* 30(3):167–86.

Vargas, Robert. 2016. *Wounded City: Violent Turf Wars in a Chicago Barrio*. Oxford: Oxford University Press.

Vaughan, Diane. 2004. "Theorizing Disaster: Analogy, Historical Ethnography, and the Challenger Accident." *Ethnography* 5(3):315–47.

PART II

WHAT TO COMPARE

CHAPTER 5

PROCESS THEORIES AND COMPARATIVE SOCIOLOGY

Some Problems and a Solution

NATALIE B. AVILES

Introduction

Postpositivist sociological theory is, in many ways, an attempt to reckon with the dynamic complexity characterizing contemporary social orders. Often positioning themselves outside the tomb of a naively scientistic "grand theory," postpositivists question the extent to which our explanations of complex social phenomena are truly generalizable. In pursuing more tempered "theories of the middle range," postpositivist sociologists sometimes promiscuously summon ontological, epistemological, theoretical, and methodological claims in their attempts to reconstruct a discipline around circumscribed processes of social ordering. Their theoretical efforts to capture the complexity and heterogeneity of social processes can then challenge the taken-for-granted tools of sociological inquiry, such as case-based comparison.

This chapter takes recent efforts to develop processual sociological theories seriously as a challenge postpositivist comparative sociology should confront. After discussing the problems for comparative sociological explanation that can arise when process theories prioritize synchronic events as objects of analysis, I explore some suggestive alternatives that preserve the basic insights of processual sociology while firmly rooting processual explanations in the discipline's pragmatist philosophical ancestors. One possible solution to the problem of comparison in processual sociology involves tracing pragmatism's theoretical commitments to where they connect with methodological approaches to analyzing meso-level social orders as comprising collective reconstructions emergent from iterative temporal sequences of problem-solving. By combining theories focused on the looping effects that diachronically constitute objects of analysis with the method of reiterated problem-solving, process theorists can develop a systematic approach to analyzing how the emergence of social phenomena is entangled with the broader ecological context for their emergence without sacrificing the possibility of gaining insights about the social world that can be generalized by comparing across model cases.

Event, Process, and Comparison

In *Logics of History*, William Sewell (2005) advanced one of the most memorable critiques of positivist historical sociology yet published. He argued that the dominant approaches to conceptualizing temporality alive in the discipline failed to account for the heterogeneity of social time and, therefore, the causal heterogeneity of social life. Sewell famously countered sociology's preoccupation with teleological and experimental interpretations of time with an emphasis on eventful temporality. For Sewell, an eventful sociology would reject the tendency to treat social structures as given causal antecedents to outcomes of interest and instead focus on how the multiplicity of structures, meanings, and a whole host of causal influences are subject to contingent transformation in the unfolding of historical happenings.

Where Sewell's eventful sociology tends to focus on how social forces contribute to the emergence of synchronic social phenomena, a similar preoccupation with correcting the troubling assumptions of positivist sociology led Andrew Abbott to advance his own more diachronic interpretation of eventful temporality. In addition to criticizing the "general linear reality" of quantitative social science characterized by flaws similar to those Sewell attributed to positivist historical sociology, Abbott's reflections upon temporality formed the basis of a more far-reaching program for processual sociology (Abbott 2001, 2016). Abbott (2016, 33) circumvents the limitations of Sewell's definition of events as distinct ruptures from the routine reproduction of social order by elaborating the "duality of temporality in the processual approach":

> On the one hand, all is changing, and therefore all is diachronic, even the entities of social process itself. Entities emerge only because historicality enables them to do so. And they emerge as lineages of events that tend to recur, and that tend thus to become the seemingly stable individuals of the traditional ontologies. . . . But, on the other hand, since everything is changing, everything is contingent. The present is all that exists, and all effects of the past must work through encoding that—combined with moment-to-moment action—has preserved those effects across the succession of contingent presents to the one present of now.

Abbott's processual sociology thus considers how events emerge in the momentary meeting of interacting elements (like institutions and biographical individuals) that operate across different, overlapping time horizons. The elements that make up events interpolate into one another in causally efficient ways, pushing temporal processes forward by enabling certain possibilities and constraining others. By allowing that events are made up of different temporal processes with different time horizons, Abbott leaves the door open for sociologists to study how order and change emerge both synchronically and diachronically from the interaction of multiple mechanisms of varied scale and duration.

Whereas Sewell's eventful sociology focuses on the apparent singularity and open-endedness of events in their synchronic becoming, the duality of temporality Abbott theorizes in his processual sociology is more deliberately oriented toward the possibility of comparison across events via their diachronic persistence in temporal lineages. In earlier works, Abbott (2001) developed the duality of temporality by drawing upon process philosophers ranging from Alfred North Whitehead to Henri Bergson and George Herbert Mead. While all of these philosophers propose that reality is a fluid and temporal process, the potential for comparison across the emergent processes that constitute social reality varies greatly from one interpretation to the next. For instance, Bergson's proto-phenomenological preoccupation with the experience of pure duration and Whitehead's emphasis on irreducible and self-generating events as the ontological primitives of the world each thwart the sociologist's search for multiple, generative mechanisms that explain the emergent outcomes of ongoing social processes, and this puts their process philosophies at odds with one of the prevailing preoccupations of the discipline.[1] The most common solution in contemporary efforts to form a comprehensive processual theory rooted in these diverse philosophical perspectives is thus faced with the need to ensure processual accounts are ultimately reconcilable with the goals of comparative sociological inquiry.

The challenge of developing a thoroughgoing processual ontology is a daunting one, and proposed solutions that swing too far in the direction of metaphysically holistic or atomistic process philosophies like those of Bergson or Whitehead can leave sociological analysis unmoored. Fortunately, there is potential for meeting this challenge in another philosophical strain already partially developed in Abbott's approach. When the influences of American pragmatist thinkers like John Dewey and George Herbert Mead are deliberately centered alongside Abbott's favored heuristic of "ecology," long-running traditions in sociological theorizing can be used to develop a distinctively sociological process theory whose philosophical commitments are more hospitable for comparative analysis.

To the extent contemporary sociologists currently use the heuristic of ecology, it is often in service of analyzing competition among organizations and other social groups over limited resources within a particular institutional niche (Abbott 1988; Hannan and Freeman 1989). Yet the focus on competition is only one interpretation of ecology; since its inception, American pragmatist thinkers from Dewey to Mead and W. E. B. DuBois have stressed another interpretation that focuses on the ways organism and environment mutually constitute life together in a dialectical process of adjustment and adaptation over generational time (Pearce 2020). This more symbiotic interpretation of ecology is already inchoate in Abbott's writings on processual sociology that explicitly embrace Mead's approach to iterative temporal change.

Indeed, Mead had already formulated a humanist interpretation of Whitehead's metaphysics that built upon his pragmatist theories of the emergence of the self. In *The Philosophy of the Present*, Mead (1932, 17–19) hints at the hinge between pragmatism and process theory in suggesting that an event-based understanding of temporal reality enables us to account for both the determinable influences of past events on the present as well as the indeterminacy evident in the irreducibility of the present to past events. This emergentist perspective emphasizes the capacity of actors to interpret the past, anticipate the future, and act in the present in communion with their environment. The process theory Mead proposes, based upon his theories of mind and self, is thoroughly humanist and perspectival, locating the crux of the event in situated persons' conduct within their environments:

> The past as it appears with the present and future, is the relation of the emergent event to the situation out of which it arose, and it is the event that defines that situation. The continuance or disappearance of that which arises is the present passing into the future. Past, present and future belong to a passage which attains temporal structure through the event, and they may be considered long or short as they are compared with other such passages. . . . The pasts and futures to which we refer extend beyond these contiguous relations in passage. We extend them out in memory and history, in anticipation and forecast. They are preeminently the field of ideation, and find their locus in what is called mind. (Mead, 1932, 23–24)

Mead's interpretation of passage allows for the duality of temporality where antecedent cause and continuity shape the conditions toward which actors respond, while preserving a present that is open, in flux, and capable of radical discontinuity in light of the way actors perceive and act toward their interpretations of the constraints of the past and the possibilities of the future.

Mead's passage proposes an environment for human action characterized by overlapping and interpenetrating strands of temporal systems, constituting a world akin to the one Emirbayer and Mische (1998, 968) characterize as "a multilevel flow of nested events." In advancing such a view of the world, Mead points toward the importance of "sociality," the ongoing coordination of organism and environment accomplished through the kind of reflexive consciousness familiar to sociologists from Mead's more popular works on the self. Mead (1932, 47) asks us to focus on how the "determining conditions" of the past create the environment actors adjust to and how the present emerges from the mutual adjustment of environment and organism. Abbott (2016, 34–35) himself seizes upon Mead's construction of temporal passage as the basis for conceptualizing the vast horizon of "linked ecologies" that can be reconstructed in synchronic accounts of action in context. Embracing Mead's concept of sociality extends ecological analysis beyond competition to include the generative and open-ended potential for cooperation, mutuality, and co-construction of social environments.

Recently, some scholars have argued that the contemporary analysis of social worlds would benefit from a reexamination of Mead's work to the extent it emphasized a processual and relational approach to social ecologies (Abbott 2007; Cefaï 2016; Joas 1996). As Daniel Cefaï (2016, 169) writes, Mead's interpretation conceives of social worlds as social orders constituted from interconnected actors who coordinate with one another to shape their environments, thus forming "a network of perspectives and perspectives on perspectives that keeps on transforming" as collective activity unfolds over time. From the perspective of one self involved in a social world, the meso-level social orders comprising their diffuse and multiple ecologies represent "perspectives on perspectives." The "objective" qualities of such meso-level social orders provide for certain stimuli in individuals' efforts to reconstruct situations through interpretation in order to act toward those situations. Yet these objective qualities are partial according to Mead's processual ontology. There is a "subjective" and emergent quality to meso-level social orders as processual, reconstructive, and experiential collective phenomena. It is this other reality of meso-level social orders as collective phenomena—as the continual transformation of these perspectives on perspectives in the context of group action—that demands our attention when reinterpreting social worlds from a Meadian perspective.

The objectivity of perspectives belonging to humans and their environments suggests that individuals change their experiential stock as well as their physical circumstances as they accommodate the experience of passage through action in the world. To better capture the mutual temporal emergence of human experience and its environment, we might substitute social worlds analysis' traditional grounding in symbolic interaction with a focus on *transaction*. Transaction is a way of looking at human conduct as involved in a transformative intersubjective exchange including the many elements constituting the environment for the exchange. In the words of Mustafa Emirbayer (1997, 287), the concept of transaction implies that "the very terms or units involved in a transaction derive their meaning, significance, and identity from the (changing) functional roles they play within that transaction." Emirbayer has been a recent advocate of transactional ontologies in sociological theory, but he adopts the term from pragmatist John Dewey. Dewey developed the idea of transaction from, and to better describe, the theoretical ontology of his good friend George Herbert Mead. Mead's conception of the self as emergent from "constitutive and developmental" experiences of biological individuals acting in their objectified environment is illustrative of a transactional approach to the self (McVeigh 2016, 222). As Mead claims, "selves can only exist in definite relationships to other selves. No hard-and-fast line can be drawn between our selves and the selves of others, since our own selves exist and enter as such into our experience only in so far as the selves of others exist and enter as such into our experience also" (quoted in McVeigh 2016, 220).

To adapt the transactional theory of self to social worlds, making affordances given the incompleteness of Mead's thoughts before his death, we could say that no hard-and-fast line can be drawn between the boundaries of the meso-level social orders that make up social worlds as they "enter into our experience"; what we subsequently identify as formal organizations, networks, or discrete social groups are reconstructions that emerge from our attempts to make sense of and construct meaning from the temporally extended processes comprising them. Transaction allows us to transcend the topographical ontology of social worlds by emphasizing the ecological nature of sociality, thus accounting for the emergence of features of an environment that can only exist as objectified products of transactional processes (Simpson 2014). For Mead, the coincidence of these different temporal strands enables the emergence and persistence of novel temporal lineages out of human actors' efforts to reshape their worlds. Other-oriented action communicated through meaningful symbols allows for the emergence of different social phenomena, whether selves (Mead 1962) or, as contemporary process theorists argue, other social things like professions, organizations, cultural artifacts, or institutions (Abbott 1999, 2001). What is crucial from Mead's perspective is that such phenomena be viewed as ongoing, temporally emergent processes rather than as given achievements to be treated abstractly, and that the analyst pay attention to the twinned material and mental processes that allow these features of the world to be shaped by meaningful human conduct.

Processual Comparison: From Looping Effects to Reiterated Problem-Solving

Embracing a pragmatist processual sociology opens the door for ecological perspectives on social construction that situate the iterative emergence of meso-level social orders in relation to their often-changing social and material context. It thus complements efforts in sociological theory that build on philosopher of science Ian Hacking's dynamic nominalism. In analyzing how psychiatric knowledge helps constitute the reality of psychiatric illness, Hacking (1995) developed dynamic nominalism to describe the processual emergence of "human kinds" (e.g., "the autistic") in terms of a "looping effect." Looping effects are processes whereby the classifications experts develop to define and study certain kinds of people feed back into the way people so classified act, opening up new ways of being for those human kinds that subsequently reconstruct the knowledge being developed about them, and so on. In sociology, Daniel Hirschman and Isaac Reed (2014) have scaled this concept to discuss the emergence of "social kinds" from historical looping effects that embody conceptual, discursive, and sociotechnical relations in their historical constitution and evolution. Processual theories inspired by dynamic nominalism call out for a method that captures the iterative and temporal nature of the emergence and change of meso-level social orders, such as communities, networks, groups, and organizations. Many theoretical advocates of this approach have found a methodological approach to the study of looping effects in reiterated problem-solving.

Jeffrey Haydu (1998) first proposed reiterated problem-solving as an alternative to analyzing recurring eventful temporal processes that were typically lumped under path dependency approaches. As a comparative historical method, reiterated problem-solving focuses on sequences of events that repeat across different time periods and revolve around attempts by historical actors to address similar problems while integrating insights from past attempts at their solution. Reiterated problem-solving encourages the analyst to theorize problems and their attempted solutions as intact pairs rather than deconstructing them into variables to compare across cases, focusing their attention on how solutions to antecedent problems shape the environments to which subsequent iterations respond. In the process, it draws the analyst's attention to the mutual entanglement of the environing factors impacting social orders as well as the constitution of these social orders themselves. It thus makes context analytically informative for interpreting outcomes and specifying causal mechanisms rather than treating context as a source of variation to be discarded.

Reiterated problem-solving has been applied to analyze the emergence of the same objects of analysis upon which Hacking developed the notion of looping effects: that is, novel disease entities like autism that are characterized by socially meaningful and evolving symptomology or sequalae. Gil Eyal shows the importance of temporality in the formation of an "autism epidemic" at the turn of the twenty-first century. Rather than asking why autism rates have risen so precipitously in recent years, Eyal (2013, 867) "suggest[s] that we ask first why autism was rare in the past." He demonstrates the iterative historical episodes whereby deinstitutionalizing children with intellectual disabilities led to the constitution of a new "institutional matrix" that attempted to solve the recurring problem of "how to define, observe, and intervene in a domain of [disease] objects that were neither [mental] illness nor retardation" (Eyal 2013, 868). It was "the combination of this new actor, the new ecology created by deinstitutionalization, and the capacity of the therapies to secure the cooperation of the patients themselves . . . [that] led to the autism 'epidemic'" (Eyal 2013, 868). Eyal shows how successive attempts by numerous lay and professional actors to define an ambiguous constellation of symptoms in relation to evolving social contexts subsumed heterogeneous disorders under the umbrella of the autism (and now autism spectrum disorder) diagnosis. In the process, the very scientific and medical object of "autism" was reconstituted as a disease entity, such that researchers now deal with a different object than the one their predecessors reckoned with only decades prior.

Similarly, Daniel Navon (2019) demonstrates how newly discovered genetic mutations with varied or ambiguous clinical manifestations become associated with new or existing syndromes through an iterative process of inquiry and interpretation involving geneticists, physicians, patient advocates, and disease organizations. Navon's within-case comparisons of the evolution of various mutations charts how this complex ecology over time allows some sources of genetic variation to classify "genomically designated" kinds of people, such as "children with 22q13 deletion syndrome," while other genetic variations fail to potentiate new communities of suffering. Successful genomic designation of new disease entities thus emerges from a process of "reiterative fact making," wherein historical actors' interpretations of recurring problems around classifying and diagnosing the medical effects of mutations that they are simultaneously studying and defining as scientific objects produce "powerful categories of human difference underwritten by complex networks of research, treatment, and social mobilization" (Navon 2019, 15–19).

Although biomedical knowledge production has provided a foundation for uniting Hacking's looping kinds with Haydu's reiterated problem-solving, the objects of analysis appropriate to this approach need not derive from scientific knowledge systems. More mundane socially constructed objects of state intervention also benefit from approaches that draw from reiterated problem-solving to show how the very things around which substantive policies evolve are emergent from processes where complex social ecologies participate in the constitution of problems and their solutions over time. As Daniel Hirschman, Ellen Berrey, and Fiona Rose-Greenland (2016, 267) argue, the "dequantification" of race-based admissions decisions at the University of Michigan resulted from "internal features of the system of quantified admissions and important conditions characterizing the relationship between that system and its larger political environment." By showing how systems of classification and evaluation around race-based admission decisions emerged in relation to the problem of ensuring a diverse student body across shifting legal and political contexts challenging affirmative action, the authors demonstrate how the University of Michigan achieved a rare outcome of *de*quantification, where qualitative and holistic decision rules replaced a system once organized around quantitative admission algorithms. Similarly, Matthew Norton (2014, 1539) uses reiterated problem-solving to analyze the emergence of a "cultural infrastructure of coercive power" in the early modern British empire. Norton's case demonstrates how the state's capacity to combat piracy was constituted by bureaucratic, legal, and cultural meanings assigned to piracy and how this capacity was itself the product of interacting historical attempts by state actors to define and mobilize against the issue of extralegal maritime violence.

Appreciating the depth of this mutual constitution of social kinds and their environing conditions, from genetic disorders to diversity initiatives, calls for a comparative sociology that contends with the ecological emergence of meso-level social order. With some modifications from processual sociological theory, reiterated problem-solving is a methodological tool fit for the task of explanation in postpositivist comparative historical sociology. It enables the sociologist to maintain a theoretical position on the temporal and processual emergence of our objects of analysis while leaving room to uncover mechanisms or theories that can be generalized to other cases.

Toward an Ecological Comparative Historical Sociology

My primary goal here has been to advocate for a greater role in postpositivist comparative analysis for process theories with a common philosophical basis in the works of processual pragmatists. Combining this processual ontology with a temporal focus on the looping effects that lead to the emergence of social kinds allows for within-case temporal comparisons that show the broad ecological influences that shape such objects of sociological analysis. Such an approach is likely to foreground "maximal interpretations" as the basis for rich comparative work that is attentive to the concerns of postpositivist explanation in sociology (Reed 2011). In mutually articulating thick descriptions of empirical cases with specifications of generalizable explanatory mechanisms, maximal interpretation constitutes a potent tool in the postpositivist explanatory arsenal. Maximal interpretation is an approach to sociological analysis that weds referential evidentiary accounting to relational theories of the social world, thereby generating explanations that serve the sociologist less like the positivist accounts Sewell criticizes and more like the model organisms operable in the life sciences today.

To belabor the comparison between social and life sciences once more, scholars of science and technology studies have found that model organisms serve a significant purpose for guiding theory and empirical analysis in life sciences where covering laws are largely absent. Model organisms are relatively simplistic species variants whose organismic qualities are used by scientists to study more general biological phenomena. Model organisms can be used toward a variety of epistemic ends, but for our purposes, their ability to represent case-based reasoning in the life sciences offers an analogue for how to think across the complex explanations postpositivist sociologists might produce in applying the frameworks covered in this chapter.

As theoretically driven index cases, model organisms are good to think through and good to think with; they enable "the proffering of observations and detailed descriptions, which may well point to testable hypotheses and explanations, particularly if they are to have an impact on the development of theory or on practice" through "creation of an epistemological space or framework within which to ask questions" (Ankeny 2007, 53). Much like the epistemic practices advocated in maximal interpretation, the use of model organisms foregrounds the analyst's own interpretive labor in extracting quasi-generalizable explanations from concrete phenomena in all their messy, meaningful, and materially embedded complexity. This abductive-style approach to explanation (see Tavory and Timmermans 2014) is more common in medicine and biology than many sociologists may suppose, as these fields often depend upon case-based reasoning to open up spaces for generating workable lines of inquiry into phenomena that are still poorly circumscribed or understood (Ankeny 2007, 55).

Recently, Monika Krause (2021, 7) has embraced the comparison of canonical cases in sociology with model organisms in biology, encouraging sociologists to consider "collective conventions and patterns and material practices" that shape how researchers select and analyze these empirical cases. Much of comparative historical sociology has focused on "privileged material research objects"—that is, events or research sites that have achieved canonical status through a history of intensive study and disciplinary convention. Thus, much as *Drosophila melanogaster* has become one of the favored model organisms in genetics, Chicago has become the privileged material research object in urban sociology. As it depends on a temporal emergentist conception of social phenomena, processual sociology would side with Krause in encouraging the proliferation of alternative material research objects. The more apt approach, then, would be more akin to evolutionary ecology, which seeks out a diversity of niches that are each studied intensively to uncover how their change over time has influenced the relational interactions among the diverse organisms that populate them.

Recently, philosopher Joseph Rouse (2015) applied the concept of niche construction to analyze how human communities alter their sociomaterial environments to enable them to pursue meaningful lines of action. Rouse proposes that social practices be conceptualized in relation to the constraints and affordances of actors' shared cultural and linguistic environments as well as their material environments, which together constitute the historically constructed niche within which such practices are intelligible and efficacious. Importantly, this approach to analyzing social practices requires attention to how social action is accountable to the normative expectations of proper performance in addition to the material constraints imposed by the environment. By highlighting past performances and future projections, niche construction dovetails with a pragmatist conception of temporality and procession that focuses on the dynamics of sociality in each successive performance of a given social practice. The extension of these practices over time, and their modifications to the environment for action in accordance with the outcomes of iterative performances, form the heart of niche construction accounts.

Advancing the evolutionary metaphor that has influenced pragmatism, niche construction firmly maintains the focus of analysis on the emergence of meso-level social orders from the iterative and looping interplay between social things and their environments. Comparing across such cases in sociology, similarly to how one might compare the emergence of ecological niches in two geographic locations in ecology, encourages analysts to look for processes that might be generalizable across cases while maintaining an epistemological appreciation for the fundamental entanglement of social things with the environments from which they emerge.

✻ ✻ ✻

A pragmatist interpretation of process philosophy, used in pursuit of studying the ecological emergence of meso-level social orders, offers distinctive advantages for comparative study relative to alternative groundings for process theories in sociology. In its attention to how meso-level orders emerge from the iterative temporal procession of situated events, pragmatist process theory remains alive to the ways human actors respond to their own environments by conceptualizing the possibilities for action in light of their present and past circumstances. Realizing the potential of a pragmatist processual sociology involves exploring the evolutionary ecological thinking that inspired process philosophies to begin with—a project that should be pursued with all the epistemic caution that a century of hard lessons about its irresponsible use should instill. Recent developments in both philosophy and sociology hold promise for an enlightened approach to the use of biological and ecological metaphors as supplements to sociological heuristics like reiterated problem-solving. Capitalizing on these developments will help postpositivist sociology advance the goals of constructing empirically adequate and commensurate accounts of complex social phenomena that attend to disciplinary concerns over leveraging comparison cases to develop mid-range theories of social order.

Notes

A primordial ancestor of this paper was presented at the 2015 Junior Theorists Symposium.
1. For an in-depth discussion of the differences between Whiteheadian and pragmatist process theories, see Rosenthal (1996).

References

Abbott, Andrew. 1988. *The System of Professions: An Essay on the Division of Expert Labor.* Chicago: University of Chicago Press.

——. 1999. *Department and Discipline: Chicago Sociology at One Hundred.* Chicago: University of Chicago Press.

——. 2001. *Time Matters: On Theory and Method.* Chicago: University of Chicago Press.

——. 2007. "Against Narrative: A Preface to Lyrical Sociology." *Sociological Theory* 25(1):67–99.

——. 2016. *Processual Sociology.* Chicago: University of Chicago Press.

Ankeny, Rachel A. 2007. "Wormy Logic: Model Organisms as Case-Based Reasoning." In *Science Without Laws: Model Systems, Cases, Exemplary Narratives,* edited by Angela N. H. Creager, Elizabeth Lunbeck, and M. Norton Wise, 46–58. Durham, NC: Duke University Press.

Cefaï, Daniel. 2016. "Social Worlds: The Legacy of Mead's Social Ecology in Chicago Sociology." In *The Timeliness of George Herbert Mead,* edited by Hans Joas and Daniel Huebner, 165–84. Chicago: University of Chicago Press.

Emirbayer, Mustafa. 1997. "Manifesto for a Relational Sociology." *American Journal of Sociology* 103(2):281–317.

Emirbayer, Mustafa, and Ann Mische. 1998. "What Is Agency?" *American Journal of Sociology* 103(4):962–1023.

Eyal, Gil. 2013. "For a Sociology of Expertise: The Social Origins of the Autism Epidemic." *American Journal of Sociology* 118(4):863–907.

Hacking, Ian. 1995. "The Looping Effects of Human Kinds." In *Causal Cognition: A Multidisciplinary Debate,* edited by D. Sperber, D. Premack, and A. J. Premack, 351–94. Oxford: Oxford University Press.

Hannan, Michael T., and John Freeman. 1989. *Organizational Ecology.* Cambridge, MA: Harvard University Press.

Haydu, Jeffrey. 1998. "Making Use of the Past: Time Periods as Cases to Compare and as Sequences of Problem Solving." *American Journal of Sociology* 104(2):339–71.

Hirschman, Daniel, Ellen Berrey, and Fiona Rose-Greenland. 2016. "Dequantifying Diversity: Affirmative Action and Admissions at the University of Michigan." *Theory and Society* 45(3):265–301.

Hirschman, Daniel, and Isaac Ariail Reed. 2014. "Formation Stories and Causality in Sociology." *Sociological Theory* 32(4):259–82.

Joas, Hans. 1996. *The Creativity of Action.* Chicago: University of Chicago Press.

Krause, Monica. 2021. *Model Cases: On Canonical Research Objects and Sites.* Chicago: University of Chicago Press.

McVeigh, Ryan. 2016. "Mead, the Theory of Mind, and the Problem of Others." In *The Timeliness of George Herbert Mead*, edited by Hans Joas and Daniel Huebner, 209–30. Chicago: University of Chicago Press.

Mead, George H. 1932. *The Philosophy of the Present*. London: Open Court.

——. 1962. *Mind, Self, and Society: From the Standpoint of a Social Behaviorist*. Edited by Charles W. Morris. Chicago: University of Chicago Press.

Navon, Daniel. 2019. *Mobilizing Mutations: Human Genetics in the Age of Patient Advocacy*. Chicago: University of Chicago Press.

Norton, Matthew. 2014. "Classification and Coercion: The Destruction of Piracy in the English Maritime System." *American Journal of Sociology* 119(6):1537–75.

Pearce, Trevor. 2020. *Pragmatism's Evolution: Organism and Environment in American Philosophy*. Chicago: University of Chicago Press.

Reed, Isaac Ariail. 2011. *Interpretation and Social Knowledge: On the Use of Theory in the Human Sciences*. Chicago: University of Chicago Press.

Rosenthal, Sandra. 1996. "Continuity, Contingency, and Time: The Divergent Intuitions of Whitehead and Pragmatism." *Transactions of the Charles S. Peirce Society* 32(4):542–67.

Rouse, Joseph. 2015. *Articulating the World: Conceptual Understanding and the Scientific Image*. Chicago: University of Chicago Press.

Sewell, William H. 2005. *Logics of History: Social Theory and Social Transformation*. Chicago: University of Chicago Press.

Simpson, Barbara. 2014. "George Herbert Mead." In *The Oxford Handbook of Process Philosophy and Organization Studies*, edited by Jenny Helin, Tor Hernes, Daniel Hjorth, and Robin Holt, 272–86. Oxford: Oxford University Press.

Tavory, Iddo, and Stefan Timmermans. 2014. *Abductive Analysis: Theorizing Qualitative Research*. Chicago: University of Chicago Press.

CHAPTER 6

DESIGNING NARRATIVES AND RECOVERING LEGAL NARRATIVITY

An Exploratory Essay

LAURA R. FORD

Meta-theoretical challenges posed by critical realists have high-lighted a narrowness in our received ideas about causality, which tend almost always to be about *efficient* causality—about causes that *make things happen* (Groff 2004, 2013). Here we often think about billiard balls knocking into one another and about causes as being necessary and suffi-cient to produce their effects. But creative developments in sociological theory, broadening our conception of causality, have suggested possibilities for revisit-ing Aristotle's four-cause theory (cf. Reed 2011), with suggestive application, for example, to the "networked public sphere" of social media (Tufekci 2017).

An alternative conception of causality might be one of *enabling things to happen*—encouraging certain things and discouraging others and facilitating new possibility sets. One benefit of exploring such an alternative is to see how narratives can be important in explicating certain causal properties of social-relational activity, particularly in institutionalized settings involving formal law. A notion of formal causality, for example, focuses our attention on aspects of design (or plan), which do not *make* things happen, in the sense of efficient causality, but nonetheless do make certain social outcomes more likely than others, some possible, and others impossible. The causality here might work at the level of an intellectually apprehended design, or plan, one that social beings respond to at the level of meaning, motivation, and affect in their social-rela-tional activities.

Narrative-based methods may be particularly important in explicating causal properties like this in long-enduring legal institutions. Here the legal "design" may have developed over an extended period of time through inter-generational activities by many social actors relating to narratively informed legal documents. To account for causal properties in institutions like nation-states or property, for example, we may need to tell "social formation stories" (Hirschman and Reed 2014) that begin quite long ago (cf. Pierson 2003).

In this chapter, I seek to explore such ideas by recovering Margaret Somers's path-breaking work on narrativity, which has been influential in sociole-gal scholarship. In particular, I seek to recover a method of *legal narrativity* (Fleury-Steiner 2002; Somers 1992, 1997; cf. Ewick and Silbey 1995). Along the way, I synthesize sociological scholarship on narrative methodology, a line of scholarly inquiry that flourished during the 1990s, with resources that remain untapped.

Narrative as the Other Method

The sociological "classics" often employed narrative. However, the irony with their narrative methods is that the broader, overarching narrative—the meta-narrative of modernity that they all offer—must be reconstructed. Part of the joy and challenge in interpreting these classical figures in sociology's canon lies precisely in reconstructing their narratives of modernity (cf. Smith 2003, 81–7; Somers 1992). For Max Weber, perhaps, it is the rise of modern, rational capitalism that constitutes the overarching, meta-narrative, whereas for Emile Durkheim, it may instead be the rise of modern individualism, within a new social cosmos of organic states and functionally divided labor. For Karl Marx, the meta-narrative is more apocalyptic and eschatological—a grand narrative of the fall of man through private property and a heavenly future to which we can look for in communism, shared property, and ultimate human flourishing (cf. Löwith 1949, 33–51; Steinmetz 1992, 502–3).

With the empiricist naturalism of the Chicago school and pragmatism, genealogy and evolutionary theory often serve the role of narrative. The social world is always in the process of becoming (Abbott 2016), with crucial dynam-ics ultimately deriving from the struggle to survive and create anew (Coser 2003; Joas 1996). We are all equally designers and designed (selves and society) in such narratives, and although a strong element of teleology (final causality) can easily smuggle itself into the picture of a processual struggle for becoming, there is really no place for formal causes (Mead 2015).

During the 1990s, in the wake of sociology's collective rebellion against Talcott Parsons, there were many "turns," among them a "narrative turn" (Abbott 1991; Sewell 1992). A recognition of this narrative turn, together with its methodological possibilities, was marked by a series of essays in *Social Science History*. Although these essays primarily focused on narratives as *objects of analysis*—as structures of meaning for social actors, contributing to identity-formation and mobilization—rather than as a *method* for sociologists to use, there was also some focus on narrative as a method (Abbott 1991; Somers 1992; Steinmetz 1992). If social actors find meaning and understanding through telling stories, presumably sociologists do, too (cf. Maines 1993; Smith 2003, 81–87).

In 1991, Andrew Abbott surveyed the possibilities for a genuinely narrative sociology, arriving at a rather pessimistic conclusion for U.S. sociology, based on an institutional analysis. Abbott showed that there were, at that time, really two separate clusters of historically focused sociological research, which had relatively little contact with each other. His analysis drew on evidence from a combination of university-based and professional organization–based affiliations and programming. Abbott's account highlighted the extent to which embrace of historical methods tended to be instrumentalist, serving a shared ambition to demolish Parsonian theory and to forge a path for left-leaning politics, particularly Marxism and feminism. There was no real rethinking of a basically Humean paradigm for causality or of the ontological model suggested by statistical methodologies, what Abbott (1988, 2001) has called "general linear reality." The overall effect, according to Abbott, was a narrowly circumscribed, thematically constituted range of possibilities for historical sociology and a refusal to genuinely embrace narrative as a sociological method (cf. Adams et al. 2005, 24n50).

A more optimistic picture was painted by William Sewell in 1992, in a brief article introducing a set of essays dedicated to the theme of "narrative and the formation of social identities" (479). The essays grew out of a 1989 panel at the Social Science History Association (SSHA) annual meeting, which generated a sufficiently enthusiastic discussion to garner support by an editor for a special edition of *Social Science History*. Five articles were ultimately published, in addition to Sewell's, authored by Janet Hart, Mary Jo Maynes, Margaret Somers, Luisa Passerini, and George Steinmetz.[1] Thematically, and as introduced by Sewell, the articles addressed the role of narrative in identity formation. Three of the five articles dealt with (working) class identity, one with gender identity, and one with national identity. As William Sewell (1992, 482–83) himself noted, the articles did not primarily address narrative as a method, but rather focused on the role of narrative in the lives of social actors, particularly in connection with processes of identity formation: "Perhaps the most important claim of these articles is that getting at the narratives in which historical actors emplot themselves is crucial for understanding the course and the dynamics of historical change" (483).

Sewell nonetheless declared an opening for narrative-based methods, inaugurated in this set of essays, an opening that was amplified by Somers (1992, 1997) and by others (e.g., Aminzade 1992; Franzosi 1998; Isaac 1997; Maines

1993). In Sewell's (1992, 480) description, social science history of the type embraced by the SSHA had previously defined itself in opposition to "traditional narrative history." Narrative, according to Sewell, is associated with the fuzzy and soft humanities, whereas analysis and quantification are associated with the hard, rigorous clarity of science (see also Griffin 1993; Hart 1992, 639; Maines 1993, 19; Somers 1992, 599; Stone 1979). Recognizing the original opposition between *narrative* history and social *science* history, Sewell nonetheless saw a new departure in a panel dedicated to narrative, hosted under the umbrella of the SSHA. Sewell also noted a fundamental ambiguity, however, in the way the category of narrative was being applied. As applied to the motivating and motivational accounts of politically engaged, social actors, might not political programs or ideologies be an appropriate, alternative name for stories of identity formation (Sewell 1992, 486–87)?

This question was amplified by George Steinmetz (1992), because, for him, it is the *coherence* of a story told by social actors—one that connects their individual lives to a larger, collective history—that makes for *success* in working-class identity formation. Steinmetz (1992, 490) thus applied evaluative criteria in forming judgments about (1) the coherence of "social narratives" and (2) the successful outcome to which they contribute. At one point, he directly identified collective narratives as a type of "ideological structure," one that is drawn upon by social actors in formulating identity narratives. Steinmetz, however, described his article as an exercise in concept formation for purposes of comparative analysis in sociology, and he engaged both explicitly and at length with literary theory in considering the category of social narratives. One enduring contribution of Steinmetz's article rests in the analysis it offers, keyed both to literary theory and to sociology, of a successful narrative (Sewell 1992).

Margaret Somers (1992) equated Steinmetz's category of *social narrative* with her alternative category of an *ontological narrative*. Somers sees in narrative the capacity to constitute social identity (e.g., class identity) for people and, therefore, to have an existential, world-forming power, which renders it ontological (Somers 1992, 603; cf. Somers 1998, 2008). Like Steinmetz, however, Somers also offered a broader analysis of narrative, one that both critiqued the implicit narratives covertly deployed within social science and that helpfully identified the causal and explanatory dimensions of *narrativity*.

In close parallel to Steinmetz, Somers (1992, 601–2) described "emplotment" as the crucial intellectual move in narrative articulation. However, with Somers, this is an explicitly *causal* emplotment that can serve explanatory functions (cf. Somers 1998, 2008). For Somers, in other words, narrative was explicitly envisioned as a sociological *method*, whereas for Steinmetz, it remained a sociological *object*. Nonetheless, because there are such close parallels between their analyses of narrative, I discuss Somers and Steinmetz together throughout this essay.

The notion that narrative analysis constitutes, at least potentially, a comparative method for sociological research was also taken up by Janet Hart (1992), in her account of Greek resistance movements during the 1940s. While her article was primarily a case study in national identity formation, Hart offered an analytical preface that was explicitly geared toward methodological use of narratives in comparative sociological research. Hart expressed agreement with Somers and Steinmetz that emplotment is fundamental to a narrative. Drawing on the literary theory of Hayden White, Hart argued that the important, explanatory function of a plot is in identifying a narrative *kind*, or type (a "kind of story"). In other words, for Hart, we should deploy a categorical scheme for narratives, one drawing upon literary *and* sociological theories. Hart (1992, 635) distinguished ontological narratives, which are more subjective and personal, from mobilizational narratives, which are shared and intersubjective, "designed by their authors to establish and support collective values and to encourage solidarity." While mobilizational narratives are primarily treated as an object of research in Hart's account, her opening and preface hint at the possibility that mobilizational narratives might also be methodologically deployed by sociologists. What I take from her article is the notion that narratives are *designed*.

Between 1993 and 1997, a cluster of articles further explored the implications of narrative as a methodological approach. Articles appeared in the *Sociological Quarterly*, a journal published by the Midwest Sociological Society, and in a thematic issue of *Historical Methods: A Journal of Quantitative and Interdisciplinary History* (Volume 30, Issue 1, 1997). In 1998, a review of these developments was published by Roberto Franzosi. One article even appeared in the *American Journal of Sociology*, although it notably reinforced a version of the "hard science" skepticism concerning narrative methods (Griffin 1993). Nonetheless, taken together, these articles proclaimed that the moment had come for a return to narrative methods in sociology and sought to explicate features of such methods, drawing on the early Chicago school and on illustrations from contemporary research (Gotham and Staples 1996; Maines 1993; cf. Abbott 2001). Authors viewed a turn to narrative in sociological research as positive, highlighting the possibilities for broader conceptions of causality (Gotham and Staples 1996), while also recognizing the need to think carefully about traditional questions of validity and reliability, as well as systematicity (Griffin 1993; Isaac 1997; cf. Maines 1993). Underlying these traditional questions, as Maines (1993, 27) pointed out, is the deeply traditional (if quixotic) quest for certainty in knowing (*scientia* in the high medieval and early modern senses).

As many have noted, there is a wide range of scholarship on narrative methods outside of sociology: in literary theory, philosophy, and the "human sciences," particularly psychology. References to Hayden White, Paul Ricoeur, and Donald Polkinghorne are frequent in surveys. Christian Smith briefly surveyed this interdisciplinary research in his 2003 book, *Moral, Believing Animals*, which focused on the moral and ontological implications of narratives, including for the discipline of sociology.

In 2007, Andrew Abbott took up a rhetorical stance "against narrative," in what I take to be an effort to show how deeply narrative forms actually structure most methodological approaches in U.S. sociology and to create a space for "lyrical" approaches that are temporally "momentaneous" and passionate (cf. Abbott 2001, 2005). Today, in any case, Abbott's 1991 prediction seems in large degree correct. Possibilities for narrative-based methodology seem to have been largely confined to particular areas of thematic research, particularly on identity. The explanation for this, I suspect, has to do with embrace of narrative methods by rational choice scholars, which revealed a widening divide on metaphysical and theoretical presuppositions, particularly with reference to causation (Calhoun 1998; Kiser 1996; Kiser and Hechter 1998; Somers 1998).

Arguably, the possibilities for narrative methodologies in sociology remain largely untapped. In the following section, I aim to synthesize insights from the sociological literature of the 1990s, focusing especially on the work of Margaret Somers, considering the methodological possibilities and implications of narrativity. In the following section, I focus specifically on implications for the study of legal institutions. Margaret Somers (1992, 1997) pointed the way forward in formulating a concept of "legal narrativity"; sociologists of law have subsequently taken legal narrativity in a more critical and constructivist direction.

Designing Narratives

At the core of narrative-based methods is a storyline, a connecting thread that links and distills a "point of the story" from selected elements. Stories have plots. In the language of Paul Ricoeur, *emplotment* is fundamental to the meaning and coherence of narrative. This emphasis on plot design has been picked up almost uniformly by the sociologists who have focused on possibilities for narrative methods. However, among the sociologists surveyed in this article, Margaret Somers (1992) has arguably gone the furthest in considering a range of features and social levels for plot design.

In her 1992 article, Somers sought to reconstruct the elements of plot design underpinning what she identified as a mistaken *master narrative* within sociology, "the classical story of English socioeconomic development" (593), deriving from Adam Smith and Karl Marx, among others, a narrative that paradoxically renders English developments anomalous while at the same time being founded upon them. This narrative was premised on a "conceptual filter" derived a priori from theory, the same a priori so dear to early pragmatist theory: social naturalism. Here is the master narrative of "self-regulating entities" and processes, invisible social hands premised on posited, "natural" capacities for intersubjective social experience, fellow feelings of empathy and sympathy that build upon one another to constitute a moral universe without any need for authorities and intellectual traditions. This master narrative is a *plot*, a carefully designed conceptual arc in a story that is told and retold to assert something very fundamental about human beings and their collective capacities. Ironically, however, the actors in the drama, according to Somers (1992), are "atemporal" abstractions: "classes, society, tradition and modernity" (594).

Somers's (1992) reconstruction of a master narrative underpinning sociology is one enduring contribution of her article, but another rests in her analysis of narrativity (599–603). Somers rejected the notion that narratives are *representations*. For her, they go deeper than this and are rather constitutive of social experience. Narratives are ontological, in that they contribute to constituting human persons as selves with identities, and they provide the foundation for our collective projects in knowing, acting, and creating (see also Smith 2003). We have social being and knowledge through narratives. This jointly ontological and epistemological conception of narratives provides the foundation for an approach that Somers labels *narrativity*.

Somers (1992, 601–3) identifies four features of narrativity and four social levels at which narrativity can operate. The four features of narrativity are (1) parts that are connected together into a relational, narrated whole; (2) a plot providing the storyline that gives meaning to the connected whole; (3) "selective appropriation," meaning that there is a narrator who designs the plot through exercising judgment about what should be included in the storyline; and (4) a spatiotemporal setting ("relational setting") that locates the plot in a time sequence and in concrete places.

"Causal emplotment," which is central to narrativity, is a modality of investigation and explanation, for Somers (1992), one in which "plot hypotheses" are judged in relation to "actual events" in order to see whether the events fit within a hypothesized plot (601). Once a plot is judged to adequately fit the events, such that it can link them together in an intelligible pattern of relational connection, meaningless events are transformed into meaningful episodes that are part of a larger story. The design of the causal plot is therefore fundamental to narrativity. Plot, for Somers, is the "logic or syntax" of narrativity (602).

The social levels at which narrativity can operate are (1) personal/ontological; (2) public, cultural, and institutional; (3) conceptual/analytic/sociological; and (4) meta. The personal/ontological level is that on which identities, selves, and personhood are formed. Narrativity at this level is fundamental both to agency and to institution building. The third and fourth levels are involved in theory building within sociology, in concept formation, and in the overarching storyline of modernity that sociologists implicitly reiterate. The second level of public, cultural, and institutional narrativity is central to what Somers briefly labels *legal narrativity*, and it is the focus of my attention in the remainder of this chapter.

It is important to stress Somers's emphasis on the interdependence of (1) personal/ontological and (2) public, cultural, and institutional narratives (see also Somers 2008). Public, cultural, and institutional narratives have a different subject than the personal/ontological, but the two types of narrative are closely related. Selves design their narrative identities (persons form their narrative personalities) in relation to a set of broader narratives that are fundamentally about the social groups with which they see themselves as being relationally situated: family, ethnic community, race, religious community, social movement, nation, state, or company (Somers 1992, 603–4; cf. Steinmetz 1992, 490). Somers mainly focused in her early work on the dependency that runs from personal/ontological to public narrative, with the former being designed in relation to the latter (cf. Somers 2008, where the direction is reversed). She describes public narratives as being designed through a "selective appropriation" and "processing" of events (Somers 1992, 602, 604; cf. Somers 2008; Steinmetz 1992, 491).

Public, cultural, and institutional narratives "comprise (breakable) rules, (variable) practices, binding (and unbinding) institutions, and the multiple stories of family, nation, or economic life" (Somers 1992, 607; cf. Somers 2008). The "practical workings of the legal system," for example, have an impact on people's experiences and, therefore, will often be incorporated into the stories they tell about themselves and the public institutions through which they mutually relate and interact (Somers 1992, 2008).

One of Somers's (1992, 606–8) priorities has been to contest the notion that identities are formed based on interests, particularly class interests. She is especially critical of the extent to which theoretical conceptions of class identity posit a uniformity of experience based on economic interest. Taking an approach of narrativity, on the other hand, we can theorize social experiences as being relational, in the sense that the experiences themselves are emplotted as episodes in personal and public narratives. Social action becomes "intelligible," therefore, through emplotted narratives (607), but the action is also constrained by the extent to which certain public and personal narratives tend to prevail in a given social context (cf. Somers 2008).

Somers (1992, 609) suggested a concept of "relational setting," rather than "society," for concretely locating the empirical study of personal and public narratives. And she further suggested that geometric metaphors may be better than mechanistic ones in designing public narratives, which will trace the interrelations of "institutional arrangements and cultural practices" in relational settings (Somers 1992, 610; Somers 2008).

It is important to note, however, that even though Somers critiqued a narrowly representational conception of narratives, she seemed in certain ways to valorize the very positivism and empiricism that she endeavored to escape. At times, Somers seems to presume that the experience of events can be treated as a collection of sense data that may be held up to the light of a coherently formed narrative (an episode), which is separately constituted at what should perhaps be understood as a cultural or consciously meaningful level.

However, when Somers (1992, 2008) writes about personal/ontological narratives, she asserts that experience itself is narrativized. There is an ambiguity or tension here that Somers did not, to my knowledge, resolve. And there is the further practical issue, not dealt with by Somers, that in primary historical sources we are usually dealing with events that are already narrativized (e.g., a monastic chronicle or records from a lawsuit). Emplotment almost always involves weaving together narrativized threads, metaphorically speaking, rather than the fictional model of the laboratory scientist working with raw sense data. For what may be institutional reasons, Somers was drawn toward an ontology of events, but this is in tension with her ontology of narrativized social experiences.

From Legal Narrativity to Neo-Marxist Ideology

In formulating a theoretical approach to narrative-based identity, Somers ended up formulating a methodology for the narrative-based study of legal institutions. This is because, according to her empirical study, English working-class identity emerged as a result of personal/ontological narratives designed in relation to large-scale legal transformations in medieval England. In these transformations, as Somers describes them, a "national public sphere" was created by constituting a national state through extension of legal institutions that were operative within cities and villages. "In legal practices the state became the city 'writ-large'" (Somers 1992, 615). The crucible, Somers argues, was likely the set of conjoined medieval institutions mandating participation in local administration. Most familiar among these is the jury, not so much the modern jury that decides facts at issue in a lawsuit, but rather the medieval body of oath-bound jurors called together to attest to local patterns of property holding and legal customs and to engage in intensive mutual scrutiny premised on solidary liability (e.g., "frankpledge" or tithing, see Downer 1972, 103; Hudson 1996, 39, 61–69). Within local relational settings, differing legal cultures prevailed. However, the overarching narrative that Somers provides is one in which local communities came, over time, to administer a "formally uniform national law," one in which "multiple narratives of community politics were institutionalized into the heart of the national legal and political apparatus" (Somers 1992, 616).

Based on her study of English working-class formation, Somers (1992) concluded that law and rights were central elements in the public narratives upon which English people drew in designing their personal/ontological narratives (611–13). "The relationship between 'the people and the law' was thus the prevailing public narrative of these working people, and the plot line which configured this narrative was that of a political culture of rights" (612). Narratives about becoming a person were fundamentally narratives about acquiring legal rights, especially property-related rights, which were closely connected to membership and citizenship (613).

In 1992 and 1997, Somers used the phrase "narrative justice" to label the "participatory system" that constituted a public narrative of rights, in relation to which English working-class identity was formed. She also, however, used the phrase "legal narrativity." Legal narrativity was then, for her, a specific public narrative, one that contributed essential conceptual forms to the personal narratives enabling working-class identity formation in England.

However, because Somers offers a set of methodological prescriptions for designing narratives that involve public narratives of legal institutions, we can also label her overall approach as one of *legal narrativity*. We can accordingly extend her methodological prescriptions into the foundation for a methodology of legal narrativity, one sketched briefly in 1992 (610–16) and reiterated in 1997.

Somers's model of legal narrativity has since been picked up and redeployed by scholars affiliated with interdisciplinary "law and society" scholarship, including sociologists of law (Ewick and Silbey 1995, 1998; Fleury-Steiner 2002; Fleury-Steiner and Nielsen 2006). Legal narrativity has, by these scholars, been elevated to the status of a *theory of legal consciousness*, a theoretical perspective on the ways that narratives reinforce structures of power and inequality, which are operative through identity-related ideologies. While Somers provides a background reference for these scholars, the basic framework is critical, constructivist, and neo-Marxist, juxtaposing hegemonic narratives about law that reinforce inequalities against subversive narratives that heroically resist and potentially transform the coercive powers of law (Ewick and Silbey 1995, 1998).

For Patricia Ewick and Susan Silbey (1998, 223–44), narratives are fundamental to the "social construction of legality," which can take one of three ideal-typical forms: (1) narratives about (respectfully) standing "before the law," (2) narratives about working strategically "with the law," and (3) narratives of resistance "against the law." Narratives, for Ewick and Silbey, reflect and encode these three forms of socially constructed legality, or legal consciousness. The first is unmasked as hegemonic ideology, the second as strategic gamesmanship, and the third is celebrated as the nonmystified and counter-hegemonic experience of law among the oppressed.

The theoretical background for this line of sociological research lies in social constructivism and in neo-Marxist theories of ideology and hegemony. An important mediator is Hayden White (1987), an authority upon whom Ewick and Silbey (1995) rely. White was also an important authority for George Steinmetz (1992, 495), who quotes with approval White's paraphrasing of Louis Althusser: Narrative is a "particularly effective system of discursive meaning production by which individuals can be taught to live a distinctly 'imaginary relation to their real conditions of existence,' that is to say, an unreal but meaningful relation to the social formations in which they are indentured to live out their lives" (quoting White 1987, x). In their 1998 book (273n8), Ewick and Silbey explicitly indicate their reliance on Althusser.

In a programmatic, methodological essay, Ewick and Silbey (1995) briefly referenced Somers (1992), primarily in order to unpack their critical strategy, which ranges hegemony and ideology along a continuum of contestation over the ways that law connects everyday social experiences to general power structures reinforcing inequalities. With hegemony, power structures are reinforced to a degree that they are taken for granted, whereas with ideology, there is contestation. Narratives either reinforce or resist, and they are accordingly either unmasked or celebrated.

In their methodological essay, Ewick and Silbey (1995, 199) described their embrace of narrative as being rooted in two important virtues of narrativity, which are connected and related to one another. The first is overtly political: narratives have the potential to "unsettle power," to give "voice" to those who are often voiceless, and "to undermine the illusion of an objective, naturalized world which so often sustains inequality and powerlessness." This revolutionary, political virtue is inseparable from the epistemological virtue of narratives, the way in which the possibility of plural narratives underwrites the "conviction that there is no single, objectively apprehended truth" (199). Because of their plurality and the ways in which they can speak for the powerless in society, narratives possess a transformative power, a power to break down existing structures of power, presumably in the hope that new and better powers will arise to replace them or that we can exit the world of social power altogether (cf. Liu 2015).

Social constructivism and the Marxist tradition of ideological critique are reinforcing one another here. But, because we are situated so firmly within neo-Marxist theory, it is the Marxist meta-narrative that is operating in the background. There is no historical development traced in the analysis. We are back, in other words, in the narrow domain of narratives as objects of study, rather than as method. And we are situated entirely in the present, as though all that matters is the present-day social experience that reinforces hegemony in respectful deference to the law or heroic resistance against the law (for a critique of the pervasive "presentism" in sociology, see Gorski 2009).

Realisms, Causal Mechanisms, and the Ironic Decline of Narrative Methodologies

During the later 1990s, a methodology of analytic narratives was embraced by rational choice scholars (e.g., Bates et al. 1998; Kiser 1996). The vigorous theoretical and methodological debate that ensued helped to bring questions of causation and ontology into the foreground of U.S. sociology. The interchange is neatly captured in a series of articles published in the *American Journal of Sociology* (Volume 104, Issue 3, November 1998), converging around a central debate between Somers and two proponents of rational choice theory (Edgar Kiser and Michael Hechter).

In her contribution to the debate, Somers identified a contested return to realism in sociology, which she saw as occurring in response to Thomas Kuhn's revolutionary portrayal of scientific practice and knowledge accumulation. The effect, according to Somers, was to undermine the legitimacy of positivist empiricism and to necessitate formulation of alternatives. Somers describes the basic response within sociology as a return to realism, albeit of two different types, which she differentiates as *theoretical* and *relational* realism.

This return to realism, as described by Somers, has entailed a greater willingness to grapple with ontological questions of causality. Strict positivists had outlawed discussion of causation as excessively metaphysical because causal relations are unobservable. However, the weakened credibility of positivism enabled (perhaps even necessitated) a greater focus on questions of ontology and metaphysics. All theories and methodological approaches depend upon metaphysical presumptions about the types of things that exist in the (social) world and about the ways those things can act and interact. The metaphysics of positivism was empiricist, in the sense that only things accessible to experiential/sensory observation were to be posited to exist as part of a valid explanation. When this strictly empiricist ontology collapsed, the big questions of metaphysics returned.

As was recognized in 1998—not only by Somers but also by other participants in the discussion (e.g., Calhoun 1998)—the debate triggered by rational choice scholars had foregrounded causal mechanisms and human personhood (through ontological assertions about rational actors and micro-foundational mechanisms) as hallmarks of good explanation in sociology. What does not seem to have been noticed, and indeed, what can perhaps only be seen in hindsight, is the extent to which discipline-wide discussion over narrative methods was a casualty of this polarized debate.

The parties to the debate very clearly had different standards for assessing narrative validity. Rational choice scholars prioritized generality and a clearly demarcated parsimony in narrative construction, while those who reacted against them stressed the ways in which rational choice scholars were reimposing positivistic criteria of explanatory validity. In the process of specifying their disagreements with rational choice narratives, moreover, divisions opened among Somers, Steinmetz, and others who had previously been aligned in their advocacy of narrative methods.

In response to a prompt from Steinmetz, Somers distanced herself explicitly from critical realism, identifying critical realists as rationalist bedfellows of rational choice scholarship. For Somers, critical realism and rational choice are variant forms of *theoretical realism*. This version of realism, as she portrays it, represents a return to precritical forms of rationalism, especially in the way that it considers human beings as agents, with reasons for action that can be efficient causes of action (Smith 2010). Somers offered instead a *relational realism*, where social agency rests in relational structures, rather than human persons. People have a limited agency through the stories that they tell, but these stories are themselves relational, presumably in the sense previously articulated, whereby personal/ontological narratives are formed in relation to public narratives.

In many ways, these debates come down to questions about characterization in narratives, and, as Somers rightly pointed out, these are metaphysical questions just as much as they are literary questions. Characters and characterization are fundamental to narrative construction (Franzosi 1998; Steinmetz 1992). Stories have villains and protagonists, and these are the characters who seem to drive the plotline. However, if we follow the Aristotelian model that has been so influential in literary theory, plot design has a priority over characterization (Ricoeur 1984; cf. Auerbach 2003).

In any case, by 2005, when Julia Adams, Elisabeth Clemens, and Ann Orloff published their influential introduction to a series of essays in historical sociology, narrative methods had been relegated to a footnote. And, strikingly, in 2008, Margaret Somers published a book on the *genealogies* of citizenship. Although Somers did focus on narratives, employing elements of her narrativity approach, she also identified her overall approach as genealogical. Narrativity became genealogy, with Michel Foucault as the defining reference. Causal narrativity was briefly mentioned, but in literary contexts that subtly pointed to its narrowed reference. Tellingly, Somers (2008, 10) defined her approach to citizenship as one involving "genealogies and narratives with causalities and meanings that only emerge by looking at the present through some very long and very wide lenses." The structural parallelism hints at the notion that genealogy is about causality, whereas narratives are about meaning. We are, once again, faced with the traditional divide between interpretive meaning and explanatory causation.

In his 1998 essay responding to the polarized debate between Somers and Kiser/Hechter, Craig Calhoun lamented the ways in which sociology seems to be fated to its own unique version of eternal return: the *Methodenstreit*. In its founding as a discipline and in its periodic return to fundamental questions about the nature of social reality, sociology seems to be destined for periodic, unresolved fights over questions of methodology. But something else happened in the *Methodenstreit* of the late 1990s. An important opportunity for systematically developing narrative-based methodologies for studying the social constitution and causality of shared institutional realities was missed. In the remainder of this chapter, I seek to metaphorically turn back the clock, recovering an awareness of legal narrativity in early and foundational legal sources.

Recovering Legal Narrativity

Societies are held together by stories; indeed, they are constituted by stories. This is the basic insight, I believe, resting at the heart of Somers's approach to legal narrativity. This basic insight is also recoverable within the framework of legal consciousness, although it may be helpful to drop some of the critical baggage, in the service of fresh and open-minded return to the legal sources.

If we reach down deeply, as deeply as we can, to the foundations of our inherited legal traditions, we find sagas and origin myths, together with etiological (causal) tales. I am speaking here of Greco-Roman legal traditions, as well as biblical legal traditions.

I offer the *Digest* (Watson 1985) as Exhibit A in my case for legal narrativity, that sixth-century compilation of jurisprudential literature from the classical period of Roman law that was assembled under the emperor Justinian. This massive collection of treasured legal wisdom begins (I.1) by presenting a world of shared law, which is founded in justice (*justitia*) and right (*jus*). This is the shared world of the *jus gentium*, the law of nations, which is common to all peoples (*gentes*). The *jus civile*, or civil law (the law that distinguishes peoples from one another), is simply a special variant of this common body of law (I.1.6). It would be hard to overstate the degree to which this vision of law has influenced modern, Western law (e.g., Blackstone 1979; Grotius 2012: I.1; Kent 1873; Pufendorf 2013; cf. Pothier 1999).

After defining the basic parameters of this shared legal world, the *Digest* presents a lengthy origin story, drawn from Gaius and Pomponius. This is a jurisprudentially inflected version of the Roman origin myth, featuring tables of stone upon which the foundational laws for constituting the Roman people were inscribed and displayed.[2] Gaius and Pomponius, writing in the second century of the common era, agreed that it was necessary to return to the beginning in accounting for the deep coherence and the obligatory character of social duties rooted in Roman law. Justinian and Tribonian, overseeing the commission that decided what was worth preserving from classical jurisprudence, agreed (on Tribonian, see Honoré 1978).

Gaius, *XII Tables, book 1*: Since I am aiming to give an interpretation of the ancient laws, I have concluded that I must trace the law of the Roman people from the very beginnings of their city. This is not because I like making excessively wordy commentaries, but because I can see that in every subject a perfect job is one whose parts hang together properly. And to be sure the most important part of anything is its beginning. (I.2.1)

Pomponius, Manual, sole book: Accordingly, it seems that we must account for the origin and development of law itself. (I.2.2)

This was an origin myth for jurists, as much as it was an origin myth for the Roman empire. Like Platonic philosophers before them (Pangle 1980, Book III) and Christians alongside them (Eusebius 1926, I.4), jurists were constituted as a people by the origin stories that they told about their vocation. Only in understanding the beginnings of the law could they rightly understand how the law cohered together, how it all made sense.

We can see the effort to understand law through its beginnings quite clearly in the antiquarian works of Varro and Cato (Cornell 2013; Drummond 2013), together with the lengthy history of Livy (Ogilvie 1965), but also on the part of provincial peoples who were drawn into the grasp of empire. At the eastern end of the empire, we can see this in the *Jewish Antiquities* of Josephus, who told the origin story of the Jewish people and of their national lawgiver, Moses, for philhellenic Roman patrons (Thackeray 1930). On the north African coast, we can see this in the Augustinian adaptation of Greco-Roman history writing, a pre-Marxist version of the alienation story, the alienation story of original sin (Dyson 1998). Laws of God and of Rome play an important role in this epic saga of two intermingled *civitates*. At the western end of the empire, meanwhile, new peoples were forming through the interaction of Roman armies with non-Roman civilians (Goffart 1980). The "barbarians" were telling stories about who they were, and those stories were given in forms that their cultural interlocutors could recognize and understand, forms in which origin myths were linked with codifications of law, written by clerics, priests, and kings working closely together (Goffart 2005).

That the transformation from Roman late antiquity to early medieval Europe occurred as part of an "age of migration" is a hoary truth now hotly contested (Noble 2006). But there is no denying that the centuries scholars struggle to classify and characterize (c. 400–800) provided the foundations for "national" lawgiving and origin myths that are still with us. From orient to occident, the rising and setting sun passed over peoples who were laying down laws for themselves, while telling origin stories about who they were as peoples. The two activities are intimately connected, both for them and for us.

The close connections between origin myths and early forms of "national" law can be seen in the regions that became Spain, France, and Italy—in the laws and stories of the Goths and Franks, and later the Alamans and Burgundians. The early literary figures who provide intriguing windows into their worlds are Cassiodorus, Jordanes, and Isidore of Seville, among others (Goffart 2005;

Wolf 2011). Cassiodorus wrote a twelve-book origin story for the Goths (which was epitomized by Jordanes), before publishing a collected volume of legal rulings from the Gothic kings (Barnish 1992; O'Donnell 1979). Isidore provided a chronicle of world history, synthesizing biblical history with the histories of the Roman empire and its "barbarian" peoples (Seville 2004). He also oversaw church councils that laid down laws for the Visigothic peoples who had recently converted from Arianism to Nicene Christianity (King 1972; Stocking 2000). His *Etymologies* left an enduring legacy of etiological tales for all manner of institutions, including law, money, and the arts (Barney et al. 2006). Meanwhile the Franks under Clovis had converted to Nicene Christianity and defeated the Visigothic king Alaric, whose *Lex Romana Visogothorum* had adopted and adapted the fifth-century Theodosian Code for his Roman peoples (Haenel 1849; Wood 2010). The Salian Frankish "law code" is among the earliest of the legal codes that have been so often interpreted as repositories of "Germanic" national consciousness (Drew 1991; Rivers 1977, 1986).

The facts about these early foundations for Western law are very hard to establish. Specialized literatures in multiple European languages make it almost impossible for language-impoverished scholars in the United States to gain entry. But translations are available. And the scholarly editions of primary sources are now readily available through sponsored projects in the digital humanities.[3] The history is incredibly complex, partly because the manuscript traditions are complex. For the nonspecialist, it is treacherous to assert anything specific about early European law, but there are certain generalities that are well supported, both in the primary literature and the secondary literature. One of these well-supported generalities is the close relationship—we might call it a semantic dependence—between law and narrative.

There is an obvious explanation for this semantic dependence between law and narrative in the fact that the people who produced legal texts in medieval Europe were almost uniformly clerics or monks, men steeped in biblical narrative traditions (Wormald 1999a, 1999b, 2014). And so it is not surprising that the biblical narrative of a chosen people, alternately blessed and punished by God, should play such a strong role in their legal writing and thinking (Wolf 2011). In the Pentateuch, the five books of legal and moral instruction (Torah), which Western clerics read in versions of Jerome's Latin translation, narratives provide interpretive foundations for legal codes and rulings, which were believed to have been recorded by the great lawgiver Moses. The mutual dependence between law and narrative in these books continues to be recognized today in Jewish, Christian, and secular scholarship (e.g., Carmichael 1996; Childs 2004; Heschel 2008).

The legal source materials for medieval Europe are almost all narrativized, in one way or another. Perhaps they are part of a medieval cartulary—a collection of legal documents for a monastery or church, accompanied by a narrative (e.g., Bouchard 1991). Or perhaps they are in original charter form, in which case the *narratio*—the narration of the events and personages providing the context for the grant contained in the charter—forms an important part of the document itself (e.g., Koziol 2012). The emperor Justinian's great codification had its own *narratio* in the prologues that declared its purposes. And the emperor Charlemagne issued partially narrativized "capitularies" as part of his legal and religious reforms (King 1987; McKitterick 2004).

Medieval European law was heavily narrativized, and we could almost tell the story of increasing formalization in European law as one whereby the narrative elements were stripped away from the formal legal texts. But legal treatises from the early modern period into the Enlightenment continued to link stories of legal development with stories in the national destinies of European peoples. And although narratives may have disappeared from modern statutory laws, they are easily recovered from the legislative documents that surround them, from the case law that interprets and often gives rise to them and in voluminous records connected with administrative documents that implement them. Very often when we need to interpret law, we turn to narratives, in one form or another.

Law as we experience and interpret it in Western legal systems is narrativized, and the question is where the narratives come from and which form they take. Another way to say this is to say that our legal consciousness has been shaped by narratives, whether these are the biblical narratives of divinely given law, the national narratives of the founding fathers and democratic processes, or the conspiratorial narratives of law in service of exploitative power. For Margaret Somers, an important question is about the way in which personal identity becomes narratively formed in relation to broader, institutional narratives about law. But her work also attests to the importance of a closely related set of questions, about where the institutional narratives come from and how they relate, in turn, to narratives given by social theory and the meta-narratives that are current in a particular sociocultural ("relational") setting.

Assuming there is some truth in these rather sweeping generalizations about semantic dependencies between law and narrative, what does it mean for methodological approaches to the historical and comparative sociology of law? At a minimum, I think it means that those methods should be attentive to narratives. This means paying close attention to narratives that are being offered in theories and empirical materials, whether the narratives are implicit or explicit. But Somers's claims were bolder than this, extending to the assertion that explanatory accounts for institutional developments themselves can (and perhaps should) be narrative in form. To fully understand certain causal properties of law in shaping our legal institutions and consciousness, we may need to tell social formation stories (cf. Hirschman and Reed 2014).

Final Thoughts on Legal Narrativity

Students of the social world are often asked, as they are trying to formulate a research project, "What is this a case of?" Leaving grammar aside, this may be a bad question for certain projects in historical and comparative research. As others have noted, the language of "cases" being deployed here is premised on the notion that social events recur as tokens of conceptually formulated types. To compare is therefore to juxtapose a number of instances, or tokens, of the same type.

But, if it is true that narratives are deeply constitutive of the social world, the language of cases may be inappropriate. At the very least, it should be conceded that another type of sociological research is legitimate: narratives that are judged according to criteria of plot design and utilization of reliable sources (Howell and Prevenier 2001).

What I have suggested in this exploratory chapter is that narratives have the capacity to reach features of causality in the social world that methods premised solely on efficient causality may not adequately address. If we are seeking to understand and explain causal features of law and legal institutions, narrative forms of explanation may be especially important because they map onto an underlying narrativity that is an important feature of the ways in which law actually impacts our cultural and institutional contexts and perhaps even our motivational frameworks of meaning. A conception of narrativity may work better here, one that conceives of narratively encrusted institutions like law as enabling and constraining social relations of various types over extended periods of time, rather than as making things happen in the narrow and probabilistic sense of efficient causality.

One role of a narrative methodology in studying the development of a legal system or institution can be to help us understand the relationship between intentional design and patterns of development. What we will often see, I think, is that early design decisions have a particular causal weight, one that is basically formal, in the sense that it defines the type of social thing that a legal institution is and therefore constrains the kinds of meaningful social action that the institution can facilitate. To paraphrase Michael Mann's (2012) paraphrasing of Max Weber, early design decisions lay the tracks from which later ones depart.

But there is nonetheless an open-endedness, even in the later stages, an open-endedness that makes path-dependency models based on concepts of efficient causality inadequate. Recursive learning processes offer a better alternative conception, and these are best described through retrospective narratives, tracing design decisions, consequences, and adaptations (Halliday and Carruthers 2007). The overall narrative that emerges can be described as a pattern of development, but it is a pattern that is designed through selection and judgment on the part of the narrator, not one that can be simplistically read off from comparisons between demarcated "events."

There is, and should be, an important methodological place for retrospective narratives in sociology. But these are designed through the exercise of human judgment, not the mechanistic outcome of perfected, methodological rules.

Notes

1. A sixth article was published by Kathleen Canning in *The American Historical Review* (1992).
2. That the story was mythical does not, of course, mean that it contains no truth.
3. For example, *Monumenta Germaniae Historica* online, sponsored by the Bavarian State Library and the German Forschungsgemeinschaft, available at https://www.dmgh.de / (accessed April 10, 2022).

References

Abbott, Andrew. 1988. "Transcending General Linear Reality." *Sociological Theory* 6:169–86.

———. 1991. "History and Sociology: The Lost Synthesis." *Social Science History* 15:201–38.

———. 2001. *Time Matters: On Theory and Method*. Chicago: University of Chicago Press.

———. 2005. "Process and Temporality in Sociology: The Idea of Outcome in U.S. Sociology." In *The Politics of Method in the Human Sciences*, edited by George Steinmetz, 393–426. Durham, NC: Duke University Press.

———. 2007. "Against Narrative: A Preface to Lyrical Sociology." *Sociological Theory* 25:67–99.

———. 2016. *Processual Sociology*. Chicago: University of Chicago Press.

Adams, Julia, Elisabeth S. Clemens, and Ann Shola Orloff. 2005. "Introduction: Social Theory, Modernity, and the Three Waves of Historical Sociology." In *Remaking Modernity: Politics, History, and Sociology*, edited by Julia Adams, Elisabeth S. Clemens, and Ann Shola Orloff, 1–72. Durham, NC: Duke University Press.

Aminzade, Ronald. 1992. "Historical Sociology and Time." *Sociological Methods and Research* 20:456–80.

Auerbach, Erich. 2003. *Mimesis: The Representation of Reality in Western Literature, Fiftieth Anniversary Edition*. Princeton, NJ: Princeton University Press.

Augustine. 1998. *The City of God Against the Pagans*. Translated by R. W. Dyson. Cambridge: Cambridge University Press.

Barney, Stephen A., W. J. Lewis, J. A. Beach, and Oliver Berghof, eds. and trans. 2006. *The Etymologies of Isidore of Seville*. Cambridge: Cambridge University Press.

Barnish, S. J. B. 1992. *The Variae of Magnus Aurelius Cassiodorus Senator*. Liverpool: Liverpool University Press.

Bates, Robert H., Margaret Levi, Jean-Laurent Rosenthal, and Barry R. Weingast. 1998. *Analytic Narratives*. Princeton, NJ: Princeton University Press.

Blackstone, William. 1979. *Commentaries on the Laws of England, Volume 1*. Chicago: University of Chicago Press.

Bouchard, Constance Brittain. 1991. *The Cartulary of Flavigny, 717–1113*. Cambridge, MA: Medieval Academy of America.

Calhoun, Craig. 1998. "Explanation in Historical Sociology: Narrative, General Theory, and Historically Specific Theory." *American Journal of Sociology* 104:846–71.

Canning, Kathleen. 1992. "Gender and the Politics of Class Formation: Rethinking German Labor History." *American Historical Review* 97:736–68.

Carmichael, Calum. 1996. *The Spirit of Biblical Law*. Athens: University of Georgia Press.

Childs, Brevard S. 2004. *The Book of Exodus: A Critical, Theological Commentary*. Louisville, KY: Westminster John Knox.

Cornell, Timothy J. 2013. "M. Porcius Cato." In *The Fragments of the Roman Historians, Volume I*, edited by Timothy J. Cornell, 191–218. Oxford: Oxford University Press.

Coser, Lewis. 2003. *Masters of Sociological Thought*. 2nd edition. Long Grove, IL: Waveland.

Downer, L. J., ed. and trans. 1972. *Leges Henrici Primi*. Oxford: Clarendon.

Drew, Katherine Fischer. 1991. *The Laws of the Salian Franks*. Philadelphia: University of Pennsylvania Press.

Drummond, Andrew. 2013. "M. Terentius Varro." In *The Fragments of the Roman Historians, Volume 1*, edited by Timonth J. Cornell, 412–23. Oxford: Oxford University Press.

Eusebius. 1926. *The Ecclesiastical History*. Edited by Kirsopp Lake. Cambridge, MA: Harvard University Press [Loeb].

Ewick, Patricia, and Susan S. Silbey. 1995. "Subversive Stories and Hegemonic Tales: Toward a Sociology of Narrative." *Law and Society Review* 29:197–226.

——. 1998. *The Common Place of Law: Stories from Everyday Life*. Chicago: University of Chicago Press.

Fleury-Steiner, Benjamin. 2002. "Narratives of the Death Sentence: Toward a Theory of Legal Narrativity." *Law and Society Review* 36:549–76.

Fleury-Steiner, Benjamin, and Laura Beth Nielsen. 2006. "Introduction: A Constitutive Perspective of Rights." In *The New Civil Rights Research: A Constitutive Approach*, edited by Benjamin Fleury-Steiner and Laura Beth Nielsen, 1–14. Aldershot, UK: Ashgate.

Franzosi, Roberto. 1998. "Narrative Analysis—Or Why (and How) Sociologists Should be Interested in Narrative." *Annual Review of Sociology* 24:517–54.

Goffart, Walter. 1980. *Barbarians and Romans (A.D. 418–584): The Techniques of Accommodation*. Princeton, NJ: Princeton University Press.

——. 2005. *The Narrators of Barbarian History (A.D. 550–800): Jordanes, Gregory of Tours, Bede, and Paul the Deacon*. Princeton, NJ: Princeton University Press.

Gorski, Philip. 2009. "Social 'Mechanisms' and Comparative-Historical Sociology: A Critical Realist Proposal." In *Frontiers of Sociology*, edited by Peter Hedstrom and Bjorn Wittrock, 147–94. Leiden, Netherlands: Brill.

Gotham, Kevin Fox, and William G. Staples. 1996. "Narrative Analysis and the New Historical Sociology." *Sociological Quarterly* 37:481–501.

Griffin, Larry J. 1993. "Narrative, Event-Structure Analysis, and Causal Interpretation." *American Journal of Sociology* 98:1094–133.

Groff, Ruth. 2004. *Critical Realism, Post-Positivism and the Possibility of Knowledge*. London: Routledge.

——. 2013. *Ontology Revisited: Metaphysics in Social and Political Philosophy*. New York: Routledge.

Grotius, Hugo. 2012. *On the Law of War and Peace*. Edited by Stephen C. Neff. Cambridge: Cambridge University Press.

Haenel, Gustavus. 1849. *Lex Romana Visigothorum*. Leipzig, Germany: Teubner.

Halliday, Terence C., and Bruce G. Carruthers. 2007. "The Recursivity of Law: Global Norm Making and National Lawmaking in the Globalization of Corporate Insolvency Regimes." *American Journal of Sociology* 112:1135–202.

Hart, Janet. 1992. "Cracking the Code: Narrative and Political Mobilization in the Greek Resistance." *Social Science History* 16:631–68.

Heschel, Abraham Joshua. 2008. *Heavenly Torah, as Refracted Through the Generations*. New York: Continuum.

Hirschman, Daniel, and Isaac Ariail Reed. 2014. "Formation Stories and Causality in Sociology." *Sociological Theory* 32:259–82.

Honoré, Tony. 1978. *Tribonian*. London: Duckworth.

Howell, Martha, and Walter Prevenier. 2001. *From Reliable Sources: An Introduction to Historical Methods*. Ithaca, NY: Cornell University Press.

Hudson, John. 1996. *The Formation of English Common Law: Law and Society in England from the Norman Conquest to Magna Carta*. London: Longman.

Isaac, Larry W. 1997. "Transforming Localities: Reflections on Time, Causality, and Narrative in Contemporary Historical Sociology." *Historical Methods* 30:4–13.

Joas, Hans. 1996. *The Creativity of Action*. Cambridge: Polity.

Kent, James. 1873. *Commentaries on American Law*. 12th edition. Boston: Little, Brown.

King, P. D. 1987. *Charlemagne: Translated Sources*. Bloomington: Indiana University.

——. 1972. *Law and Society in the Visigothic Kingdom*. Cambridge: Cambridge University Press.

Kiser, Edgar. 1996. "The Revival of Narrative in Historical Sociology: What Rational Choice Theory Can Contribute." *Politics and Society* 24:249–71.

Kiser, Edgar, and Michael Hechter. 1998. "The Debate on Historical Sociology: Rational Choice Theory and Its Critics." *American Journal of Sociology* 128:785–816.

Koziol, Geoffrey. 2012. *The Politics of Memory and Identity in Carolingian Royal Diplomas: The West Frankish Kingdon (840–987)*. Turnhout, Belgium: Brepols.

Liu, Sida. 2015. "Law's Social Forms: A Powerless Approach to the Sociology of Law." *Law and Social Inquiry* 40:1–28.

Löwith, Karl. 1949. *Meaning in History*. Chicago: University of Chicago Press.

Maines, David R. 1993. "Narrative's Moment and Sociology's Phenomena: Toward a Narrative Sociology." *Sociological Quarterly* 34:17–38.

Mann, Michael. 2012. *The Sources of Social Power Volume 1: A History of Power from the Beginning to AD 1760*. 2nd edition. Cambridge: Cambridge University Press.

Maynes, Mary Jo. 1992. "Autobiography and Class Formation in Nineteenth-Century Europe: Methodological Considerations." *Social Science History* 16:517–37.

McKitterick, Rosamond. 2004. *History and Memory in the Carolingian World*. Cambridge: Cambridge University Press.

Mead, George Herbert. 2015. *Mind, Self, and Society: The Definitive Edition*. Chicago: University of Chicago Press.

Noble, Thomas F. X., ed. 2006. *From Roman Provinces to Medieval Kingdoms*. New York: Routledge.

O'Donnell, James J. 1979. *Cassiodorus*. Berkeley: University of California Press.

Ogilvie, R. M. 1965. *A Commentary on Livy Books 1–5*. Oxford: Clarendon.

Pangle, Thomas L., trans. 1980. *The Laws of Plato*. Chicago: University of Chicago Press.

Passerini, Luisa. 1992. "A Memory for Women's History: Problems of Method and Interpretation." *Social Science History* 16:669–92.

Pierson, Paul. 2003. "Big, Slow-Moving, and . . . Invisible: Macrosocial Processes in the Study of Comparative Politics." In *Comparative Historical Analysis in the Social Sciences*, edited by James Mahoney and Dietrich Rueschemeyer, 177–207. Cambridge: Cambridge University Press.

Pothier, Robert Joseph. 1999. *A Treatise on Obligations Considered in a Moral and Legal View*. Translated by Francois-Xavier Martin. Union, NJ: Lawbook Exchange.

Pufendorf, Samuel. 2013. *Two Books of the Elements of Universal Jurisprudence*. Edited by Thomas Behme. Indianapolis, IN: Liberty Fund.

Reed, Isaac Ariail. 2011. *Interpretation and Social Knowledge: On the Use of Theory in the Human Sciences.* Chicago: University of Chicago Press.

——. 1984. *Time and Narrative.* Translated by Kathleen McLaughlin and David Pellauer. Chicago: University of Chicago Press.

Rivers, Theodore John. 1977. *Laws of the Alamans and Bavarians.* Philadelphia: University of Pennsylvania Press.

——. 1986. *Laws of the Salian and Ripuarian Franks.* New York: AMS.

Seville, Isidore of. 2004. *Chronicon.* Translated by Kenneth B. Wolf. Roger Pearse, www.tertullian.org.

Sewell, William H., Jr. 1992. "Introduction: Narratives and Social Identities." *Social Science History* 16:479–88.

Smith, Christian. 2003. *Moral, Believing Animals.* Oxford: Oxford University Press.

——. 2010. *What Is a Person?* Chicago: University of Chicago Press.

Somers, Margaret R. 1992. "Narrativity, Narrative Identity, and Social Action: Rethinking English Working-Class Identity Formation." *Social Science History* 16:591–630.

——. 1997. "Deconstructing and Reconstructing Class Formation Theory: Narrativity, Relational Analysis, and Social Theory." In *Reworking Class,* edited by John R. Hall, 73–105. Ithaca, NY: Cornell University Press.

——. 1998. "Symposium on Historical Sociology and Rational Choice Theory: 'We're No Angels': Realism, Rational Choice, and Relationality in Social Science." *American Journal of Sociology* 104:722–84.

——. 2008. *Genealogies of Citizenship: Markets, Statelessness, and the Right to Have Rights.* Cambridge: Cambridge University Press.

Steinmetz, George. 1992. "Reflections on the Role of Social Narratives in Working-Class Formation: Narrative Theory in the Social Sciences." *Social Science History* 16:489–516.

Stocking, Rachel L. 2000. *Bishops, Councils, and Consensus in the Visigothic Kingdom, 589–633.* Ann Arbor: University of Michigan Press.

Stone, Lawrence. 1979. "The Revival of Narrative: Reflections on a New Old History." *Past and Present* 85:3–24.

Thackeray, H., ed. and trans. 1930. *Josephus in Nine Volumes, Volume IV.* Cambridge, MA: Harvard University Press [Loeb].

Tufekci, Zeynep. 2017. *Twitter and Tear Gas: The Power and Fragility of Networked Protest.* New Haven, CT: Yale University Press.

Watson, Alan, ed. 1985. *The Digest of Justinian.* Philadelphia: University of Pennsylvania Press.

White, Hayden. 1987. *The Content of the Form: Narrative Discourse and Historical Representation.* Baltimore, MD: Johns Hopkins University Press.

Wolf, Kenneth Baxter. 2011. *Conquerors and Chroniclers of Early Medieval Spain.* 2nd edition. Liverpool: Liverpool University Press.

Wood, Ian. 2010. "Nachleben and the Code in Merovingian Gaul." In *The Theodosian Code: Studies in the Imperial Law of Late Antiquity,* 2nd edition, edited by Jill Harries and Ian Wood, 159–77. Bristol, UK: Bristol Classics.

Wormald, Patrick. 1999a. *Legal Culture in the Early Medieval West: Law as Text, Image, and Experience.* London: Hambledon.

——. 1999b. *The Making of English Law: King Alfred to the Twelfth Century.* Oxford: Blackwell.

——. 2014. "Papers Preparatory to the Making of English Law Vol. II: From God's Law to Common Law, edited by Stephen Baxter and John Judson." *Early English Laws.* Accessed August 15, 2018. http://www.earlyenglishlaws.ac.uk/reference/wormald/.

CHAPTER 7

COMPARISON, CONTEXT, AND THE POWER OF MODERN CORRUPTION

NICHOLAS HOOVER WILSON

Introduction

Corruption is a hard thing to study and an even harder thing to compare using orthodox social-scientific methods. This is because, like some other important social-scientific concepts, "corruption" is a composite of technical jargon and lived political and moral categories. It is a label, in other words, that only becomes sensible when invoked and evoked in specific contexts. This evocation in turn gives corruption power as a *form of moral accusation*, attaching moral condemnation to whatever acts or entities it is applied. But that power remains contextual; it works only in situations when an audience is present that is alive to its claims.

Given that corruption is a tricky, embedded concept, how can we compare it? Dominant strands of the social-scientific literature decontextualize it prior to analysis. Whether done in the service of institutional or macro-comparative analysis, this approach strips away the meaning actors attach to their action and instead concentrates on purportedly objective behavioral standards. As I argue in this chapter, although draining the moral significance from "corruption" as it is lived and invoked may create a seemingly stable ground for comparing it in different times and places, it also creates striking conceptual tensions.

This drawback of decontextualizing corruption prior to analysis leads me to propose a different strategy. Like other contributions to this volume,[1] I focus on corruption itself and *also* the practicing comparative analyst's need to balance among fidelity to the phenomenon itself, an anticipated readership, and existing scholarship about it, all while seeking to intervene in and reshape all three domains.[2]

From this starting point, the question of "what to compare" becomes two-fold. On the one hand, the analyst must make clear what it is about "corruption" that gives it a general power or capacity in the social world—that is, the ability to influence or affect states of affairs (Dupré 1995; Little 2009). On the other hand, the analyst must also focus on how the very study of corruption and, in particular, assertions that it reflects universal causes and consequences represent the capacity of modern corruption to simultaneously invoke social contexts and render them similar and comparable. In other words, although corruption in general has energetic potential in social life, modern corruption is a particular *nomological machine*, or "a fixed (enough) arrangement of components, or facts, with stable (enough) capacities that in the right sort of stable (enough) environment will, with repeated operation, give rise to the kind of regular behavior that we represent in our scientific laws" (Cartwright 1999, 50). Achieving a reflexive balance among all of these competing demands is perhaps beyond the ability of any analyst. However, the best work makes the attempt, and below I suggest that these burdens are shouldered using two narrative strategies familiar to historians. Some emphasize the continuity of the nomological machine of modern corruption over time ("lumping" its interactions with local contexts together); others, meanwhile, stress the discontinuities in its course ("splitting" them apart).

In this chapter, I first show that scholarship on corruption expresses an analytic tension between behavior and social norms. Next, I explore various responses to this tension, including the dominant macro-comparative and institutionalist strands and some of their most important variations. After introducing the concept of nomological machines, I then briefly enumerate four specific elements of the nomological machine of corruption–moral accusation, abstraction, escalation of conflict, and moral biography, while drawing examples from two sterling recent books on the subject, Zephyr Teachout's *Corruption in America* (2016) and Stephen Pierce's *Moral Economies of Corruption* (2016). Finally, I focus on how both works exhibit the strategies of lumping and splitting the nomological machine of modern corruption—as well as their tensions—in order to cope with the difficulty of comparing its behavior in American and Nigerian history, respectively.

What Is Corruption and How Do You Compare It?

Crack open any example of the efflorescent scholarship on the subject and in its early pages you will find a troubled meditation on corruption's definition. This is because "corruption" is a term of *both* lived political use and analytically specific meaning; for instance, when introducing their mammoth edited volume on political corruption, Arnold Heidenheimer, Michael Johnston, and Victor LeVine (1989) outline the nine definitions of corruption provided by the *Oxford English Dictionary* before lamenting that academic scholarship narrows them into just three classes. "Public-office-centered definitions" centralize "the concept of the public office and . . . deviations from norms binding upon its incumbents" (8). Definitions that focus on markets, meanwhile, think corruption occurs when a "civil servant regards his public office as a business" (9, quoting Van Kalveren). A third group of scholars, finally, defines corruption as official behavior that "does damage to the public and its interests" (10, quoting Friedrich).

These definitions appear different, but as Heidenheimer, Johnston, and LeVine recognize, they are all indebted to Joseph Nye's ur-definition of corruption in 1967 as "behavior which deviates from the formal duties of a public role because of private-regarding (personal, close family, private clique) pecuniary or status gains; or violates rules against the exercise of certain types of private-regarding influence" (originally Nye 1967; in Heidenheimer et al. 1989, 966). This definition is assigned to the "public office" category above, but it is remarkable because, like the market and public interest definitions as well, it is purely formal. "Corruption" is whatever counts as a violation (whether by the standards bureaucrats are to be held, the laws of market and state behavior, or the "public interest"). This, of course, leaves the substances of each category open and subject to tremendous empirical variation (Heidenheimer et al. 1989, 11–13).

Why define corruption in such an austere, formal way? In the 1967 *American Political Science Review* article from which his famous definition is usually excerpted, Nye gives us a clue. As he writes, his definition stipulates a Western, modern definition to the exclusion of a wider definition of corruption as "perversion or a change from good to bad, [which covers] a wide variety of behavior from venality to ideological erosion" (Heidenheimer and Johnston 2002, 966) because his narrower definition sidesteps the empirical reality that "in less developed countries, there are two standards regarding such behavior, one indigenous and one more of less Western, and the formal duties and rules concerning most public roles tend to be expressed in terms of the latter."[3] For Nye, this move is a feature, not a bug, since "it has the merit of denoting specific behavior generally called corrupt by Western standards . . . thus allowing us to ask what effects this specific behavior has under different conditions" (Heidenheimer and Johnston 2002, 967). Yet while this may enable one kind of comparison,[4] the "Western standards" of modern bureaucracy—that is, the actual content used to judge something or someone as "corrupt" or "virtuous"—have been abstracted from the contexts of their implementation and stipulated prior to analysis!

Thus an early and influential definition of corruption has a tension at its heart: it seeks a comparative search for general causes, yet in order to generalize, it empties "corruption" of substantive meaning while still implicitly relying on it. Subsequent threads of the corruption literature recognize this tension and have responded to it. In the following sections, I review two of the most important threads—macro-comparative and institutionalist approaches to corruption—and argue that both struggle to resolve the tension inherent in Nye's definition.

Macro-Comparative Studies

James Scott directly addresses the comparative problems in Nye's narrowed definition of corruption in his 1972 standard-setting book, *Comparative Political Corruption*. The central object of the book is to treat corruption as "a special case of political influence" and, "because an adequate understanding of corruption generally requires a grasp of an entire network of influence, we shall try to deal with corruption in a way that embeds it contextually in a broader analysis of a regime's political dynamics" (Scott 1972, 6). This goal is extraordinarily analytically demanding, and it leads to a dramatic passage, worth quoting at length, in which Scott attempts to preserve *both* the sense in which corruption is defined by local, contextual sets of norms (that can be formal or informal) *and* the sense in which the general complex of norms to which "corrupt" and "virtuous" behavior belong can change dramatically over time (and especially after the emergence of Western political modernity):

> Much corruption is in a real sense a product of the late eighteenth and nineteenth centuries. Only the rise of the modern nation-state, with its mass participation, broadly representative bodies, and elaborate civil service codes, signaled the transformation of the view of government office, and even kingship, from a private right into a public responsibility.
>
> How, then, can we handle historical comparisons? If, for example, we wanted to compare the practice of bribing to gain appointment to the bureaucracy in transitional England with the same practice in modern England, we could classify such an act as corrupt in the modern period by not in the traditional period, where it often occurred openly and legally. We will want, nonetheless, to compare *practices* that are corrupt only by modern standards and ask what their causes are in different periods, how they affect the composition of the elite, and so forth. If nepotism or bribery have similar causes and consequences in early France as in contemporary India, that is an important subject for analysis, notwithstanding the fact that legal codes and public standards have changed so much that what was tolerated (not corrupt) in early France is

now forbidden by law (corrupt) in India. For our comparative purposes, then, we will refer to pre-nineteenth-century practices which only became "corrupt" in the nineteenth century as "*proto-corruption*." This convention will allow us to analyze the comparative causes and effects of similar behavior while recognizing that such earlier practices did not contravene the existing norms of official conduct and thus cannot be considered corruption as we have chosen to use the term. (Scott 1972, 7–8, emphasis original)

This is, of course, a brilliant means of squaring the circle for the purposes of comparison and enables Scott to compare regimes as diverse as seventeenth-century England and mid-twentieth-century Thailand, Indonesia, Haiti, and many other cases. And it leads him to the monumental insight that corruption functions as a form of political influence like any other, and its incidence is thus dependent upon the institutions that provide political access to wealthy elites (see especially, chapter 2).[5]

Note the cost of this strategy, however. To gain analytic purchases on the function of corruption when it is embedded in a large sociopolitical context, Scott must sever the connection between corruption as a behavior seeking influence and our sense of it as a moral transgression. To resupply this moral sense, though, Scott must (somewhat uncomfortably) reintroduce our own situated views as readers or analysts back into the complex of judgment, as in the following passage:

> *Our feeling* about corruption often depends on whether this "uninstitutionalized" influence of wealth [exhibited by corrupt activity on political distribution] is undermining a formal system *of which we approve or disapprove.* Thus, corruption in eighteenth and early nineteenth-century England *seems less contemptible to us* than modern corruption since it involves the subversion of an aristocratic or status-based monopoly of government. Corruption in modern liberal democratic or socialist regimes, on the other hand, seems especially damaging since it undermines both *the egalitarian assumptions of majority rule* and the principles of even distribution of civil and social rights *of which we normally approve.* (Scott 1972, 34, emphasis added)

In this passage, Scott directly confronts the tension that remains in his study of corruption. Severing practice from norms—as he does by introducing "proto-corruption"—may well aid functionalist analysis of the politics of influence and how they are organized. But this tells us little about corruption per se; to recover the special sense in which corruption appears as a moral transgression, a violation of explicit or implicit norms, Scott must rely on the reader's reaction and their importation of their own moral sensibility to ground an analytic judgment, as he assumes it will be in "the egalitarian assumption of

majority rule and the principles of even distribution of civil and social rights"
(34). In other words, Scott's macro-comparative approach recapitulates the tension in contemporary understandings of corruption and resolves it only by
depending on the assumptions of a socially and historically situated reader.

Institutionalist Studies

If Scott seeks to resolve Nye's definitional tension by macro-analysis—that is,
by comparing whole systems of influence or whole political regimes to one
another—another popular response to Nye has pursued equally ambitious substantive goals via a more modest analytic strategy. Rather than attempt the analysis of entire societies, two varieties of institutionalism seek to instead study the
dynamics of individual and organizational interactions within specific social
structures and hence to show the specific conditions under which corruption is
likely to occur. This kind of institutional analysis of corruption usually comes
in more or less economistic flavors. Whatever their variations, however, I group
them together because they represent, from the perspective of how they address
Nye's definitional tension, a fundamentally similar resolution: they both stipu-
late basically universal norms in place of empirical variation.

Susan Rose-Ackerman's *oeuvre* on corruption is one of the most influential in
modern scholarship.[6] From her *Corruption: A Study in Political Economy* (1978)
to more recent work, she has striven to deploy the tools of rational-choice economics into the study of corruption. In such studies, "corruption" essentially
means bribery—"payments . . . illegally made to public agents with the goal of
obtaining a benefit or avoiding a cost" (Rose-Ackerman 1999, 9)—of a public
official by another individual or a business. As with Scott's analysis, the prevalence of corruption is thus a function of how certain institutional arrangements
alter the cost-benefit schemes faced by both bribers and those being bribed.

This kind of analysis is extraordinarily powerful for all of the reasons that
rational choice approaches usually are: it allows analytic simplification to gain
extraordinary breadth in application, and it provides tools for mathematical
formalization and simulation. It is, in other words, a great "first cut" at much
analysis (Adams 1999). But such an approach, as is also familiar, depends on a
heroic simplification of human action and flattening of the ontological landscape of analysis. As Rose-Ackerman (1999, 2) herself states with admirable
clarity: "Obviously, subtle differences in culture and basic values exist across
the world. But there is one human motivator that is both universal and central
to explaining the divergent experiences of different countries. That motivator is self-interest, including an interest in the well-being of one's family and
peer group. Critics call it greed. Economists call it utility maximization. Whatever the label, societies differ in the way they channel self-interest. Endemic

corruption suggests a pervasive failure to tap self-interest for productive pur-poses." In other words, the idea here is to shrink the variation in social norms to the analytic vanishing point of "subtle differences," while affirming that *the* major explanation for corruption is to be found in the "universal" and "central" mechanism of utility maximization.

Yet a glance at Rose-Ackerman's work shows that norms and their variation can't be dismissed so easily. By 1999's *Corruption and Government*, the anal-ysis of culture is given an odd prominence.[7] Rose-Ackerman (1999, 5) writes that she sees her role in the following way: "My aim is not to set a universal standard for where to draw the legal line between praiseworthy gifts and ille-gal and unethical bribes. It will be enough to isolate the factors that should go into the choice. Culture and history are explanations, not excuses. As an economist, I cannot provide an in-depth analysis of the role of culture and history, but I can point out where they legacy of the past no longer fits modern conditions."[8]

Yet even with this caveat, *how* Rose-Ackerman goes about the sustained analysis of culture is telling. In the conclusion to a chapter in which she distin-guishes among prices, gifts, bribes, and tips, Rose-Ackerman (1999, 110) offers an oblique resolution to Nye's tension: "The definition of bribes and gifts is a cultural matter, but 'culture' is dynamic and constantly changing. If behavior labeled 'corrupt' by some observers is, nevertheless, viewed as acceptable gift giving or tipping within a country, it should simply be legalized and reported. If, however, these practices are imposing hidden or indirect costs on the pop-ulace, analysts can clarify and document these costs. Definitions of acceptable behavior may change once people are informed of the costs of tolerating pay-offs to politicians and civil servants."

If Scott injects the moral significance back into "corruption" via an invitation to the reader's sympathies, Rose-Ackerman anchors her return in the univer-salism of the economistic perspective. The persistence of corruption (at least its cultural toleration) is simply a matter of people's ignorance of its costs. Thus, "clarification" is in order, as supplied by economistic assessments of cost and benefits. Moreover, this resolution also simply wishes away what Nye centralized: that normative standards are *rarely* held by societies as a whole, and the story of the developing world is not simply that, as a whole, behaviors should be legalized or forbidden, but rather that their administrative and political realities reflect the collision of two very different systems of understanding (McDonnell 2017).

Perhaps because of the waning fortunes of rational-choice analysis and its supplanting by various strands of behavioral economics, another variety of institutional analysis has grown in popularity in recent years. This approach is best represented by Bo Rothstein's *Quality of Government* approach (2011, usually abbreviated QoG).

From one vantage point, Rothstein's departure from Nye is strikingly different from Rose-Ackerman's.[9] Whereas Rose-Ackerman stipulates that human beings are fundamentally self-interested, "impartiality" lies at the heart of Rothstein's "procedural" approach. Impartiality means, simply, that "when implementing laws and policies, government officials shall not take into consideration anything about the citizen/case that is not stipulated beforehand in the policy or the law" (Rothstein 2011, 13). Rothstein forcefully argues that this basic norm of impartiality in the execution of government policy can be derived from a careful reading of normative political philosophy, that the approach holds advantages over other attempts to give such a procedural foundation (replacing "impartiality" with "democracy," for example), and that it is amendable to criticism of its austere, hyper-Weberian appearance (Rothstein 2011, 12–30). But most importantly for our purposes, impartiality supplies a universal foundation for judgment among societies and hence comparison. As Rothstein writes,

> [The dominant definition of corruption, à la Nye] makes no reference to what kind of acts constitute the "misuse" or "abuse" of public office, which makes the definition of corruption relativistic. Without a basic norm (such as impartiality), these definitions simply avoid the question of what should count as corruption or, to be more precise, what is the norm or practice that is being "abused." . . . [A definition of corruption based on violating impartiality] has the advantage that what counts as a breach of impartiality is fairly universally understood and thus not related to how things like "abuse" or "misuse" of public power are defined in different cultures. (Rothstein 2011, 14–15)

Rothstein goes on to use this definition to undertake a rich comparative program, ultimately arguing that poor QoG and concomitant corruption are the result of a collective action problem, in which people cannot trust one another to act impartially and hence will not do so regardless of their judgment of corruption. Put differently, the problem is institutional design, not the possession of different social norms toward specific, corrupt behaviors.

Yet for all its empirical productivity, the original tension in Nye's definition of corruption lingers even in Rothstein's analysis. This can be seen most clearly in Rothstein's discussion of where impartiality should apply. Using Michael Walzer's (1983) notion of "spheres of justice," Rothstein argues that *every* decision made by a bureaucrat or in a society need not be impartial because "norms should be different in different societal spheres, [and] we should recognize that the same individuals often operate simultaneously in different spheres and are carriers of different norms about what is appropriate in these different spheres" (Rothstein 2011, 19). Thus, impartiality is fine, even admirable, during market activity or parenting, but "those who exercise public power need to know and acknowledge the boundaries between what norms apply in different moral spheres" (Rothstein 2011, 19). Yet at the same time, Rothstein argues that Walzer's theory of spheres is itself too particularistic since, for Walzer, the boundaries among spheres are "defined by reference only to historical particularities" (Rothstein 2011, 19). In place of these historical particulars, Rothstein presents a two-by-two table of (presumably universal) moral spheres, divided according to the "scope of interest" for actors and their "type of interest."

This is an extraordinarily attractive way of providing a foundation for analysis because it both recognizes the historical and internal heterogeneity of societies *and* allows their direct comparison to one another against the "objective" standard of how well they achieve impartiality. Yet this comes at a high cost. On the one hand, although the norm of impartiality is hard to argue against *in principle*, its role in the analysis is simply to supply another universal sensibility for people in place of self-interest: all people, Rothstein seems to argue, believe that the best governments execute policies impartially. On the other hand, this style of analysis simply transposes the particularity inherent in the definition of corruption from people's foundational motivations and beliefs to where the (still particularistic and historical) boundaries among particular spheres are to be drawn. This yields arguments that seem to recapitulate the original problem of relativism, as in Rothstein and Torsello's analysis of anthropologists' notes about bribery in preindustrial societies:

> Differences in what is understood as corruption lie in the variation of what counts as (and is the extension of) public goods in cultures, and to variation in whether it is morally wrong to turn a public good into a private good. Hence, our hypothesis is that in a culture in which private and public goods are neatly separated both conceptually and customarily . . . there will be fewer problems in distinguishing what is corruption and what is not. . . . Corruption will be a relevant issue whenever private and public goods overlap or are easily converted by those who have access to them. (Rothstein and Torsello 2014, 265; see also 279–80)

Thus, although macro-comparativists as well as economic and noneconomic institutionalists have grappled with tensions expressed in the corruption literature by Nye, each solution they offer recapitulates the tension. Scott, employing the macro-comparative approach, resupplies the moral sense of "corruption" via his readers' imaginations; Rose-Ackerman extinguishes culture as a significant analytic category (while admitting its empirical importance); and Rothstein displaces the question of variation in norms from the sense that "corruption" is wrong to the question of where boundaries of institutional domains are to be drawn.

Corruption as a Nomological Machine

All of the previously discussed approaches to corruption grapple with the problem of how to think about the relationship between behaviors that violate social norms when those norms vary considerably across social space and time. My approach is grounded in this tension, too, but it moves in a different direction. Rather than *analytically* disembedding corruption from its context (albeit in various ways), I suggest that a useful starting point to analysis is to treat decontextualization and disembedding as aspects of the phenomenon of modern corruption itself.

To undertake this approach is to begin from a very different ontology: rather than *flattening* this reality into a world of interrelated variables (Abbott 1988), this view thinks of the world as populated by various *kinds of things* endowed with different *capacities and powers*, which is to say, entities that have capabilities and influences that operate on other entities in the world in different ways. By this view, atomic mechanisms[10] are composed into arrangements such that the overall composition has emergent properties (i.e., capacities and powers that are not reducible to the addition of their component elements but rather emerge in combination) (Bhaskar 2008; Elder-Vass 2010; Harré and Madden 1975).

To grasp this distinction, I have found Nancy Cartwright's concept of *nomological machines* particularly useful. Cartwright's view of reality is similar to the "chunky" or "ontologically heterogeneous" view I have described earlier (she prefers the term "dappled"), but she also wants to be able to explain how it is that there are in fact causal regularities that can be observed and measured. This regularity is achieved by a variety of "arrangements," ranging from the controls of scientific experiments to the performative aspects of modern economic measurement, that produce the regularities that are usually taken as the basic phenomena to be explained by scientific explanation. But why can't they just be called "mechanisms"?[11] Cartwright uses an excellent analogy to explain the difference:

> Consider the lever that constitutes my car's throttle. Pushing on that lever makes the object the lever sits on accelerate. This causal law is true in my car and probably in yours and it's typically invariant across cars and trucks and even tractors. And it is a law that supports a strategy that most of us depend on many times a day, day in and day out. But this law is not true for most levers. Take a random sample of levers in the world and almost none of them will make the object they sit on accelerate. This important law is local, local to specific kinds of structures that give rise to it. I call structures like this, "nomological machines." (Cartwright 2009, 12).

In this example, the "mechanism" is the individual lever, but for it to have a predictable function—for it to produce a regularity that we would normally identify as an object of explanation—it must be embedded in a much larger order of mechanisms, a machine. To me, this distinction gets to the heart of what is missing in the study of modern corruption: too often, the analytic strategy is to isolate the individual mechanisms of corruption (whether directly through things like randomized controlled trials or intellectually by composing models and testing their implications given a body of data) to the neglect of how they are composed together (and the effects of that composition).

Of course, this strategy presents important comparative challenges, but before discussing them, I will first outline and briefly illustrate the mechanisms of corruption's nomological machine as well as how their composition takes on a specifically *modern* composition endowed with distinctive powers and properties.

The Mechanisms of Corruption

The nomological machine of corruption has four central components: it emphasizes the moral dimension of human and organizational conduct; it abstracts behavior from its immediate context; it involves an appeal to an audience; and it invokes an agent's moral biography and vocabularies of motive. Working in combination, these mechanisms endow corruption with the capacity to supply the moral boundaries of social spaces and to highlight ambiguous "edges" of those spaces for special scrutiny and social action. My claim is that none of these four mechanisms is reducible to any of the others and that none is most "fundamental" or "essential."

To illustrate each of the mechanisms described in the following sections, I draw from two recent, excellent analyses of corruption as a nomological machine.[12] Zephyr Teachout's *Corruption in America* (2016) focuses on legal history and on the deep continuities in American public and legal traditions.[13] For Teachout, American senses of "corruption" have revolved around a capacious "conflict of interest" understanding of the concept, in which any *appearance* of corrupt conflict was to be avoided. This understanding, argues Teachout, has anomalously and disastrously been narrowed by courts in the second half of the twentieth century—culminating in the *Citizens United* ruling by the Supreme Court in 2010—to an understanding of "corruption" as a mere quid pro quo in which all elements of the exchange are explicit. Meanwhile, Stephen Pierce, in *Moral Economies of Corruption* (2016), traces the "corruption complex"— encompassing legal definitions of corruption, actual practices, and cultural norms—of Nigeria from its colonial origins through its modern-day political economy. For Pierce, Nigeria's corruption complex was originally a tool for colonial control (Indigenous leaders would typically only be treated as "corrupt" as a pretext to remove them once their positions had become politically untenable for some reason), but after Nigerian independence, it became intertwined with Nigeria's ethnic and federal politics while also drawing from contemporary technocratic vocabularies.

Morality

Corruption is an irreducibly moral accusation. Rather than an argument about, say, the utilitarian inefficiency of a particular action, to call someone, their behavior, or an institution *corrupt* is to attack it more deeply. As Alan Ryan (2013, 978–79) has put it, "questions about corruption are enmeshed in questions about individual character; the notion of an objectively perfectly decent person engaging in objectively utterly corrupt behavior makes little sense." A person of "good" character behaving in a corrupt way would make so little sense because corruption is inherently a *strong evaluation*, or a judgment that, by virtue of its invocation of goodness and badness as criteria of evaluation, touches on fundamental understandings of proper and right *being* and action. According to Charles Taylor (1985, 25–26), "to characterize one desire to inclination as worthier, or nobler, or more integrated, etc. than others is to speak of it in terms of the kind of quality of life which it expresses and sustains. . . . Strong evaluation is not just a condition of articulacy about preferences, but also about the quality of life, the kind of being we are or want to be."

To this individualistic conception of the groundwork of corruption, I would add that corruption accusations go farther. As Ryan (2013, 978) writes, "any discussion of corruption requires a firm grip on what we think an uncorrupt political system looks like and what a 'clean' economy looks like" (see also Wuthnow 1987).

Corruption, simply put, is *a moralized evocation of the social order and an accusation that one's obligations and responsibilities in this order have been violated.*

One of the best examples of corruption's irreducibly moral valence comes from Teachout's discussion of how juries' judgments of what was and wasn't "corrupt" came to dominate corruption prosecutions in mid-twentieth-century America (Teachout 2016, chap. 10). In Teachout's account, this dominance began with the prosecution of Louisiana official Abraham Shushan under an 1872 federal mail fraud statute. Prosecutors employed the broadly worded statute simply because the underlying corrupt act—involving conflicts of interest on interest rates for bonds issued by the City of New Orleans—did not yield provable harm to the city (Teachout 2016, 196). Shushan was convicted by a jury, and the appeals court issued an extraordinary judgment in upholding his conviction:

> It held that "no trustee has more sacred duties than a public official and any scheme to obtain an advantage by corrupting such an one [sic] must in the federal law be considered a scheme to defraud." . . . Even if the city had not

been hurt by the sale, the harm lay in this kind of faithlessness, whether or not there was material harm in the form of public monetary loss. Was there corrupt intent? What was corruptness? The *Shushan* court concluded that the requisite intent was that "there must be purpose to do wrong with is inconsistent with moral uprightness." (Teachout 2016, 198)

This decision, amplified by the early antiracketeering Hobbs Act of 1934, led to confusion over just how juries were to be instructed over what acting "corruptly" or with "corrupt intent" actually meant: Was " 'corruptly' a separate element of an offense that needed to be found, a superfluous adjective, or an essential adjective" (Teachout 2016, 202)? As Teachout argues, how exactly to resolve these questions, and thus how to supply the ineradicable moral content to "corruption," lay with juries. In short, until a different legal understanding took over, "the job of policing political morality in close cases was a jury matter" (Teachout 2016, 203). And for our illustration, this conflict over "corruption's" peculiar rhetorical force in law coupled with its fundamental ambiguity speaks to its fundamental moral character.

Abstraction

In part because it is moral and moral judgments and accusations mean attempting to get at some *fundamental* structuring essence of a particular situation (Abend 2008, 2014), corruption also involves abstraction. By "abstraction," I simply mean that "something concrete becomes abstract when certain properties, which belong to the 'real thing' (and that make it concrete), are taken away from it" (Bailer-Jones 2008, 33).[14]

This understanding of abstraction, of course, is common to the building of scientific models, comparative analysis, and the everyday deployment of heuristics and stereotypes in perception and interaction. Indeed, as Donald Levine has recognized for the use of "univocal" language (1988, especially chapter 2), James Scott (1998) and Jonathan Wyrtzen (2016) have seen for the modern and colonial states, respectively, and Timothy Mitchell (1999) and Damon Mayrl and Sarah Quinn (2016) have argued for modern institutions of governance, this abstraction is powerfully intertwined with the organization of modern life, as it supplies the backbone of rationalization.

But when specifically seen as a mechanism of corruption, abstraction works in at least two important ways. First, when I accuse someone of corruption, I am inviting a reduction and simplification of their behavior into a moral judgment. Other (perhaps mitigating) aspects of the situation drop away, and what is left is the moralized significance: Was that behavior corrupt or pure? Is that person's character virtuous or corrupt? Is that institution tainted or impartial?

Second, as implied by the list of examples I just supplied, corruption's abstraction is binary. No matter how complex the actual circumstances of an action are, corruption invites us to bifurcate it into *either* "virtue" or "corruption." Put differently, while it's easy to envision *circumstances* that are ambiguous with reference to corruption, the *accusation* of corruption is unambiguous and is meant precisely to wipe away the ambiguous circumstances.

An excellent illustration of this property can be found in Pierce's discussion of Nigerian First Republic politics in the early 1960s. These politics took place in the shadow of Nigeria's 1954 constitutional reorganization, which federalized political competition between Nigeria's different regions (and ethnicities) among different "marketing boards" responsible for brokering the sale of Nigerian commodities on the global market (Pierce 2016, 88–90). As competition over these new national boards intensified, so too did accusations and investigations of corruption. Pierce recounts how an investigation of one marketing board—that of the western region of Nigeria—was found to be in deficit and investigated and the man found responsible, who happened to be a political rival of those in power, was discredited (Pierce 2016, 93–99). From our vantage point, the extraordinarily complex details of the case and its investigation are less the point than the exaggerated clarity that the corruption investigation itself brought. As Pierce writes:

> The rights and wrong of the government's case against Chief Awolowo were less important than its general tenor. It is not unreasonable to suppose Awolowo was ultimately responsible for systematically diverting the marketing board's funds for the benefit of his party and his supporters—not just in a ministerial sense of collective responsibility but in the sense of having crafted the policy. Nonetheless, the specifics of the case against him were more suggestive than definitive, and they depended on a literal hermeneutics of suspicion: damning testimony was balanced by exculpatory testimony or by absence of other forms of direct evidence. Chief Awolowo's guilt in specific instances was demonstrated by the miasma of misconduct emanating from the totality of the transactions under investigation. . . . The commission's report . . . tends to construe corruption as being a set of nefarious plots orchestrated by singular villains. . . . The more obvious conclusions would have been that sweetheart deals and public funds diverted to political parties and to corporations controlled by their members were a more-or-less universal feature of First Republic politics. (Pierce 2016, 97–98)

Mobilization

As noted earlier, in addition to being an act of moral abstraction, corruption is also fundamentally an *accusation*. That is, its power as a lived category stems not from its incorporation into actors' own identities, but rather as a slur used against political, social, and economic enemies in a given domain of struggle. There are few, if any, cases in which actors avow themselves as "corrupt" in the thick of a moment's particular struggle.[15]

With this in mind, "corruption" becomes the name for a certain style of moralized, abstracting appeal given at least two actors locked in a social struggle with one another. Following the work of E. E. Schattschneider (1975, especially chapters 1 and 2), these appeals are thus oriented around expanding the scope of conflict by inviting the audience to a conflict to join it on the side of the actors making the appeal. Crucially, it is thus almost always the *losers* of a local round of conflict who seek to expand the scope of a conflict by publicizing, appealing to, or invoking the resources of outsiders via the accusation of "corruption."[16] Because it is moral and abstracting, moreover, modern corruption is an especially potent appeal to make, especially insofar as the "audiences" for a struggle are often legal, political, and economic institutions with enormous power to intervene (Harrison 1999).

This dynamic is amply illustrated by Pierce's discussion of the marketing board investigations outlined in the previous section. Pierce notes wryly that "it is far-fetched that a panel as distinguished as the Coker Commission [who investigated the boards] would have reached its conclusions without any awareness of their political convenience to the government" (Pierce 2016, 97–98). And indeed, the abstraction discussed in the previous section ran in two directions—at the same time that, by publishing its report on corruption, the Coker Commission escalated the conflict between Awolowo and the government to a new audience, so too did it *suppress* the conflict between Awolowo and his "deputy, successor, and rival" S. N. Akintola by, in Pierce's view, wholly implausibly interpreting Akintola's own corrupt behavior during the same episode as having been solely at the behest of Awolowo (Pierce 2016, 95)!

Biography

Finally, a corruption accusation contains some argument not only about a given act itself but also of actors—whether people or organizations. That is, although a given economic exchange may be "inappropriate" or a gift "in poor taste," "corruption" contaminates the actors in the exchange themselves that taint is carried beyond any individual interaction. Actors in complex societies tend to circulate among domains with different norms and styles of exchange (Padgett and Powell 2012) and attempt to create narratives that synthesize an identity narrating that circulation (Ricoeur 1995; Somers 1994), and these narratives often contain moralized "vocabularies of motive" (Mills 1940) explaining behavior. Accordingly, corruption struggles are often not only moral accusations abstracting from a given context to mobilize observers into a conflict; they are also struggles over the "character" of people and organizations and how to reconcile potentially aberrant behavior with claims about either virtue or corruption.

Given the importance of biography as a grounding for modern corruption accusations, the accusers can find themselves in a difficult position. On the one hand, to be persuasive, they must demonstrate concrete knowledge of the behavior of those they are accusing—they have to have witnessed wrongdoing or at least have proof of it. On the other hand, such knowledge, especially in domains that are esoteric or unfamiliar to the audience, is often only obtained by participating in some way in the very activities being labeled as corrupt. Since a part of one's credibility is the consistency in their biography, corruption accusers often express the trope of *moral conversion* to resolve this tension. For instance, Jack Abramoff, in his memoir *Capitol Punishment*, is at pains to explain how he became an anticorruption reformer at the end of his prison term for bribery and violation of campaign finance laws:

> Often I would sit alone by the prison camp ball field, or walk the uneven and unpaved perimeter track in solitude. I had a lot of thinking to do. How had I wound up in this place? What had I not seen where I was headed? After I crashed, I began to see the road signs that might have warned me off the dangerous cliff I eventually drove off, but why was I so blind at the time? . . . Human beings have limits, but I refused to recognize mine and, instead, used my creativity, intellect, work ethic, and the power of manipulation to get what I wanted. It didn't matter that I believed my actions were for the good of my clients; they were wrong—I was wrong. Moreover, not only were some of my actions illegal, many of them were corrupt despite their legality. (Abramoff 2011, 269–70)[17]

The Powers of Modern Corruption: An Excursus

Morality, abstraction, mobilization, and biography are all key mechanisms of corruption in general. But how do they come together to create specific regularities, and what does this have to do with comparison? For this question, we should at least distinguish *modern* from *nonmodern* forms of corruption. Here, a qualification I have made—describing the object of discussion as *modern* corruption—is crucial. For the purposes of thinking about and comparing the nomological machine of corruption, Alina Mungiu-Pippidi offers a useful starting point by distinguishing contemporary forms of corruption from all others insofar as modern ones rely on "ethical universalism." This "is the state's *modus operandi*: government is impartial and, when implementing laws and policies, treats citizens as mere individuals" (Mungiu-Pippidi 2015, 15). Of course, this definition is essentially Weber's contrast between patrimonialism and bureaucracy (as Mungiu-Pippidi [2015, 15] acknowledges) and tends to take for granted the emergence of good government as an evolutionary output of a given institutional design.[18]

But what exactly does the structure of a nomological machine of modern corruption have to look like for such institutional accounts to hold? To answer this question, we can look to Pierre Bourdieu's account of the rise of "the interest in disinterest"—or the emergence and ratification of *claims to* ethical universalism and disinterested judgment by particular actors at particular times (see Bourdieu 1998; and 2000, 122–27). As Bourdieu (2000, 123, emphasis original) describes in his characteristically circuitous prose, "If the universal does advance, this is because there are social microcosms which, in spite of their intrinsic ambiguity, linked to their enclosure in the privilege and satisfied egoism of a separation by status, are the site of struggles in which the prize is the universal in which agents who, to differing degrees depending on their position and trajectory, have a *particular interest in the universal,* in reason, truth, virtue, [and] engage themselves with weapons which are nothing other than the most universal conquests of the previous struggles."

This passage implies states for each of the mechanisms of corruption to make the resulting nomological machine "modern" and distinguish it from nonmodern varieties. The "morality" of the machine must not rest on particular circumstances or local conditions but rather refer to ethical universals such as "public interest" or "markets."[19] In the act of anchoring themselves to such ethical universals, corruption accusations must also be stark and binarizing in their abstraction; as Bourdieu notes, part of the power of the reference to universals is that they leave behind the "intrinsic ambiguity" of particularities. Third, because the "social microcosms" proliferate as societies grow more complex yet remain embedded in a larger "field of power," the likelihood is that mobilizing appeals made from those microcosms will be made to an audience unfamiliar with the details of the behaviors at stake in classification. Fourth, and finally, mobilizing appeals made in a stark moral language across such microcosms will need to contain some reconciliation of a unitary moral biography—after all, the claim to *universal* ethics implies that one ought to behave, or be accountable for one's behavior, in terms of a single standard. (I summarize these distinctions in table 7.1.)

Combined together in the nomological machine of modern corruption, these four mechanisms express two powers crucial to any attempt to compare corruption. First, because any accusation of corruption invoking the modern nomological machine refers to a purportedly universal ethical space, it is therefore also an act of commensuration and comparison insofar as it holds a given behavior in comparison to a universal standard. Second, and Bourdieu implies,

TABLE 7.1 Nomological machines of corruption and their mechanisms

	Type	
Mechanism	Modern	Nonmodern
Moral reference	Universalistic	Circumstantial
Abstraction	Binarizing	Contingent
Mobilizing audience	Unfamiliar	Familiar
Biography	Unitary	Fragmented

the nomological machine helps produce another phenomenon that has proliferated in modernity: ethically "disembedded" spaces capable of making ethical demands on their occupants and rationalized in their own terms (Polanyi 1944; Weber 1946).

Comparing Corruption: Lumping, Splitting, and Articulation

So just *how* are we supposed to compare the nomological machine of modern corruption, given that there are significant variations over time and space about what is considered corrupt? Beyond the ordinary methodological questions involved in comparison, this question is especially difficult for two reasons. First, one important property of nomological machines, as Cartwright emphasizes, is that they *produce* the very empirical regularities normally considered *inputs* of the comparative method. Thus, for instance, post-Soviet societies may exhibit an "inevitable corruption of transition" (Scheppele 1999) less because of changes in actual behaviors and more because those behaviors are newly categorized by the nomological machine of modern corruption (see also Harrison [1999]).[20] Second, as I stressed at the outset of this chapter, "corruption" is a composite concept, describing behavior itself and also contextual categories applied to that behavior. To rephrase this distinction slightly, invoking the concept of "corruption" puts the tension between "objective" and "subjective" accounts of social action at the center of analysis (Fourcade 2018), and a particular challenge of comparison is to hold both of these dimensions in frame.

Grappling with these two comparative difficulties means departing from the orthodox positivist terrain of comparison, wherein (in its classical formulations) a variety of cases supply measurements, which are then compared using a given method to yield stable causal pathways of one kind or another explaining their similarity to or difference from one another (Ragin 1989, 2000; Skocpol 1979). Along with many of the other contributors to this volume, my suggestion is that we instead consider comparison as a *practice*[21] meant to balance at least three complicated real[22] demands.

1. **Fidelity to the phenomenon under study.** First, any comparative scholar must balance fidelity to the most accurate possible interpretation of their phenomenon with the recognition that any given phenomenon is rarely "cleanly" expressed *across* all cases being compared. One easy solution to this dilemma is to say simply, "Your argument must be constrained by what the evidence shows," and such a statement lies at the heart of the scientific ethos (Daston and Galison 2014; Merton 1979). But such an injunction rapidly becomes complicated when we ask, first, *how* to delimit the body of evidence relevant to a given claim or comparison and, second, whether the empirical surface of observations is "really" the whole of the matter in a given phenomenon. Of course, classical empiricism supplies an extremely strenuous test for any theory (and comparison) that rarely holds in the actual practice of research; instead, a variety of "theoretical" (Kiser and Hechter 1991), "depth" (Harré 1996), "constructive" (Gorski 2004), and "relational" (Somers 1998) realisms all claim in one way or another that the "actual" level of apparent observation hardly matches the "real" level of the phenomenon itself. In such cases, comparison is a critical tool for revealing how mechanisms operate in different contexts (Steinmetz 2004), but the question of how to balance empirical comparability with realist fidelity presents an ongoing challenge that can only be resolved by reflection on the purpose of comparison in the first place.[23]

2. **An anticipated audience or readership.** Even if an analyst *were* to somehow strike a perfect comparative balance and do justice to all relevant nuances of their cases while also perfectly articulating the operation of a phenomenon under study, the result would likely resemble the famed, and useless, exhaustively detailed map of a terrain that is identical to the terrain itself. Indeed, to *communicate* what they have learned from comparison, a scholar must transform their findings into a publication of some kind. To do this, they must employ an abstraction, which, with Damon Mayrl, I have elsewhere called an "analytic architecture" (Mayrl and Wilson 2020), to make their mixture of evidence and theory legible to their readers. This point, in turn, begs the question of "Which readers?" And the answer is complicated. On the one hand, an analyst must choose an analytic architecture that is at least somewhat legible to some community, lest their publication seem inscrutable and subject to the dreaded question "Who is this for?" On the other hand, however, scholars usually seek to intervene and reshape scholarly debates, acting as brokers among fields, addressing themselves to audiences that "need to hear what they have to say," and even seeking to "shake up" an established scholarly order. In other words, the goal is to be intelligible enough to be read by an audience but also to stimulate them to say, "That's interesting!" (Davis 1971).

3. **An existing body of scholarship.** In undertaking comparisons of some phenomenon and communicating their findings about them to some audience, scholars do so with reference to existing bodies of scholarship, whether called "canons," "paradigms," or something else. Here there is a similar tension as with the scholarly audience: an existing body of scholarship provides theories, arguments, and even stock comparative choices[24] that provide a groundwork of knowledge that a scholar seeks to inform, yet the progress of paradigms and bodies of knowledge is built on play at the boundaries of what is known, either by making common comparisons in novel ways or creating uncommon comparisons to test received wisdom.

Lumping and Splitting

Balancing all of these demands perfectly is an impossible challenge for any scholar, and it is well beyond the scope of this chapter to trace *every* means by which this web of demands affects the act of comparison.[25] Instead, I will focus on a pair of strategies common in historical and macro-comparative studies and that seem especially important for comparing the nomological machine of modern corruption since they make construction of a scholarly work indissoluble from consideration of the phenomenon under study: lumping and splitting.[26] Although "lumping" and "splitting" may have originated in taxonomy and have received excellent treatments within sociology (see especially Zerubavel 1996), the distinction is most common in history.[27] Jack Hexter was one of the first to deploy the term in print, as part of a critique of Christopher Hill's work:

> The most consequential line of division among historians is not the one that separates quantifiers from non-quantifiers, comparativists from national historians, Marxists from non-Marxists from anti-Marxists; it is . . . the one that separates the lumpers from the splitters. Historians who are splitters like to point out divergences, to perceive differences, to draw distinctions. They shrink away from systems of history and from general rules, and carry around in their heads lists of exceptions to almost any rule they are likely to encounter. They do not mind untidiness and accident in the past; they rather like them.
>
> Lumpers do not like accidents; they would prefer to have them vanish. They tend to ascribe apparent accidents not to the untidiness of the past itself, but to the untidiness of the record of the past or to the untidiness of mind of splitting historians who are willing to leave the Temple of Clio a shambles. Instead of noting differences, lumpers note likeness; instead of separateness, connexion. The lumping historian wants to put the past into boxes, all of it, and not too damn many boxes at that, and then to tie all the boxes together into one nice

shapely bundle. The latter operation turns out to be quite easy, since any prac-
tised lumper will have so selected his boxes in the first place that they will fit
together in a seemly way. Hegel, Marx, Spengler, and Toynbee have at least so
much in common: each of their systems possesses a large measure of internal
coherence. It is the initial step, the packing of the clutter of evidence around
them and their sayings and doings in the past into an appropriately small number of boxes, that causes the trouble. (Hexter 1975, 1251–52)

The way Hexter deploys the distinction has a variety of uses for the purpose
of comparing the nomological machine of modern corruption. For one thing, it
recognizes that *the same* datum—an historical event or document, say—could
have very different significances for different scholars. A "lumper" looking at
the English revolution from 1642 to 1660, for instance, might downplay the
importance of the English "revolution," while a "splitter" might see a series of
ruptures in seventeenth-century English history and might even insist that the
Glorious Revolution in 1688 was even more important! In addition, thinking of
lumping and splitting embeds any act of comparison in a causal account, both
at the level of the author's own narrative and potentially also in a given theoretical "system" like Marxism or Whiggism. And finally, as Hexter implies, "good
history" lies somewhere between radical lumping (in which case, one loses
fidelity to the phenomenon) and radical splitting (in which case, comparison
is impossible given history's radical particularity). *All* history and, I would add,
all comparison are a mixture of acts of lumping and splitting.

Two Examples of Lumping and Splitting

But of course, to say that any reasonable social-scientific comparative scholarship mixes acts of lumping and splitting in its analysis is not to say that they
are mixed in equal proportion or importance, as a comparison of Teachout and
Pierce's approaches illustrates.[28]
One way of reading Teachout is that she is recounting the history of how
the nomological machine of modern corruption intertwines with another—the
law. This history, in turn, fundamentally relies on lumping for its coherence:
Teachout's central claim is that there is a more or less coherent approach in
America to what constitutes corruption, that this is different ("more expansive") than other places, and that the course of this understanding was wrongly
diverted by fundamentally mistaken Supreme Court decisions culminating in
Citizens United. This basic continuity, she argues, was present from the concerns expressed during the constitutional convention, ran through the political
dilemmas of the early American republic, was the lay understanding of citizens
who served as jurors in the middle of the twentieth century, and supplies the

best road map for restoring confidence in our political institutions today. It is, in short, "a particularly demanding notion of corruption that has survived through most of American legal history" that "is the foundation of the architecture of our freedoms" (Teachout 2016, 2).

But of course, to establish this master continuity in American understandings of corruption requires many smaller acts of comparative "splitting." Teachout's argument about *how* Americans' understanding of corruption became so "demanding," for instance, relies on an argument about how early American political life self-consciously differentiated from a "corrupted" Europe of gifts, bribery, and patronage, undertaking the radical project of realizing Montesquieu's vision of human nature. And sustaining her argument about the fundamental continuity of Americans' concept of corruption requires another act of splitting: this time comparing the present state of jurisprudence on corruption with an ideal counterfactual of what the jurisprudence *could have been* in the absence of poor rulings. Thus, as she summarizes near the end of the book, "our concept of corruption, too, is corrupted, dismembered, the component parts taken out" (Teachout 2016, 291).

Teachout's strategy to emphasize lumping and the continuity of the sense of "corruption" in America while employing splitting to buttress her point, though, carries characteristic tensions. First, empirically, in one sense, the book revolves around chapter 15, wherein Teachout explains that the intellectual groundwork for *Citizens United* was laid by the "law and economics" movement (championed by, among others, Susan Rose-Ackerman),[29] which views citizens as "self-interest maximizing, and people are primarily conceived of as consumers instead of citizens" (Teachout 2016, 261). To explain *how* this movement became so powerful and created a situation in which Supreme Court justices simply could "see" the consequences of their rulings, however, Teachout falls back to ad hoc reasons. She suggests that there is a striking complacency on the modern court, a disdain for democracy, and a biographical disconnection of justices from politics, but hedging words such as "may" and "perhaps" abound throughout the chapter. And her sole allusion to the origins and organizational operations of the movement is the unfootnoted sentence: "The legal impact of this movement, which began in the late 1950s and gained force throughout the 1960s and 1970s, is well documented" (Teachout 2016, 260).[30]

The balance Teachout strikes between lumping and splitting in her analysis of corruption also creates a striking tension around the question of "What is to be done?" The book is self-consciously a call for reform (see, e.g., Teachout 2016, 276), but at the end of an excursus on the power of America's legal tradition to shape our political life and reduce political corruption, partly because of that very emphasis on continuity, Teachout oddly argues *against* direct intervention in the courts: "the same history that teaches us that corruption was a foundational principle teaches us that structural changes are possible even within the constraints of a misinterpreted Constitution. We can fundamentally rearrange power dynamics and improve representative democracy *even without a new Court, or court packing*" (Teachout 2016, 298, emphasis added). In other words, at the end of a book about legal history, the answer has little to do with the law.

If Teachout emphasizes lumping to give her account of the nomological machine of corruption coherence and uses splitting to emphasize particular points, Pierce does the converse. *Moral Economies of Corruption*—as the plural in the title suggests—fundamentally splits as its basic comparative act, emphasizing both the particularity of Nigeria's different nomological machines of corruption and also the uniqueness of its experience in a variety of ways. At the same time, Pierce gestures toward lumping Nigeria in with other ethnically federated and postcolonial states; he writes, for instance, that one of Nigeria's anticorruption commissions "captures in microcosm a general tendency of the Nigerian state, *perhaps of all states*" (Pierce 2016, 196). Yet this balance between lumping and splitting, like Teachout's, generates characteristic tensions, which Pierce admirably addressed head-on in the last paragraph of the book:

> What does this tell us about corruption as a comparative phenomenon? The argument of this book is that corruption discourse has a long history as a global occurrence, and that history is well known. There is also a long history of articulations between that global discourse and its political use in particular locales. Understanding corruption requires understanding this history of intellectual and political interaction around the world, all taking place as if corruption were applied to a discrete and coherent object. The history of corruption around the world is a history of global politics, and it is a history bringing together myriad local histories. This relatively grand claim about historical processes can coexist with a number of more modest practical implications. For reformers, ameliorating corruption will require dealing with issues fundamental to the logic of local political culture, and these will vary tremendously from context to context. In Nigeria, the issues involve the intersection of patronage and political life and the distributive issues of revenue across a culturally diverse country. Instead of attempting to prevent officials from diverting public revenue to self-interested ends, Nigerians must face a constitutional challenge: how can public ends be served by accommodating patronage as a fundamental political principle? Exhortation is ineffective, as are investigations and judicial interventions. Instead, the constitutional order must be brought into alignment with political culture. Webs of patronage must be able to constrain official behavior and demand more from it, and the needs of regions must be brought into harmony. That is easier said than done. (Pierce 2016, 229)

The final sentence of this passage, "That is easier said than done," applies both to the concrete reforms Pierce discusses and to the analytic project of comparison. If Nigeria represents a fundamentally particular instance of the nomological machine of corruption, it is one of the "myriad local histories" that can be "brought together" into "a history of global politics." And this project can "coexist" with an injunction that, essentially, any corruption-reform project will "vary tremendously from context to context" and will only come with fundamentally remaking the alignment between "the constitutional order" and "political culture." Again, my aim here is not to argue with the substance of these points, but simply to emphasize the pressure Pierce's splitting puts on terms like "brought together," "coexist," and "bring into alignment with."

* * *

Even though I have emphasized the tensions in both Teachout's and Pierce's accounts of the nomological machine of corruption, both are stellar recent attempts to expand our social-scientific view of the phenomenon. With specific reference to the problem of *comparing* the phenomenon of corruption in its expanded sense, I have argued that a profitable way forward, as exhibited in both books, is to think of corruption as a nomological machine, which, in its modern varieties, has the characteristic of producing the purportedly universal regularities of behavior and judgment that are usually taken as a priori assumptions in social-scientific investigations.

By way of conclusion, this essay is a reminder of three sets of arguments. First, social reality is composed of many different kinds of things, and one important phenomenon is that of nomological machines themselves because their operation at least attempts to order and homogenize domains of that reality. To that extent, it may prove useful to further investigate whether such machines also operate for other morally laden concepts, such as abuse, exploitation, and so on.

Second, there are two ways of reading the point that nomological machines play an important role in corruption and hence must be a part of a comparison of it. The more orthodox reading is that there is simply a second order of contextual variables that must be taken into account when comparing corruption—say, the presence or absence of a robust legal tradition, the structure of the public sphere in a country, or the extent to which individualism is normative, and so on. A more radical reading, though, is also possible: here, nomological machines stand between "forming" causes that bring entities into being and "forcing" causes familiar to traditional epistemology (Abbott 1995; Abend 2022; Hirschman and Reed 2014). In this reading, since the very natures of the entities under study transform at different points in the investigation, it is not possible to subsume them into generalized laws or causal statements. Whichever of these readings one prefers, the general argument of this essay can be stated simply—*Ceteris non paribus!*—and the points of contact between the nomological machine of corruption and the rest of a social structure need to be central parts of comparison.

As might be implied by the previous paragraph, a final argument of this essay has been for scholarly reflexivity. Comparison is one of the many scholarly acts we undertake, and any piece of corruption scholarship, and indeed, any piece of scholarship at all, is caught in a web of trade-offs. It is *not possible* for a scholar to maintain perfect fidelity to corruption in one particular instance or any other, while remaining intelligible to their readership and transcending disciplinary boundaries—to say nothing of influencing the policy community and the public.[31] Rather, to compare corruption and to undertake the study of the complex, composite phenomena that abound in the social world, it would be useful to develop vocabularies that clarify our standpoints with reference to these trade-offs and facilitate dialog across the different communities interested in corruption. This chapter has sought to make a modest contribution to this end.

Notes

1. See especially chapters by George Steinmetz (chapter 8) and Jonah Stuart Brundage (chapter 9).
2. See Emirbayer (1997) and Erikson (2013). Of course, this focuses on the *academic* comparative study of corruption. A parallel analysis of the policy, nongovernmental organization, and consulting parts of the field would emphasize different influences on the comparative study of corruption, like the attractiveness of comparisons to donors, governments, and compatibility with ongoing development efforts.
3. See McDonnell (2020) for a recent, fantastic exploration of this point.
4. Nye imagines an accretion of general understanding of the causes and consequences of corruption through analysis of variables and their relationships populating a "general linear reality" (Abbott 1988) and even supplies a speculative regression table (Nye 1967, 976).
5. This perspective is similar to Merton's (1979, 73, 76) famous observation on the latent functions of corrupt political machines: "The functional deficiencies of the official structure [of formal politics in the United States] generate an alternative (unofficial) structure [of political bossism] to fulfill existing needs somewhat more effectively. . . . The political machine persists as an apparatus for satisfying otherwise unfulfilled needs of diverse groups in the population. . . . To adopt an *exclusively* moral attitude toward the 'corrupt political machine' is to lose sight of the very structural conditions which generate the 'evil' that is so bitterly attacked" (emphasis original). Perhaps because of Merton's stronger note of functional necessity, Scott does not cite Merton.
6. See Fisman and Golden's *Corruption: What Everyone Needs to Know* (2017), which is heavily indebted to Rose-Ackerman.
7. I say "odd" because chapter 6, "Bribes, Patronage, and Gift Giving," is accorded one of four "Parts" of the book, "Corruption as a Cultural Problem," but it is the only part containing only a single chapter.

8. This statement echoes the language of "virtuous" and "vicious" institutional cycles, the analysis of which has been championed by Daron Acemoglu and James Robinson (2013).

9. Rothstein (2011, 21) avows the difference: "Social science should not be based on the idea that society is dominated by agents with only one script of human behavior or a single set of moral norms, be it self-interest, the principle of care, rent seeking, bureaucratic ethics, feelings of community, altruism, or for that matter impartiality. According to this model, humans have a greater repertoire than being only self-regarding, and they understand that what is appropriate in one sphere is fundamentally wrong in another."

10. *Atomic* here means the scholar's arbitrary judgment of whatever level can be taken as fundamental for the purposes of analysis.

11. See, for example, Gross (2009).

12. Neither Teachout nor Pierce use the vocabulary I do. Teachout refers to the "traditional [American] conception" of corruption, and Pierce to the "corruption complex," but I believe both of their analyses resemble the approach I advocate.

13. As I note below, the law itself is a nomological machine and is distinct from "corruption," even as the law intertwines with it.

14. Note the similarity here with several other contributions to this volume focusing on typologizing.

15. As I note below, however, it *is* sometimes the case of modern corruption that an actor will admit to *having been* corrupt in the past.

16. See Adut (2008) for more on these dynamics.

17. Abramoff, at the time of this writing, had also just been indicted again for corrupt undeclared lobbying.

18. Again, McDonnell (2017) is a brilliant exception to this trend, as is Gupta (1995).

19. In other words, the condition of morality in modern corruption is reference to something like Walzer's "spheres of justice" (1983). But rather than deploy Walzer as Rothstein does (and as I criticize earlier), I emphasize contingency: the boundaries among the different spheres are not normatively set or derived, but rather an historical accomplishment!

20. Likewise, corruption studies typically struggle over whether "grand" (i.e., elite) and "petty" (i.e., undertaken by ordinary people) are the same kind of thing. From the perspective of corruption as a nomological machine, the question is less whether a given act is definitionally "corrupt" in some similar or different way, but rather how the nomological machine of corruption operates on such acts during and after a classification struggle over them takes place.

21. Cite your favorite postpositivist philosopher of science or science-studies don or doyenne here!

22. A classic positivist response to this suggestion is to argue, simply, that the analyst's job is to reveal the mechanisms or properties of a phenomenon "as it really is," reducing the scholar to a cypher for empirical reality. My response is that this reality is indeed an essential and crucial tether for any empirical work of scholarship, but the anticipated readership for a piece of scholarship, the body of understanding to which it is explicitly and implicitly addressed, and the narrative structures that provide its coherence are no less "real" and cannot be wished away by fiat.

23. See Mayrl, chapter 2 in this volume.

24. See Beck (2017) for a brilliant analysis of the relationship among cases in macro-comparative scholarship.

25. The entire volume is focused on this in different ways, but see especially chapters by Newman (chapter 10), Bargheer (chapter 1), and Steinmetz (chapter 8).
26. While this distinction bears a family resemblance to Xu's "comparison as deconstruction and reconstruction" in this volume (chapter 3), my focus incorporates Ford's focus on how these comparative practices play out in the service of different master narratives.
27. Another reason to prefer Hexter's voicing to Zerubavel's is that Zerubavel lacks Hexter's polemical spittle flecks.
28. To even compare Teachout and Pierce is, of course, itself an act of both lumping and splitting. It is "lumping" in the sense that "Western" corruption is only rarely compared directly with "developing world" corruption as exhibitions of the same nomological machine, and it is splitting in the sense that I am arguing each author pursues a different course in their analysis.
29. Teachout's (2016, 261–62) discussion of the tension inherent in Rose-Ackerman's concept of corruption is brilliant.
30. My point here is not that such an account is *not possible*, or even that it is not easily accessible to the curious, but rather that this sentence plays an important role in Teachout's particular account. The absence of a footnote is telling because it presupposed a particular readership; namely, one for which the "law and economics" movement is so familiar as to need no further explanation.
31. For example, someone with philosophical training or a particularly hard-nosed social-scientific analyst might read the previous paragraph and find it hopelessly wishy-washy. "There are multiple readings?!?" they might ask. "Which one *did you mean?*"

References

Abbott, Andrew. 1988. "Transcending General Linear Reality." *Sociological Theory* 6:169–86.
——. 1995. "Things of Boundaries." *Social Research* 62(4):857–82.
Abend, Gabriel. 2008. "Two Main Problems in the Sociology of Morality." *Theory and Society* 37(2):87–125.
——. 2014. *The Moral Background: An Inquiry Into the History of Business Ethics*. Princeton, NJ: Princeton University Press.
——. 2022. "Making Things Possible." *Sociological Methods and Research* 51(1):68–107.
Abramoff, Jack. 2011. *Capitol Punishment: The Hard Truth About Washington Corruption from America's Most Notorious Lobbyist*. Washington, DC: WND.
Acemoglu, Daron, and James A. Robinson. 2013. *Why Nations Fail: The Origins of Power, Prosperity, and Poverty*. Reprint edition. New York: Currency.
Adams, Julia. 1999. "Culture in Rational-Choice Theories of State-Formation." In *State/Culture: State Formation After the Cultural Turn*, edited by George Steinmetz. Ithaca, NY: Cornell University Press.
Adut, Ari. 2008. *On Scandal: Moral Disturbances in Society, Politics and Art*. Cambridge: Cambridge University Press.
Bailer-Jones, Daniella. 2008. "Standing Up Against Tradition: Models and Theories in Nancy Cartwright's Philosophy of Science." In *Nancy Cartwright's Philosophy of Science*, edited by Stephan Hartmann, Carl Hoefer, and Luc Boevens. New York: Routledge.
Beck, Colin J. 2017. "The Comparative Method in Practice: Case Selection and the Social Science of Revolution." *Social Science History* 41(3):533–54.
Bhaskar, Roy. 2008. *A Realist Theory of Science*. New York: Taylor & Francis.

Bourdieu, Pierre. 1998. "Is a Disinterested Act Possible?" In *Practical Reason*, 75–91. Stanford, CA: Stanford University Press.

——. 2000. *Pascalian Meditations*. Translated by Richard Nice. Stanford, CA: Stanford University Press.

Cartwright, Nancy. 1999. *The Dappled World: A Study of the Boundaries of Science*. Cambridge: Cambridge University Press.

——. 2009. "How to Do Things with Causes." *Proceedings and Addresses of the American Philosophical Association* 83(2):5–22.

Daston, Lorraine, and Peter Galison. 2014. *Objectivity*. New York: Zone.

Davis, Murray S. 1971. "That's Interesting! Towards a Phenomenology of Sociology and a Sociology of Phenomenology." *Philosophy of the Social Sciences* 1(2):309–44.

Dupré, John. 1995. *The Disorder of Things: Metaphysical Foundations of the Disunity of Science*. Cambridge, MA: Harvard University Press.

Elder-Vass, Dave. 2010. *The Causal Power of Social Structures: Emergence, Structure and Agency*. Cambridge: Cambridge University Press.

Emirbayer, Mustafa. 1997. "Manifesto for a Relational Sociology." *American Journal of Sociology* 103(2):281–317.

Erikson, Emily. 2013. "Formalist and Relationalist Theory in Social Network Analysis." *Sociological Theory* 31(3):219–42.

Fisman, Ray, and Miriam A. Golden. 2017. *Corruption: What Everyone Needs to Know*. New York: Oxford University Press.

Fourcade, Marion. 2018. "The Will to Progress and the Twofold Truth of Capital." In *Destabilizing Orders: Proceedings of the Maxpo Fifth Anniversary Conference*. Vol. 18. 1st Series. Paris: Maxpo Discussion Papers.

Gorski, Philip S. 2004. "The Poverty of Deductivism: A Constructive Realist Model of Sociological Explanation." *Sociological Methodology* 34(1):1–33.

Gross, Neil. 2009. "A Pragmatist Theory of Social Mechanisms." *American Sociological Review* 74(3):358–79.

Gupta, Akhil. 1995. "Blurred Boundaries: The Discourse of Corruption, the Culture of Politics, and the Imagined State." *American Ethnologist* 22(2):375–402.

Harré, Rom. 1996. "From Observability to Manipulability: Extending the Inductive Arguments for Realism." *Synthese* 108(2):137–55.

Harré, Rom, and Edward H. Madden. 1975. *Causal Powers: A Theory of Natural Necessity*. Rowman and Littlefield.

Harrison, Graham. 1999. "Corruption as 'Boundary Politics': The State, Democratisation, and Mozambique's Unstable Liberalisation." *Third World Quarterly* 20(3):537–50.

Heidenheimer, Arnold J., and Michael Johnston, eds. 2002. *Political Corruption: Concepts & Contexts*. 3rd edition. Piscataway, NJ: Transaction.

Heidenheimer, Arnold Joseph, Michael Johnston, and Victor T. LeVine. 1989. *Political Corruption: A Handbook*. Piscataway, NJ: Transaction.

Hexter, Jack. 1975. "The Burden of Proof: On the Historical Method of Christopher Hill." *Times Literary Supplement*. 25 October.

Hirschman, Daniel, and Isaac Ariail Reed. 2014. "Formation Stories and Causality in Sociology." *Sociological Theory* 32(4):259–82.

Kiser, Edgar, and Michael Hechter. 1991. "The Role of General Theory in Comparative-Historical Sociology." *American Journal of Sociology* 97(1):1–30.

Levine, Donald N. N. 1988. *The Flight from Ambiguity: Essays in Social and Cultural Theory*. Chicago: University of Chicago Press.

Little, Daniel. 2009. "The Heterogeneous Social: New Thinking About the Foundations of the Social Sciences." In *Philosophy and the Social Sciences*, 154–78. Cambridge: Cambridge University Press.

Mayrl, Damon, and Sarah Quinn. 2016. "Defining the State from Within: Boundaries, Schemas, and Associational Policymaking." *Sociological Theory* 34(1):1–26.

Mayrl, Damon, and Nicholas Hoover Wilson. 2020. "What Do Historical Sociologists Do All Day? Analytic Architectures in Historical Sociology." *American Journal of Sociology* 125(5):1345–94.

McDonnell, Erin Metz. 2017. "Patchwork Leviathan: How Pockets of Bureaucratic Governance Flourish Within Institutionally Diverse Developing States." *American Sociological Review* 82(3):476–510.

——. 2020. *Patchwork Leviathan: Pockets of Bureaucratic Effectiveness in Developing States*. Princeton, NJ: Princeton University Press.

Merton, Robert K. 1979. "The Normative Structure of Science." In *The Sociology of Science: Theoretical and Empirical Investigations*, 267–78. Chicago: University of Chicago Press.

Mills, C. Wright. 1940. "Situated Actions and Vocabularies of Motive." *American Sociological Review* 5(6):904–13.

Mitchell, Timothy. 1999. "Society, Economy, and the State Effect." In *State/Culture: State Formation After the Cultural Turn*, 76–90. New York: Cornell University Press.

Mungiu-Pippidi, Alina. 2015. *The Quest for Good Governance*. Cambridge: Cambridge University Press.

Nye, J. S. 1967. "Corruption and Political Development: A Cost-Benefit Analysis." *American Political Science Review* 61(2):417–27.

Padgett, John F., and Walter W. Powell. 2012. *The Emergence of Organizations and Markets*. Princeton, NJ: Princeton University Press.

Pierce, Steven. 2016. *Moral Economies of Corruption: State Formation and Political Culture in Nigeria*. Durham, NC: Duke University Press.

Polanyi, Karl. 1944. *The Great Transformation*. New York: Beacon.

Ragin, Charles C. 1989. *The Comparative Method: Moving Beyond Qualitative and Quantitative Strategies*. Berkeley: University of California Press.

——. 2000. *Fuzzy-Set Social Science*. Chicago: University of Chicago Press.

Ricoeur, Paul. 1995. *Oneself as Another*. Translated by Kathleen Blamey. Reissue edition. Chicago: University of Chicago Press.

Rose-Ackerman, Susan. 1978. *Corruption: A Study in Political Economy*. New York: Academic Press.

——. 1999. *Corruption and Government: Causes, Consequences, and Reform*. Cambridge: Cambridge University Press.

Rothstein, Bo. 2011. *The Quality of Government: Corruption, Social Trust, and Inequality in International Perspective*. Chicago: University of Chicago Press.

Rothstein, Bo, and Davide Torsello. 2014. "Bribery in Preindustrial Societies: Understanding the Universalism-Particularism Puzzle." *Journal of Anthropological Research* 70(2):263–84.

Ryan, Alan. 2013. "Conceptions of Corruption, Its Causes, and Its Cure." *Social Research* 80(4):977–92.

Schattschneider, Elmer Eric. 1975. *The Semisovereign People*. New York: Dryden.

Scheppele, Kim Lane. 1999. "The Inevitable Corruption of Transition." *Connecticut Journal of International Law* 14:509–32.

Scott, James C. 1972. *Comparative Political Corruption*. Englewood Cliffs, NJ: Prentice-Hall.

——. 1998. *Seeing Like a State: How Certain Schemes to Improve the Human Condition Have Failed*. New Haven, CT: Yale University Press.

Skocpol, Theda. 1979. *States and Social Revolutions: A Comparative Analysis of France, Russia, and China*. Cambridge: Cambridge University Press.

Somers, Margaret R. 1994. "The Narrative Constitution of Identity: A Relational and Network Approach." *Theory and Society* 23(5):605–49.

——. 1998. " 'We're No Angels': Realism, Rational Choice, and Relationality in Social Science." *American Journal of Sociology* 104(3):722–84.

Steinmetz, George. 2004. "Odious Comparisons: Incommensurability, the Case Study, and 'Small N's' in Sociology." *Sociological Theory* 22(3):371–400.

Taylor, Charles. 1985. *Human Agency and Language*. Cambridge: Cambridge University Press.

Teachout, Zephyr. 2016. *Corruption in America: From Benjamin Franklin's Snuff Box to Citizens United*. Cambridge, MA: Harvard University Press.

Walzer, Michael. 1983. *Spheres of Justice: A Defense of Pluralism and Equality*. New York: Basic Books.

Weber, Max. 1946. "Religious Rejections of the World and Their Directions." In *From Max Weber*, edited by H. H. Gerth and C. Wright Mills, 323–59. New York: Oxford University Press.

Wuthnow, Robert. 1987. *Meaning and Moral Order: Explorations in Cultural Analysis*. Berkeley: University of California Press.

Wyrtzen, Jonathan. 2016. *Making Morocco: Colonial Intervention and the Politics of Identity*. Ithaca, NY: Cornell University Press.

Zerubavel, Eviatar. 1996. "Lumping and Splitting: Notes on Social Classification." *Sociological Forum* 11(3):421–33.

PART III

HOW TO COMPARE

CHAPTER 8

COMPARATIVE SOCIOLOGY, CRITICAL REALISM, AND REFLEXIVITY

GEORGE STEINMETZ

Introduction

This paper examines the evolution of sociological approaches to comparison over the past two centuries, arguing that the dominant approaches have emerged from contexts of *vernacular* or *lay* comparison. In line with the theories of science developed by Émile Durkheim, Gaston Bachelard, and Pierre Bourdieu, the starting point for this paper is epistemic wariness vis-à-vis reliance on spontaneous prenotions in conducting social research. The paper argues instead for a reflexive approach to knowledge production, along the lines proposed by Bourdieu (2004, 2022a, 2022b). Reflexivity requires a historical socioanalysis of the genesis of spontaneous forms of thought—both those of the researchers and those of the people they are studying, regardless of whether one is studying the past or present. The approach that dominated early social science was cross-cultural comparativism, which relied on universal metrics of societal modernization and progress, against which societies were assessed. The most popular social scientific approach to comparison during the last decades of the twentieth century was based on John Stuart Mill's methods of difference and agreement and was compatible with neo-positivist epistemology, as defined by critical realism (Steinmetz 2004, 2005). The defining tenets of cross-cultural comparativism and Millian comparativism—universal metrics of societal modernization and positivist epistemology—were grounded in different dimensions of common sense. After presenting these arguments, this chapter turns to a third approach to comparison, the critical realist philosophy of science, based on the philosophy of Roy Bhaskar. Like Bachelard and Bourdieu, the critical realist approach is critical of standpoint epistemologies that derive epistemic categories in an unmediated way from spontaneous practices, although it acknowledges that particular social standpoints may provide opportunities for knowledge (Bourdieu and Mammeri 2013; New 1998). Critical realism rejects two doctrines that seem ubiquitous in contemporary common sense, both inside and outside of science: empiricist ontology and positivist epistemology. In so doing, critical realism autonomizes itself from the leading approaches to comparison in society at large and within social scientific disciplines that are still permeated by neo-positivism.

The chapter's conclusion argues that this approach can be combined with a limited opening to standpoint epistemology. Both Bourdieu and critical realism recognize that sociology should maintain a foothold in common sense and prereflexive thought.[1] Bourdieu underscored the importance of circling back to spontaneous epistemologies following the initial breaks with sociologists' prenotions and with the objectification of the object of study. Critical realists recognize that subjects' social positions may present them with specific opportunities for knowledge, even if they do not automatically take advantage of these opportunities. Critical realist comparison maps closely onto the existing, nonreflexive practices of many historians, for this reason, even if most historians do not reflect explicitly on the philosophy of science.[2]

This chapter is organized into three parts. The first section briefly examines comparison as a universal aspect of human thought and social existence. Leading theories in the human and social sciences describe social life as having always been permeated by comparative practices and judgments. The second section examines the emergence of *sociological* comparativism from practices of *social* comparison, focusing on the two methods that were most influential in comparative sociology, until recently: cross-cultural comparativism, followed by Mill's methods of difference and agreement. By focusing on the contexts in which these two methodologies emerged, we can better perceive the interpenetration of social and scientific comparison. Early versions of sociological comparativism resulted from the rivalry among states and empires and from colonial settings in which policy was guided by the inherently comparative "rule of colonial difference" (Chatterjee 1993; Steinmetz 2007, 2014). The cross-cultural evolutionary forms of comparativism that were popular in the nineteenth century—Henry Maine, Herbert Spencer, Edward Tylor, and so on (Burrow 1966; Tenbruck 1992)—like their modernization-theoretical descendants in the twentieth century, reflected this overarching imperial context. Like cross-cultural comparativism, the so-called Millian method approach also emerged from a context of social comparison, but one that was internal to sociology. Key here were the competitive and therefore comparative interactions among sociologists within the disciplinary field. Sociologists struggle among themselves over theories, concepts, methods, and rankings.

The critique of these practices of sociological comparison is therefore also part of a more general criticism of social scientific reliance on spontaneous, unreflected categories in generating methods, concepts, and theories. I will return to this critique in the third section, which discusses a third approach to comparison, grounded in the critical realist philosophy of science. In the conclusion, I turn to the question of critical realism as a kind of immanent critique of historians' and social scientists' unreflected practices. This involves a definition of social standpoints as opportunities for knowledge rather than positions of epistemic privilege.

Comparison as a Basic Structure of Human Cognition and Social Life

Comparison, as a process of cognition . . . or as a process of ordering knowledge . . . is omnipresent in philosophy and science.

—Schenk and Krause (1971, 677)

Social comparisons have been decried as odious since the early modern era (Mitchell 1996; Steinmetz 2004). Critics have proposed various alternatives to comparison, ranging from nonhierarchical practices of "transculturalism" and "comparativity" (Xie 2001) to the anticomparative stance organized around the notion of "incommensurability" (Lyotard 1983; Steinmetz 2004). However, most philosophers argue that knowledge per se is impossible without seeking to identify similarities and differences between mental and/or real objects (Eggers 2016). For Plato, knowledge involves comparing empirical precepts to forms (*eidê* or *ideai*). Comparison is ubiquitous in Aristotle's thought. According to Aristotle's theory of scientific knowledge, any "definition must contain both the genus and the specific difference; that is to say, what the thing defined has in common with other things, and what distinguishes it from other things," such that "without similitude and difference, there could not . . . be knowledge of any thing" (Burnett 1774, 68). In his theory of economic exchange, Aristotle writes that "all things that are exchanged must be somehow comparable" (1941, para. 1133a). Regarding social status, Aristotle suggests that "comparison is easier when the persons belong to the same class, and more laborious when they are different" (1941, para. 1165a). Diderot's *Encyclopédie* carries a lengthy entry on comparison, according to which "there is nothing the human spirit does more often than to make comparisons. . . . It attempts to discover the relations among objects" (Diderot and d'Alembert 1778, vol. 3, 719). For Kant, "*Comparation*," the "comparison of representations with one another" (*die Vergleichung der Vorstellungen unter Einander*), is one of three basic "logical acts of understanding," alongside reflection and abstraction (Kant 1923, 94). Thinking involves comparing things in order to establish their "uniformity or diversity, their agreement [and] conflict with one another" (*Einerleiheit oder Verschiedenheit, die Einstimmung [und der] Widerstreit*) (Kant [1787] 1922, 291).[3]

Alongside this recognition of comparison as a basic operation of human cognition, social theorists have argued that *social comparatism* is a universal aspect of social existence. In English, the words comparatism and comparativism are used without any clear differentiation. In this chapter, I use social *comparatism* to designate vernacular practices of social comparison and scientific *comparativism* to designate social-scientific methodologies.

Marx analyzed capitalism as a veritable commensurating machine. Practices of comparative judgment are built into the core structures of modern capitalism—the commodity form, value form, monetary form, economic markets, social structure and class struggle, and so on. Marx argues that classification and the establishment of equivalences and differences take a specific form under capitalism—one in which *qualitatively* different practices and products are transformed in ways that allow their *quantitative* measurement and ranking. Capitalism also generates pervasive logics of competition at all levels of the class hierarchy, undercutting interpersonal solidarities and generating logics of comparison *tous azimuts*. Following suggestions made by the Frankfurt School, theorists of the "value theory of labor" (Elson 1979; Fleetwood 2001; Postone 1993) have argued that social relations and practices in general, including temporal practices, are reconfigured along the lines of abstract labor, which means that they are arranged in ways conducive to comparison.

We can look briefly at three other branches of the human sciences to illustrate the centrality of comparison:

1. **Linguistics:** Scottish philosopher James Burnett, Lord Monboddo, who helped found the first explicitly comparative scholarly field, comparative historical philology, believed that the faculty of comparison, which consisted of discovering "similitude and difference," was what "the ancient philosophers called the rational or logical faculty." Comparison was "the foundation of intellect and of all the intellectual powers of the human mind" (Burnett 1774, 179, 68) and was intrinsic to language, which evolved along with the development of human society. Comparison plays a central role in Ferdinand Saussure's linguistics (even though Saussure was opposed to historical linguistics and comparison across languages). Language, for Saussure, is organized around comparative judgments of the similarities and differences among phonemes or signifiers within a given language (Culler 1986). Structuralist

semiotics, which is part of linguistics (Barthes 1967, 11), is premised on the model of contrastive signifiers.

2. **Psychoanalysis and psychology:** Comparisons are ubiquitous in psychic life, according to Sigmund Freud. Freud argues that the unconscious operates via comparisons, in symptoms, fantasies, dream symbols, identifications, and compulsions. One familiar example is Freud's notion of the narcissism of small differences (*Narzissmus der kleinen Differenzen*; Freud 1962). According to Freud's analysis of the family novel of the neurotic, for example, some children compare their real parents to people with "higher social standing" (Freud 1909, 228). Psychologists have also been interested in the role of comparison in mental life. For Leon Festinger, there was a "universal drive for self-evaluation and the necessity for such evaluation being based on comparison with other persons," usually others judged to be close to oneself "with respect to opinions and abilities" (1954, 138).

3. **Sociology:** Comparisons have long played a central role in sociologists' theories. Durkheim's sociology of classification foregrounds the social determination of the categories actors use to define one another and the objects in their environment. Social comparison is central to Max Weber's theory of the increase in social action guided by instrumental rationality (Swedberg and Agevall 2016, 286). This parallels Marx's theory of the all-encompassing recoding of use values into exchange values. Weber argues further that social life is shot through with struggles for honor (*Ehre*)—a comparative category *par excellence*.

Bourdieu's (1979, 2013b) approach transformed Durkheim's sociology of classification and Weber's theory of status conflict into an analysis of the ways in which actors located in the same social space or field classify, evaluate, and rank one another. Such comparative struggles are central to Bourdieu's basic understanding of social existence. Participants in any given social field or space engage in constant, ongoing, reciprocal evaluations of one another, giving rise to ever-changing distributions of *symbolic* or *cultural capital*. These symbolic resources are irreducible to economic resources and indeed are sometimes orthogonal to or more significant than economic capital. Bourdieu suggests that symbolic capital is not specific to "modern" society in his analysis of struggles for honor in colonial-era Kabyle society (Bourdieu 1965). Bourdieusian studies suggest that reciprocal evaluation is characteristic of social practices in many different historical contexts, from Qing China (Will 2004) to the contemporary United States (Bourdieu 1991). The modern "aristocracy of culture" differs from capitalist elites, whose social power is grounded in economic capital. Bourdieu also argued that it was becoming increasingly possible to accumulate symbolic capital by obtaining objectified markers of symbolic capital that were less dependent on the ongoing, interactive judgments of value or on inculcation into individual habitus. Together with Marxist analyses of the value form and commodification and earlier discussions of distinction strategies by Thorstein Veblen (1899), Bourdieu's approach paved the way for discussions of present-day society as the "age of comparison" (Heintz 2016).

The Relations Between Social Comparatism and Sociological Comparativism

Taken consistently, [reflexivity] implies the need for every philosophy, if it is to be adequate, to be capable of reflectively situating itself—which entails its own production and context as well.

—Bhaskar (1997b, 141)

In my view, the history of sociology, understood as an exploration of the scientific unconscious of the sociologist through the explication of the genesis of problems, categories of thought, and instruments of analysis, constitutes an absolute prerequisite for scientific practice.

—Pierre Bourdieu (Bourdieu and Wacquant, 1992, 213–14)

A *reflexive* approach to comparative social science begins with a rupture with spontaneous conceptions of social practice and epistemology. One method of bringing the "unthought" to light is to trace the genealogy of the concepts that dominate the scientific field and snap judgments of epistemic and methodological issues. The historical sociology of science is therefore the centerpiece of sociological reflexivity (Bourdieu 2004, 2022a, 2022b; Steinmetz 2022, 2023a). In the present discussion, this approach would recommend that we examine the connections between the comparative methods embraced by sociologists and the social contexts that generated and subtended these ideas.

In this section, I will focus on two approaches to *comparativism* that have been extremely influential in sociology, and I will suggest that they were shaped by practices of *social comparatism*. In the first example, official and public comparisons among empires and states gave rise to social-scientific forms of intercultural comparison. These social-scientific approaches perpetuated some of the assumptions of "lay" cross-cultural comparatism, including the belief in generalized progress and a social ontology organized around nation-states. Postwar American modernization policies provided this nineteenth-century formation with a second lease on life in sociology and neighboring social sciences.

My second example is the adoption of Mill's natural science methodology by historical sociologists and political scientists in the 1980s. Unlike the first

example, this did not involve any direct reproduction of vernacular comparative practices. Instead, the enthusiasm among qualitative sociologists for the
Millian method was stoked by their marginal status with a discipline dominated by quantitative and positivist methods (Calhoun 1996). The Millian
method provided a positivist solution to the problem of comparison within
"small N" research. The Millian method assumed that it was possible to identify
generalized causal regularities at the macro-sociological scale. The plausibility
of this idea stemmed in part from the relative social and geopolitical stability of the postwar, Cold War United States and world, or more precisely, the
description of that social stability in the public culture of the time. This context allowed sociologists to perceive resonances and analogies between, on the
one hand, the "constant conjunctions of events" at the heart of neo-positivist
epistemology and, on the other hand, their immediate experiences of stability
in their private and professional lives, the perceived stability of global political
events due to the Soviet-American condominium, and the repetitive patterns of
postwar Fordist economic growth and prosperity (Steinmetz 2004). Two types
of context lent credibility to Millian comparativism, one "meso-level," entailing
comparisons among sociologists within the disciplinary field, and the other
"macro-level," involving arrangements of capitalist regulation and geopolitical
diplomacy.[4]

The Comparative Method as Cross-Cultural Sociology

The determination of the cross-cultural comparative method by lay practices
of comparison had important consequences for various aspects of this method,
including the definition of analytic units, the understanding of the directionality of history, and the vision of the dominated, peripheral polities and
societies in the world system. Societies have always been connected through
the circulation of goods, ideas, and people, and as a result, they have always
compared themselves to one another. Cross-societal comparison was "part of
theological and historical literature from the beginning" (Tenbruck 1992, 16).
This is evident in ancient philosophers and historians such as Herodotus, Poly-
bius, and Tacitus, in Al Biruni and Ibn Khaldun (Karataşlı and Clark, 2022),
and in Vico, Montesquieu, and Tocqueville in the era leading up to the rise
of modern social science. Throughout history, states and empires have been
embedded within global power systems whose dynamics were both coopera-
tive and competitive, generating comparative imperatives (Speich-Chassé 2020;
Steinmetz, 2019a, 2019b). *Fields* of international relations exist where a group of
states agrees on common stakes of competition for field-specific forms of symbolic capital, where each state recognizes the others as belonging to this field
and where each refuses membership to outsiders. In settled international fields,

all of the players concur on an ordinal ranking of states (Bigo 2011; Steinmetz 2008, 546; 2017a).

The organic intellectuals of empires tend to think comparatively and globally. One of the main factors leading states to acquire overseas empires and colonies and guiding their understanding of their imperial mission was comparison with their precursors and competitors. Julia Hell (2019) analyzes the ways in which European imperial rulers for two millennia compared their histories to the fall and ruination of the Roman empire, leading to an array of katechontic strategies. Other historians examine bilateral comparisons: European colonizers compared themselves to other colonial powers, compared among the colonies making up their empires, and compared the Indigenous groups within a single colony. Imperial ministries and officials compared the "native policies" in their colonies to the practices of rival colonizers (Steinmetz 2007). Anticolonial Europeans engaged in interimperial comparisons, or contrasted their state's overseas policies with normative ideals, decrying "un-British rule" in "Anglo-India" (Darwin 2009, 180) or attacking the League of Nations mandates system for failing to live up to its promises (Pedersen 2015).

Once Europe embarked on its project of overseas imperial expansion in the fifteenth century, the old frameworks of civilization and barbarism were reworked into a massive new comparative edifice. America, East Asia, Africa, and the Near East and their cultures, religions, and peoples provided the foil for this comparative imagination (Steinmetz 2007). European control over the terms of comparison, the *tertium comparationis*, operated as a tool of intellectual imperialism. Europeans who wrote cross-cultural comparative texts between 1500 and the mid-twentieth century were situated at the dominant pole of an imperial relationship between polities, although they dealt with this condition in differing ways. Some Europeans rejected claims to cultural superiority; some recognized difference without positing a hierarchy of values; and some attempted to understand the foreign culture on its own terms (Merle 1969; Steinmetz 2014). Cultural comparativism emerged from everyday *comparatism* in imperial situations. Sociology, emerging in the nineteenth century, retained the ontology of separate, competing, self-enclosed states and the category of "society" as a correlate of these states (Tenbrück 1992). American postwar modernization theory and politics reaffirmed these ontological and methodological assumptions. During the twentieth century, intellectuals and politicians in the European colonies experimented with ideas of pan-Africanism, pan-Asianism, and pan-Arabism and nonaligned politics. Yet this experimental phase quickly came to an end after the last colonies became independent around 1962 and the bipolar Cold War schism of the United States and Soviet Union came to completely dominate the global geopolitical imagination. The independent postcolonies now reaffirmed political nationalism; social thought in the core countries pulled back into the metropoles.

The 1960s was therefore the heyday of the cross-cultural comparative approach in the United States and countries like Germany that had been occupied, militarily and intellectually, by the United States. According to the postwar German sociologist Erwin Scheuch, "if there is one feature that sets off the sociology of the 1960's from that of the preceding decades, it is the sudden increase of interest in cross-cultural comparisons" (1967, 10). An American sociologist wrote around the same time that "interest in the comparative method today springs from the tremendous surge in cross-national or international research on the part of rural sociologists and other social scientists" and, in particular, from "the increasing international participation of the United States in foreign areas, which has opened many new opportunities to social scientists for study and research" (Suchman 1964, 124). U.S.-based social scientists received enormous sums of military funding to carry out "comparative" studies geared toward American foreign policy (Cullather 2002; Gilman 2003; Rohde 2013). Modernization theory reflected "the expansion of American political, military, and economic interests throughout the world" (Tipps 1973, 208). The "increasing international participation of the United States in foreign areas" was also a euphemism for counterinsurgency research (Robin 2001). Yet the torrent of cross-cultural comparative research narrowed to a thin rivulet by the end of the 1960s. Modernization theory was now decried as imperialist and racist (Mazrui 1968). A survey of books scanned by Google reveals that the term "comparative sociology" peaked around 1969 and reached a nadir in 1995 (Deville 2016, 19).

Several factors contributed to the decline of cross-national and cross-cultural research. Alongside the critique of science subordinated to military and diplomatic goals was the reemergent critique of positivism (Bryant 1975; Giddens 1974). Antipositivism in the social sciences had always rejected universal laws of societal development and definitions of social progress (Steinmetz 2020a). Rising awareness of globalization and transnationalism eroded confidence in the cross-cultural comparative paradigm. A final factor undermining modernization theory was growing disagreement among its practitioners (Knöbl 2003, 104). Rather than reconfiguring comparativism to take transnational flows and circuits into account, most social scientists simply abandoned macro-comparison. That said, theories rarely disappear entirely in the social sciences; rather, they continue to haunt the scientific unconscious and reappear in new guises. Examples are recent theories of the "reflexivity of modernity" and cultural "neo-institutionalism," which reproduce many of the assumptions of classic American modernization theory, including the idea that the United States (or Europe) is "the archetypal modern society" and that "Western history is to be understood as a process of modernization or convergence on the American" or European archetype, "thanks to the diffusion of American-style economic and political organizational forms" and secularized individualism

(Woodiwiss 2007, 112). Because of the power of comparativism in the geopolitical imaginary of the United States, imperial ideologies are extremely likely to resurface periodically in U.S. social thought.[5] Resistance to lay ideology is weakened even further in American sociology due to its willful embrace of self-heteronomization in forms like "public sociology" and "policy sociology" (Burawoy 2005). U.S. sociology's aggressive parochialism, conflation of scientific reflexivity with self-identity (see below), and hostility to any sustained discussion of epistemology render it poorly equipped even to recognize the resurgence of these modernization-theoretic topoi and tenets.

"Chemical" Comparativism—The "Millian" Method

Neo-positivist epistemology and quantitative methods began to dominate the American sociology field in the 1970s.[6] This was the same period in which an alternative comparative approach based on Mill's methods of difference and agreement was proposed to historical sociologists (Skocpol 1979). This method was presented as acceptable to a positivist discipline and as not being susceptible to the critiques of modernization theory. Cross-cultural social research now also turned toward survey statistics, "within-nation differences" (Rokkan and Valen 1966), and "microfoundations" (Przeworski and Teune 1970). However, the most influential approach was the Millian one, since it was compatible with small Ns and qualitative sources.

In 1980, Theda Skocpol published a highly influential article with Margaret Somers that presented three different approaches to comparative macro-sociology. The authors described the first two approaches, "contrast of cases" and "parallel demonstration of theory," as being uninterested in "making causal inferences." The third approach, which the authors preferred, was labeled "macro-causal analysis," emphasizing *causal* inference. Skocpol and Somers went on to further specify this "macro-causal" approach by referring to John Stuart Mill's discussion of the methods of chemistry in his *System of Logic*:

> Logically speaking, Macro-analysts proceed according to one of two basic analytic designs, or a combination of these. On the one hand, Macro-analysts can try to establish that several cases having in common the phenomenon to be explained also have in common the hypothesized causal factors, although the cases vary in other ways that might have seemed causally relevant. This approach was once labelled by John Stuart Mill the "Method of Agreement." On the other hand, Macro-analysts can contrast cases in which the phenomenon to be explained and the hypothesized causes are present to other ("negative") cases in which the phenomenon and the causes are both absent, although they

are as similar as possible to the "positive" cases in other respects. This procedure Mill called the "Method of Difference." (Skocpol and Somers 1980, 183)

Mill's approach, they continued, was exemplified by Barrington Moore, Jr.'s
Social Origins of Dictatorship and Democracy (1966) and Skocpol's *States and
Social Revolutions* (1979).

I do not intend to revisit the various critiques of Skocpol's use of the Millian
approach. It is probably enough to recall that Mill himself argued that "in the
Social Science experiments are impossible," the "Method of Difference inapplicable," and "the Methods of Agreement, and of Concomitant Variations,
inconclusive" (Mill 1843, Book VI).[7] The positivist Durkheim agreed that Mill's
"method of agreement and the method of difference are scarcely usable" in
sociology (Durkheim 1982, 150–51). In the most damning critique, William
Sewell, Jr. (1996) pointed out that the three cases in Skocpol's *States and Revolutions* can hardly be considered independent trials, as required in a true experiment, since each revolution influenced the subsequent ones.

The rise of the Millian approach can also be understood as another example
of the effects of social contexts of comparatism on scientific change. Unlike
cross-cultural comparison, however, the key context shaping theory choice in
this instance was not a macro-historical one but was located within the competitive field of U.S. sociology itself. The pressure on sociologists to prove that they
were truly scientific became more intense in the decades after World War II,
given the triumph of military science, technical advances in computing, and the
weakening of systematic challenges to methodological positivism (Steinmetz
2005). There was no "positivism debate" in U.S. sociology. Historicism and historical Marxism were evacuated from U.S. sociology during the McCarthy era,
as even Robert K. Merton renounced *Wissenssoziologie* and warned that any
investigation of "the connections between sciences and society consititute[d]
a subject matter which ha[d] become tarnished for academic sociologists who
know that it is close to the heart of Marxist sociology" (Merton 1952, 15). In the
1970s and 1980s, Marxist sociology tended to adopt a positivist epistemology.
It was within this context that Skocpol argued that the goal of comparative
historical research was "to identify invariant causal configurations" (Skocpol
1984, 378). Skocpol and Somers praised the Millian methods of difference and
agreement precisely because they "resemble multivariate hypothesis-testing"
(1980, 175). Deployment of Mill's method for chemistry was aimed at winning
acceptance in a discipline with many members who were powerfully identified
with the ego ideal of the natural sciences and its supposed methods. Adoption
of the Millian method represented an attempt to mimic the dominant methods
in the field of sociology. Mimicry itself is an inherently comparative practice
(Bhabha 2004).

The Millian approach remained influential within comparative historical sociology (CHS) during a relatively brief period, compared to the earlier cross-cultural comparative approach, but this was the foundational period for CHS, as it is still known.[8] Its prominence after 1980 is largely responsible for the fact that "historical sociology" does not exist apart from "comparative sociology" as a section in the American Sociological Association. As Sewell points out, the conjunction of "historical" and "comparative" sociology "places as much emphasis on comparative method as on historical subject matter. In this respect, historical sociologists reveal themselves to be in the mainstream of American sociology. By stressing comparative method, they participate eagerly in the discipline's obsessive concern to justify itself as a science. Comparative method, after all, is the standard alternative to mainstream statistical methods when the number of cases is insufficiently large" (Sewell 1996, 246). More than four decades later, historical sociology remains yoked to comparative sociology, which still often engages in comparisons across "societies" or states and relies on the Millian method.

Despite these critiques, the "Millian" episode represented an important moment in the maturation of comparative methodologies in sociology insofar as it did not replicate comparative methodologies found outside social science in the "real" world but was an entirely intrafield affair. Methodological nationalism was not inherent in the Millian method. Nor did this method assume that societies evolved progressively along the lines of Europe or the United States. Indeed, the Millian method was shorn of all substantive commitments and political assumptions, like American social science (and art, music, literature, and criticism) in the McCarthy era, concerned mainly with formal, technical issues (Steinmetz forthcoming). Historical sociology's links to discussions of overdetermination, ontology, and normativity in the 1920s and 1930s were broken; disciplinary collective memory was damaged (Steinmetz 2020b).

By the 1990s, the Millian approach was said to be in terminal demise. Yet like the previous comparative method, it continued to inhabit the netherworld museums of defunct ideas, ready to reemerge when needed. A more important lasting effect was the gesture of wrenching historical material out of its contexts and forcing it into formats that could be legible to the discipline's positivist core. Mill *flattened* history into a table of variables, just as other approaches froze history into linear and curvilinear equations, immobile network diagrams, rigid models, multivariate data tables, and so on. Ontology, normativity, processual fluidity, and contingency—the hallmarks of the first wave of truly historical sociology in Weimar Germany (Steinmetz 2020a)—were nowhere to found.[9]

As I will argue below, a reflexive social science needs to first separate itself as much as possible from its social contexts and unexamined "prenotions" in order to consciously construct its object, before finally circling back to its starting point. The Millian method made a first break with spontaneous knowledge, an "objectifying" break, but it did not complete the reflexive circle, and it made this break in reaction to a dominant other. Before discussing this Bourdieusian theory of reflexivity, however, I want to present an alternative to the cross-cultural and Millian methods based on the critical realist philosophy of science. After presenting this approach, I will ask whether it, too, was related to contexts, including contexts of lay comparativism.

Critical Realism and Comparative Social Science

A different understanding of the problem of comparison can be derived from the critical realist philosophy of science.[10] Critical realism begins by arguing that the worlds studied by natural science are stratified *open systems*, insofar as a multiplicity of causal mechanisms interact both contingently and in semi-regular ways, generating empirical events. Causal mechanisms are defined as structures or entities with powers that may be possessed unexpressed or expressed unperceived. Reality is stratified ontologically along two dimensions. First, it is stratified into the levels of real mechanisms and empirical events; second, it is stratified into real levels emerging from other real levels.

The causal mechanisms of the human sciences differ ontologically from those in the natural sciences in three main ways (Bhaskar 1979, 1986). First, social structures are activity dependent, meaning that they do not exist independently of the practices they govern. Second, they are concept dependent, meaning that the practices constituting a social structure do not exist independently of the meanings associated with them. Social things are thing-like only in a very particular way. They are thing-like in Durkheim's sense (i.e., meaning that they are emergent from physical and biological strata and cannot be reduced to the latter). They may even exercise *downward causation* on those lower levels. But social mechanisms are *not* thing-like insofar as they cannot even be described without determining what they mean to the actors who bear them or carry them out. Third, social mechanisms are time and space dependent; that is, they vary across history and geography. Critical realism is the exact opposite of an approach that believes that theory "provides an objective base . . . that is applicable to [all] settings, cultures and times" (Baert 2005, 194). Critical realism is interested precisely in discovering how far a given causal mechanism can travel in time and space and where the limits are located. As Heikki Patomäki (2020, 441) writes, for critical realism, "the object of study . . . may be geo-historically specific, liable to diversity within any given world-historical epoch, and open to further changes and new forms of emergence in the future." Social scientific concepts are therefore *historical concepts*, concepts linked to particular times and places.

If the world studied by the natural sciences is an open system, and the social is emergent from the physical and biological levels, then it follows that the social must also be an open system with a rainforest-like plethora of causal mechanisms, events, and processes. Social events will therefore be overdetermined in complex, contingent ways and cannot be explained in terms of a single cause or uniform conjunction of causes. Social scientists may well identify small-scale patterns or *demi-regularities*—the "occasional, but less than universal, actualization of a mechanism, or cluster of mechanisms, over a definite region of time-space" (Lawson 2013, 149). These demi-regularities are valuable, however, *not* as evidence of a constant conjunction or general law, though they may "provide a prima facie indication of an occasional, but less than universal, actualization of a mechanism or tendency" (Hartwig 2007, 116). Rather, demi-regularities are the markers of a temporary stabilization of social practices and a temporary suturing of symbolic systems.

That said, social scientists cannot be restricted to the study of demi-regularities. They should also be interested in historical processes and changes, including crises and catastrophes, turning points, and singular, unique events. None of these event types is subsumable under the category of a universal empirical regularity or general law. Indeed, one important type of historical event is one that *destroys* social entities with generative powers (Steinmetz 2008). The processual, neo-historicist sociologists of Wilhelmine Germany and the Weimar Republic understood this, from Wilhelm Dilthey through Karl Mannheim and Hans Freyer, but this insight was resisted by most American sociologists, with the partial exception of pragmatists like John Dewey and early critical realists like Roy Wood Sellars (Steinmetz 2020a, 2020b).

How, then, does critical realism *explain*? Critical realism embraces the idea of causality, but it understands *cause* in a distinctive way. Causal mechanisms in both the social and natural sciences are described as real entities or structures with specific powers and tendencies that may be possessed without being exercised or realized or realized without being perceived (Bhaskar 1997a, 184).[11] The unconscious in psychoanalytic theory is an example of an underlying causal mechanism that possesses particular causal powers and that tends to produce empirically observable symptoms. However, the events (i.e., symptoms) produced by the inherent powers of the unconscious may be suppressed by other causal mechanisms. Awareness of such events may also be suppressed. In open systems, multiple causal mechanisms also coexist and interact with one other, producing streams of events or ongoing processes. The other distinction, mentioned earlier, is that social structures do not exist separately from practices and the meanings imposed on them by actors but are consubstantial with practices and meanings.

Theories in critical realism are distinguished from *explanations*. A single event or process may be explained, but explanation will usually involve a panoply of causes. Each causal mechanism becomes the focus of a specific theory. Theories are concepts, pictures, models, or narratives that describe particular causal entities as having specific structures, powers, and tendencies (Mumford and Anjum 2011). Theory is not situated at the empirical level of events, as in some pragmatic approaches, even though social structures only exist in the form of practices. The goal of science is generalization, as in positivism, but generalization consists not in the form of constant conjunctions of events but in the form of statements about the inherent powers of causal mechanisms with powers that may or may not be expressed, depending on the context, interacting in a particular constellation at a particular moment.

The explanation of a unique event involves constructing a plausible model of the unique conjuncture of causes that combined to generate the event. The historian or social scientist engages in *retroductive* (not inductive or deductive) analysis in order to assess the model's plausibility. *Retroduction* is defined as "inference from effects to explanatory structures." It is a form of "inference to the best explanation" that infers by answering the question "What made X possible?" (Hartwig 2007, 257). A retroductive argument is one that necessitates "the building of a model of the mechanism which, if it were to exist and act in the postulated way, would account for the phenomenon concerned" (Bhaskar 1986, 61). Some of these mechanisms will be familiar from other case studies or theoretical discussions. Some causes may be familiar from existing analyses of demi-regularities. The creation of a model involves *analogy*, which is a subtype of comparison because the conjectured structure that is being modeled is unknown and not directly observed (Bhaskar 1986, 61). As Mario Bunge notes (2004), "because mechanisms are largely or totally imperceptible, they must be conjectured." The movement of analysis is not from the particular to the universal, but from the concrete to the abstract and back again.

Nor is analysis a one-time operation. Instead, analysis involves a continual cycling between new empirical material and new retroductive inferences, and then back to new empirical checks on the plausibility of the model. Theoretical construction is therefore, like psychoanalysis, an "interminable" process. There always remains a hiatus between concept and real object—an "irrational hiatus" in the neo-Kantian sense between theoretical concept and the object of which it is the concept. Critical realism, like pragmatism, is firmly wedded to a *fallibilist* understanding of knowledge (Elder-Vass 2022).

How does this relate to sociological comparison? In contrast to natural sciences like chemistry, it is impossible to carry out genuine controlled experiments in the social sciences, for ontological and ethical reasons. Comparative sociology instead takes two main forms under a realist description, focused alternatively on the ontological levels of the *real* and the *empirical*. Logics of case selection vary according to which of these levels is prioritized. Bhaskar distinguishes between the domains of the *real* and the *actual*, which correspond respectively to the realms of causal mechanisms and events, and between the actual and the empirical, noting that mechanisms may be realized (at the level of the actual) without being perceived (at the level of the empirical).

The first approach compares cases in which the common factor is some causally efficacious structure, process, or mechanism that figures as the *tertium comparationis* across multiple empirical cases. Two events that are remote from one another in time or space may therefore be usefully and fruitfully compared as long as they are suspected of having one or more causal mechanisms in common. There is no requirement that the compared events belong to the same empirical category. This approach warrants comparisons between "unrelated societies"—to use Marc Bloch's (1928) phrase. We may be interested in the causal impact of the introduction of capitalist social relations in two otherwise very different social spaces or historical periods, for example. We may be interested in the impact of the bipolar Cold War geopolitical structure on different locations in the Global South. This approach is inherently autonomous from spontaneous sociology since it requires looking beyond and beneath surface-level appearances and positing the existence of underlying causes.

The second approach takes a form that is more familiar within spontaneous sociology. Here, the cases being compared belong to the same empirical category—as revolutions, empires, genocides, pandemics, collapsed states, authoritarian governments, social movements, economic crises or boom periods, and so on. Critical realism cautions that a different causal nexus may explain each instance of a single event type. Such causal variability is consistent with what we know about the openness of social systems and the universality of contingent causation (Knöbl 2016; Steinmetz 1998; Vogt 2011; Windelband 1870). Indeed, comparison may be used to identify and point to contingency and to call attention to the absence of universal laws. Comparison can demonstrate that different conjunctures of causes lead to similar empirical events or that the same set of causes is associated with different empirical events. Comparing units of a single empirical category and finding causal variation leads to counterintuitive narratives and thus, once again, to enhanced autonomy from spontaneous forms of thought. Adopting critical realism tends to enhance researchers' analytic autonomy.

Given the earlier discussion, the reader might ask how critical realism is related to its contexts, including contexts of lay comparativism. In contrast to the Millian method, it is difficult to argue that critical realism emerged as a strategic move within sociology. Its main institutional location between the 1970s and early 2010s was, first, British philosophy and then other British and a few Scandinavian social science disciplines. Although the main venue for discussions of critical realism, *Journal for the Theory of Social Behaviour*, was coedited in the United States, it was extremely marginal to sociology. Only since the mid-2010s has critical realism had any effect on discussions in U.S.

sociology, gaining traction as neo-positivism fades away and declares its defeat in the face of a "culminating crisis in sociology" rooted in post-positivism (e.g., House 2019) or relinquishes reasoned argument, lashing out with obscenities (Healy 2017). The specific role of critical realism within discussions of comparative and historical sociology is only starting to be felt, for example in the present collection.

There is a different way to consider the question of critical realism's relations to its contexts, however. Critical realism seems esoteric to some sociologists, due to Bhaskar's deployment of Kantian and Hegelian logics and language. Some sociologists complain about the complexity of critical realism's ontological furniture and recommend pragmatism as being oriented toward everyday language and solving immediate problems and as "anti-intellectualist" (James 1907, 41). It is far from obvious, however, that "anti-intellectual" languages closer to spontaneous understandings are the best place to begin even if one wants to solve immediate problems. There is a different answer, which is that critical realism may map closely onto the philosophy of science that undergirds much of the work done by excellent historians, even when they avoid epistemological discussions (Steinmetz 1998). It is simply putting that more spontaneous epistemology, rooted in centuries of historiographic research, into a language that can be abstracted from the practices of any one discipline.

What about historians? I may seem to have just argued that historians' spontaneous epistemologies are already adequate for carrying out historical research. Does this mean there is a "historians' standpoint," akin to György Lukács's "proletarian standpoint" or Sandra Harding's "feminist standpoint"? I will have more to say in the next section about the proper place for "standpoints" and immanent knowledge. Critical realism does function as a form of reflexivity for (social) scientists but has not worked out a satisfactory answer to the question of the place of spontaneous knowledge in social science. This is where Bourdieu's theory of epistemic reflexivity can complement critical realism.[12]

Epistemic Reflexivity, Spontaneous and Implicit Knowledge, and Comparison

As history moves forward, this space of possibilities closes in, among other reasons because the alternatives from which the historically established choice emerged have been forgotten. And one of the forces of historical necessity that is exerted by way of objectivation and incorporation bears on the fact that the co-possible possibilities [or] lateral possibilities, those possibilities that surround the possibility actually realized, are not only discarded, but discarded as possibilities. The realized possibility has a kind of destiny effect. One of the

virtues of historical sociology or social history is precisely to reawaken these
dead possibilities, the lateral possibilities, and offer a certain freedom.

—Pierre Bourdieu, *On the State* (January 24, 1991)

Bourdieu's approach steers clear of narcissistic, solipsistic, and confessional versions of reflexivity centered on identity, including scientists' identities. This does not mean that Bourdieu ignores the possibility that individuals may gain more conscious, reflexive control over their own conditions of existence. Indeed, this is a central goal of social science, in his view. One means of enhancing self-control involves reshaping the habitus through "repeated exercises . . . like an athletic training" (Bourdieu 2000, 172). However, Bourdieu's most significant thinking about reflexivity is directed at scientists. The term *reflexivity* in Bourdieu's writings refers mainly to the "epistemic vigilance" necessarily to conduct social research (Bourdieu and Heilbron 2022).

Bourdieu suggests that sociological researchers should make two epistemological "breaks" in analyzing social practices. The first is a break with their own categories, that is, with the scientific prenotions with which they enter the discipline or which they find ready at hand within the sociological field. Carrying out this first break necessitates a historical sociology of the scientific field or subfield in which one is active. By studying the history of battles, revolutions, and settlements within the field, one can understand its configuration at the moment of analysis.

The sociologist also needs to enact a second break with the spontaneous categories of the people they are studying, rather than assuming that they live in a world untroubled by symbolic conflict and logics of symbolic domination. This entails a reconstruction of the genesis of the categories guiding our research subjects' practice. If our subjects are past social scientists, we will need to identify the social location of the speakers within the disciplinary field and the hidden presuppositions and arrangements of power within that field at the time of their utterances.

Reflexivity does not involve tracing simple correlations between a thinker's social origins or demographic properties and their ideas. Social origins are rarely irrelevant for intellectual work, but they may be less important than the history of the thinker's socialization and the history of the fields in which they are active. Habitus is reworked within the scientific field in an ongoing way, along with dynamics and struggles and movements within the field space. Aging and various contexts outside the scientific field also account for transformations.[13]

Bourdieu also suggested the need for a third break with the sociologist's initial "objectification" of the research object (Bourdieu 1972, 2). This may involve a distancing from the "scholastic" representation (statistical or otherwise) used to make a first break with spontaneous ways of mentally organizing social reality. Bourdieu's redeployment of his early essay on the Kabyle house as an "Appendix" in *Logic of Practice* (1990, 317n1) illustrates both the second and third epistemological "breaks." Bourdieu presents this essay as evidence for the evolution of his theory as an ongoing process moving from prenotions to scientific objectification, on to a more adequate final product. The static structural analysis of "The Kabyle House" represented a necessary first stage of "objectivist reconstruction" en route to the "more complete and more complex" final interpretation centered on practice as strategy (Bourdieu 1990, 317n1). In other words, the original Kabyle house essay is reprinted (in Bourdieu 1990) to illustrate both the second, objectifying break and the third, practice-theoretic reinterpretation.

The third break may also entail a rapprochement with the initial forms of "spontaneous" knowledge from which the analyst originally distanced themselves. According to Bourdieu, "there are extraordinary advantages in the fact of being native, on condition one knows what this implies, that is, everything it hides" (2013a, 207). The feminist critical realist Carolyn New (1998) makes a similar point, writing that nonscientific standpoints may provide access to knowledge while also blocking knowledge.

Sociological reflexivity differs from standpoint theory, then, without rejecting it entirely. Both Bourdieu and critical realism reject the definition of reflexivity as an "exercise of introspection" (Bourdieu and Heilbron 2022, 13), a confession of intimate secrets, or a recitation of the speaker's demographic origins and properties. The idea of a knowledge standpoint based on first-hand experience can be a part of reflexivity, but it cannot be the starting point and is inadequate in and of itself. There is, strictly speaking, no "proletarian standpoint," no "feminist standpoint," no "subaltern standpoint," if standpoint is defined (e.g., Go 2016, 159) as a "social position of knowing." Or rather, it may be a social position of some sort of knowing, but it is not in itself a social position granting access to reflexive, social scientific knowledge. Indeed, the *spontaneous standpoint* is likely to have encoded societal and field-level symbolic settlements of previous battles and to have accepted the "destiny effect" as described by Bourdieu in the epigraph to this section. Spontaneous thought is likely to have discarded as possibilities all of the "lateral possibilities" that once surrounded the "possibility that was actually realized," the path that was actually taken. Lukács's original formulation of standpoint theory was not oriented toward accepting proletarian's *spontaneous* perspectives, which were mired in reification. For Lukács, the possibility of attaining knowledge of capitalism stemmed from the fact that the proletariat shared its reified ontological status with the commodities that constitute the essential structure of capitalism (Lukács 1971, 168).

Turning back to the question of comparativism, we can now summarize the approach pursued in this chapter. The first step was a genealogy of the vernacular and the sociological approaches to comparison. This helped us understand the ways in which scientific approaches bear the traces of past and present contexts located both inside and outside the scientific field. Sociological comparativism needed to make two breaks: with spontaneous social ontologies and epistemologies that were state-centric and progressivist and with comparative methods that were epistemologically positivist. Critical realism broke more decisively with its contexts and has been correspondingly more autonomous. By reconnecting the genealogy of alternative methods of comparison, we become more attuned to resurgent forms of epistemic imperialism (e.g., contemporary theories of reflexive modernity), epistemic positivism, methodological nation-statism, empire-ism, or society-ism.

Notes

1. This is especially clear in the realm of ethics, where the only alternatives to the derivation of norms via imminent critique are deductivism and relativism (Steinmetz 2017b).
2. It is paradoxical that the more deliberate discussions of methodology among sociologists and political scientists have tended to immunize them against these spontaneous forms of insight.
3. Kant also addressed the related concept of *analogy*, which I understand as a subtype of comparison. Analogy is "the equivalence of two qualitative relations, or a complete similarity between fully dissimilar things" (Brockhaus 1822, 206). I do not have space here to deal separately with analogy as a concept, but see Griffiths (2016).
4. On the determination of social knowledge by social contexts located at different scales and degrees of social proximity to the point of intellectual production, see Steinmetz (2023a, 2023b).
5. Indeed, one of the most prominent examples of an imperialist imposition of American comparativism on the non-American world involves the ostensibly anticolonial ideologies of African American internationalism, which imposes American concerns on the history of nonalignment (Vitalis 2013, 269).
6. As I argued in Steinmetz (2005), the various elements of the full-fledged "methodological positivist" configuration in sociology were elaborated in earlier periods. This configuration had three key elements: epistemological positivism, ontological empiricism, and methodological scientism. The constellation emerged in full force after 1945, but it did not come to completely dominate the discipline until the 1970s and 1980s.
7. Skocpol's contradiction of Mill's own guidance on the use of his methods was pointed out by Lieberson (1994, 1226).
8. A different alternative based on Boolean algebra and fuzzy set theory was elaborated by U.S. sociologist Charles Ragin (1987, 2008).
9. In this original formation of historicist historical sociology, social processes were no longer simply seen merely as being historical but as being fully processual, even "in their molecular structure," as Freyer (1930, 171) put it. Historical social process, according to Alfred Weber, had to be conceived of as a "life stream" (*Lebensstrom*), not as a snapshot or a series of discrete events, much less as universal, teleological trajectories (Weber 1927, 16–17, 39). Karl Mannheim spoke of the "the reality of the fluid basis" (*Faktum der gleitenden Basis*) in human existence, thought, and philosophy, defending

a position he called "dynamic relationalism" (Mannheim 1929, 821, 825). These positions differed not only from teleological narratives of historical progress but also from positivism, which requires ontological stability.

10. Critical realism was initially introduced by Roy Bhaskar and carried forward by a number of British sociologists and philosophers and is now being developed by an international network of scholars; see http://criticalrealismnetwork.org/. Critical realism was introduced to the social sciences in Bhaskar's doctor of philosophy thesis in 1972, published as Bhaskar (2018); it was introduced into comparative historical sociology in Steinmetz (1993).

11. The argument that a generative mechanism may be possessed unexercised and exercised unrealized is at the core of critical realists' rejection of Popperian falsificationism as a guide to theory choice.

12. For a different use of Bourdieu's theory of reflexivity to elucidate Bhaskar's view of the transformation of nonscientific actors' "proto-theories into formal models of social structure," see Singh (2018).

13. Bourdieu's approach differs sharply from Beck, Giddens, and Lash (1994), who describe "modernity" as an era in which social classes, structures, and distributional conflicts are replaced by individualism, identities, and what they call "reflexivity" (Woodiwiss 2007).

References

Aristotle. 1941. "Nichomachean Ethics." In *The Basic Works*, edited by Richard McKeon, 935–1126. New York: Modern Library.

Baert, Patrick. 2005. "Towards a Pragmatist-Inspired Philosophy of Social Science." *Acta Sociologica* 48(3):191–203.

Barthes, Roland. 1967. *Elements of Semiology*. London: Cape.

Beck, Ulrich, Anthony Giddens, and Scott Lash. 1994. *Reflexive Modernization: Politics, Tradition and Aesthetics in the Modern Social Order*. Stanford, CT: Stanford University Press.

Bhabha, Homi. 2004. *The Location of Culture*. New York: Routledge.

Bhaskar, Roy. 1979. *The Possibility of Naturalism: A Philosophical Critique of the Contemporary Human Sciences*. New York: Humanities.

——. 1986. *Scientific Realism and Human Emancipation*. London: Verso.

——. 1997a. *A Realist Theory of Science*. London: Verso.

——. 1997b. "On the Ontological Status of Ideas." *Journal for the Theory of Social Behaviour* 27(2/3):139–47.

——. 2018. *Empiricism and the Metatheory of the Social Sciences*. New York: Routledge.

Bigo, Didier. 2011. "Pierre Bourdieu and International Relations: Power of Practices, Practices of Power." *International Political Sociology* 5(3):225–58.

Bloch, Marc. 1928. "Pour une histoire comparée des sociétés européennes." *Revue de synthèse historique* 46:15–50.

Bourdieu, Jérôme, and Johan Heilbron. 2022. "De la vigilance épistémologique à la réflexité." In *Retour sur la réflexivité*, edited by Pierre Bourdieu, 9–29. París: Editions de l'Ecole des Hautes Etudes en Sciences Sociales.

Bourdieu, Pierre. 1965. "The Sentiment of Honour in Kabyle Society." In *Honour and Shame: The Values of Mediterranean Society*, edited by John G. Peristiany, 191–241. London: Weidenfeld and Nicholson.

——. 1972. *Esquisse d'une théorie de la pratique*. Genéve, Switzerland: Librairie Droz.

——. 1979. *La distinction: Critique sociale du jugement*. Paris: Les Éditions de Minuit.

——. 1990. *The Logic of Practice*. Stanford, CA: Stanford University Press.

——. 1991. "On the Possibility of a Field of World Sociology." In *Social Theory for a Changing Society*, edited by Pierre Bourdieu and James S. Coleman, 373–87. Boulder, CO: Westview.

——. 2000. *Pascalian Meditations*. Cambridge: Polity.

——. 2004. *Science of Science and Reflexivity*. Chicago: University of Chicago Press.

——. 2013a. "The Right Use of Ethnology, Interview with Mahmoud Mammeri." In *Algerian Sketches*, edited by Pierre Bourdieu, 203–23. Cambridge: Polity.

——. 2013b. "Séminaires sur le concept de champ, 1972–1975." *Actes de la Recherche en Sciences Sociales* 200:4–37.

——. 2022a. "Réflexivité narcissique et réflexivité scientifique." In *Retour sur la réflexivité*, edited by Pierre Bourdieu, 45–60. París: Editions de l'Ecole des Hautes Etudes en Sciences Sociales.

——. 2022b. *Retour sur la réflexivité*. Paris: Editions de l'Ecole des Hautes Etudes en Sciences Sociales.

Bourdieu, Pierre, and Loïc Wacquant. 1992. *An Invitation to Reflexive Sociology*. Chicago: University of Chicago Press.

Bourdieu, Pierre, and Mahmoud Mammeri. 2013. "The Right Use of Ethnology, Interview with Mahmoud Mammeri." In *Algerian Sketches*, edited by Pierre Bourdieu, 203–23. Cambridge: Polity.

Brockhaus. 1822. "Analogie." In *Allgemeine deutsche Real-Encyclopädie fur die gebildeten Stände (Conversations-Lexikon)*, 5th edition, 205–6. Leipzig: F. A. Brockhaus.

Bryant, Christopher. 1975. "Positivism Reconsidered." *Sociological Review* 23(May):397–412.

Bunge, Mario. 2004. "How Does It Work? The Search for Explanatory Mechanisms." *Philosophy of the Social Sciences* 34(2):182–210.

Burawoy, Michael. 2005. "Provincializing the Social Sciences." In *The Politics of Method in the Human Sciences: Positivism and Its Epistemological Others*, edited by George Steinmetz, 508–25. Durham, NC: Duke University Press.

Burnett, James, Lord Monboddo. 1774. *Of the Origin and Progress of Language*, 2nd edition. Edinburgh, Scotland: J. Balfour.

Burrow, J. W. 1966. *Evolution and Society: A Study in Victorian Social Theory*. London: Cambridge University Press.

Calhoun, Craig. 1996. "The Rise and Domestication of Historical Sociology." In *The Historic Turn in the Human Sciences*, edited by Terrence J. McDonald, 305–38. Ann Arbor: University of Michigan Press.

Chatterjee, Partha. 1993. *The Nation and Its Fragments*. Princeton, NJ: Princeton University Press.

Cullather, Nick. 2002. "Damming Afghanistan: Modernization in a Buffer State." *Journal of American History* 89(2):512–37.

Culler, Jonathan D. 1986. *Ferdinand de Saussure*. Ithaca, NY: Cornell University Press.

Darwin, John. 2009. *The Empire Project: The Rise and Fall of the British World-System, 1830–1970*. Cambridge: Cambridge University Press.

Deville, Joe, ed. 2016. *Practising Comparison: Logics, Relations, Collaborations*. Manchester: Mattering.

Diderot and d'Alembert. 1778. *Encyclopedie, ou Dictionnaire raisonné des sciences, des arts et des métiers*. 3rd edition. Geneva, Switzerland: Jean-Léonard Pellet.

Durkheim, Émile. [1895] 1982. *The Rules of Sociological Method and Selected Texts on Sociology and Its Method*. London: Macmillan.

Eggers, Michael. 2016. *Vergleichendes Erkennen: Zur Wissenschaftsgeschichte und Epistemologie des Vergleichs und zur Genealogie der Komparatistik*. Heidelberg, Germany: Universitätsverlag Winter.

Elder-Vass, Dave. 2022. "Pragmatism, Critical Realism and the Study of Value," *Journal of Critical Realism* 21:261–87.

Elson, Diane. 1979. "The Value Theory of Labour." In *Value: The Representation of Labour in Capitalism*, edited by Diane Elson, 115–80. London: CSE.

Festinger, Leon. 1954. "A Theory of Social Comparison Processes." *Human Relations* 7(2):117–40.

Fleetwood, Steve. 2001. "What Kind of Theory Is Marx's Labour Theory of Value? A Critical Realist Inquiry." *Capital and Class* 25(1):41–77.

Freud, Sigmund. [1909] 1941. "Der Famlienroman der Neurotiker." In *Gesammelte Werke, chronologisch geordnet*, Vol. 7, edited by Sigmund Freud, 227–31. London: Imago.

———. [1930] 1962. *Civilization and Its Discontents*. New York: Norton.

Freyer, Hans. 1930. *Soziologie als Wirklichkeitswissenschaft: Logische Grundlegung des Systems der Soziologie*. Leipzig, Germany: B. G. Teubner.

Giddens, Anthony. 1974. "Introduction." In *Positivism and Sociology*, edited by Anthony Giddens. London: Heinemann.

Gilman, Nils. 2003. *Mandarins of the Future: Modernization Theory in Cold War America*. Baltimore, MD: Johns Hopkins University Press.

Go, Julian. 2016. *Postcolonial Thought and Social Theory*. Oxford: Oxford University Press.

Griffiths, Devin. 2016. *The Age of Analogy: Science and Literature Between the Darwins*. Baltimore, MD: Johns Hopkins University Press.

Hartwig, Mervyn. 2007. *Dictionary of Critical Realism*. London: Routledge.

Healy, Kieran. 2017. "Fuck Nuance." *Sociological Theory* 35(2):118–27.

Heintz, Bettina. 2016. "'Wir leben im Zeitalter der Vergleichung': Perspektiven einer Soziologie des Vergleichs." *Zeitschrift für Soziologie* 45:305–23.

Hell, Julia. 2019. *The Conquest of Ruins: The Third Reich and the Fall of Rome*. Chicago: University of Chicago Press.

House, James S. 2019. "The Culminating Crisis of American Sociology and Its Role in Social Science and Public Policy: An Autobiographical, Multimethod, Reflexive Perspective." *Annual Review of Sociology* 45:1–26.

James, William. 1907. *Pragmatism: A New Name for Some Old Ways of Thinking*. New York: Longmans, Green.

Kant, Immanuel. [1787] 1922. *Kritik der reinen Vernunft*. 12th edition. Leipzig: Felix Meiner.

———. 1923. "Logik." *Kant's gesammelte Schriften*, edited by Königlich Preussischen Akademie der Wissenschaften, Vol. 9, 1–150. Berlin: de Gruyter.

Karataşlı, Şahan Savaş, and Derek Clark. 2022. "Labor, Race, and Antinomies of Modernity: Non-Debates Between Ibn-Khaldun and Modern Social Theory." Paper presented to Social Theory Workshop, University of Michigan, March 23.

Knöbl, Wolfgang. 2003. "Theories That Won't Pass Away: The Never-Ending Story of Modernization Theory." In *Handbook of Historical Sociology*, edited by Gerard Delanty and Engin F. Isin, 96–107. London: Sage.

———. 2016. "Das Problem der Kontingenz in den Sozialwissenschaften und die Versuche seiner Bannung." In *Die Ungewissheit des Zukünftigen: Kontingenz in der Geschichte*, edited by Frank Becker et al., 119–37. Frankfurt, Germany: Campus.

Lawson, Tony. 2013. "Economic Science Without Experimentation/Abstraction." In *Critical Realism*, edited by Margaret Archer et al., 144–85. London: Routledge.

Lieberson, Stanley. 1994. "More on the Uneasy Case for Using Mill-Type Methods in Small-N Comparative Studies." *Social Forces* 72:1225–37.

Lukács, Georg. 1971. "Reification and the Consciousness of the Proletariat [1923]." In *History and Class Consciousness*, edited by Georg Lukács, 82–222. London: Merlin.

Lyotard, Jean-François. 1983. *Le différend*. Paris: Editions de Minuit.

Mannheim, Karl. 1929. "Zur Problematik der Soziologie in Deutschland." *Neue Schweizer Rundschau* 36/37:820–29.

Mazrui, Ali A. 1968. "From Social Darwinism to Current Theories of Modernization." *World Politics* 21(1):69–83.

Merle, Marcel. 1969. *L'Anticolonialisme européen, de Las Casas à Karl Marx*. Paris: A. Colin.

Merton, Robert K. 1952. "Foreward." In *Science and the Social Order*, edited by Bernard Barber, 7–20. Glencoe, IL: Free Press.

Mill, John Stuart. [1843] 1856. *A System of Logic*. London: J. W. Parker.

Mitchell, William J. T. 1996. "Why Comparisons Are Odious." *World Literature Today* 70(2):321–24.

Moore, Barrington. 1966. *Social Origins of Dictatorship and Democracy: Lord and Peasant in the Making of the Modern World*. Boston: Beacon.

Mumford, Stephen, and Rani Lill Anjum. 2011. *Getting Causes from Powers*. Oxford: Oxford University Press.

New, Caroline. 1998. "Realism, Deconstruction and the Feminist Standpoint. *Journal for the Theory of Social Behaviour* 28(4):349–72.

Patomäki, Heikki. 2020. "On the Historicity of Social Ontology." *Journal of the Theory of Social Behaviour* 50:439–61.

Pedersen, Susan. 2015. *The Guardians: The League of Nations and the Crisis of Empire*. New York: Oxford University Press.

Postone, Moishe. 1993. *Time, Labor, and Social Domination: A Reinterpretation of Marx's Critical Theory*. Cambridge: Cambridge University Press.

Przeworski, Adam, and Henry Teune. 1970. *The Logic of Comparative Social Inquiry*. New York: Wiley.

Ragin, Charles C. 1987. *The Comparative Method: Moving Beyond Qualitative and Quantitative Strategies*. Berkeley: University of California Press.

——. 2008. *Redesigning Social Inquiry: Fuzzy Sets and Beyond*. Chicago: University of Chicago Press.

Robin, Ron. 2001. *The Making of the Cold War Enemy: Culture and Politics in the Military Intellectual Complex*. Princeton, NJ: Princeton University Press.

Rohde, Joy. 2013. *Armed with Expertise: The Militarization of American Social Research During the Cold War*. Ithaca, NY: Cornell University Press.

Rokkan, Stein, and Henry Valen. 1966. "Archives for Statistical Studies of Within-Nation Differences." In *Comparing Nations: The Use of Quantitative Data in Cross-National Research*, edited by Richard L. Merritt and Stein Rokkan, 411–18. New Haven, CT: Yale University Press.

Schenk, G., and A. Krause. 1971. "Vergleich." In *Historisches Wörterbuch der Philosophie*, Vol. 11, edited by Joachim Ritter, 676–80. Basel, Switzerland: Schwabe.

Scheuch, E. K. 1967. "Society as Content in Cross-National Research." *Social Science Information* 6(5):7–23.

Sewell, William H., Jr. 1996. "Three Temporalities: Toward an Eventful Sociology." In *The Historic Turn in the Human Sciences*, edited by Terrence J. McDonald, 245–80. Ann Arbor: University of Michigan Press.

Singh, Sourabh. 2018. "Anchoring Depth Ontology to Epistemological Strategies of Field Theory: Exploring the Possibility for Developing a Core for Sociological Analysis." *Journal of Critical Realism* 17(5):429–48.

Skocpol, Theda. 1979. *States and Social Revolutions: A Comparative Analysis of France, Russia, and China*. Cambridge: Cambridge University Press.

——. 1984. "Emerging Agendas and Recurrent Strategies in Historical Sociology." In *Vision and Method in Historical Sociology*, edited by Theda Skocpol, 356–39. Cambridge: Cambridge University Press.

Skocpol, Theda, and Margaret Somers. 1980. "The Uses of Comparative History in Macrosocial Inquiry." *Comparative Studies in Society and History* 22(2):174–97.

Speich-Chassé, Daniel. 2020. "Der Staatsvergleich in historischer Perspektive: Warum, seit wann und wie werden politische Mächte miteinander verglichen?" In *Global beobachten und vergleichen: Soziologische Analysen zur Weltgesellschaft*, edited by Hannah Bennani, Martin Bühler, Sophia Cramer, and Andrea Glauser, 79–111. Frankfurt, Germany: Campus.

Steinmetz, George. 1993. *Regulating the Social: The Welfare State and Local Politics in Imperial Germany*. Princeton, NJ: Princeton University Press.

——. 1998. "Critical Realism and Historical Sociology." *Comparative Studies in Society and History* 40(1):170–86.

——. 2004. "Odious Comparisons: Incommensurability, the Case Study, and 'Small N's' in Sociology." *Sociological Theory* 22(3):371–400.

——. 2005. "Scientific Authority and the Transition to Post-Fordism: The Plausibility of Positivism in American Sociology Since 1945." In *The Politics of Method in the Human Sciences: Positivism and Its Epistemological Others*, edited by George Steinmetz, 275–323. Durham, NC: Duke University Press.

——. 2007. *The Devil's Handwriting: Precoloniality and the German Colonial State in Qingdao, Samoa and Southwest Africa*. Chicago: University of Chicago Press.

——. 2008. "*Logics of History* as a Framework for an Integrated Social Science." *Social Science History* 32(4):535–54.

——. 2014. "Comparative History and Its Critics: A Genealogy and a Possible Solution." In *A Companion to Global Historical Thought*, edited by Prasenjit Duara, Viren Murthy, and Andrew Sartori, 412–36. New York: Wiley.

——. 2017a. "The Octopus and the *Hekatonkheire*: On Many-Armed States and Tentacular Empires." In *The Many Hands of the State*, edited by Kimberly Morgan and Ann Orloff, 369–94. New York: Cambridge University Press.

——. 2017b. "What Does It Mean to Be Critical in Social Science? Immanent Critique, Scientific Autonomy, and the American University." Unpublished paper, presented at symposium on Critical Sociology, University of California-Berkeley, January 12.

——. 2020a. "Historicism and Positivism in Sociology: From Weimar Germany to the Contemporary United States." In *Historicism: A Travelling Concept*, edited by Herman Paul and Adriaan van Veldhuizen, 57–95. London: Bloomsbury.

——. 2020b. "Historismus und Positivismus in der Soziologie: Eine begriffsgeschichtliche Recherche vom Wilhelminischen Deutschland bis in die Gegenwart der Vereinigten Staaten von Amerika." *Mittelweg* 36(3):37–68.

——. 2022. "The History of Sociology as Scientific Reflexivity." In *The Palgrave Handbook of the History of Human Sciences*, edited by FM Collyer, section editor, in D. McCallum, series editor, *The History of Sociology*. London: Palgrave Macmillan.

——. 2023a. *The Colonial Origins of Modern Social Thought: French Sociology and the Overseas Empire*. Princeton, NJ: Princeton University Press.

——. 2023b. "Response to My Readers." *Social Science History* 47(4).

——. Forthcoming. "Diplomatic Non-Alignment and Intellectual Autonomy in the Early Cold War and the Late Colonial Era." *Social Science History*.

Steinmetz, Willibald. 2019a. "Above/Below, Better/Worse or Simply Different? Metamorphoses of Social Comparison, 1600–1900." In *The Force of Comparison: A New Perspective on*

Modern European History and the Contemporary World, edited by Willibald Steinmetz, 80–112. New York: Berghahn.

——, ed. 2019b. *The Force of Comparison: A New Perspective on Modern European History and the Contemporary World*. New York: Berghahn.

Suchman, E. A. 1964. "The Comparative Method in Social Research." *Rural Sociology* 9(2):123–37.

Swedberg, Richard, and Ola Agevall. 2016. *The Max Weber Dictionary: Key Words and Central Concepts*. 2nd edition. Stanford, CA: Stanford Social Sciences.

Tenbruck, Friedrich H. 1992. "Was war der Kulturvergleich, ehe es den Kulturvergleich gab?" In *Zwischen den Kulturen? Die Sozialwissenschaften vor dem Problem des Kulturvergleichs*, edited by Joachim Matthes, 13–36. Göttingen, Germany: O. Schwartz.

Tipps, Dean C. 1973. "Modernization Theory and the Comparative Study of Societies: A Critical Perspective." Comparative Studies in Society and History 15(2):199–226.

Veblen, Thorstein. 1899. *The Theory of the Leisure Class: An Economic Study in the Evolution of Institutions*. New York: Macmillan.

Vitalis, Robert. 2013. "The Midnight Ride of Kwame Nkrumah and Other Fables of Bandung (Ban-doong)." *Humanity: An International Journal of Human Rights, Humanitariansim, and Development* 4(2):261–88.

Vogt, Peter. 2011. *Kontingenz und Zufall: Eine Ideen- und Begriffsgeschichte*. Berlin: Akademie Verlag.

Weber, Alfred. 1927. *Ideen zur Staats- und Kultursoziologie*. Karlsruhe, Germany: G. Braun.

Will, Pierre Étienne. 2004. "La distinction chez les mandarins." In *La liberté par la connaissance: Pierre Bourdieu (1930–2002)*, edited by Jacques Bouveresse and Daniel Roche, 215–32. Paris: Odile Jacob.

Windelband, Wilhelm. 1870. *Die Lehren vom Zufall*. Berlin: F. Henschel.

Woodiwiss, Anthony. 2007. "Rescuing Reflexivity: From Solipsism to Realism." In *Critical Realism and the Social Sciences: Heterodox Elaborations*, edited by Jon Frauley and Frank Pearce, 97–116. Toronto: University of Toronto Press.

Xie, Ming. 2001. *Conditions of Comparison: Reflections on Comparative Intercultural Inquiry*. New York: Continuum.

CHAPTER 9

HISTORICIZING COMPARISONS IN HISTORICAL SOCIOLOGY

JONAH STUART BRUNDAGE

Historical sociologists frequently urge us to "historicize" our objects of study. The task, we are told, is one of "historicizing social theory" (Calhoun 1996, 306), producing a "historicized sociology" (Adams, Clemens, and Orloff 2005, 11; Clemens 2007) attuned to "historicizing its objects of enquiry" (Go and Lawson 2017, 15). Some advocate a "fully historicized social science" (Abbott 1991, 202; see also Abrams 1982).

But what exactly does "historicization" mean? And how should sociologists go about it? This chapter emphasizes *comparison* as an essential—yet underappreciated—tool. Despite the designation "comparative historical sociology," the comparative and historicizing dimensions of sociological research are all too often seen as separate. Early proponents of macro-comparison ignored what made historical sociology historical (Ragin 1987; Skocpol and Somers 1980). Conversely, champions of processual concerns like sequence and temporality have downplayed comparison itself (Abbott 2001; Griffin 1992; Isaac 1997).[1] Historical sociology's global, transnational, and postcolonial turns are sometimes framed as alternatives to comparison (Go 2014, 127–32; Go and Lawson 2017, 5; Quisumbing King and White 2021, 7–9).

Many forms of comparison are indeed unhistorical. Yet such uses hardly exhaust its potential. Comparison, at its best, serves to denaturalize what appears given or inevitable. I refer to this mode as "historicizing comparison," and I argue that it is central to a historicized sociology. I make my case, negatively at first, by showing what goes wrong when historical accounts lack the sensibility that historicizing comparisons afford. In so doing, I revisit three canonical works of historical sociology: Theda Skocpol's (1979) *States and Social Revolutions*, Charles Tilly's (1990) *Coercion, Capital, and European States, AD 990–1990*, and the first volume of Michael Mann's (1986) *The Sources of Social Power*. Despite their many merits, each of these works develops arguments that are ahistorical in major respects. Critically, these ahistoricisms do not follow from a privileging of comparative over historical methods—in fact, it is only Skocpol's text that employs explicit comparisons at all. Nor are they explained by a mistaken approach to temporality per se (cf. Sewell 2005).

Instead, I argue, the fault resides in something that is typically praised in these works: the way they depict *contingent relations* between *multiple causal factors*, especially political and economic factors. This is ironic because a basic sense of "contingency"—a sense that history could have been otherwise—is surely crucial to a historicized sociology. In the absence of historicizing comparison, however, two different meanings of contingency become conflated.[2] The version to which these works commit themselves invokes a multiplicity of irreducible domains, structures, factors, causes, or mechanisms. This makes contingency a matter of complexity: since domains are irreducible, their combinations are unpredictable. What is contingent is thus the set of *relations between* entities. Such entities are contingently, or externally, related; no necessary, or internal, relation obtains.[3]

There is, however, another sense in which contingency is at work in historical sociology. The entities that enter into contingent relations in historical sociologists' accounts are themselves contingent rather than universal; their very existence as objects is *historically* contingent. Contingency here does not express a type of relation; it references the quality of *time-space dependence*, defined in opposition to a transhistorical presence. After all, if the world were already fully formed, then it would not be truly contingent.

Of course, any object may be irreducible in its effects and yet transient in its being (Hirschman and Reed 2014; Rutzou and Elder-Vass 2019). The problem with Skocpol, Tilly, and Mann is that the domains that populate their causal models—separate-but-interacting political and economic domains in particular—*also* constitute the historical outcomes for which they seek to account. Functioning both as explanans and as explanandum, at once a set of contingently related causes *and* a historically contingent effect, the distinction between the political and the economic begs the question. It presupposes that which demands explanation.

It is against this backdrop that I develop the idea of historicizing comparisons, with the help of two positive examples, in the final part of the chapter. Most comparative strategies compare across social things (e.g., "outcomes," "events,") and their causes (or "conjunctures" of causes). By contrast, historicizing comparisons compare across the *conditions of possibility* of causes themselves. Specifically, they compare across the *sociohistorical* conditions that make some causal mechanisms pertinent just as they make others unrealizable.

Ahistorical Explanation in Historical Sociology: The "Autonomy" of the Political

As is well known, comparative historical sociology emerged in the United States (and elsewhere) between the 1960s and 1980s as an effort to resensitize social science to social transformation. But as this epistemic formation—"second-wave" historical sociology as some call it (Adams et al. 2005)—broke apart, it too came under fire for insufficient historicity (Abbott 1991; Calhoun 1996; Sewell 2005). Largely ignored in these assessments, however, is the most ironic limitation of historical sociology's classics: their tendency to account for historical change using ahistorical *causal models*. Indeed, the crucial offender is a concept that comes in for praise even in critical accounts. I am referring to the master explanatory device of second-wave historical sociology: the *relative autonomy of the political*, sometimes understood as the relative autonomy of the state, sometimes understood in broader terms.[4] Attributing a degree of autonomy to a political sphere, especially its autonomy from the economic sphere, would seem a progressive—if still too limiting—move, a "pluralistic" advance beyond "reductionism." Yet a close examination of texts by three figures whom we might take as metonymic[5] of second-wave historical sociology—Theda Skocpol, Charles Tilly, and Michael Mann—casts this strategy in a very different light.

Theda Skocpol: The Ahistorical Autonomy of the State

Skocpol's (1979) masterpiece, *States and Social Revolutions*, proposes a novel theory of social revolution (as occurred in France, Russia, and China) founded on a claim about the "potential autonomy of the state"—from society in general and from ruling-class interests in particular. As she develops her model, potential autonomy becomes actual (if partial) autonomy, a causally relevant feature of social-revolutionary situations (Skocpol 1979, 31, 284). The postulated autonomy of states undergoing social revolutions thus licenses Skocpol's signal contribution to the explanation of these events: the identification of *state breakdown* as an essential cause of social revolution, rather than a mediating variable by means of which underlying social contradictions wrought their revolutionary consequences. As she puts it at her most theoretically explicit: "the political crises that have launched social revolutions have not at all been epiphenomenal reflections of social strains or class contradictions. Rather they have been direct expressions of contradictions centered in the structures of old-regime states" (Skocpol 1979, 29).

Crucially, Skocpol's point of departure for the notion of state autonomy was an ongoing Marxist debate over the nature of the "capitalist state" (Poulantzas 1973), or the "state in capitalist society" (Miliband 1969), which had hinged precisely on locating its "relative autonomy," albeit in ways that Skocpol found inadequate. Rather than offering an alternative resolution to a common problem, however, Skocpol's intervention was to shift the level of abstraction at which the problem was posed: whereas Marxists were debating a certain *kind* of state—the modern, capitalist kind—Skocpol's theoretical framework applies to states in general, lacking any historical parameter.[6] This is interesting because when Skocpol does turn to history, it becomes clear that her object of explanation is the very formation of modern states (indeed, the formation of a modern, capitalist state in the case of the French Revolution). In other words, Skocpol derives a key component of her explanatory model by generalizing a concept whose boundaries—as originally defined—are internal to her explanatory outcome.

Can the state autonomy concept be extended in this way? Skocpol's own evidence suggests that it cannot, at least not to the contexts that produced her revolutions of interest. By her own description, these "old regimes"—the agrarian-imperial formations of France, Russia, and China—were amorphous configurations that blurred the boundaries between the state and a dominant class that enjoyed literal property in political power and legal jurisdiction (through venality of office, for instance). As Skocpol (1979, 49) correctly recognizes, "such appropriation of surpluses indirectly through state office-holding had become very important in old-regime France, Russia, and China alike." Skocpol (1979, 56) even argues, about the French case, that *all* surplus appropriation was political-juridical in nature: "This surplus appropriation occurred through a mélange of rents and dues enforced in part by landlord-dominated judicial institutions, and through the redistribution of revenues collected under the aegis of the monarchical state" (in a similar vein, and for all three cases, see Skocpol 1979, 52–53, 59, 68, 86, 167). In fact, at least for France, her analysis inadvertently shows that revolution was not the effect but the cause of state autonomization. As Timothy Mitchell (1991, 92) has noted, Skocpol details "a transformation in which the army and bureaucracy . . . became permanent, professional organizations whose staffs were *for the first time* set apart from other commercial and social activities" (emphasis added; see Skocpol 1979, 196–205).

Skocpol's concept of state autonomy thus provides a poor description of her evidence. And it provides an ahistorical—more specifically, a teleological— explanation of one of her key outcomes because her presumption of state autonomy renders it a self-generating accomplishment. Mitchell (1991, 91) captures this well: Skocpol, he says, is "unable to offer a historical explanation of the appearance of the modern state" because, for her, "the state must be an independent cause of events, even when those events . . . involve the very birth of a modern, apparently autonomous state." To put it somewhat differently, while Skocpol's empirical account of how "state breakdown" facilitated social revolution in France, Russia, and China may or may not remain valid, the causal significance that she attributes to this phenomenon is misleading either way. She has never *demonstrated* that it was an independent cause, one whose presence varied sufficiently independently of the "social" contradictions of old regimes to earn that title. Rather, she *presupposes* its independence.

What relation does comparison bear to these problems? Might they stem from Skocpol's commitment to comparative methods over other, more specifically historical strategies? Not exactly. True, Skocpol's comparisons have been rightly criticized for the way that they present in a synchronic array, subject to uniform causes, what were actually linked events in a historical-developmental series (Burawoy 1989; Sewell 2005, 91–100). For purposes of the present discussion, however, her major cases really do have a certain equivalence: all three "old regimes" constitutively fused state and ruling class. This is an ironic equivalence given Skocpol's theory of state autonomy. But her use of comparison, in itself, does no violence to this particular reality. Yet it offers no leverage either: comparison, as deployed by Skocpol, remains indeterminate with respect to the problems described here. As I will show later, it is capable of much more.

Charles Tilly: The Ahistorical Separation of Coercion from "Capital"

At first glance, Charles Tilly's (1990) *Coercion, Capital, and European States, AD 990–1990* fares better on the grounds of historicization. If Skocpol takes the formation of modern states as a by-product of social revolutions, Tilly takes it as his explicit object of explanation. In so doing, he makes no assumption about causal uniformity. Rather, Tilly identifies *multiple causal paths*, alternative routes to the modern state. Given conditions of endemic warfare in late medieval and early modern Europe, Tilly argues, all rulers attempted to extract resources from their subject populations as a means to military mobilization. In the process, they pursued varying strategies, determined by their variable access to "concentrated capital" and "concentrated coercion." These competing strategies produced different organizational forms: a "capital-intensive" path led to city-states, a "coercion-intensive" path led to agrarian empires, and a "capitalized coercion" path led to what Tilly identifies as national states (e.g., France and England). Gradually, however, the balance of capital and coercion found in national states gave the latter a competitive advantage at war because they were uniquely able to field and fund large armies. Through combination or mimicry, other states conformed to the structure of the national state—or else they were eliminated altogether (Tilly 1990, 15, 30–31, 90–91, 183–91).

In schematic terms, Tilly traces a process of heterogeneous organizational emergence, determined by a contingent interaction of multiple causal forces (uniform military pressures mediated by variable combinations and levels of capital and coercion), which is followed by organizational convergence, determined by an environmental selection mechanism (those same military pressures heightened by the "success" of one particular organizational type). The latter half of this argument—the moment of convergence—is easily criticized. Some note the persistence of heterogeneity throughout the early modern period (Teschke 2003); others stress alternative selection mechanisms (Spruyt 1994). At any rate, Tilly's "national states" were themselves empires when seen from a global perspective (Go 2014, 125–27). Perhaps, then, the former moment of heterogeneity—with its causal multiplicity—displays a more sophisticated analysis better suited to the contingency of history.

On closer inspection, however, the contingency in Tilly's argument is restricted to a complex interaction *between* what he takes as preformed objects (contingency in the first sense of an external, or contingent, relation). Tilly never inquires whether these objects are *historically* contingent (in the second sense of time-space dependent). Rather, the distinctiveness of entities called "capital" and "coercion" is always already presumed.[7] Consider Tilly's depiction of the relevant entities. Capital includes "any tangible mobile resources, and enforceable claims on such resources. Capitalists, then, are people who specialize in the accumulation, purchase, and sale of capital. Capitalists have often existed in the absence of capitalism. . . . *Through most of history*, indeed, capitalists have worked chiefly as merchants, entrepreneurs, and financiers, rather than as the direct organizers of production." Coercion, by contrast, "includes all concerted application, threatened or actual, of action that commonly causes loss or damage to the persons or possessions of individuals or groups. . . . Where *capital defines a realm of exploitation, coercion defines a realm of domination.*" Finally, while capital and coercion sometimes merge, "for the most part, however, they remain *sufficiently distinct to allow us to analyze them separately*" (Tilly 1990, 17, 19; emphasis added).

This distinction between separate-yet-interacting concentrations of coercion and capital is no more viable than Skocpol's distinction between state and society—given the very historical context that Tilly studies. A vast literature shows that merchant, entrepreneurial, and financial activities in late medieval and early modern Europe were utterly coercive processes, forms of forced profit-taking to the last, whether that involved military control of trade routes, legal privileges and monopolies like tax farms and chartered companies, or—perhaps the most obvious—colonial plunder and the slave trade (see, among many others, Adams 2005; Anievas and Nisancioglu 2015; Brenner

1985; Teschke 2003). Hence this "capital," which, according to Tilly, predated the systematic organization of production for exchange via wage labor—his definition of *capitalism*—was, for that very reason, predicated instead on causing just the sort of "loss or damage" to the "persons or possessions" of others that Tilly associates with "coercion." Conversely, wielders of coercion did not pursue domination for its own sake, as Tilly sometimes implies. Rather, early modern European "rulers" (whom Tilly [1990, 19] correctly associates with the landholding nobility) deployed coercion as an "economic," class-like strategy: because peasants controlled their own means of production, the material reproduction of ruling families required forcible extraction (internal coercion); and because land was a fixed quantity—and inheritance practices produced ever-new dynastic appendages—their reproduction tended to forcible expansion as well (external coercion, i.e., war) (Anderson 1974; Brenner 1985; Teschke 2003). Thus "capital" was invariably tied to coercion, and "coercion" was invariably tied to exploitation (though not necessarily to capital in any meaningful sense).

As with Skocpol, this is not to suggest that Tilly's narrative of the sequence of events that issued in modern states is prima facie invalid. Many of Tilly's core empirical claims—that war was endemic to Europe, that it induced efforts to build fiscal machinery, and that these efforts were enabled and constrained by polities' degree of integration into trading networks, their variable property arrangements, and the sheer size of their peasantries—surely contain considerable truth. Just as Tilly's distinction between coercion and capital poorly describes this empirical detail, however, it leads him to frame his explanation in teleological—indeed, tautological—ways. Yet another instantiation of the autonomy of the political from the economic, this distinction transforms the state into a theoretical prior when it is the very thing whose historical existence Tilly is trying to explain.

Consider the category "ruler," which supplies Tilly's narrative with its chief protagonist. For Tilly (1990, 131), rulers are the critical agents of state formation: "rulers form and transform states." Now Tilly (1990, 34) admits, rather disarmingly, that he is resorting to "metonymy" by speaking of "'rulers' . . . as if they represented a state's entire decision-making apparatus." Yet the issue is not so much the act of abstraction as what the abstraction presupposes—that the state's decision-making apparatus is conceptually distinguishable from the outset. This is a strange premise for a work that takes the development of the state's decision-making apparatus as its central historical outcome (Tilly 1990, 2, 164). The problem with the shorthand "rulers," then, is not that it simplifies what would otherwise be appreciated for a more complex and nuanced process. The problem is that it obfuscates the circularity of Tilly's process itself: the fact that, in his account, the agents of state formation are also its products. In this way, Tilly's *explanatory model* presumes an analytical distinction between state and society, which then doubles as a structural differentiation of state from society in his *object of explanation.*

The confusion generated by this move is most visible in the case of warfare, the primary motor of state formation for Tilly. Given the tremendous causal weight that Tilly places on this phenomenon,[8] it is puzzling that he has no historical-sociological account of war itself (Teschke 2014, 18). Rather, he responds to the question "Why did wars occur at all?" with a universal claim that positions war as an unmoved mover: "The central, tragic fact is simple: coercion *works*" (Tilly 1990, 70; emphasis original). Of course, what Tilly means to say is that coercion works provided that rulers are interested in internal extraction and external aggrandizement. But because he never accounts for these interests, they appear as self-evident—and self-generating.

It is in this sense that Tilly's explanation for the rise of the modern state as a structurally distinct organization assumes the prior existence of a state-like realm that can only be regarded as a conceptual product of this later structural distinction. As we have seen, war results not from historically contingent pressures, in Tilly's account, but from the domain-specific interests of rulers (whose domain is, of course, the state). And yet war, for Tilly (1990, 183), is what produces a state-specific domain in the first place: it "generated as by-products *centralization, differentiation, and autonomy* of the state apparatus" (emphasis added). Teleology and tautology are the unavoidable consequences. As Benno Teschke (2014, 22–23) sums it up in an important critique, "Tilly transhistoricises the very *results* [of state formation] while re-deploying and retro-activating them as causal categories, each endowed with their own 'logic of action', to explain this very same process" (emphasis original). Tilly's explanation—or at least his theoretical gloss on his explanation—is circular. It begs the question in the technical sense of that phrase.

It should be clear, much more for Tilly than for Skocpol even, that one cannot blame a positivist, atemporal use of comparison for the lack of historicity in this respect. As Abbott (1991, 210, 232) has noted, Tilly actually sits uneasily among the founders of "comparative historical sociology" in that comparison was never quite as central to his empirical work. But I would go further: perhaps if Tilly *had* pursued systematic comparisons of European state formation, some of these problems could have been avoided.

For example, Tilly (1990, 137–60) does compare countries to flesh out his capital-intensive, coercion-intensive, and capitalized-coercive pathways, but this is mostly for illustrative purposes: cases are assigned to different combinations of categories ("capital," "coercion") that are derived entirely in advance. If, however, he had employed comparison to locate the *historical boundaries* of his categories, a different picture would have emerged. We could have seen, for instance, that England and France—Tilly's paradigmatic and thus interchangeable cases of capitalized coercion—actually differed with respect to the very distinctiveness of capital and coercion as historical objects. Thus in England, the organizational bases of coercion and capital really did become somewhat disembedded from each other at a much earlier date, and in a much more gradual way, than in France, where—as Skocpol showed us—there was little separation at all until the transformative event of the French Revolution (for this contrast, see especially Bloch 1960; Brenner 1985; Wood 1991). Alternatively, even within a single national case (say, France), if Tilly had explicitly compared different periods of time (using such a conventional historical boundary as, say, the French Revolution), he might have better identified the specificity of each period's "regime of causality" (Abbott 2001, 291; cf. Haydu 2010, 29)—not just contingent *interactions* between his posited causes but the *historically* contingent character of those causes themselves.[9] In that way, he might have avoided conflating his causal model with the outcomes that it was meant to explain.

Michael Mann: The Ahistorical Distinctiveness of Social-Power Sources

The first volume of Michael Mann's (1986) *The Sources of Social Power* is the most historically sophisticated of the three works considered here. Nevertheless, as I will show, it also takes the relative autonomy of the political to its logical conclusions and, in so doing, lays bare its limitations as an explanatory device. Mann's text is especially useful because it is such a hard case for accusations of anachronism. Sewell (2005, 114–23) discerns in Mann's narrative an "eventful temporality" that the former regards as essential to the craft of history and finds lacking in Mann's historical-sociological peers, including Skocpol and Tilly. Mann is also the most rigorously Weberian of the three in his use of analytical categories as ideal types, which immunizes him somewhat from the critique that his categories lack descriptive realism. Even then, rather than taking this as a license to ahistorically generalize, Mann's methodological statements argue for the constant disciplining of analytical constructs by historical observations. In fact, he warns against anachronistic applications of static typologies: "Categories . . . lose their discriminating power if applied too broadly across the historical spectrum. This is not primarily because history is infinitely varied (though it is), but because history *develops*" (Mann 1986, 525; emphasis original).

It is thus paradoxical that Mann's *theoretical* framework is just such an a priori, transhistorical set of categories. These are what Mann calls the four principal networks, organizational means, or simply "sources" of social power: ideological, economic, military, and political power (the IEMP model for short). Mann thus generalizes the second-wave emphasis on the autonomy of the political, embedding it in a four-part typology of mutually irreducible—and contingently interacting—categories. To be sure, his use of these types is much

more sophisticated than standard "multifactor" accounts, which he readily criticizes. But significantly, Mann objects to the language of "factors" (or "dimensions" or "levels") not because he questions the analytical separations that they
imply; rather, he simply denies that the separate parts form a demarcated whole
or totality because, in fact, "societies are constituted of multiple overlapping
and intersecting socio-spatial networks of power" (Mann 1986, 1).

Here, however, Mann makes two moves at once. Starting from the unob-
jectionable premise that society is irreducible to a monolithic organization or
a single network, he then imposes the strong assumption that societies' distinct organizations and networks at least *tend* to reflect distinct types of power.
Otherwise, the typology would fail to capture even the most general empirical
truth. Mann is a Weberian, not an idealist: as he assures the reader at the outset, "a broad division of function between ideological, economic, military, and
political organizations *is ubiquitous*, popping up again and again through the
interstices of more merged power organizations" (Mann 1986, 18; emphasis
added). But why should the second move follow from the first? Why, that is,
should the undeniable multiplicity of observable *organizations* even approximate an equivalent division of *functions* throughout history? We could just as
easily envision a world in which each existing organization tended to combine
different "types" of power internally. It is my view that Mann's evidence better
supports the latter conclusion.

Once again, this is clearest with the category of political power, which Mann,
like Skocpol and Tilly, grants a conceptual distinctiveness independent of historical context. According to Mann (1986, 11), "political powers are those of
centralized, institutionalized, territorial regulation" (see also Mann 1986,
26–27). The problem with this definition is that, *by Mann's own admission*,
centralized, territorial states are the exception rather than the rule in human
history. In fact, the *only* organization that has successfully centralized and
institutionalized regulation over an extensive territory is the modern state. As
Mann (1986, 512) argues, it is not the modern, centralized state but the "territorially federal state" that characterized "almost all previous extensive societies.
Hitherto rule had been a compromise between central and provincial power
arenas." But despite the historical ubiquity of central-provincial collaboration,
Mann's definition of the political restricts it to the central. In short, Mann has
adopted a definition of the political with only one pure example in human
history yet insists on regarding it as a transhistorical category. What is more,
because the one pure example, the modern state, happens to be the political
outcome of Mann's account, his commitment to the distinctiveness of the political presupposes the historical object whose emergence he is trying to explain.[10]

Indeed, from here on in, Mann's account of the rise of the modern state
exhibits the same explanatory circularity as Tilly's *Coercion, Capital, and European States*. Much like Tilly, Mann (1986, 511) identifies war and preparation for

war as the primary motors of state formation, an "overwhelmingly military and overwhelmingly geopolitical rather than economic and domestic" process (see generally Mann 1986, 416–517). As we have already seen, this claim bears little resemblance to the historical context out of which the modern state supposedly emerged. For in early modern Europe, war was an overwhelmingly "economic" strategy—a strategy aimed at the acquisition of land and its associated peasants in the interest of appropriating their surpluses. This is not at all to "reduce" war to economics in a causal sense. We could just as well reduce economics to war in this instance. The point is that we are dealing with a context in which the categories "geopolitical" and "economic" simply do not index separate things. The plausibility of their separation hinges on the prior emergence of distinctively geopolitical organizations: namely, states. But then, that is what Mann has set out to explain in the first place.[11]

By presupposing the thing to be explained, Mann ends up selecting his data in a way that risks making his argument unfalsifiable. Thus his claim that the fiscal demands of warfare determined the emergence and form of the modern state is, in part, the artifact of an empirical focus on the finances of the state's central administration, where such demands were extremely visible. Because the political is, by definition, a centralized instance for Mann, this is a logical measurement strategy. Yet considering that centralized governance is the exception in history—and that the exception in question is Mann's historical *outcome*—it is deeply problematic as evidence of that outcome's *determinant*. Anticipating this problem, Mann (1986, 486) argues that even if he were to include all local administration in his analysis, civil (as opposed to military) expenditures in England—his primary empirical case—would still amount to just 25 percent of total government spending prior to 1820. This does not resolve the issue, however, because the key agents of local English administration in the period before 1820 were unremunerated, amateur officials. These included, most prominently, the justices of the peace (JPs), whose ability to regulate an exceptionally pacified society was all the more impressive for the lack of "public" financial resources at their disposal—though they enjoyed significant private wealth in land (Braddick 2000). As Derek Sayer (1992, 1406) has argued, "until the 19th century, for most English people and most practical purposes, J.P.'s *were* the state" (emphasis original). In sum, Mann's explanation for the rise of the modern state, like those of Skocpol and Tilly, runs into trouble because its causal categories have conditions of possibility that include the existence of the modern state.

As I have suggested, however, Mann's ahistoricisms are the most paradoxical of those considered here because in other respects he is far more sensitive to historicity than his contemporaries. In fact, Mann's views on *comparison* come strikingly close to the historicizing approach that I am advocating. Like Tilly, he eschews the kinds of systematic, cross-national comparisons favored by Skocpol, but Mann's reasons for this are much more self-conscious and critical. For in place of standard comparative methods, he offers something called "historical comparison"—diachronic comparison across time—designed to grasp the intrinsically dynamic nature of social reality: "It is not that history repeats itself. Precisely the opposite: World history develops. Through historical comparison we can see that the most significant problems of our own time are novel" (Mann 1986, 32). Perhaps, then, if Mann's narrative of European state formation had adhered more closely to his method of historical comparison and less to the static assumptions of the IEMP model, he could have avoided the conflation of explanandum with explanans to which he, too, falls victim.

Contingent Relations and Historical Contingency

To sum up this extended detour into works of "second-wave" historical sociology, we can conclude that despite the apparent appeal of its pluralistic antireductionism, the foundational analytical separation of the political from the economic in these works is ultimately an anachronistic move inducing explanations that are teleological (self-causing outcomes) and, at times, tautological as well (circular and true by definition). Pluralism functions here as an a priori assumption, a dogmatic commitment: it is not anchored in any empirical observation about the "pluralized" nature of the object under study. Not only that, it forecloses the possibility of explaining how coercive-exploitative structures *became* pluralized in the first place, splitting (if only formally) into differentiated political and economic spheres. The result is a paradoxical mirror image of what Polanyi (1977) called the "economistic fallacy." Whatever the merits of the "relative autonomy of the political" for explaining sociological outcomes *within* the historically specific complex of liberal capitalism, parliamentary democracy, and the bureaucratic state—its initial point of reference—adopting this concept as an explanatory device was an exceedingly odd choice for historical sociologists concerned with explaining the very emergence of capitalism, democracy, and bureaucratic authority.

Of course, more than a generation of historical-sociological scholarship has intervened since Theda Skocpol, Charles Tilly, and Michael Mann penned their canonical texts. Yet even as newer work broadens its substantive foci considerably, historical sociology has invested more than ever in the explanatory *form* of contingent relations between distinct and irreducible causes. The tendency is thus to generalize the relative autonomy of the political—a move that Mann had already initiated with the IEMP model—so as to encompass the relative autonomy of *all* dimensions of one's account, which are then said to constitute separate-but-interacting factors.

Clemens (2005, 501) summarizes this approach well: "The current atten-tion to contingency is grounded in an imagery of multiple domains or orders or institutions that cannot be reduced—in 'the last instance' or otherwise—to some master logic" (see also Abbott 2001, 147; Clemens 2007, 540; Padgett and Powell 2012, 3, 12; Steinmetz 1998, 173, 177). Agnostic about the content of these domains, such an imagery is structurally equivalent to the contingent inter-action of state and class, or of coercion and capital, or of all four social-power sources in the works of Skocpol, Tilly, and Mann. Sewell (2005, 118) makes this connection explicit, since Mann's "conception of societies as concatenations of overlapping organizational networks . . . builds in the possibility of *contingent temporal conjunctures between such networks*" (emphasis added).

No doubt contingent relations between domains or networks or factors are powerful explanatory tools; they serve sociologists well in many respects. The problem is that absent a rigorous specification of the sociohistorical conditions of possibility—or what Steinmetz (2005a, 111) has called in a different context the "social structures of plausibility"—of the *particular* domains or networks or factors in question, an emphasis on their distinctiveness and irreducibility risks transposing them to a transhistorical realm. In other words, by locating contin-gency in the interactions of things, it conceals the historicity of the things that do the interacting (see also Hirschman and Reed 2014).

Historicization as a Strategy of Comparison

What, then, is to be done? Redeployed as a historicizing strategy, comparison offers a way forward. At this point, it is useful to make my terminology explicit. "Historicizing comparisons" turn on a distinction between two ontological sets or imageries. First is a set of claims about things that populate the world and mechanisms that bring them about—claims involving explananda and expla-nans. We can call these the "ontology of causal production," because they are, among other things, the order on which causal explanations operate. Sociolog-ical analyses, including the historical-sociological variety, are in the business of making empirically verifiable claims about the ontology of causal production. Entailed by such imageries, however, is a second ontology, a set of presupposi-tions about what "enables" or "makes possible" our specific claims about cause and effect (Abend 2022). These are what I have described as the *conditions of possibility or plausibility* of any given causal mechanism or social domain. We might call this second set a "background ontology."[12]

Three implications follow. First, an issue of logical priority: the ontology of causal production is necessarily contained or embedded within the background ontology. Causes have conditions of possibility; the former set presupposes the latter. Second, and quite obviously, the ontology of causal production is heterogeneous. There are many things in the world, and not all things have the same cause. Different outcomes are often explained by different mechanisms (or conjunctures of mechanisms). Even the same outcome may be brought about in more than one way. Together, these ideas constitute the well-worn image of "multiple conjunctural causation" (Ragin 1987). And it is here that the notion of contingency as a contingent or external relation does its useful work.

Third, and finally, the background ontology varies as well (see also Abend 2022, 72). This is not as obvious. But unless we are prepared to accept that all causal entities are, in principle, possible in all sociohistorical settings regardless of observable effects, we must assume instead that conditions of possibility are themselves spatiotemporally rooted and variable. Although some realist-minded scholars seem to treat ontological conditions of possibility, like Kant's epistemological categories, as universals, I see no reason why realism requires such a move (indeed, on the time-space dependence of mechanisms, see Gorski 2009, 166; Steinmetz 2004, 382). It is in this sense that causes are not just contingently related but *historically* contingent.

Most comparative methodologies are designed to capture variation in the ontology of causal production. This is what the "method of difference" claims to do by comparing cases to isolate a critical causal factor that is present in one case and absent in another (Skocpol and Somers 1980, 183). In a very different way, it is the goal of what Steinmetz (2004, 392) calls "depth-realist comparison," whereby researchers compare across constellations of mechanisms to explain the variable events that they sometimes produce. What distinguishes historicizing comparison, by contrast, is that here the goal is to compare *ontological backgrounds themselves*. In so doing, it responds to Abend's (2022, 81) recent challenge to address conditions of possibility "comparatively and historically, because you might discover illuminating variation at the level of enablers"— what I am calling background ontologies.

Doing so could take a synchronic or a diachronic form. Thus we might compare geographically demarcated cases to locate a *sociospatial* boundary between different conditions of possibility. Or we might compare longitudinally delineated periods within a single "case" to identify a *sociotemporal* boundary between such backgrounds. Of course, this suggests that we think of historical periods as cases themselves, arrayed across sociohistorical time rather than across sociogeographical space (Haydu 1998). Diachronic historicizing comparisons also have the peculiar feature that the causal mechanisms embedded in one background ontology may help to explain the formation, over time, of an entirely new background ontology. Whether and how they do so is a matter of theoretical assessment and empirical specifics, however; it is not implied by the notion of background ontologies.

Indeed, historicizing comparisons are no panacea. Rather, they are useful when the analytically pertinent task is spatiotemporal *specification*, locating differences across space or time where one would have expected to observe uniformities. In this mode, comparison serves a de-universalizing purpose, checking "the temptation to think that everything happens 'quite naturally,'" as that most classical of comparativists Marc Bloch (1967, 67) put it (see also Knafo and Teschke 2020, 20). Unlike the method of difference, however, establishing these specificities need not involve any assumption about case "independence." Quite the contrary, identifying ontological boundaries becomes all the more fruitful the more closely related are the cases. Shared context and influence are what render the discovery of boundaries so puzzling in the first place. Far from disallowing comparison, then, the links between cases—as recently stressed by global and transnational sociologists—form its necessary starting point.[13]

Furthermore, what is being specified in historicizing comparison is a puzzle, a surprising deviation that demands explanation. Historicizing comparison thus enters the research process as a strategy of *case selection* and *problem definition* (and, if comparing over time, *periodization*). It also becomes a means of *eliminating* alternative accounts that depict implausible ontologies of causal production—causes that are not embedded in the relevant background ontology established by comparison. A necessary condition of many explanations, then, historicizing comparison is never sufficient.[14] Explanation always requires additional empirical and theoretical resources. However, this goes for all forms of comparison (see chapter 2 in this volume).

Framed in terms of historicizing comparison, the negative examples of Skocpol, Tilly, and Mann appear in a new light. The problem arose because these scholars embedded their (implicit) background ontology *within* their (manifest) ontology of causal production—contingently related political and economic causes in this case—rather than doing the reverse. This is the sense in which their causal explanations quite literally explained themselves. Such a problem is more common than we might expect; it is a risk whenever researchers fail to make explicit the historicity of their background ontology, indeed, whenever they fail to recognize that their background ontology *is* historically specific.

Do positive examples of historicizing comparison exist, even if they have not been named as such?[15] Here I discuss two works that respectively illustrate the synchronic and diachronic forms of historicizing comparison. For the sake of consistency, my examples take politico-economic problems as their explananda.

The exemplary instance of synchronic historicizing comparison in historical sociology is Richard Biernacki's (1995) effort, in *The Fabrication of Labor*, to document the differing "cultural definitions" of labor as a commodity in late nineteenth-century Germany and Britain. Tellingly, Biernacki selects cases whose relevant causal mechanisms appear, at first blush, as similar as possible—labor fully commodified, its subsumption to capital complete, factory production in its pre-Fordist phase in both contexts. Yet despite these common pressures, Biernacki shows that the very labor in question was conceptualized in a strikingly different way in each case: as embodied and materialized in its products (and thus exchanged like any other commodity) in Britain and as the capacity to work (as labor *power*) in Germany. Such conceptions were not at all self-contained ideas but rather "signifying practices" (Biernacki 1995, 13, 68, 485), lodged at the point of production and shaping everything from the physical organization of the workplace to the demands of labor movements. In short, Biernacki identifies a puzzling difference between two *ontological backgrounds*—a variation in the conditions of possibility for the execution of wage labor as meaningful practice—backgrounds that are puzzling because their boundary transects a seemingly uniform context.[16]

To be sure, Biernacki's stated goal is an intervention into debates about the relationship between culture and action, a rather universal problematic.[17] Nevertheless, his most important findings, for my purposes, involve the way that his comparative strategy leads him to *historicize* the category of labor itself. For instance, he historicizes Smithian and Marxian labor theories of value, showing how the difference between these frameworks is explicable in terms of real historical differences. Thus, in contrast to Friedrich Engels's claim that Karl Marx's discovery of the appropriation of surplus value through wage labor came to him like "a thunderbolt that struck out of a clear blue sky," Biernacki (1995, 279–85) shows that the kernel of this notion emerges precisely by combining German folk concepts with the categories of British political economy—that is, the socio-biographical-intellectual trajectory of Marx himself. (Among other things, such an interpretation of the relationship between ideas and historically emergent being is truer to Marx's own theoretical system than is Engels's quip.)[18]

Note that Biernacki's use of historicizing comparison adheres to the two limits that I described earlier. Its purpose is *specification*: the surprising fact that labor was apprehended differently in contexts where we would expect uniformity of perception. Again, however, this does not mean that historicizing comparison treats cases as independent. Part of what makes Biernacki's findings so surprising is that differences persisted despite constant dialogue between the two countries (via their respective management theorists, labor movements, etc.). Unbeknownst to themselves, these actors were talking past each other. Second, historicizing comparison is deployed to *identify a puzzle* that demands explanation, but it does not amount to an explanation on its own. This is why Biernacki's (1995, 213–347) account of how labor came to be defined differently in Britain and Germany, which consumes the middle part of the book, reverts to a more conventional imagery of macro-conjunctural causation and differential timing. Historicizing comparisons bear no intrinsic relation to any particular explanatory approach.

By contrast, Julia Adams's (2005) investigation of the gendered dimension of state formation, in *The Familial State*, illustrates a diachronic historicizing comparison, although this aspect of her comparative design is mostly implicit. Adams starts from the premise that all hitherto existing states—at least those that interest political theorists—have been gendered in important ways. One of her contributions, however, is to *historicize* this process, identifying a historically specific form of gendered state power that took hold in European patrimonial empires between the sixteenth and eighteenth centuries. This is what Adams (2005, 29) calls the "familial state," one institutionalized nexus of male domination and political rule among others with the distinguishing feature that it "awards men precedence and power on the basis of paternal status." Much of the book is devoted to tracing some of the permutations of this *ontological background*, which Adams does by comparing three early modern European states/empires—the Dutch, English, and French—that illustrate its variable forms.

Note, then, that Adams's synchronic comparisons are not themselves historicizing: all three cases are internal to the background ontology that is the familial state. Nevertheless, what distinguishes this ontology—what makes it historically bounded rather than generic—is a longitudinal, if less explicit, comparison that Adams pursues vis-à-vis the modern state to come. As Reed and Adams (2011, 258) elaborate elsewhere, the gendered character of the latter is best described as a "symbolic contract among brothers." No less masculinist, it is not, strictly speaking, patriarchal in the delimited sense of "father rule" that had characterized the familial state.

As with Biernacki, the goal of Adams's historicizing comparison is an increase in specificity.[19] Thus she criticizes feminist theories that adopt too broad a definition of patriarchy "in which the term designates all forms of institutionalized male dominance" (Adams 2005, 32). Obviously, Adams does not deny the general merit of such accounts, and her most pointed critiques are reserved for those theories of state formation that ignore gender altogether. One must already take masculine domination as a problem for her work of specification to acquire its utility.

Even as she emphasizes particularity, it is noteworthy that Adams expresses ambivalence about a certain particularizing strategy with which her own generation of "third-wave" historical sociology is commonly associated: the proliferation of contingently related, causal factors. Although the book "may be read as one of many texts that seek . . . to bring this or that additional factor 'back in'"—an explicit reference to the way that Skocpol, Tilly, and Mann brought autonomous politics "back in"—Adams (2005, 200) concludes that "patriarchy cannot simply be added as an asterisk to fiscal-military preoccupations that remain otherwise undisturbed." The reason they cannot remain otherwise undisturbed, I believe, is that the relationship between patriarchal authority and fiscal-military power is *not* contingent for Adams. It is rather a necessary, internal relation in which the patriarchal character of early modern European social formations entered into the deepest workings of fiscal and military mechanisms—and vice versa. And yet, what is *historically* contingent in this account, what requires de-universalization and denaturalization, is patriarchy itself.

Finally, just as Biernacki's synchronic historicizing comparison did not suffice to explain the variation between German and British understandings of labor, Adams's diachronic historicizing comparison does not explain the transition from familial to modern states on its own. Because her comparison is longitudinal, however, certain features of the first background ontology are relevant to explaining the emergence of the second: internal contradictions within the patriarchal-patrimonial mode of governance that helped to bring about its military defeat (Netherlands) and revolutionary destruction (France), and which English elites managed to escape only through a self-transformation of the bases of rule (Adams 2005, 137–63, 187–96). But this explanation rests on prior theory and intracase evidence as much as it does on comparison.

Historicizing comparison pertains to many topics beyond those discussed here. To take one last example, recent sociological interest in the origins of modern racism and its relation to capitalism (Go 2021; cf. Robinson 2000) necessarily entails a comparison across background ontologies. Precisely to explain how race came to exist, we must be able to imagine a world in which race did *not* yet exist. Accordingly, and regardless of how early in history we end up discovering racialized things—an empirical and probably a definitional question—historicizing comparison, with its strategic bias toward what Stuart Hall (2018, 202) called "the premise of historical specificity," checks the teleological tendency to presuppose what one is trying to explain, a tendency latent in any origin story. It thereby supports a historical sociology of race and racism committed not to "taking racial categories as given but rather studying the processes of construction and change" (Quisumbing King and White 2021, 6).

✳ ✳ ✳

As actual research practice, then, historicizing comparison is hardly new. My intention, however, is to make this practice explicit so that researchers can frame their projects around it. Much of what comparison is thought to involve is either impossible or incidental in the case of historicizing comparisons. This obviously includes a quasi-experimental isolation of causes in the positivist mode, but it still includes some sort of variation at the level of what I have called "ontologies of causal production" in most postpositivist depictions. The former is impossible in, and the latter incidental to, historicizing comparison. By comparing "background ontologies" instead, historicizing comparison is nonetheless a legitimate and frequently necessary endeavor. I have tried to show that it is the best way to avoid ahistorical—especially teleological—explanatory claims. The more we deploy historicizing comparison, the more sociology will become a "fully historicized social science."

It also has implications for understanding the present. By identifying the sociohistorical conditions under which causal mechanisms or social domains exist, we are better able to notice when they have ceased to exist, their distinct contours fading back into the flux of history. In that respect, a fully historicized sociology's fundamental contribution lies not so much in drawing lessons from the past for the present but in radically historicizing the present itself. As Michael Mann (1986, 32) would say, it reveals in just what way "the most significant problems of our own time are novel."

Acknowledgments

I would like to thank Edwin Ackerman, Graham Hill, Damon Mayrl, Dylan Riley, Tad Skotnicki, Paige Sweet, William Welsh, and Nick Wilson for their feedback on earlier drafts of this chapter.

Notes

1. Haydu (1998, 2010) and Sewell (2005) are exceptions in this regard.
2. For the multiple meanings of "contingency" in contemporary historical sociology, see Ermakoff (2015).
3. For a lucid explication and critique of this style of reasoning as applied to cultural sociology, see Knight and Reed (2019).
4. As Adams et al. (2005, 17) summarize matters: "The questions posed by the second wave were derived from a Marxist theoretical agenda; its answers pushed beyond, informed by an engagement with Weber, to embrace 'the relative autonomy of the political.'"
5. See Adams (2005, 199).
6. Interestingly, Skocpol (1979, 27, 300n69) cites Perry Anderson's (1974) work on the early modern European "absolutist state" to suggest that the Marxist problematic of relative autonomy is not exclusively limited to modern capitalist societies. It is thus telling that Anderson (1974, 16, 18), contra Skocpol, largely *rejects* the state's autonomy in the historical context of absolutism, maintaining that, far from a "counterpoise" between nobility and bourgeoisie, the absolutist state was an *instrument* of noble class rule.
7. See Teschke (2014, 21–22) for a clear exposition of this point.
8. War "underlay both the creation and the ultimate preponderance of the national state," according to Tilly (1990, 191).
9. As Sewell (2005, 91) points out, it is strange that even in Tilly's work on contentious politics (e.g., Tilly 1986), which centrally includes revolutionary politics, he downplays the epochally or qualitatively transformative character of the French Revolution.
10. Mann did seek to account for the autonomy of political power, rather than taking it as given, in an article published shortly prior to the first volume of *The Sources*. However, the main conclusion of that piece—that "state autonomy . . . flows principally from the

state's unique ability to provide a *territorially-centralised* form of organization" (Mann 1984, 185; emphasis his)—proves my point, since centralized, territorial states are specifically modern according to Mann.

11. Nor is it clear why state formation was a "geopolitical" rather than a "domestic" process when the very separation between domestic and international realms assumes the prior existence of territorially bounded states—the product of state formation yet again.

12. I thank Nick Wilson for suggesting that this is what I was actually arguing. For the distinction between first-order claims and their second-order "backgrounds," see Abend (2014).

13. For an alternative approach to defending comparative history while incorporating insights from the transnational critique, see Steinmetz (2014).

14. This is what distinguishes my approach from what Hirschman and Reed (2014) call "formation stories." Like historicizing comparisons, formation stories "offer an empirical, historically traceable reason why the scope conditions of a given analysis are what they are" (Hirschman and Reed 2014, 274). However, formation stories are meant as causal explanations in their own right. Because my concern is comparison rather than explanation, I am agnostic about what causal idiom is most appropriate in this context.

15. Of those methodologists already discussed, works by Abend (2014) on "moral backgrounds" in the history of U.S. business ethics, Bloch (1960) on servile labor in late medieval England and France, and Steinmetz (2005a, 2005b) on the epistemological implications of the transition from Fordism to post-Fordism all exemplify this approach in variously synchronic and diachronic degrees.

16. It may appear strange to refer to these as ontological backgrounds, since Biernacki ostensibly asks questions about how labor is *perceived*. However, I take his emphasis on signifying *practice* to be a particularly strong claim as to the location of social concepts within social reality, that is, of epistemological questions within ontological ones.

17. It is his effort to isolate culture as an independent variable of sorts that motivates Biernacki's highly controlled comparison of the British and German wool textile industries. In the process, however, all of the features that he "holds constant" across cases can be fruitfully reread as helping to establish the puzzle of his historicizing comparison. This is similar to what Aviles and Reed (2017, 726) describe as the "mechanistic" aspect of Biernacki's argument, a machine-like regularity that he then shows to be differentially "interpreted" by actors in the two cases.

18. The quotation from Engels is found in Biernacki (1995, 42n4). Biernacki (1995, 260) is by no means agnostic about the relative *analytical* merits of these competing conceptions, suggesting that German understandings were "perhaps more penetrating" than those of the British.

19. Important aspects of Adams's (2005) argument not considered here also stress historical continuities.

References

Abbott, Andrew. 1991. "History and Sociology: The Lost Synthesis." *Social Science History* 15(2):201–38.

——. 2001. *Time Matters: On Theory and Method.* Chicago: University of Chicago Press.

Abend, Gabriel. 2014. *The Moral Background: An Inquiry Into the History of Business Ethics.* Princeton, NJ: Princeton University Press.

——. 2022. "Making Things Possible." *Sociological Methods and Research* 51(1):68–107.

Abrams, Philip. 1982. *Historical Sociology*. Ithaca, NY: Cornell University Press.

Adams, Julia. 2005. *The Familial State: Ruling Families and Merchant Capitalism in Early Modern Europe*. Ithaca, NY: Cornell University Press.

Adams, Julia, Elisabeth S. Clemens, and Ann Shola Orloff. 2005. "Introduction: Social Theory, Modernity, and the Three Waves of Historical Sociology." In *Remaking Modernity: Politics, History, and Sociology*, edited by Julia Adams, Elisabeth S. Clemens, and Ann Shola Orloff, 1–72. Durham, NC: Duke University Press.

Anderson, Perry. 1974. *Lineages of the Absolutist State*. London: New Left.

Anievas, Alexander, and Kerem Nisancioglu. 2015. *How the West Came to Rule: The Geopolitical Origins of Capitalism*. London: Pluto.

Aviles, Natalie B., and Isaac Ariail Reed. 2017. "*Ratio via Machina*: Three Standards of Mechanistic Explanation in Sociology." *Sociological Methods and Research* 46(4):715–38.

Biernacki, Richard. 1995. *The Fabrication of Labor: Germany and Britain, 1640–1914*. Berkeley: University of California Press.

Bloch, Marc. 1960. *Seigneurie française et manoir anglais*. Paris: A. Colin.

——. 1967. "A Contribution Towards a Comparative History of European Societies." In *Land and Work in Mediaeval Europe: Selected Papers*, translated by J. E. Anderson, 44–81. Berkeley: University of California Press.

Braddick, Michael J. 2000. *State Formation in Early Modern England, c. 1550–1700*. Cambridge: Cambridge University Press.

Brenner, Robert. 1985. "The Agrarian Roots of European Capitalism." In *The Brenner Debate: Agrarian Class Structure and Economic Development in Pre-Industrial Europe*, edited by T. H. Aston and C. H. E. Philpin, 213–327. Cambridge: Cambridge University Press.

Burawoy, Michael. 1989. "Two Methods in Search of Science: Skocpol Versus Trotsky." *Theory and Society* 18(6):759–805.

Calhoun, Craig. 1996. "The Rise and Domestication of Historical Sociology." In *The Historic Turn in the Human Sciences*, edited by Terrence J. McDonald, 305–37. Ann Arbor: University of Michigan Press.

Clemens, Elisabeth S. 2005. "Afterward: Logics of History? Agency, Multiplicity, and Incoherence in the Explanation of Change." In *Remaking Modernity: Politics, History, and Sociology*, edited by Julia Adams, Elisabeth S. Clemens, and Ann Shola Orloff, 493–515. Durham, NC: Duke University Press.

——. 2007. "Toward a Historicized Sociology: Theorizing Events, Processes, and Emergence." *Annual Review of Sociology* 33:527–49.

Ermakoff, Ivan. 2015. "The Structure of Contingency." *American Journal of Sociology* 121(1):64–125.

Go, Julian. 2014. "Occluding the Global: Analytic Bifurcation, Causal Scientism, and Alternatives in Historical Sociology." *Journal of Globalization Studies* 5(1):122–36.

——. 2021. "Three Tensions in the Theory of Racial Capitalism." *Sociological Theory* 39(1):38–47.

Go, Julian, and George Lawson. 2017. "Introduction: For a Global Historical Sociology." In *Global Historical Sociology*, edited by Julian Go and George Lawson, 1–34. Cambridge: Cambridge University Press.

Gorski, Philip S. 2009. "Social 'Mechanisms' and Comparative-Historical Sociology: A Critical Realist Proposal." In *Frontiers of Sociology*, edited by Peter Hedström and Björn Wittrock, 147–94. Leiden, Netherlands: Brill.

Griffin, Larry J. 1992. "Temporality, Events, and Explanation in Historical Sociology." *Sociological Methods and Research* 20(4):403–27.

Hall, Stuart. 2018. "Race, Articulation, and Societies Structured in Dominance." In *Essential Essays, Volume 1: Foundations of Cultural Studies*, edited by David Morley, 172–221. Durham, NC: Duke University Press.

Haydu, Jeffrey. 1998. "Making Use of the Past: Time Periods as Cases to Compare and as Sequences of Problem Solving." *American Journal of Sociology* 104(2):339–71.

———. 2010. "Reversals of Fortune: Path Dependency, Problem Solving, and Temporal Cases." *Theory and Society* 39(1):25–48.

Hirschman, Daniel, and Isaac Ariail Reed. 2014. "Formation Stories and Causality in Sociology." *Sociological Theory* 32(4):259–82.

Isaac, Larry W. 1997. "Transforming Localities: Reflections on Time, Causality, and Narrative in Contemporary Historical Sociology." *Historical Methods* 30(1):4–12.

Knafo, Samuel, and Benno Teschke. 2020. "Political Marxism and the Rules of Reproduction of Capitalism: A Historicist Critique." *Historical Materialism* 29(3):1–30. https://doi.org/10.1163/1569206X-00001441.

Knight, Carly R., and Isaac Ariail Reed. 2019. "Meaning and Modularity: The Multivalence of 'Mechanism' in Sociological Explanation." *Sociological Theory* 37(3):234–56.

Mann, Michael. 1984. "The Autonomous Power of the State: Its Origins, Mechanisms and Results." *European Journal of Sociology* 25(2):185–213.

———. 1986. *The Sources of Social Power, Volume I: A History of Power from the Beginning to A.D. 1760.* Cambridge: Cambridge University Press.

Miliband, Ralph. 1969. *The State in Capitalist Society.* London: Weidenfeld and Nicolson.

Mitchell, Timothy. 1991. "The Limits of the State: Beyond Statist Approaches and Their Critics." *American Political Science Review* 85(1):77–96.

Padgett, John F., and Walter W. Powell. 2012. *The Emergence of Organizations and Markets.* Princeton, NJ: Princeton University Press.

Polanyi, Karl. 1977. "The Economistic Fallacy." *Review (Fernand Braudel Center)* 1(1):9–18.

Poulantzas, Nicos Ar. 1973. *Political Power and Social Classes.* Translated by Timothy O'Hagen. London: New Left.

Quisumbing King, Katrina, and Alexandre I. R. White. 2021. "Introduction: Toward a Global Historical Sociology of Race and Racism." *Political Power and Social Theory* 38:1–22.

Ragin, Charles C. 1987. *The Comparative Method: Moving Beyond Qualitative and Quantitative Strategies.* Berkeley: University of California Press.

Reed, Isaac Ariail, and Julia Adams. 2011. "Culture in the Transitions to Modernity: Seven Pillars of a New Research Agenda." *Theory and Society* 40(3):247–72.

Robinson, Cedric J. 2000. *Black Marxism: The Making of the Black Radical Tradition.* Chapel Hill: University of North Carolina Press.

Rutzou, Timothy, and Dave Elder-Vass. 2019. "On Assemblages and Things: Fluidity, Stability, Causation Stories, and Formation Stories." *Sociological Theory* 37(4):401–24.

Sayer, Derek. 1992. "A Notable Administration: English State Formation and the Rise of Capitalism." *American Journal of Sociology* 97(5):1382–415.

Sewell, William H., Jr. 2005. "Three Temporalities: Toward an Eventful Sociology." In *Logics of History: Social Theory and Social Transformation,* 81–123. Chicago: University of Chicago Press.

Skocpol, Theda. 1979. *States and Social Revolutions: A Comparative Analysis of France, Russia, and China.* Cambridge: Cambridge University Press.

Skocpol, Theda, and Margaret Somers. 1980. "The Uses of Comparative History in Macrosocial Inquiry." *Comparative Studies in Society and History* 22(2):174–97.

Spruyt, Hendrik. 1994. *The Sovereign State and Its Competitors: An Analysis of Systems Change.* Princeton, NJ: Princeton University Press.

Steinmetz, George. 1998. "Critical Realism and Historical Sociology." *Comparative Studies in Society and History* 40(1):170–86.

——. 2004. "Odious Comparisons: Incommensurability, the Case Study, and 'Small N's' in Sociology." *Sociological Theory* 22(3):371–400.

——. 2005a. "The Epistemological Unconscious of U.S. Sociology in the Transition to Post-Fordism: The Case of Historical Sociology." In *Remaking Modernity: Politics, History, and Sociology*, edited by Julia Adams, Elisabeth S. Clemens, and Ann Shola Orloff, 109–57. Durham, NC: Duke University Press.

——. 2005b. "Scientific Authority and the Transition to Post-Fordism: The Plausibility of Positivism in U.S. Sociology Since 1945." In *The Politics of Method in the Human Sciences: Positivism and Its Epistemological Others*, edited by George Steinmetz, 275–323. Durham, NC: Duke University Press.

——. 2014. "Comparative History and Its Critics: A Genealogy and a Possible Solution." In *A Companion to Global Historical Thought*, edited by Prasenjit Duara, Viren Murphy, and Andrew Sartori, 412–36. Malden, MA: Wiley Blackwell.

Teschke, Benno. 2003. *The Myth of 1648: Class, Geopolitics, and the Making of Modern International Relations*. London: Verso.

——. 2014. "IR Theory, Historical Materialism and the False Promise of International Historical Sociology." *Spectrum: Journal of Global Studies* 6(1):1–66.

Tilly, Charles. 1986. *The Contentious French*. Cambridge, MA: Belknap.

——. 1990. *Coercion, Capital, and European States, AD 990–1990*. Cambridge, MA: Basil Blackwell.

Wood, Ellen Meiksins. 1991. *The Pristine Culture of Capitalism: A Historical Essay on Old Regimes and Modern States*. London: Verso.

CHAPTER 10

HOW NOT TO LIE WITH COMPARATIVE HISTORICAL SOCIOLOGY

A Realist Balance Sheet

SIMEON J. NEWMAN

Introduction

Milton Friedman (1953, 14), champion of positivist social science, decries the idea that we should carve away at existing social research methodologies in an effort to improve them, calling the impulse "fundamentally wrong and productive of much mischief." He would find this chapter fundamentally mischievous. For I assume here that we ought to interrogate the adequacy of our methodologies and even reconfigure them to better suit our scientific ends.

The ends I assume are realist ones. This position in the philosophy of the social sciences maintains that there is a mind-independent reality;[1] that substantive phenomena and processes are the result of entities endowed with (or linked to) causal powers;[2] and that our explanatory models and theories are (or should be) symbolically mediated renderings of how these entities generate the phenomena or processes of interest.[3] Realists contrast their position to positivism (often defined as the empiricist search for constant conjunctions of events and/or the idea that such regularities conform to laws) as well as strong constructionism (a form of philosophical idealism denying that reality is independent of the knower) (Bhaskar 1998; Bourdieu, Chamboredon, and Passeron 1991, 6–7; Marx 1973, 100–101; Sayer 1992; Steinmetz 1998). Distinguishing scientific realism from strong constructionism involves defending the possibility of empirically informed knowledge and thus of science itself—a position advanced mainly on philosophical grounds. But realists' disputation with positivism revolves around their distinctive vision for the scientific enterprise and thus comes into sharpest relief in their views about the purpose of scientific methodologies.

Realists think our methodologies should support us in developing *causal models* shown to be *empirically adequate* (Gorski 2004, 20–21). At first glance, this position may seem uncontroversial. But if we grant that social causation is complex (e.g., that there are numerous potential causes of any given substantive phenomenon or process or that there is a single cause but it is nondeterministic), its implications can readily be seen to conflict with other values held dear in the positivism-influenced social sciences. Thus, by privileging accounts of real causation (Elias 1983; Sayer 1992; Steinmetz 1998; Tilly 2008, chaps. 7, 11), we tend to sacrifice empirical generalizability.[4] And by opting to develop models that we feel confident are empirically adequate (Bhaskar 1998, 12, 21, 45–46, 129; Demetriou 2009; Gorski 2004), we shortcircuit the pursuit of ones with explanatory power.[5] We may, therefore, have to pay a price to pursue empirically adequate causal models—in other words, to avoid lying.

And yet precisely *how* we are to do so remains somewhat unclear. The only full-fledged realist comparative historical methodology prescribes comparing both causal entities (often hidden from view) *and* their effects (phenomena and processes) across multiple cases (Steinmetz 2004). But merely selecting different cases that share the same underlying causes, to say nothing of completing a study of them, borders on impossible.[6] We may, therefore, be justified in wondering about the alternatives. Specifically, are the methodologies developed to furnish empirically generalizable models or to increase existing theories' explanatory power irredeemably flawed from the perspective of realism, or can they be used, albeit perhaps judiciously? What are the epistemic hazards?

My inquiry into this question concerns the *comparative* dimension of comparative historical social science more than the *historical* one. Nearly all satisfying explanations seem to account for some amount of change over time (or, conversely, continuity despite contrary expectations) and are thus somewhat unavoidably "historical." Comparison, in contrast, raises potential problems. By definition, comparative conclusions represent synthetic insights gleaned through juxtaposition. None rest on a single case (however construed); all instead straddle cases. It is precisely this hammock-like quality that seems to make comparative conclusions empirically generalizable and apt for pursuing models with explanatory power. So it is also this quality that forces us to ask whether by comparing we sometimes sacrifice the empirical adequacy of our explanatory models.

I take it as a given that we can scrutinize existing comparative historical methodologies on *epistemic grounds*. My critique is therefore pitched slightly above the "analytic architectures" to which researchers may freely appeal in pursuit of scientific credibility and professional success (Mayrl and Wilson

2020). But I do not aim so high as to dismiss all existing methodologies as reflections of an "episteme" that cuts across the entire discursive field and whose influence the researcher cannot hope to escape (Foucault 1970). Our methodologies enable and constrain, although different ones do so in different ways and thus harbor different implications in regard to the pursuit of empirically adequate causal models.

It will be useful at this point to define several terms that I use over the course of my discussion. I use the term "comparison" in two ways. By *local comparison*, I mean simultaneous or successive examination of multiple cases with reference to one another (see chapter 2 in this volume). By *global comparison*, I refer to juxtapositions of the cases directly studied to existing explanatory theories based on other cases (see chapter 8 in this volume). (I use these terms in a metaphorical sense, not at all a geographical one.) I use both "theory" and "model" to denote abstract renderings of processes and structures that have at least one explanans (that which does the explaining) and an explanandum (that which is explained). I use the two terms slightly differently, however, to track a practical difference. By *theory*, I mean one of these abstract renderings that the researcher inherits and may choose to put to use. By *model*, I mean one that the researcher constructs and advances as a contribution. (In practice, the researcher *consumes* theories but *produces* models.)

Different comparative historical methodologies leverage different kinds of comparisons. As I elaborate below, the so-called Millian method[7] calls for local comparison. In this, it contrasts with each of the other methodologies I survey, which call for leveraging global comparisons of different kinds, sometimes along with local comparison. In the *negative-case method*,[8] the theory's explanans matches the case(s) but its explanandum does not; in what I call the *alternative-factors approach*,[9] the theory's explanans does not match the case(s) but its explanandum does; and in the approach we may call *inference from absence*,[10] neither the theory's explanans nor its explanandum match the case(s), but the researcher nevertheless compares findings with the theory en route to drawing conclusions.[11]

Based on an analysis of applications of each research strategy, I argue that these methodologies differ significantly in terms of the empirical adequacy of the explanatory models they lead the researcher to develop. As I try to show, neither the Millian method nor inference from absence is an adequate means for developing empirically adequate explanatory models; instead, the models advanced on the basis of these strategies reflect dogmas. The negative-case method and the alternative-factors approach fare considerably better; although they each ultimately incline the researcher to contort explanatory models in ways that are not based on evidence, they nevertheless do serve as means to develop ones that are by and large empirically adequate, especially if these contortions are checked.

I proceed as follows. I assess the locally comparative Millian method and then each of the globally comparative approaches—inference from absence, the negative-case method, and the alternative-factors approach—based on a critical assessment of exemplar books that employ each respective strategy. I conclude with a discussion of what we can accomplish by using the negative-case and alternative-factors strategies; namely, we can progressively elaborate and expand our understanding of the social totality. This is where scientific models and theories meet reality, and it thus borders and bears upon normative questions of politics and ethics.

What's Wrong with the Millian Method?

The so-called Millian method was once and perhaps continues to be considered the gold standard for comparative historical research. Theda Skocpol popularized the strategy in her *States and Social Revolutions* (1979). Indeed, this method was so prominent and so closely associated with Skocpol's book that the ensuing methodological debate was aptly described as a series of answers to the question "What's wrong with Theda Skocpol?" (Paige 1999, 789). I further scrutinize the Millian method in this section based on a critique of how it played out in practice in Skocpol's remarkable and ambitious attempt to identify the causes of social revolutions, which she defines as profound alterations of a society's government and class structure.

In comparative historical sociology, the Millian method is used to explain specific outcomes on the basis of two kinds of local comparison. The *method of agreement* allows us to make causal inferences when at least one cause is present and the outcome of interest occurs in each of the cases we examine. The mechanics are as follows: our hunch or hypothesis is that A causes B; we look to cases in which A' is present and find that B' occurs; and we infer that A caused B, which we take as confirmation. (It is perfectly well for A' to coincide with other, extraneous factors when employing the method of agreement, and indeed, this increases our credence.) The *method of difference* allows for causal inferences when variation in the putative cause correlates with variation in the outcome of interest. It proceeds as follows: our hunch or hypothesis is that A causes B; we look to one or more cases in which A' is present and find that B' occurs *and also* one or more cases in which A' is not present and find that B' does not occur; and we infer that A caused B, which we take as confirmation. (It is preferable for extraneous factors to be constant across cases when employing the method of difference, as a nonconstant value would mean that these factors could also correlate with the outcome and thereby weaken credence in the inference.)

Skocpol employs both the method of agreement and the method of difference to argue that the French, Russian, and Chinese revolutions were the product of three variables: government crisis, rigid agrarian class structure, and peasant insurgency. First, take government crisis. The French Revolution broke out amid the government's financial doldrums, itself attributable to its attempts to compete with England; the Russian Revolution erupted in the context of government decay during the First World War; and the Chinese Revolution emerged after Japanese incursions and the Second World War had taken their toll on the government.

Government crises only led to social revolution, Skocpol argues, because they were accompanied by insurrectionary peasant movements facing off against elites in the context of a rigid agrarian class structure. Peasant insurrections occurred in cases with a particularly large and united middle peasantry. And they only segued to social revolution, in turn, when faced with agrarian elites who had prevented the government from carrying out agrarian reform. In such cases, a peasant insurrection broke out and destabilized the old regimes. (Crucially, peasant insurrections did not result when the middle peasantry was either weak or nonexistent or when the landed elite exercised little influence over the government, as in England, Japan, and Prussia.) Since France, Russia, and China were in crisis due to external factors as well, the result was social revolution.

So what is wrong with Skocpol? Commentaries on Skocpol's use of the Millian method are as extensive as her book is famous, and some are exceptionally insightful. Observers note, as Skocpol (1984, 378) herself admits, that the Millian method requires that one assume causal factors are deterministic rather than probabilistic (Hall 2003, 382; Lieberson 1992)—an assumption that, some argue, can and should be jettisoned (Ragin 1987). This method leads researchers to register diffusionary processes in case-bound terms, which serves to obscure and misconstrue them (Sewell 1985, 81–84; Tilly 2008, 86, chap. 11; cf. Abbott 2001, chap. 5). And it assumes unit homogeneity in order to gaze upon completely dissimilar cases and processes with the same analytic lens (Burawoy 1989, 782; cf. Ragin 1987, 38). These criticisms identify problematic *ontological assumptions*, each of which is undeniably an issue.

But they have not quite hit on what I consider the most serious problem with the Millian method. The biggest problem, in my view, is that it dictates *substantive conclusions*. Its methodological procedures obstruct empirical adequacy because they entail that the *number of cases* included in an analysis bears upon the nature of the conclusions that can be drawn, at least when combining both the method of agreement and the method of difference. The Millian method only allows the researcher to draw conclusions in which the number of variables said to be causes of the outcome of interest are equal to or fewer than the number of negative cases. Consider what it would have taken for Skocpol to conclude that a fourth variable, together with the three she identifies, was also a cause of social revolutions: she would have needed to select an additional *negative* case, featuring positive values for state crisis, peasant insurrection, and rigid agrarian class structure and a *negative* value for the fourth variable. Only in this way could she use this method to determine that the absence of the fourth variable correlates with the failure of the outcome and thereby affirm that it *is* indeed a cause of the outcome in cases in which both the variable and the outcome correlate positively (positive cases).

The fact that the number of cases included in the analysis bears directly on substantive conclusions has monumental implications. Thus, having considered only three negative cases, Skocpol heroically reduces the causes of social revolutions to *three*. The Millian method left her no alternative.[12] Had Skocpol included a fourth negative case, the method would have allowed her to conclude that social revolutions are the product of four main causal variables; and had she included five, it would have let her conclude that they are the product of five causes.

Now, the French, Russian, and Chinese revolutions were caused by whatever number (and whatever kind) of causes that caused them. This has little to do with the number of failed social revolutions and absolutely nothing to do with the number of such cases included in a given study. How the world actually works is a substantive question and cannot be adjudicated by dictates stemming from any methodology per se. Because the Millian method sets the researcher in train to develop causal models that reflect the methodology, we have no reason to think the models are empirically adequate. They are not entirely erroneous, to be sure, but are almost certainly fundamentally incomplete because they reflect pro-omission dogmas borne of the methodology.

Inference from Absence

Miguel Angel Centeno's ambitious book, *Blood and Debt: War and the Nation-State in Latin America* (2002), exemplifies what I call *inference from absence*. Using this strategy, the researcher draws from existing theory to point to something that was present in the cases upon which the theory was based but *not* present in the cases studied, and then concludes that this absence accounts for the fact that the outcome did not result in the cases of study. Its chief feature is that neither the theoretical explanans nor the explanandum matches the cases of study. It draws a conclusion only by assuming that there is a causal relationship between both absences. This assumption is epistemically treacherous. Centeno juxtaposes a prominent theory—bellicist theory, which was developed to account for Western European state formation and which posits that "war made the state, and the state made war" (Tilly 1975, 42)—with the case of nineteenth- and twentieth-century Latin America (excluding Central America). He highlights the fact that neither the theoretical explanans—"large-scale war"—nor the explanandum—"state development"—matches the cases he studies: "these countries have mostly avoided large-scale war," and "the states have only minimally developed" (Centeno 2002, 11). And he *assumes* that the *lack* of large-scale wars *caused* the *lack* of state development.

Before criticizing the methodology behind this book's model, let me say that Centeno's insights into the region's modern political, economic, and social history are legion. Latin American states emerged principally due to the collapse of the Spanish colonial system, making the new republics "fragments of empire" (Centeno 2002, 25). The *caudillos*, or strongmen, who helped midwife national independence, thereafter vied with bureaucratic state organizations for political control, trouncing their attempts to extract taxes from society. *Caudillos'* wealth stemmed from their control of rural property, whose exploitation was based on repressive labor regimes in agriculture continuous with the colonial period. Since governments were largely complicit in this, they amounted to institutions of racial domination (Centeno 2002, 64). Thus, the inherited "colonial race hierarchy" became Latin America's "postcolonial impediment to nation-state formation" (Centeno 2002, 272). Since few social groups identified with the state, Latin America's most salient cleavages were not *between* nation-states, as in Europe, but *within* national territories.

These insights could have been developed into an empirically adequate explanatory model. But use of inference from absence leads Centeno to contrast Latin America with bellicist theory, resulting in inferences that lack an evidentiary basis. The first step involves conceptualizing Latin America in terms of the absence of the theory's explanans: war.[13] Centeno provides two kinds of reasons for their absence in Latin America. First, Latin American countries were "born" into a world in which Great Powers already existed (Centeno 2002, 25). Not only did this make it impossible for Latin American states to become Great Powers themselves; Great Powers also provided Latin American governments with credit on the condition that they not challenge great authority (Centeno 2002, 127). Second, when Latin American governments did opt for military action against a neighboring country, they did not do so in a vacuum. *Caudillos* obstructed the state's extraction of taxes from the population—which could otherwise have been used to finance state initiatives such as war. This, of course, reinforced the importance of borrowing to finance conflict (Centeno 2002, 118). Together, these factors prevented states from marching further and further in the direction of total war with one another.

The second step in inference from absence is to leverage a global comparison to draw the conclusion that the absent explanans accounts for the absence of the theory's explanandum in the cases studied. Having accounted for the absence of total wars in modern Latin America, Centeno addresses bellicist theory's explanandum—the formation of powerful states—by concluding that the absence of the theory's explanans caused the lack of state formation across

Latin America: the explanandum. Because Latin American states did not extract resources from their populations in coercion-extraction cycles comparable to those bellicist theory says were central to European state formation, Centeno (2002, 130) maintains, they did not grow powerful. He is crystal clear about the relationship he posits between cause and effect in his model: "total wars seem to produce richer, more powerful states" than do "limited wars" (Centeno 2002, 22). And he even offers scope conditions within which war can be expected to lead to state formation (Centeno 2002, 275–76). But there is a hitch: never does he show that his model is empirically adequate.

Indeed, Centeno's evidence suggests that two other factors were responsible for the outcome of interest, and he does not provide any reason to think they were related to war. First, *caudillos* prevented states' efforts to extract resources from societal elites; and second, international lines of credit gave states an alternative means of financing war, making it unnecessary to develop bureaucracies that would be capable of extracting resources from society. These are the proximate causes Centeno himself points to in his narrative as explanations for a lack of state formation. He nevertheless insists the absence of large-scale war was the fundamental factor blocking this outcome in Latin America. To demonstrate that his model is empirically adequate, Centeno would need to show that the lack of large-scale war was a distal cause behind one or both of these proximate causes: that it caused *caudillos* to be powerful[14] and/or that it made international lines of credit available to Latin American states.[15] He demonstrates neither. Thus, in formal terms, Centeno claims that causation runs from ~A (lack of war) to ~B (blocked state formation); he provides evidence that p (powerful *caudillos*) and q (international credit) led to ~B; but he fails to provide evidence that ~A caused p or q.

Centeno's conclusion that the absence of large-scale war causes a lack of state formation requires treating his theory of choice as a statement of general laws, undertaking global comparison of the theory with the cases of study, and making causal inferences based on the absence of both explanans and explanandum: the *absence* of state-organized conflicts "links the infrequency of wars with the weakness of states" (Centeno 2002, 277); formally, ~A causes ~B. Note that this kind of statement, which John Stuart Mill might subsume to what he calls the method of residues, has no direct evidentiary criteria.[16] Such models rest on a belief that inexistent things are, much as theists posit, ontic gatekeepers.

If entities that do not exist are capable of preventing things from occurring, one can explain miracles. Thus Centeno opines that mass conscription to populate armies for total wars produces democratic states replete with liberal citizenship rights, and that because there was no mass conscription in Latin America, there was, consequently, no citizenship (Centeno 2002, 238). Yet if it is based on inference from absence, the model that sustains these conclusions is not empirically adequate. One indicator of this from Centeno's book is that this particular miracle is at odds with evidence provided, which suggests that entrenched ethnoracial hierarchies were inhospitable to liberal citizenship regimes and that, because they were so powerful, *caudillos* and other economic elites—who depended on ethnoracial hierarchies for their repressive labor regimes—prevented the advent of liberal citizenship.

The problem lies with epistemic hazards inherent to the methodological strategy of inference from absence, not its application in this or any other instance. Indeed, to his credit, Centeno casts doubt on "encompassing general laws" (2002, 18, see also 260). Nevertheless, inference from absence requires that he embrace them, which he does explicitly (264, 279), obliquely (104, 107, 264), and implicitly, as the very basis of his inferential approach. Once one accepts general laws, they can lean into global comparison, employing covering-law logic to derive conclusions about how the lack of an explanans was responsible for the lack of an explanandum—inference from absence. But no matter how nuanced or restricted such conclusions may be, models about causal relationships between inexistent things cannot make sufficient recourse to evidence to be empirically adequate. For this reason, they make the researcher susceptible to invoking spirits as spurious causes. We must admit that there *could* be secondary movers just as there could be a prime mover. But because it is invoked on grounds of dogma rather than evidence, any alleged cause identified using such a methodology would be a "philosophical monstrosity . . . that can be defined as an entity but that [likely] doesn't exist" (Abbott 1992, 433), and if it does exist, it is likely to be "trivial" and "unimportant" (Mahoney, Kimball, and Koivu 2009, 127).

The impulse to highlight unimportant factors does not stem from an interest in bellicist theory per se, nor from opting to study the political development of modern Latin America. It stems, instead, from the *combination* of the two because neither the theoretical explanans nor explanandum matches these cases. By engaging with bellicist state-formation theory, one may be able to contribute empirically adequate explanatory models (although for explanatory misfiring in Tilly's classic bellicist account, see chapter 9 in this volume). But applying bellicist theory to nineteenth- and twentieth-century Latin America requires that one draw conclusions sheerly based on global comparison, thus forgoing the opportunity to draw conclusions informed by evidence about Latin American political development. It is only in spite of the methodology that Centeno provides prescient insights in his discussion of Latin America's colonial legacy, *caudillos*, ethnoracial hierarchy, and world-scale political economy that could be built upon to develop an empirically adequate model of the region's political development. Indeed, Centeno is the first to highlight how this research avenue is more promising "than any adjustment of the bellicist theory of political development" (2002, 163).

The Negative-Case Method

Dylan J. Riley's audacious book, *The Civic Foundations of Fascism in Europe: Italy, Spain, and Romania, 1870–1945* (2010), exemplifies the negative-case method, a powerful strategy for studying a phenomenon that clearly had an impact in one or more cases but not as rendered by a theory of interest. That is, this strategy starts with a *tension* between theory and cases in which the theoretical explanans matches the cases but the explanandum does not. Since the theory in question is based on other cases, the negative-case method is inherently globally comparative. One follows the explanans to find what it produced in the cases of study. In principal, the cases could vary in regard to the explanandum, allowing for conclusions based also on local comparison. But at least one case of study must exhibit anomalous evidence, which is then leveraged as license to reconstruct the theory. The result is a new explanatory model. As I aim to show, the resulting model is empirically adequate, although the methodology does set the researcher up to make gratuitous claims about the cases upon which the original theory was based.

Riley opts for neo-Tocquevillian theory about civil society and liberal democracy and selects a set of three parallel cases—interwar Italy, Spain, and Romania—whose political development does not confirm the theory: the theory's explanans (robust civil society), but not its explanandum (liberal democracy), matches the cases. In Riley's model, the efflorescence of civil society—in the absence of elite-masses political polarization and liberal democratic institutions—led to fascism in interwar Italy, Spain, and Romania.

Let me start by outlining the two chief empirical features of the cases. First was a lack of elite cohesion and nationalist solidarity. For reasons that vary somewhat by case, none of these countries' elites had political parties that united the distinct fractions organically and allowed them to project a unified agenda as a national program. The second factor present across all three of Riley's cases is class organization among the masses amid an absence of between-class struggle. Given the first factor, the second one precipitated fascism in each of the cases. In Italy, civil society organizations proliferated and politicized. The left was politically ineffective, allowing the fascist movement to arise in civil society, transform into a party-militia, repress workers, and trigger a wave of mobilization, giving rise to "societal fascism." In Spain, civil society also grew rapidly, spearheaded mostly by agrarian elites and Catholics. A republican-socialist coalition initiated a leftist political alternative. Elites were outraged. But since they were also ineffective, military officials took the reins and established a "traditionalist" fascist regime. Finally, in Romania, civil society also expanded rapidly, while the government collapsed. This allowed the deposed monarch to justify a return to power; it also contributed to the rise of a grassroots fascist movement. After both political parties imploded, this movement metamorphosed into a terrorist organization, prompting the monarch to install "statist fascism" from above.

One could juxtapose these cases to theory in at least two ways. One alternative involves finding a theory whose explanans does not match the cases but whose explanandum does, which is characteristic of the alternative factors approach, discussed in the next section. Riley opts, instead, for the negative-case method and juxtaposes his cases to Tocquevillian theory. Whereas Tocquevillian theory posits a positive relationship between robust civil society (the explanans) and liberal democracy (the explanandum), in the cases Riley examines, civil society was associated instead with fascism. This leads Riley to conceive of his cases as negative cases—negative, that is, vis-à-vis the Tocquevillian view that civil society's telos is liberal democracy—and to take the mismatch between theory and cases as indication of a "need for theoretical reconstruction" (Riley 2010, 18). Based on his analysis, and drawing conceptual inspiration from Gramsci, he reconstructs Tocquevillian theory into a new explanatory model.

Riley's explanatory model is based on contrasting the pattern of political development in these cases with a realpolitik-inflected, relational, three-stage conception of class formation—tacitly based on the Western European and perhaps U.S. cases—at the center of which is a tripartite developmental conception of hegemony: the advent of interclass hegemony, involving a political party that unifies the elite; followed by interclass hegemony, a broad acceptance of that party's rationale for ruling; and then (hopefully) counterhegemony, wherein civil society ascends to political leadership. But, crucially for Riley's argument, civil society can also develop in the *absence* of hegemonic politics—when the antecedent stages have not occurred. Such scenarios—which Gramsci called "Organic Crises"—are characterized by traditional parties' inability to "represent" and "lead" because "they are no longer recognized by their class (or fractions of a class) as its expression" (Riley 2010, 17, quoting Gramsci). The consequences of civil societal resurgence under such conditions are very different from those under hegemonic development. In Italy, Spain, and Romania, when "the 'traditional parties' and the forces of opposition were outstripped by a rapidly developing civil society," fascist movements stepped in and created "a regime that claims to represent the people or nation but rejects parliamentary institutional forms" (Riley 2010, 17). Such a scenario is anomalous vis-à-vis Tocquevillian theory. In each of the cases studied, Riley shows, a failure of intraclass hegemony undermined interclass hegemony, which, in turn, led their respective efflorescent civil societies to develop in a fascist direction.

The upshot is that the causal model is empirically adequate. Individually and collectively, Riley's cases show that when civil society weighs in on the political balance of forces without being structured by counterhegemony, political opportunists will seize the day and fascism will result. This empirical adequacy means that the negative-case method is compatible with realism.

However, application of this methodology raises thorny questions about the empirical adequacy of the *new* model for the *old* cases upon which the original theory was based. The negative-case method seeks explanatory power. The idea is to "reconstruct" an existing theory such that it can account for anomalous evidence, expanding the theory's range. But, of course, to account for substantive anomalies, the researcher must substantively alter the theory. And it must be conceded that, insofar as it is actually altered, a "reconstructed" theory is a somewhat *different* causal statement than the original theory. Whether the difference is so slight that the new causal statement is essentially the same theory or so significant that it represents a new explanatory model cannot be settled a priori. Nevertheless, the extended-case method prescribes viewing all such statements as versions of the original theory (for only in this way can the theory be said to explain the evidence upon which it was originally based *and* the anomalous evidence). There is obviously a problem when the theory is altered significantly, for the method would lead the researcher to erroneously deem a new causal model merely a new version of the original theory, replete with the complete record of success of the original theory plus whatever else has been explained by its "reconstructed" version.

This epistemic hazard seems to encourage Riley to compromise his otherwise empirically sound conclusions. Riley essentially concedes that Tocquevillian theory accounts for positive cases and conceives of his cases in terms of failed hegemonic political development, thereby reserving the conceptual space of successful hegemony for the positive cases. While the great bulk of his efforts are dedicated to developing his model, Riley also seems inclined to take the additional step that the negative-case method prescribes. Thus, he not only argues that his model can explain another case of fascism—German Nazism (Riley 2010, 186–87)—as we might expect him to do, but also suggests that the success of hegemonic politics may best explain England's and France's transitions to liberal democracy (22). Riley furnishes no evidence for this last contention; it is, instead, borne entirely of use of the negative-case method, because the methodology leads the researcher to conceive of what they do in terms of *reconstructing* theories thought to perform well at explaining positive cases. It is to Riley's credit that he resists saying more, instead allocating this problem to a subsequent book (2010, 212).

The negative-case method's globally comparative moment thus pushes the researcher to reach for conclusions that are not based on empirical evidence. This is attributable to the *methodology*, not the researcher who applies it, and has been since first proposed. The idea that we can alter an existing theory, which is based on positive cases, by making adjustments to accommodate evidence gleaned from negative cases, is premised on the assumption of causal homogeneity across the universe of cases—that is, that the *same* factors are responsible for the outcome in *both* sets of cases (Emigh 1997, 658). The negative-case method does allow the researcher to develop empirically adequate causal models. But because it also entails this assumption, the researcher who uses the methodology is inclined to project new explanatory models back onto previously theorized cases. All such projections are artifacts of the methodology. And since the explanatory model will not necessarily be empirically adequate to sustain any of them, they represent epistemic hazards.

The Alternative-Factors Approach

Jeffery M. Paige's prescient book, *Coffee and Power: Revolution and the Rise of Democracy in Central America* (1997), is an excellent example of what I call the *alternative-factors approach*, a research strategy that is widely espoused but rarely assessed. Like the negative-case method, the alternative-factors approach starts with a tension between theoretical expectations and the case(s) examined, but whereas the tension for the former concerns the explanans, for the latter, it concerns the explanandum. Paige's theorist of choice is Barrington Moore, who maintains that the bourgeoisie (explanans) drives democratization (explanandum); as Moore (1966, 418) puts it, "no bourgeoisie, no democracy." The tension lies in the fact that Paige's cases, Costa Rica, El Salvador, and Nicaragua, all converged on democracy even though the bourgeoisie did not impel the process.

Paige uses this observation as license to develop an alternative explanatory model capable of accounting for the "same" outcome. Paige shows that although these cases differed dramatically from one another in the first half of the twentieth century, their elites—the most powerful of whom were coffee elites—converged on liberal democracy (and neoliberalism) by the 1990s. His model is based on two kinds of comparison: first, by leveraging global comparison, he shows that these cases represent an alternative pathway to democracy besides the bourgeois-led one that Moore identified; and, second, based on local comparison, he shows that the Central American coffee elites' political aims were a consequence, not a cause, of political (and economic) rupture, itself driven by peasant insurrection.

The fact that Moore's explanans fails to fit these Central American cases could have led Paige to seek out a theory whose explanans fared better. But he opts instead to identify through his research the alternative factors responsible for Central America's transition to liberal democracy. His first step is to conceptualize the elite. Moore assumes that there are two kinds of social elites: the agrarian nobility and the industrial bourgeoisie. Paige observes, however, that in twentieth-century Central America the landed elite was not a separate class from the industrial bourgeoisie; the elite was, instead, a single class, in that those who employed crude, labor-repressive agricultural production techniques interpenetrated with agro-industrialists, whose production was better mechanized (Paige 1997, 54–55). Over the course of his analysis, Paige shows that it took the threat of socialist revolution to divide the elite and thereby force it to accede to democracy. Having substantiated this conclusion empirically, Paige develops an explanatory model that is general enough to capture changes in elites' political ideology. Since the model is intended to represent a generalization cutting across cases that differed considerably at the macroscopic level, however, it necessarily highlights relatively microscopic factors. I return to how this microscopic bias represents an epistemic hazard below.

But let me first relate Paige's conclusions, starting with how these countries compared prior to converging on democracy. The political dynamics stemming from the economic crisis of the 1930s led these countries' political economies to develop in very different ways. However, during the postwar bonanza, they gradually converged. All three countries' agrarian sectors grew increasingly mechanized, generating a growing semi-proletarian workforce by the late twentieth century. Did this political-economic development cause the elite to behave democratically, as Moore's theory suggests? No, the political-economic convergence was a mere background condition. The precipitating causes for the three countries' political convergence on democracy and neoliberalism were, first, the economic crisis set off by the oil shocks of the 1970s and, second and most importantly, the revolutionary peasant movements that took shape by the 1980s. Over the course of the 1980s, the Costa Rican agrarian elite remained amenable to democracy, Salvadoran elites fought it to the end, after which they capitulated, and Nicaragua agrarians cycled from collaboration to opposition, until they found themselves in power, at which time they ceded the basic trappings of democracy in an effort to end the revolutionary civil war.

As an instance of the alternative-factors approach, Paige's conclusions rest largely on global comparison. He accepts Moore's explanandum of liberal democracy but concludes that Moore's explanans, the allegedly democratic inclinations of the bourgeoisie, does not describe these cases. Only under the pressure of armed struggle did agro-industrialists break ranks with traditional agrarians in El Salvador and Nicaragua and support democracy (Paige 1997, 329). The revolutionary socialist movements did not successfully take power in El Salvador or stay in power in Nicaragua. They let it fall to the agro-industrial elite. Agro-industrialists were not, however, pro-democracy; they were *forced* to accept democracy. Together with related work (Eley 1984; Rueschemeyer, Huber Stephens, and Stephens 1992), this conclusion "calls into question" the theory of "bourgeois democratic revolution" (Paige 1997, 323). Moore's theory cannot explain Paige's cases. But rather than reconstruct it, Paige elaborates a different, historically conditional explanatory model (see Paige 1999). His "new

model of democratic transition . . . through socialist revolution from below"
(Paige 1997, 7) explains why El Salvador and Nicaragua converged with Costa
Rica: because the elite faced an existential political threat.

The upshot is that this explanatory model is empirically adequate. Paige's
analysis shows that political economy was insufficient to cause elites to opt for
democracy and that only an existential threat was enough. So the alternative-
factors approach is compatible with realist ends.

And yet, having identified the factor that accounts for the outcome in the
cases he studies—socialist revolution from below—Paige is left with a question:
How *is* the bourgeoisie related to democracy? Answering this question provides Paige with a way of addressing Moore's explanans on his own terms. Paige
shows that elite narratives were anchored to key aspects of nineteenth-century
Latin American liberalism. Because they clung to these narratives to justify
rabid anticommunism during much of the revolutionary epoch, the narratives hampered the advent of democracy. But as the old order collapsed, elites
resigned themselves to a future they had not wanted. This change did not arise
spontaneously from class structure; it was induced via classist civil war.

Elite political ideology was therefore quite important in Central America,
but not in the way Moore's theory suggests. This observation—drawn from
Paige's cases but focused on Moore's explanans—allows Paige to place his model
alongside Moore's theory. But this examination of the cases studied, guided by
the theory's explanans (which, in the original form, was found not to obtain in
the cases studied), harbors an inherent epistemic hazard: the miniaturization
of the causal factors posited in the model. If the researcher opts to elaborate
a causal model emphasizing factors common to the cases studied and those
captured in the original theory, they must typically emphasize relatively microscopic ones. (This is because, among cases that are heterogeneous, the larger the
number of cases to which one compares, the smaller will be the fraction of the
compared case that matches the cases to which it is compared, ceteris paribus.)
It is to Paige's credit that he does not lean in. He does, however, seem affected:
he emphasizes smaller causal factors in his model than those that feature in
Moore's theory. Whereas Moore maintains that class structure is the proximate
cause of elite political preferences, Paige's model suggests that it is actually elite
narratives, or the stories they tell themselves about who they are, and that class
structure is a distal cause that only indirectly affects elite ideology.

The cause of any outcome common to a set of cases is what caused the
outcome in those cases, and not necessarily the cause of the "same" outcome
in other cases. The size of a cause does not contravene this principle. Thus,
the empirical adequacy of a model suffers to the degree that it arbitrarily
miniaturizes the explanans. Any method that leads the researcher to do so
is burdened with an epistemic hazard. Elites' ideology—a miniature factor—
did not cause democratization in Central America. To the contrary, in Paige's

model, the drivers of the transition to democracy are macroscopic processes: political-economic transformations prepare the ground, and peasant insurrection from below precipitates it. Elite political-ideological change is just an interesting addendum. Although certainly important in its own right, to stress these narratives in the causal model would, therefore, be to make the causal model less empirically adequate.

Where Does This Leave Us?

Both the negative-case method and the alternative-factors approach are compatible with the scientific realist ends of generating empirically adequate explanatory models. As Riley and Paige, respectively, implement them, neither strategy requires the assumption of ontological determinism; both are capable of giving due recognition to the causal interdependence of cases; and neither requires the belief that a given cause-effect sequence will play out similarly regardless of context—unlike the Millian method. They instead work by leveraging a tension between theory and cases. This tension keeps the researcher engaged in existing theory while simultaneously allowing them to be honest about how the cases of study diverge from expectations and to capture that divergence in new explanatory models. But the theory-cases disjuncture is not so vast as to lead the researcher to fall into the chasm of arbitrary belief, as with inference from absence.

The theory-case(s) tension is the opposite for each of these successful methodologies. For the negative-case method, the tension is between theoretical *explanandum* and case(s); accordingly, researchers employing this method effectively ask, "What is wrong with Theory A?" They then *follow the processes borne of the explanans* to show why it did not lead to the outcome Theory A predicts, but rather to another. Since these accounts—explanatory models—reflect the causation in question, they are empirically adequate. Meanwhile, for the alternative-factors approach, the theory-case(s) tension is between the theoretical *explanans* and the case(s); its practitioners ask, similarly, "What is wrong with Theory B?" They then *follow antecedent processes up to the explanandum* to show how it resulted and why this was possible despite the absence of Theory B's explanans (cf. Hall 2003, 391–95). And because these accounts—explanatory models—also reflect the causation in question, they are also empirically adequate.

These respective strategies need not be used in precisely the way that Riley and Paige use them. In a given negative-case analysis of more than one case, the cases could be negative vis-à-vis more than one theory. And when we limit our consideration to just one theory, cases are not always parallel with one another in regard to presence of explanans and absence of explanandum; for a given two cases, one case might exhibit this pattern while the other does not. The complexities arising from these considerations may be one of the reasons Emigh (1997, 656, emphasis added) recommends the negative-case method "to examine a *single* historical trajectory." Similarly, the alternative-factors approach need not be used, as Paige does, to examine multiple cases. Along with a given theory and the case it is based on, a single additional case study can be sufficient to demonstrate that an alternative set of factors can result in the "same" outcome.

Regardless of precisely how they are used, however, these strategies harbor epistemic hazards borne of the global comparisons for which they each call. The negative-case method inclines the researcher to assume they can explain the cases upon which the original theory was based. Even if one compares multiple cases that are negative vis-à-vis different theories, this will still be the case insofar as one follows the method's prescription of leveraging findings to "distinguish between important and irrelevant" factors for the kind of outcome in question (Emigh 1997, 658). And in regard to the alternative-factors approach, even if one only studies a single case, they will still be inclined to embrace "smaller" explanatory factors to the extent that they put these conclusions into dialogue with the original theory through global comparison.

So both of these methodologies entail a risk of drawing conclusions based on methodological strictures rather than evidence—a problem that, in a more severe form, renders the Millian method inadequate. Such conclusions are independent of evidence and are therefore gratuitous. Indeed, this can be demonstrated—because findings arrived at via the one strategy can (often) also be arrived at via the other. Let me demonstrate that this is the case before discussing the epistemic implications.

To redo Riley's analysis with the alternative-factors approach requires first selecting a theory whose explanandum (but not explanans) matches the cases, such as Moore's (1966, 435–36, 447–50) conceptualization of fascism as a reactionary and plebeian mass democracy that embraced hierarchy and romanticized small peasant producers, which protected the interests of agrarian and industrial elites. Second, we specify the alternative set of factors responsible for the outcome through study of the cases: efflorescence of civil society amid weak liberal democratic institutions produced a political vacuum into which opportunist fascist political organizations stepped. Finally, we offer a model that captures how these alternative factors led to the "same" outcome: in addition to a revolution from above, as Moore theorized, fascism can also result from a surfeit of civil society when it overflows existing political institutions and pushes opportunists to pioneer such bold new political initiatives. It is important to note that although this rendering of the conclusion captures the gist of Riley's findings, there is nothing about it that leads us to question English or French political development, as Riley seems inclined to do out of belief in the idea that "reconstructed" theories can explain the cases upon which the original theory was based.

To redo Paige's account as a negative-case analysis requires first selecting a theory whose explanans (but not explanandum) matches the cases, such as Moore's theory that armed peasant revolts lead not to liberal democracy but to communism. Second, we "reconstruct" the theory to account for the anomalous evidence: the relationship between peasant revolts and political outcome—be it communism or liberal democracy—is mediated by political-economic processes that can proletarianize peasantries and prime some elites to sympathize with democratic causes. When peasantries mobilize for socialism, these elites may temporarily ally with them, making their mobilization the impetus for a transition to democracy. Finally, we show how the theory accounts for the cases. El Salvador and Nicaragua emerged from the postwar bonanza with similar class structures, reinforcing class polarization in El Salvador and giving rise to an agro-industrial elite in Nicaragua. This, along with the economic shocks of the 1970s, drove the peasantry to armed struggle. But it also made agro-industrial elites break ranks with landed elites and collaborate with the rebels up to a point. As soon as they could, these elites took power and steered away from communism and toward liberal democracy. This explanatory model, albeit derived from the negative-case method, confirms Paige's substantive conclusions, accounting for the Central American cases. And nothing about this rendering leads to a miniaturization of causes, as Paige is inclined to since he addresses Moore's explanans (elite ideology).

That conclusions produced via the negative-case method can be "replicated" using the alternative-factors approach, and vice versa, harbors important epistemic implications. Yes, such consilience would justify greater credence in the findings. But more to the point for my purposes is that it suggests that we should have more confidence in both *research strategies* in regard to their ability to generate empirically adequate explanatory models. The fact that the gist of the conclusion arrived at using the one strategy can also be arrived at using the other means that each, in essence, vouches for the other's honesty. Both are good options if we wish to avoid lying.

Putting the one researcher's methodology to work explaining the other's cases also serves to highlight the epistemic hazards inherent to each—and suggests what would be necessary to counteract them. Because the negative-case method proceeds by "reconstructing" theory to enhance its explanatory power, it inclines the researcher to assume the "reconstructed" theory can still explain the cases upon which the original theory was based, for enhanced explanatory power is the methodology's goal. However, when we use the alternative-factors approach to draw the same substantive conclusion, we are not inclined in the same way, exposing this inclination as an epistemic hazard borne solely of the research strategy. Similarly, because the alternative-factors approach proceeds by showing how different causes can produce the "same" outcome, it inclines the researcher to hew toward smaller factors in an effort to generate a generalizable explanatory model. However, when we reconstruct these studies using the negative-case method, we can confirm the substance of the explanatory model without endorsing the idea that microscopic factors are more important than macroscopic ones. This suggests that the inclination to emphasize small causes is also an epistemic hazard borne of this research strategy.

By guarding ourselves against these epistemic hazards, comparative research may be better brought into line with realist ends. It is clear that instances in which different causes lead to the "same" outcome (alternative paths), as well as instances in which causes said to lead to certain outcomes do not in fact lead to them (negative cases), can be accommodated by a mechanisms-based, realist approach to explanation (e.g., Sayer 1992, 108). But comparative research can, at least potentially, do considerably more: it can gradually describe more and more of the social totality (cf. McMichael 1990). This was one of the original goals that Bhaskar (1998, 31, 43–44; cf. Lukács 1971) sought to accomplish by promoting realism in the social sciences, but it has been forgotten by most recent proponents, dwarfed amid pursuit of the interim goal of finding mechanisms—even though what needs improved understanding is sometimes quite large (for an instance of this condition, see chapter 7 in this volume). To fail to aggregate our models into a theory of the totality would be to remain committed, albeit perhaps implicitly, to positivism: to the view that there is in principle a hiatus between our models about observable social configurations, elaborated in conjunction with observations, and how the social world is configured. Whether under the description of "looping effects," the "double hermeneutic," or any other term, we have long known this position to be invalid for the social sciences: conceptions about the world inform behavior, and that can and often does change the world. A theory of the totality is how we do something else in light of that knowledge.

In view of this ambitious goal, however, it is worth reflecting on the limitations of both of these approaches. Both the negative-case method and the alternative-factors approach are, in a sense, epistemically conservative: because they both lean heavily on existing theories, they are incapable of truly revolutionary theoretical breakthroughs (on this problem more generally, see chapter 3 in this volume). They are limited to saying that familiar factors act or are acted upon in unfamiliar ways. Nevertheless, such caution and judicious use of explanatory categories may be prudent in light of the allure of theoretical fads and flagrant anachronistic projection of contemporary assumptions into inquiries of the past (on this problem more generally, see chapter 9 in this volume). Moreover, toggling back and forth between these strategies may allow us to not only shed mistaken beliefs but also amass a body of substantive findings that move us progressively toward fundamentally new understandings: because the latter allows us to identify un(der)appreciated causes and the former to identify un(der)appreciated consequences, a future study could relate the two un(der)appreciated factors in service of what would, at that point, be wholly new conclusions.

Acknowledgments

I would like to thank James Mahoney, Nick Wilson, and Robin Zheng for comments on earlier versions of this chapter. I alone, though, take responsibility for the arguments advanced.

Notes

1. The mind independence of social reality is sometimes mistaken for the concept dependence of all things social, generating immense confusion. The fact that green lights can be arbitrarily defined to mean "go," thus helping constitute social reality, reflects the fact that social relations and actions are concept dependent. But unless one is prepared to accept that now *red* lights mean "go" just because I say "red lights mean go," one must view reality as mind independent. Mind independence maintains *that* there is a fact of the matter; concept dependence helps us explain *what* it is.

2. This perspective is not reducible to essentialism (Bhaskar 1998, 28–37; Sayer 1992, 104–9, 162–65). There certainly are essentialist versions, especially those focused on *persons* (see Sweet 2018). But the basic and widely held view says that *social structures* have "causal powers in their own right, which arise from the combination of individuals and relations that constitute them" (Elder-Vass 2007, 40; cf. Bourdieu, Chamboredon, and Passeron 1991, 17–18). There is also a more sophisticated view dubbed "moderate essentialism," which sees essences not as givens but rather as potentialities (Sayer 1997, 462).

3. Only some realists take the additional step of asserting that models mirror reality. Most instead insist that they are more than conceptual heuristics (that, in a sense, they represent reality) but less than claims to have definitively ascertained the "truth" (that, as mere representations, they are fallible).

4. If reality is heterogeneous, attempts to enhance generalizability by tailoring our models to a larger sample size, expanded geographic scope, or extended period of study are likely to obscure the relationship between the causal factors and the outcome or process of interest *within* each population, area, and epoch, thereby compromising our causal models.

5. If causation is subject to equifinality, increases in across-case explanatory power are likely to come at the expense of within-case empirical accuracy (regardless of how cases are defined).

6. It would require completing an event-level analysis of phenomena or processes as well as an inferential procedure capable of identifying the entities causing the events for each of the cases *considered* for inclusion in the study, all before starting research in earnest. This could easily take one's entire lifetime.

7. The philosophical lineage of the Millian method traces to John Stuart Mill's canons of induction, although, ironically, Mill recommended against their use for social research (Tilly 2008, 83–84; see also chapter 12 in this volume).

8. The major philosophical inspiration for the negative-case method is Lakatos's (1978) description of and prescription for natural science, centering around the *reconstruction* of existing theories to incorporate anomalous evidence (Emigh 1997).

9. The foremost philosophical statement consistent with this strategy is Mackie's (1965) theorization of historical explanation, emphasizing equifinality, according to which the "same" outcomes may be caused in more than one way. Numerous social scientists share this view (George and Bennett 2005, 157–62; Hall 2003, 382; Ragin 1987, 15, 20, 25–26; Tilly 2008, 88–89, 137, 156–57).

10. The broad philosophical school licensing this procedure is theism.

11. I omit from discussion comparisons in which both the theory's explanans and explanandum match the case (for a discussion, see George and Bennett 2005, chap. 9).

12. Lieberson (1992, 117, see also 112) makes an analogous point from a probability-theoretic (empiricist) perspective, noting that in Mill's method, "the methodological needs are generating the theory, rather than vice versa."

13. Centeno conceptualizes the explanans as large-scale war, or total wars, in contrast with Tilly's argument that European state formation resulted from considerably less significant wars.

14. This is essentially impossible, because, on Centeno's account, *caudillos* arose as powerful actors during the struggle for independence and its immediate aftermath—before nation-states existed and thus before national wars even became a possibility.

15. The opposite was probably the case: the amount of war financing available must have correlated positively with the intensity of conflicts. For who would extend a loan for a fake war?

16. It is for this reason that Mackie (1980, 311–12), who treats the idea with considerable generosity, considers them unable to infer causation, even in delimited domains, insofar as multiple causes jointly produce the outcome.

References

Abbott, Andrew. 1992. "From Causes to Events: Notes on Narrative Positivism." *Sociological Methods and Research* 20(4):428–55.

——. 2001. *Time Matters: On Theory and Method.* Chicago: University of Chicago Press.

Bhaskar, Roy. 1998. *The Possibility of Naturalism: A Philosophical Critique of the Contemporary Human Sciences.* 3rd edition. New York: Routledge.

Bourdieu, Pierre, Jean-Claude Chamboredon, and Jean-Claude Passeron. 1991. *The Craft of Sociology: Epistemological Preliminaries.* Translated by Richard Nice. Berlin: Walter de Gruyter.

Burawoy, Michael. 1989. "Two Methods in Search of Science: Skocpol Versus Trotsky." *Theory and Society* 18(6):759–805.

Centeno, Miguel Angel. 2002. *Blood and Debt: War and the Nation-State in Latin America.* University Park: Pennsylvania State University Press.

Demetriou, Chares. 2009. "The Realist Approach to Explanatory Mechanisms in Social Science: More Than a Heuristic?" *Philosophy of the Social Sciences* 39(3):440–62.

Elder-Vass, Dave. 2007. "For Emergence: Refining Archer's Account of Social Structure." *Journal for the Theory of Social Behaviour* 37(1):25–44.

Eley, Geoff. 1984. "The British Model and the German Road: Rethinking the Course of German History Before 1914." In *The Peculiarities of German History: Bourgeois Society and Politics in Nineteenth-Century Germany,* edited by David Blackbourn and Geoff Eley, 39–155. Oxford: Oxford University Press.

Elias, Norbert. 1983. "Sociology and History." In *The Court Society*, 1–34. New York: Pantheon.

Emigh, Rebecca Jean. 1997. "The Power of Negative Thinking: The Use of Negative Case Methodology in the Development of Sociological Theory." *Theory and Society* 26(5):649–84.

Foucault, Michel. 1970. *The Order of Things: An Archaeology of the Human Sciences*. New York: Vintage.

Friedman, Milton. 1953. *Essays in Positive Economics*. Chicago: University of Chicago Press.

George, Alexander L., and Andrew Bennett. 2005. *Case Studies and Theory Development in the Social Sciences*. Cambridge, MA: MIT Press.

Gorski, Philip S. 2004. "The Poverty of Deductivism: A Constructive Realist Model of Sociological Explanation." *Sociological Methodology* 34:1–33.

Hall, Peter A. 2003. "Aligning Ontology and Methodology in Comparative Politics." In *Comparative Historical Analysis in the Social Sciences*, edited by James Mahoney and Dietrich Rueschemeyer, 373–404. Cambridge: Cambridge University Press.

Lakatos, Imre. 1978. *The Methodology of Scientific Research Programmes: Philosophical Papers*. Cambridge: Cambridge University Press.

Lieberson, Stanley. 1992. "Small N's and Big Conclusions: An Examination of the Reasoning in Comparative Studies Based on a Small Number of Cases." In *What Is a Case? Exploring the Foundations of Social Inquiry*, edited by Charles C. Ragin and Howard Saul Becker, 105–18. Cambridge: Cambridge University Press.

Lukács, Georg. 1971. *History and Class Consciousness: Studies in Marxist Dialectics*. Translated by Rodney Livingstone. Cambridge, MA: MIT Press.

Mackie, J. L. 1965. "Causes and Conditions." *American Philosophical Quarterly* 2(4):245–64.

——. 1980. *The Cement of the Universe: A Study of Causation*. Oxford: Clarendon.

Mahoney, James, Erin Kimball, and Kendra L. Koivu. 2009. "The Logic of Historical Explanation in the Social Sciences." *Comparative Political Studies* 42:114–46.

Marx, Karl. 1973. *Grundrisse*. Translated by Martin Nicolaus. London: Pelican.

Mayrl, Damon, and Nicholas Hoover Wilson. 2020. "What Do Historical Sociologists Do All Day? Analytic Architectures in Historical Sociology." *American Journal of Sociology* 125:1345–94.

McMichael, Philip. 1990. "Incorporating Comparison Within a World-Historical Perspective: An Alternative Comparative Method." *American Sociological Review* 55(3):385–97.

Moore, Barrington, Jr. 1966. *Social Origins of Dictatorship and Democracy: Lord and Peasant in the Making of the Modern World*. Boston: Beacon.

Paige, Jeffery M. 1997. *Coffee and Power: Revolution and the Rise of Democracy in Central America*. Cambridge, MA: Harvard University Press.

——. 1999. "Conjuncture, Comparison, and Conditional Theory in Macrosocial Inquiry." *American Journal of Sociology* 105(3):781–800.

Ragin, Charles C. 1987. *The Comparative Method: Moving Beyond Qualitative and Quantitative Strategies*. Berkeley: University of California Press.

Riley, Dylan J. 2010. *The Civic Foundations of Fascism in Europe: Italy, Spain, and Romania, 1870–1945*. Baltimore, MD: Johns Hopkins University Press.

Rueschemeyer, Dietrich, Evelyne Huber Stephens, and John D. Stephens. 1992. *Capitalist Development and Democracy*. Chicago: University of Chicago Press.

Sayer, R. Andrew. 1992. *Method in Social Science: A Realist Approach*. 2nd edition. London: Routledge.

——. 1997. "Essentialism, Social Constructionism, and Beyond." *Sociological Review* 45(3):453–87.

Sewell, William H., Jr. 1985. "Ideologies and Social Revolutions: Reflections on the French Case." *Journal of Modern History* 57(1):57–85.

Skocpol, Theda. 1979. *States and Social Revolutions: A Comparative Analysis of France, Russia, and China*. Cambridge: Cambridge University Press.

——. 1984. "Emerging Agendas and Recurrent Strategies in Historical Sociology." In *Vision and Method in Historical Sociology*, edited by Theda Skocpol, 356–91. Cambridge: Cambridge University Press.

Steinmetz, George. 1998. "Critical Realism and Historical Sociology: A Review Article." *Comparative Studies in Society and History* 40(1):170–86.

——. 2004. "Odious Comparisons: Incommensurability, the Case Study, and 'Small N's' in Sociology." *Sociological Theory* 22(3):371–400.

Sweet, Paige L. 2018. "The Feminist Question in Realism." *Sociological Theory* 36(3):221–43.

Tilly, Charles. 1975. "Reflections on the History of European State-Making." In *The Formation of National States in Western Europe*, edited by Charles Tilly and Gabriel Ardant, 3–83. Princeton, NJ: Princeton University Press.

——. 2008. *Explaining Social Processes*. Boulder, CO: Paradigm.

CHAPTER 11

HISTORICAL CAUSATION AND TEMPORALLY SENSITIVE COMPARISONS

YANG ZHANG

Introduction

Explaining the origins and outcomes of macro-historical change calls for both a deep understanding of causality and a suitable modeling of temporality. Indeed, models of causation are so deeply shaped by explicit or tacit conceptualizations of temporality that causal explanation is adequate only if a viable temporal structure of causation can be identified. The causal-temporal nexus also importantly shapes our conceptualization of crucial terms such as contingency, agency, and path dependence (Abbott 2001; Ermakoff 2015; Hall 1999; Mahoney 2000; Sewell 2005). For comparative studies, the temporality of causation further influences what we compare, how we compare, and what we compare for.

The word "causation" is diversely used in everyday life as well as in a range of academic fields (Kern 2009); related concepts such as causes, causality, causal conditions, causal factors, causal relations, causal power, causal process, and causal explanation are likewise defined in different ways (Cartwright 1999).[1] The investigation of causation can be traced back to as early as Aristotle's four causes—the material, formal, efficient, and final causes (Aristotle 1929)— although the contemporary conceptualization of causality is mostly associated with the "efficient cause." Notably, the reduction to efficient cause has limited our causal imaginaries. As Heidegger once lamented, "The *causa efficiens*, but one among the four causes, sets the standard for all causality", not to mention "Why are there just four causes?" (Heidegger 1977, 6–7).[2]

Instead of examining causation in general, this chapter focuses on how causation is conditioned by temporality and how two opposite versions of historical causation shape different strategies of comparison. It first examines the prevailing model—conjunctural causation—and finds it unsatisfactory in articulating the temporal dimensions of historical change. Drawing upon a diverse set of works from philosophy and sociology, this essay then develops a theory of sequential causation in historical change. Historical causation is sequential in nature because of *a periodic confluence of causes, simultaneous causal effects, nonlinear causal orders, causes as iterative properties,* and the *reflexivity of relational agency.* By examining recent works in comparative historical sociology, this chapter further discusses how such sequential causation can be established in a variety of temporally sensitive comparisons as well as supplementary methods such as narrative and counterfactual analysis.

Conjunctural Causation and Its Limitations

Theda Skocpol's application of Millian logic was a defining moment—somewhat an awkward one—for comparative historical sociology as a professional discipline. Above all, John Stuart Mill made clear that the methods of agreement and difference were inapplicable in the social sciences (Mill [1843] 1950, book VI). Furthermore, the deterministic, law-seeking nature of methodological positivism is inconsistent with the endeavor of Skocpol's empirical inquiries, which are historically specific and context dependent, thus making her findings less generalizable as she claimed. Finally, and ironically, Skocpol's actual historical analysis is much more subtle and sophisticated than her methodological statements.

Since the 1980s, a more sophisticated model of causation—conjunctural causation—has been developed beyond this deterministic structural causation.[3] It lays a more solid foundation for comparison and is compatible with some postpositivist epistemology. The conjunctural causation conceptualization constituted the foundation for comparative methodology in classical works of the 1980s (Ragin 1987; Skocpol 1984; Tilly 1984) and their intellectual heirs in the 2000s (Mahoney and Rueschemeyer 2003; Mahoney and Thelen 2015).

Conjunctural Causation

The building block of conjunctural causation is what philosopher John Mackie (1974) called an INUS condition. Simply put, given that an outcome (A) can be sufficiently caused, under different situations, by alternative causal complexes (C, D, E) that are themselves constituted by multiple conditions

(C1, C2, C3, . . .; D1, D2, D3, . . .; E1, E2, E3 . . .), any single condition (Ci, Di, Ei) in the causal complexes is an INUS condition: an Insufficient and Nonredundant part of a complex that is an Unnecessary but Sufficient cause for the outcome in question (Mackie 1974, 62). Notably, John Stuart Mill realized that social causes were often INUS conditions in *A System of Logic*: "The cause, indeed, may not be simple; it may consist of an assemblage of conditions," and it is not the case that "there was only one possible assemblage of conditions from which the given effect could result" (Mill [1843] 1950, 239). This wisdom has been well received in modern philosophy: before Mackie formally used the term "INUS" in 1965, Mill's ideas had been developed in *Causation in the Law* (Hart and Honoré [1959] 1985) and *The Structure of Science* (Nagel [1961] 1979).[4] Clearly, it is neither necessary conditions nor sufficient conditions but INUS conditions that constitute the nuts and bolts for causal explanations. In other words, Skocpol (1979) misinterpreted and misused the methodology of Mill (and also Nagel) as necessary and sufficient conditions, although her actual application of the Millian method is more sophisticated.

The INUS condition undergirds the conceptualization of multiple, conjunctural causation: "the conjunctural nature of social causation is not the only property of social phenomena that makes them complex. Typically, there are several combinations of conditions that may produce the same emergent phenomenon or the same change" (Ragin 1987, 25). Therefore, the concept of conjunctural causation not only means that the same outcome can be explained by alternative "constellations of causal factors" but also highlights how these causal factors interact, rather than act independently (Abbott 2001, 147; Steinmetz 1998, 177). Accordingly, conjunctural causation limits the applicable scope of any individual cause: in a given situation—for example, causal complex D results in singular historical outcome A—any condition within D (D1, D2, D3 . . .) is a "contingently necessary condition" for the occurrence of the final outcome (Nagel [1961] 1979). Contingent upon each other, they are "necessary" conditions only in specific situations but not in others where similar outcomes may be generated without them. As such, the causal power of each (INUS) condition can only be effective in combination with other (INUS) conditions in a given context (Ragin 1987, 25–27; Steinmetz 1998).[5]

In conjunctural causation, there is also a place for contingency, which is often theorized as *chance* or *agency* (Ermakoff 2015; Hall 1999; Sewell 2005).[6] Although structural conditions highlight causal determinacy and regular patterns, contingency points to causal indeterminacy produced by chance coincidence and human freedom (Veyne [1970] 1984, 95–97). Unlike structural models that consider contingency idiosyncratic, historically significant chance coincidences, or what Sewell called "contingent, unexpected, and inherently unpredictable events" are structurally transformative, causally significant, and durable (Sewell 2005). They hence join conjunctural conditions in causing historical change. Moreover, if any single causal factor is a *contingent necessity* in certain types of contexts (Nagel 1961), the distinction between "fundamental" and "contingent" factors is artificial, highlighting a specific variable or factor at the cost of suppressing other factors. A structural factor in one circumstance may well become a contingent factor in another.

Furthermore, given human actions are purposeful and effortful, agency is regarded as "causal carrier" in some conjunctural explanations (Menzies and Price 1993). It becomes even more *critical to* and *causal of* the moments of indeterminacy characterizing certain historical ruptures (Ermakoff 2015; Foucault 1984; Hall 1999; Veyne [1970] 1984). In some philosophical accounts, agency is given higher order than (structural) causality: "In the 'race' between causation and agency, the latter will always win. It is a contradiction in terms to think that agency could be completely caught in the nets of causality" (Danto [1963] 1985, 81). Therefore, agency (or effortful action) has a unique and sometimes central role in conjunctural explanations of historical change: "Specific sequence patterns are not always simply matters of chance or the configurational interaction of factors and events; they also can depend on effortful actions that construct the unfolding play of temporality" (Hall 1999, 164). Some scholars further introduce an element of rationality by arguing that an uncertain but critical rupture causes actors to be more aware of their constraints, incentives, and options and thus "creates the possibility for instrumental rationality" (Ermakoff 2010, 541).

Taken together, "conjunctural explanation emphasizes that a particular combination of structural causes and events, in a particular time and place, may create unique outcomes that will not necessarily be repeated in other contexts" (Paige 1999, 782). Conjunctural causation is consistent with mainstream comparative methods, as long as it is used to build "historical conditional theory" rather than general laws (Paige 1999). Comparison, in this regard, is used to identify alternative causal configurations under different contexts. Employing methods such as Boolean analysis to compare multiple cases, some scholars even attempt to discover a full list of preexisting conditions in explaining historical change like revolutions (Foran 2005; Ragin 2000). In a less positivist fashion, such a contextualized, conjunctural conception of causation considers the relationship between different comparative units (encompassing comparison), focuses on one single case by situating it in a universe of similar shadow cases, or highlights the interactive effects of different conditions and contingencies in varying contexts (Tilly 1984). In deviant case study, for example, historical contingency is used to falsify certain taken-for-granted structural conditions.

The Unspecified Temporality

Except for showing the role of historical contingency, however, the idea of conjunctural causation has not fleshed out the temporal dimension of causal

explanation. Above all, INUS condition and conjunctural causation conceive of causation as a static configuration of causes, rather than an examination of their actual interplay over time. "The interaction of the conditional
variables . . . says nothing about this sequence" (Somers 1996, 81). The Boolean method represents a view of static causation precisely because of the lack
of temporal order, pace, and effects in the empirical analysis. Therefore, such
a notion of conjunctural causation "is fully compatible with a deterministic
understanding of conjunctures" (Ermakoff 2015, 71).

Furthermore, in line with David Hume's ([1748] 1993) conceptualization of
causality, conjunctural causation suggests that causes precede effects by using
terms like "antecedent conditions," thus overlooking causality in the short term
or the *simultaneous* appearance of causes and effects. Given that structural
conditions continuously shift over the course of historical change, it is crucial
to be attentive to processual dynamics since the causes of important things can
be short-term and emergent processes.

Moreover, when conjunctural causation is treated as a combination of "necessary" conditions rather than merely alternative causal complexes of INUS
conditions, it is close to the neo-positivist conception of causality. This type of
structural explanation is often entrapped in determinism and teleology (Sewell
2005, 83–85). In these accounts, contingency has been reduced to residuals of
the more important structural factors, not only "random" and "accidental" but
also "nonexplainable," just like "residuals" in the regression model.

Even when contingency is given causal significance as exogenous shocks in
some conjunctural explanations, the temporal nature of such contingency has
not been articulated because "in numerous instances, accidents are endogenous to the action system that they disrupt" (Ermakoff 2015, 74). For example,
assassination of a ruler by his elite rivals would probably be part of a sequence
of elite conflicts rather than an accidental event. Even the causal effects of some
truly "accidental" events—for instance, the sudden death of a ruler in an air-
plane crash that results in civil war—are still enmeshed in larger and longer
sequences, such as elite struggle, the lack of a regular succession mechanism,
or the fragmentation of power. After all, it is not accidental that the death of
a ruler becomes influential in some circumstances but not in others. In effect,
reducing historical causation to chance accidents limits our ability to trace
causal connections across historical process; it is not discrete events but their
connectedness that makes historical change causally intelligible and meaningful. It is therefore indispensable to develop a more sequential view of causation
and contingency.

Likewise, individual agency—however crucial—is always enmeshed in a
web of social relations and historical sequences. Even the actions of the most
important individual involve reaction to and interaction with others. Thus, the
egocentric perspective of agency should be replaced by an interactive perspective, while the rational assumption of agency should be revised by a relational

one (Somers 1998, 749–51). A choice is not necessarily a rational choice, and a purposive action is not necessarily a rational action. In causally indeterminate ruptures, key individuals' choices are indeed critical but not always "rational" or "strategic." After all, whether actors behave rationally is an empirical question and cannot be presumed (Weber 1949).

Finally, one specific version of conjunctural causation is "temporally layered causation": historical causations are temporally layered often into two tiers, structural/underlying causes and immediate/transient causes (Pierson 2004). Lawrence Stone (1972) even divided causes of revolution into three temporal layers: *long-term preconditions, middle-term precipitant,* and *short-term triggers.*[7] Although this idea is attentive to the temporal dimension of causality and gives analytic weight to short-term causes, this temporally causal dichotomy/trichotomy is much like the structure/agency dualism in conjunctural explanations: it divides causes into different temporal spans, but the distinction between underlying and transient causes is undertheorized.

Sequential Causation of Historical Change

Historical causation is not only *singular* but also *sequential* in nature. Historical causation is simultaneously evolving (with outcomes), periodic, iterative, nonlinear, and relationally reflexive. Specifically, historical outcomes are often the becoming, rather than the being, of actual entities; various causes sequentially enter the stream of historical change to affect outcomes; causes may appear simultaneously with effects; early outcomes may become causes for later outcomes iteratively; and relational actors often adjust their positions in interactive processes of interpretations and decision making.

The idea of sequential causation is rooted in processual philosophy, German historicism, and American pragmatism. Despite its long history from Heraclitus to Georg Hegel, processual philosophy was not systematically formulated until the late nineteenth century (Nietzsche [1887] 2015; Whitehead [1929] 1978). It was Friedrich Nietzsche who explicitly pointed out that "being" is defined by "becoming" and an actor is defined by ongoing action: "There is no 'being' behind doing, effecting, becoming" (Nietzsche [1887] 2015, Essay I, para. 13). Later, Alfred Whitehead's process philosophy emphasized the central role of temporality, change, and passage in our world: "that the actual world is a process, and that the process is the becoming of actual entities" (Whitehead [1929] 1978, 22). These philosophers maintained that historical change is a continuous process of becoming; an evolving, indeterminate, open-end transformation; and emergent in essence.[8] From here, two slightly different processual views have been developed. On the one hand, German historicism highlighted the unique, singular, and segmented nature of historical causation on the world-historical scale (Beiser 2011). On the other hand, American pragmatism focused on shorter-term processes: past experience cannot predict alternative patterns of the future; human reflexivity and creativity may open up new possibilities under similar circumstances; and human political and economic experiments are recursive, unpredictable, and endless (Dewey 1922; Mead 1932).[9]

In sociology, both Max Weber and Barrington Moore notably not only pointed out historical causation is concrete, singular causal relationship but also paid sufficient attention to the temporal positioning and sequential nature of causal factors in their empirical inquiries (Moore 1958; Weber 1949). Precisely because historical causation is sequential, Arthur Stinchcombe (1978) and Charles Tilly (1995) argued for investigation of "ideal sequences," "molecular processes," and "deep analogies" between specific episodes of historical cases. For example, Stinchcombe (1978, 17) maintained that "causation does not operate at the grand level . . . but on the segmented level." Likewise, Tilly (1995, 1601) pointed out that regularities "do not operate in the form of recurrent structures and processes at a large scale." Other sociologists have noticed that historical change is sequentially sensitive, patterned by timing, pace, duration, and so on (Abbott 2001; Aminzade 1992; Haydu 1998; Isaac and Griffin 1989; Pierson 2004). One methodological implication of these interventions is an emphasis on causal mechanisms,[10] now broadly considered as the cornerstone for causal explanation of recurrent processes across historical episodes (Gross 2009; Stinchcombe 1991). Despite different epistemological foundations, recent treatments often urge attention to the processual, emergent nature of historical causation (Ermakoff 2019).

However, a surprising gap remains: a processual causal imagery has never been fully developed in the current literature. In the following subsections, I will draw upon both philosophical and sociological works to elaborate five essential aspects of sequential causation: periodic confluence of causes, simultaneous causal effects, nonlinear causal orders, causes as iterative properties, and reflexivity of relational agency. Each subsection also illustrates the empirical value of this theorization by referring to notable episodes of historical change.

Periodic Confluence of Causes

My point of departure is that causes are *periodic* and not necessarily *preexisting*: historical causation entails a progressive confluence of multiple sequences of events rather than a preexisting configuration of (INUS) causal conditions. Various causes enter the stream of history and affect outcomes in a contiguous way. Such temporal moderation of causation is more than the temporal order or duration that has been addressed by the "temporally layered causation" view (Aminzade 1992; Pierson 2004).

Historical change unfolds through alternative confluences of multiple streams of causal series. Conjunctural causation makes sense only if it is reframed in sequential terms: identifying certain conjunctural conditions is merely the first step of any historical inquiry; it is more important to locate these conditions within the temporal flow of historical change. After all, conjunctural conditions are not necessarily prior conditions but can enter gradually into history. For example, geopolitical crisis as a condition for social revolution is usually something that progressively unfolds, interplaying with domestic revolutionary processes.

It is interesting to refer to the analogy of culinary art: if we treat structural factors as a chef's ingredients, their effects are dependent upon the order and timing with which they are put together and the duration of their co-mingling (Pierson 2004, 1). This analogy can be extended further: there are multiple ways to make a good dish, just as there are multiple causal complexes to a given outcome, and each of these ways requires not only a particular combination of "ingredients" (like INUS conditions) but also appropriate order, timing, and duration of treating those ingredients (like the temporality of INUS conditions). Thus, these ingredients become effective only when they are added *periodically* at appropriate times. In each specific dish, the value of an ingredient relies not only upon what the other ingredients are but also its temporal relation with those other ingredients. This does not mean that it is "accidental" for a chef to cook a great dish; quite the contrary, both the "ingredients" and their "temporal relations" are highly regular, although there are various ways of regularity. The process is sophisticated but not messy. Likewise, to the extent that there are multiple patterned causal pathways for certain outcomes, historical causation of social change is sequential in addition to conjunctural.

Simultaneous Causal Effects

More than being periodic, historical causation is often "simultaneous": causes and effects are not two discontinuous events but aspects of a single ongoing process and can appear simultaneously (Mandelbaum 1977; Mumford and Anjum 2011; Salmon 1984). In other words, causes do not necessarily occur before effects; the two often appear simultaneously as historical change unfolds. Together with periodic causal confluence, the idea of simultaneous causation directly contradicts the Humean temporality of causality—which views causes and effects as two separate stages and assumes causes always precede effects—and therefore undermines the causal foundation of structural models of historical change.

Conceptualizing cause and effect as a continuously unfolding process hence undergirds the dynamism of historical change. For certain historical causes (e.g., geopolitical crisis) and outcomes (e.g., revolution), both the occurrence of the cause and its effects take time and simultaneously unfold over time. As such, we view "a cause and its effect as linked together in such a way that they may be said to constitute aspects of a single ongoing process, rather than being distinct events," and "the cause is complete only when the effect occurs" (Mandelbaum 1977, 75–76, 95).

Surprisingly, a notable example comes from Skocpol's "structural" account of social revolutions. Although her book is built upon Humean causation and has misunderstood Millian comparative logic, in Skocpol's empirical analysis of the Chinese Revolution, causation became periodic and simultaneous, as she clearly states: "uniquely in the Chinese case, peasant revolution and the consolidation of national power by a revolutionary elite were so intertwined as to be virtually indistinguishable" (Skocpol 1979, 154). In Skocpol's empirical account, therefore, the "artificial separation of cause and consequence" at the core of her causal schema was given up (Burawoy 1989, 772).

Nonlinear Causal Orders

Furthermore, the validation of historical causation is often not linear but sequentially interdependent. In other words, the effects of a cause sometimes become significant because of the occurrence of other sequences of events *at a later time*—the cause becomes effective not immediately but subsequently. Nonlinearity means that the causal order of historical change is woven back and forth into a network of events rather than flowing chronologically. As Paul Ricoeur nicely put it, "It might seem, then, that a subsequent event transforms a prior one into a cause, therefore that a sufficient condition for the earlier event is produced later than the event" (Ricoeur 1984, 146).

Because the effects and meanings of a past event may be transformed by future events in unanticipated ways, causal effects that we observe at a later point cannot be isolated from subsequent sequences. It also means that effects and meanings of past events can never really be stable and are in effect continually reshaped by future history. For example, the 1914 shot that killed Archduke Franz Ferdinand became truly significant only when the Habsburg Empire decided to retaliate despite Serbia's serious compensation efforts. Without this later and unexpected development, the assassination might have been just like many other similar events rather than the "trigger" of a world war (Lebow 2000).

Causes as Iterative Properties

In addition, historical causation is often iterative: intermediate outcomes have feedback effects. Therefore, early outcomes can become causes for later outcomes of the historical change. With the language of nonlinear mathematics, we may imagine "the current value of the dependent variable to determine in part or altogether the dependent variable's subsequent values over time" (Roth 1992, 204). Iterative causation is thus an extension of periodic and simultaneous causation, but with further emphasis on the reciprocal flow of causes and effects over time. To be noted, iterative causation is different from the cascading nature of events—"historical events produc[ing] more events" (Sewell 2005)—because iterative causation refers to the recursive nature of the cause-effect relationship rather than of events.

Causal iteration (or recursivity) thus indicates that emerging configurations may causally affect subsequent configurations in historical change. Historical causal inquiry thus not only means inserting a new variable in the nominal/ordinal sense but also identifying new configurations of processes. Even more critically, shifting from conjunctural causation to sequential causation requires a change of the *causal agent*: shifting from factors/variables to processes/sequences.

Revolutionary movements, for example, feature iterative, dynamic processes because subsequent actions are often produced in reaction to early events. My own study (Zhang 2021) of nineteenth-century elite insurrections during the Taiping Civil War in China is a case in point. In the wake of the Taiping Rebellion, elite-led forces were competitively organized in many areas and their identities were made, unmade, and remade in reaction to their major allies and opponents in rapidly changing political contexts. Some of them continually diverged as state allies or enemies in a fractal way.

Reflexivity of Relational Agency

The iterative nature of historical causation functions alongside another feature: the reflexivity of relational agency. In historical change, key actors have multiple opportunities to interpret and to act reflexively, but also relationally, in critical moments. On one hand, because historical causation is periodic, simultaneous, iterative, and nonlinear, human agency becomes even more pivotal insofar as key actors have many chances to reflect on the situations and reshape their directions. During moments of indeterminate rupture, the iterative interpretations and choices of some actors are hence causally significant (Ermakoff 2015; Reed 2011). On the other hand, agency is intrinsically relational and temporally embedded: actors adjust their positions and behaviors in response to each other within "temporal-relational contexts" (Emirbayer and Mische 1998, 969). It is the relational situations, rather than individuals, that should be taken as the primary unit of analysis because actors are embedded in such situations in interactive processes.

In historical change, this reflexivity of agency is fundamentally relational, as multiple actors simultaneously adjust their strategies and positions by responding to their allies, rivals, and other related actors (Tilly 1995). Accordingly, "the basic units of social analysis" are "neither individual entities (agent, actor, person, firm) nor structural wholes (society, order, social structure) but the relational processes of interaction between and among identities" (Somers 1998, 766–67).[11] Furthermore, the causal carrier is not agentive in the sense of being a *rational* actor but in the sense of being a *relational* one, whose actions are contingent upon the moves of others over time. It is this ongoing interaction that destabilizes recurring relational patterns while creating new ones—to the extent of making even structural transformation possible. The transformation of economic systems throughout human history serves as a helpful example: innovative ways of economic production are often produced in the mutual learning, competition, and even conflicts of heterogeneous and previously disconnected actors (Padgett and Powell 2012). As nicely put by Randolph Roth (1992, 204), most social change "is governed by a reflexive, dialectical process that allows causes and effects to interact."

To summarize, causes periodically enter into the stream of historical processes, causes and effects sometimes occur simultaneously in the unfolding of historical change, and historical causation may be iterative and nonlinear. A sequential view of causation thus implies "that causality is the internal linkage of a continuous process, that generalizations in the form of laws are to be inserted into singular causal explanation, and that causal necessity is conditional and does not imply a belief in determinism" (Ricoeur 1984, 202). By conceptualizing historical causation in sequential terms, we gain a better understanding of the dynamism of historical change, that change is often gradual rather than abrupt, and that transformative change is embedded in and occasionally emerges from the shifting relationships of key actors.

It is worth noting the difference between sequential causations and eventful causation. Eventful causation attributes the event with significantly more independent causal power. It is true that transformative events are often defined by their incidental nature and ability to shift patterns of relations (Sewell 2005), but it is more accurate to consider such incidental happenings less as exogenous, unexpected events than as the nexus of sequences that involve interactions among key actors. Simply put, in the eventful account, events swallow sequences; while in the sequential account, events are embedded in larger sequences. Sequential causation thus helps overcome the long-existing dualism between structure and event and the co-determinism of structure and agency. When addressing the "chains of historical causation," Moore commented that "it is very difficult to believe seriously that the sequence of historical events is purely random, or that anything can happen at any time" (Moore 1958, 151).

Identifying Causation Through Temporally Sensitive Comparisons

The previous discussion highlights the importance of temporal components in historical explanations. In historical sociology, therefore, causal explanation is not only variation-seeking but also constitutive and generative. The variations among comparative units do not explain the different outcomes in a self-evident way. A truly causal explanation should reveal the causal mechanisms and processes through which certain factors/conditions produce the outcome. Needless to say, individual works may focus on certain aspects of historical causations rather than reveal all causal configurations exhaustively.

To explore generative, sequential causation, historical sociologists and comparative political scientists have respectively emphasized the techniques of narrative and process-tracing methods. In this section, I argue for another effective strategy in temporally sensitive comparisons: comparing episodes, processes, and events rather than entities, places, or substances. These comparisons require appropriate casing, periodizing, and sequencing strategies to achieve specific analytic objectives (Clemens 2007; Haydu 1998). This section outlines a typology of temporally sensitive comparisons, illustrated by recent examples from historical sociology, and explains how these comparative strategies can help establish causal explanations. Finally, I propose narrative and counterfactual analysis as complementary methods for identifying sequential causation.

Temporally Sensitive Comparisons: A Typology

Adding temporal dimensions to comparison enriches comparative strategies. Temporally sensitive comparisons put casing strategy at the heart of the research: rather than comparing entities such as states, scholars analyze dynamic processes such as formation, emergence, encounter, incorporation, mobilization, and interactions over time (i.e., "a number of 'episodes' of major structural transformation") (Mann 1986, 3). Such "neo-episodic" comparison can generate contextualized, specific causal explanations. In practice, researchers periodize single or multiple cases in comparisons. Furthermore, these periods of each case may be considered as independent or connective (Haydu 1998). Table 11.1 outlines a simple typology of temporally sensitive comparisons based on the two dimensions.[12]

First, in the basic form of temporal comparisons, a few (and sometimes separate) periods of a single case are compared to identify either variations or common patterns across time periods. Notable examples include Roger Gould's (1995) comparison of the mobilizing structure in the 1848 revolution and 1871 Paris Commune and Ho-fung Hung's (2011) comparison of different protest

TABLE 11.1 A typology of temporally sensitive comparison

		Connectedness of periods	
		Independent	Connective
Casing strategies	Single case	Identifying variations or common patterns across time (Gould 1995; Hung 2011)	Temporally connected comparison, or "reiterated problem solving" (Clemens 2020; Haydu 1998)
	Multiple cases	Pattern matching or variation seeking across parallel trajectories (Arrighi 1993; Go 2012)	Encompassing and temporally embedded comparison (Anderson 2021; Mudge 2018)

repertories in three time periods (1740–1759, 1776–1795, and 1820–1839) in the Qing Dynasty of China. This strategy allows researchers to control the variation as much as possible to flesh out the possible causal explanation of the temporal change. Gould's (1995) comparison of two revolutions in Paris led to his findings of class or community as two types of mobilizing structure. This basic comparative strategy hence helps locate the periodic positions of historical causes—the very first characteristic of sequential causation.

Second, scholars may select multiple cases and periodize them to find analogous patterns over time across those cases, or demonstrate divergence, reversal, or alternative transformation of similar units over time. These comparative cases may or may not occur simultaneously. For example, Julian Go (2012) compares the British Empire and the American Empire, which experienced similar trajectories and dynamics of hegemonic ascendency, maturity, and decline, but at different times. Kenneth Pomeranz (2001) compares the economic development pathways of two simultaneous cases: England and the Lower Yangzi Delta of China before 1820 and their divergent trajectories since then. Comparing such parallel periods of multiple cases may lead to the findings of generic causal mechanism but alternative causal sequences, given historical causation is the sequential unfolding of different INUS conditions. Furthermore, the comparative cases may be relatively independent or deeply connected, and such connectedness may itself be the causation of divergence: in Giovanni Arrighi's (1993) analysis of hegemonic transitions in world history, the shift of manufacturing capacity from the hegemons to the hegemonic challengers is a key driver of hegemonic competition. Demonstrating connectedness thus also established simultaneous causal effects of historical change.

Third, scholars may treat periods as internally connected sequences and conduct temporally connected comparisons. In spatially encompassing comparison, the key is to demonstrate the relationship between different units and "explaining their characteristics as a function of their varying relationships to the system as a whole" (Tilly 1984, 83), and "connections or transfers should be theorized as causes and should also be compared" (Steinmetz 2014, 414).[13] Likewise, in temporally connected comparison, different periods will be considered as internally and causally interrelated. The changing outcomes are thus treated as the result of key actors' iterative problem-solving (Haydu 1998). Elisabeth Clemens employs this method to study how civic voluntarism contributed to American nationhood over two hundred years. She selects several episodes and compares them as "historically linked moments of 'iterated problem solving' in which each partial resolution changes the terms for the next round of" possible articulations (Clemens 2020, 19). Notably, comparing periods and iterative problem-solving are not mutually exclusive options. Scholars can compare periods while paying attention to their connectedness, as such temporal connectedness is part of the causation for subsequent development. This is the key strategy to reveal historical causation as iterative properties because previous responses to certain problems or crises may create new structures that produce new problems and solutions.

Notably, the broadly used path dependency model is but one type of temporally connected comparison, as it often divides the historical trajectories into two periods by a turning point, or a critical juncture. Before the critical juncture, multiple possible outcomes could result from initial structures; after the critical juncture, in contrast, some endogenous mechanisms sustain a series of events that produce the final outcomes (Goldstone 1998, 834; Mahoney 2000, 535). Although such path-dependent development is possible, its treatment of the temporal-causal link is oversimplified. First, the path dependency model is simultaneously "too contingent and too deterministic" (Thelen 1999, 385), and the identification of the critical juncture is often arbitrary (Haydu 1998, 352). Second, a critical juncture is rarely entirely contingent or exogenous; it is often constrained or facilitated by some earlier sequences of interactions. Third, in the path dependency model, endogenous causation is often infused with the power to exclude new causes, to freeze historical possibilities, and to determine all subsequent events, but there is seldom an "endogenous" period when external causes cease to matter. Overlooking this, path dependency explanations "rarely deal with multiple switch points that form more encompassing sequences" (Haydu 1998, 353). Therefore, path dependency should not be a given, but may be one of many possibilities of temporally connected periods.

Fourth, in the final and most sophisticated form, scholars may choose multiple and often interrelated cases and periodize them as connected stages to conduct spatially and temporally encompassing comparisons. Although it sounds complicated, pioneering scholars such as Barrington Moore and Alexander Gerschenkron applied this method in their masterpieces: political and economic development of each country was not only shaped by the temporal order of their encounter with modernity but also unfolded sequentially.

This comparative strategy has also been employed in some recent works. For example, Stephanie Mudge (2018) conducts a comparative study of the changing course of leftism in the West by selecting four interrelated cases: the Swedish and German Social Democrats, the British Labor Party, and the American Democratic Party. She periodizes their development into three critical junctures in the twentieth century and analyzes their responses to successive crises, which resulted in the crystallization of three dominant "isms": socialism, Keynesianism, and neoliberalism. These successive solutions were not independent but rather connected to past experiences and solutions.

In another recent study, Elisabeth Anderson (2021) juxtaposes several sequentially connected cases to investigate the causal effects of child labor reform and the origins of the welfare state. She selects two groups of sequentially connected cases, 1820s–1830s Prussia and 1870s imperial Germany and Massachusetts in the 1830s–1840s and 1860s–1870s, as well as three other cases (France, Belgium, and Illinois). In so doing, she conducts "an in-depth and historically contextualized tracing of the temporal sequence of events that led to the outcome in question" (Anderson 2021, 24). Notably, she does not aim to identify any macro-causal factors, but instead shows temporally sensitive and context-specific causal mechanisms and thus reveals varying causal pathways of how child labor reform brought about the modern welfare state. Furthermore, Anderson, like Mudge, highlights the causal significance of the relational agents—policy entrepreneurs—in responding to changing situations and producing policy outcomes.

Another use of this comparative strategy is the identification of causal significance of multiple contingencies over time. Researchers may compare events across sequences and cases to evaluate which events have more independent causal power and whose causal effects are more dependent upon the occurrence of other sequences. Sequential causation implies that contingence rarely pivots on any single chance or choice but has sequential properties. Historical contingency thus often occurs as a coincidental encounter of otherwise relatively independent sequences of events. The occurrence of an event produces consequential and durable effects on historical change because of the occurrence of other prior, simultaneous, or subsequent events. Contingency thus may be better referred to as *contingent sequence*, as it comprises a series of chances and choices and its causal effects are often reinforced by simultaneous or subsequent conjunctures with other events. Similarly, a turning *point* is better called a turning *period*: it is a series of turning points rather than a single turning point as critical juncture that sequentially change the course and switch the direction of historical change. Comparison of those contingencies or turning points help identify their causal significance and interdependence. For example, Ivan Ermakoff (2008) carefully compares three major events in 1933 to determine which one was the most causally consequential for Hitler's rise to absolute power. Likewise, Zhang and Shi (2023) compare a few key moments in 1989 to identify the breaking point for the relationship breakup between two reformist Chinese leaders.

It should be noted that the comparative strategies outlined earlier are not mutually exclusive, and researchers may prioritize one strategy in the main case(s) while employing another in supplementary cases. Further, iterative comparison across different temporal spans and spatial units sometimes can be very informative because any historical sequence can simultaneously be an event of larger historical sequence and a confluence of multiple events of shorter time spans (Ricoeur 1984, 170; Veyne [1970] 1984).

Comparison Versus Mechanism, Narrative, and Counterfactual Analysis

To flesh out sequential causation, temporally sensitive comparison is complementary with other analytic strategies. Put another way, the nature of sequential causation mitigates certain unnecessary tensions between macro-historical comparison and mechanism-based comparison, between comparison and narrative, and between comparison and counterfactual analysis. In practice, empirical research can assemble temporally sensitive comparisons with strategies such as mechanism seeking, narrative, and meticulous counterfactual analysis to offer persuasive causal explanation of historical change.

First, sequential causation reduces the unnecessary tensions between macro-historical comparison and middle-range comparison of ideal sequences with the rise of mechanism-centered historical sociology. The two methods are respectively rooted in historicism and pragmatism, but the two philosophical principles can be supplementary in empirical inquiries. It is true that comparing ideal sequences "generate[s] historically specific general ideas" (Stinchcombe 1978, 4), or mechanisms, but this method does not necessarily contradict the singular causation approach based on macro-historical comparisons (e.g., the comparison of two revolutions). Quite the contrary, such middle-range mechanisms offer building blocks for the singular explanation of macro-historical changes (Gross 2018). As complementary analytic strategies, researchers may focus on a mechanism of ideal-typical sequences across numerous contexts or examine the temporal conjunction of several causal mechanisms and the confluence of several sequences in significant case(s). After all, we have multiple cognitive needs: we want to know both why the French and Chinese revolutions occurred and why there was a scale shift or radicalization during these revolutions.

In addition, specifying sequential causation also mitigates the tension between comparison and narrative of historical events (e.g., Haydu 1998;

Stryker 1996). For standard causal inference, identifying variables that are causally significant is the ultimate goal, while narrative is used as a supplementary,
nonessential part to justify the causal adequacy of certain variables. The analytic part of those works is often approving the causal effects of certain variables
by excluding other intervening variables. In contrast, identifying causal factors is merely the starting point for a historical causation, while reconstructing
the causal processes and sequences by situating the causal factors in adequate
temporal locations is the primacy of analysis. Insofar as temporal locations,
orders, sequences, and relations are critical to the causal explanation, narrative is the appropriate apparatus to organize events into causal emplotment
(Ricoeur 1984), just as regression is the apparatus to organize variables into
causal explanations in quantitative social sciences. Overall, temporally sensitive
comparison and narrative are complementary rather than contradictory tools
in articulating such configurational causes.

Finally, specifying sequential causation helps illuminate comparison and
counterfactual analysis as two supplementary methods. While counterfactual
and comparison are ultimately the same thing (Gould 2019; Nagel 1961, 588–92),
technically there is a trade-off between the two methods because of their
respective constraints. Comparison of actually existing cases cannot control all
major confounding factors, although it can show their analogous conditions;
in contrast, counterfactual analysis may perfectly control irrelevant factors
as it often alters one condition while holding other factors constant, but the
alternative outcome is not the actually observed outcome. Causal explanation
becomes even more complicated when the temporality of causal factors is considered: for case comparison, a given causal condition may have varying and
even opposite effects with its different temporal locations; for counterfactual
analysis, the alternation of one given condition may result in a chain of change
because of causal interdependence and causal connectedness over time (Zhang
2019). As such, neither comparison nor counterfactual analysis alone can lead
to convincing causal imputation. As a matter of practice, we need to first master both extensive knowledge of other relevant cases and thorough knowledge
of the events related to the alternative scenarios of the primary case(s) and
then combine the two imperfect methods together to cautiously evaluate the
causal impacts of certain factors over time. Hence, both comparison and counterfactual analysis should be conducted in an open-ended way by "adopting a
forward-looking outcome" (Ermakoff 2019, 595). In brief, we need to compare
cases processually and think about counterfactuals sequentially.

✳ ✳ ✳

This chapter first reviews the prevailing model of conjunctural causation and
finds it unsatisfactory in explaining historical change. Other than vaguely contending historical change is caused by a conjunctural combination of causal

conditions and events, this model has not articulated the temporal components of causality. Drawing upon a diverse set of philosophical and sociological works, I demonstrate that historical causation is sequential because of the periodic confluence of causes, simultaneous causal effects, nonlinear causal orders, causes as iterative properties, and the reflexivity of relational agency. To identify such sequential causation of historical change, this chapter then outlines a typology of temporally sensitive comparison and exemplifies these comparative strategies with recent works in historical sociology. These comparative methods, as discussed earlier, are supplementary with mechanisms, narrative, and counterfactual analysis in causal explanation of historical change.

Empirically, sequential causation can be applied across temporal and spatial scales: the Polynesian War in the Fijian Islands in the mid-nineteenth century is not unlike the Peloponnesian War in ancient Greece in terms of their origins and genesis (Sahlins 1991). After all, historical inquiry cannot be reduced to a quest into the structural origins or spectacular events; it instead requires revealing the geometry and genealogy of human relationships over time. To establish historical causation, temporally sensitive comparison offers us useful analytic tools to the arsenal of comparative historical sociology.

Acknowledgments

Early versions of this chapter were presented at the Social Science History Association annual meeting in 2017, the Historical International Studies Research Cluster in American University and Comparative Methods Conference at Yale University in 2018, and the Workshop on Frontier Issues in Historical Sociology in Zhejiang University in 2019. The author thanks helpful comments and suggestion from Keith Darden, Frieder Dengler, Ivan Ermakoff, Mark Gould, Patrick Jackson, Marcus Kreuzer, Damon Mayrl, Randy Persaud, Guoquan Seng, Matthew Taylor, Libby Thompson, Nicholas Wilson, and anonymous reviewers.

Notes

1. Scholars have provided a short history of causation in philosophy (Psillos 2002), its various applications in the social sciences (Marini and Singer 1988), and its history in sociology and, in particular, in American sociology (Abbott 1998; Bernert 1983).
2. In sociology, one recent critique comes from the rediscovery of *forming* cause in addition to *forcing* cause, which is similar to the efficient cause (Reed 2011).
3. Meanwhile, the neo-positivist version of causality has its own development (e.g., Goldthorpe 2001; King, Keohane, and Verba 1994). Some new moves in this vein, such as the experimental manipulation theory of causality (e.g., Morgan and Winship 2014; Woodward 2003), are not helpful for historical social science, as this approach

requires that "causal factors" be controllable and experimentally manipulated by the researcher—as shown in the motto "No Causation without Manipulation" (Holland 1986, 959). Certain techniques, such as natural experiment, regression discontinuity, and difference-in-difference design, have been developed to identify the causal effects of certain variables, factors, or events in history, but these methods still regard "time" as Cartesian background (for critiques, see Abbott 1988, 1998; Gorski 2004; Hirschman and Reed 2014, 262–63; Martin 2011, 24–73; Steinmetz 2004).

4. Mill's theory also had an (indirect) influence on Max Weber's methodology, although Weber's reception was ambivalent (Heidelberger 2015; Strand and Lizardo 2022).

5. The INUS condition as the basic unit of causation also makes Popperian (Popper 1963) falsification unlikely if not impossible in most social explanations (Gorski 2004; Zhang 2007).

6. Paul Veyne divided causes into three types: material causes, chances, and freedom (Veyne [1970] 1984, 95–97). My treatment of contingency is closer to his interpretation of contingency as "chances" or "freedom" (or agency) (Aron 1961; Ricoeur 1984). In sociology, Hall (1999) and Ermakoff (2015) have reviewed four ways to conceptualize contingency: conjunctural causations, period and sequence effects, chance, and agency.

7. For example, this temporally layered causation is seen in the study of the cause of war by Thucydides, above all in his powder keg metaphor: structural contradictions provided "the inflammatory material" and the final crisis was a "spark" that eventually led to the explosion (Kagan 1989, 354).

8. The processual philosophy has been further developed in different ways (Carr 1986; Mandelbaum 1977; Mumford and Anjum 2011; Salmon 1984; Veyne [1970] 1984).

9. Notably, there were tensions between German historicism and the initial versions of American pragmatism (Ross 1991). Such tensions have been mitigated in the recent synthesis of the two traditions in historical sociology (e.g., Abbott 2001; Tilly 1995).

10. This article focuses on the use of mechanism by historical sociologists in the traditions of critical realism, pragmatism, and/or relationalism. Alternatively, mechanism can also be taken up as the micro-foundation of macro-level change, a reductionist view often associated with rational choice theory and methodological individualism (e.g., Elster 1989). For critiques of mechanism as micro-foundation, see Stinchcombe (1991), Gross (2009), and Hirschman and Reed (2014).

11. As Elder-Vass finds (2022), one vital difference between critical realism and pragmatism is their divergent view over the invocation of structural power in causal explanations.

12. Elsewhere, scholars have urged "unbound comparison" for different explanatory or heuristic purposes and "oscillating comparison" across spatial and temporal scales throughout the research (Anderson 1998, 31; Bodnár 2019).

13. For discussions about the relationship between comparative history and integrative/connected history, see Bodnár (2019).

References

Abbott, Andrew. 1988. "Transcending General Linear Reality." *Sociological Theory* 6:169–86.
——. 1998. "The Causal Devolution." *Sociological Methods and Research* 27:148–81.
——. 2001. *Time Matters: On Theory and Method*. Chicago: University of Chicago Press.
Aminzade, Ronald. 1992. "Historical Sociology and Time." *Sociological Methods and Research* 20:456–80.

Anderson, Benedict. 1998. *The Spectre of Comparisons: Nationalism, Southeast Asia, and the World*. London: Verso.

Anderson, Elisabeth. 2021. *Agents of Reform: Child Labor and the Origins of the Welfare State*. Princeton, NJ: Princeton University Press.

Aristotle. 1929. *The Physics*. Vol. 1. Translated by P. H. Wicksteed and F. M. Cornford. London: Heinemann.

Aron, Raymond. 1961. *Introduction to the Philosophy of History: An Essay on the Limits of Historical Objectivity*. Translated by George J. Irwin. New York: Poston.

Arrighi, Giovanni. 1993. *The Long Twentieth Century: Money, Power, and the Origins of Our Times*. London: Verso.

Beiser, Frederick C. 2011. *The German Historicist Tradition*. Oxford: Oxford University Press.

Bernert, Christopher. 1983. "The Career of Causal Analysis in American Sociology." *British Journal of Sociology* 34:230–54.

Bodnár, Judit. 2019. "Comparing in Global Times: Between Extension and Incorporation." *Critical Historical Studies* 6(1):1–32.

Burawoy, Michael. 1989. "Two Methods in Search of Science: Skocpol Versus Trotsky." *Theory and Society* 18:759–805.

Carr, David. 1986. *Time, Narrative, and History*. Bloomington: Indiana University Press.

Cartwright, Nancy. 1999. *The Dappled World: A Study of the Boundaries of Science*. Cambridge: Cambridge University Press.

Clemens, Elisabeth S. 2007. "Toward a Historicized Sociology: Theorizing Events, Processes, and Emergence." *Annual Review of Sociology* 33:527–49.

——. 2020. *Civic Gifts: Voluntarism and the Making of the American Nation-State*. Chicago: University of Chicago Press.

Danto, Arthur. [1963] 1985. *Narration and Knowledge*. New York: Columbia University Press.

Dewey, John. 1922. *Human Nature and Conduct*. Carbondale: Southern Illinois University Press.

Elder-Vass, Dave. 2022. "Pragmatism, Critical Realism and the Study of Value." *Journal of Critical Realism* 21:261–87.

Elster, Jon. 1989. *Nuts and Bolts for the Social Sciences*. Cambridge: Cambridge University Press.

Emirbayer, Mustafa, and Ann Mische. 1998. "What Is Agency?" *American Journal of Sociology* 103:962–1023.

Ermakoff, Ivan. 2010. "Theory of Practice, Rational Choice and Historical Change." *Theory and Society* 39:527–53.

——. 2015. "The Structure of Contingency." *American Journal of Sociology* 121:64–125.

——. 2019. "Causality and History: Modes of Causal Investigation in Historical Social Sciences." *Annual Review of Sociology* 45:581–606.

Foran, John. 2005. *Taking Power: On the Origins of Third World Revolutions*. Cambridge: Cambridge University Press.

Foucault, Michel. 1984. "Nietzsche, Genealogy, History." In *The Foucault Reader*, 76–100. New York: Pantheon.

Go, Julian. 2012. *Patterns of Empire: The British and American Empires, 1688 to the Present*. Cambridge: Cambridge University Press.

Goldstone, Jack A. 1998. "Initial Conditions, General Laws, Path Dependence, and Explanation in Historical Sociology." *American Journal of Sociology* 104:829–45.

Goldthorpe, John H. 2001. "Causation, Statistics, and Sociology." *European Sociological Review* 17:1–20.

Gorski, Philip. 2004. "The Poverty of Deductivism: A Constructive Realist Model of Socio-logical Explanation." *Sociological Methodology* 34:1–33.

Gould, Mark. 2019. "History Is Sociology: All Arguments Are Counterfactuals." *Journal of Historical Sociology* 32(1): e1–e10.

Gould, Roger V. 1995. *Insurgent Identities: Class, Community, and Protest in Paris from 1848 to the Commune.* Chicago: University of Chicago Press.

Gross, Neil. 2009. "A Pragmatist Theory of Social Mechanisms." *American Sociological Review* 74:358–79.

——. 2018. "Pragmatism and the Study of Large-scale Social Phenomena." *Theory and Society* 47:87–111.

Hall, John R. 1999. *Cultures of Inquiry: From Epistemology to Discourse in Sociohistorical Research.* Cambridge: Cambridge University Press.

Hart, H. L. Adolphus, and Tony Honoré. [1959] 1985. *Causation in the Law.* Oxford: Oxford University Press.

Haydu, Jeffrey. 1998. "Making Use of the Past: Time Periods as Cases to Compare and as Sequences of Problem Solving." *American Journal of Sociology* 104:339–71.

Heidegger, Martin. 1977. *The Question Concerning Technology, and Other Essays.* New York: Harper & Row.

Heidelberger, Michael. 2015. "From Mill via von Kries to Max Weber: Causality, Explanation, and Understanding." *Max Weber Studies* 15:13–45.

Hirschman, Daniel, and Isaac Ariail Reed. 2014. "Formation Stories and Causality in Sociol-ogy." *Sociological Theory* 32:259–82.

Holland, Paul W. 1986. "Statistics and Causal Inference." *Journal of the American Statistical Association* 81:945–60.

Hume, David. [1748] 1993. *An Enquiry Concerning Human Understanding.* New York: Hackett.

Hung, Ho-fung. 2011. *Protest with Chinese Characteristics: Demonstrations, Riots, and Peti-tions in the Mid-Qing Dynasty.* New York: Columbia University Press.

Isaac, Larry W., and Larry J. Griffin. 1989. "Ahistoricism in Time-Series Analyses of Histor-ical Process: Critique, Redirection, and Illustrations from US Labor History." *American Sociological Review* 54:873–90.

Kagan, Donald. 1989. *The Outbreak of the Peloponnesian War.* Ithaca, NY: Cornell University Press.

Kern, Stephen. 2009. *A Cultural History of Causality: Science, Murder Novels, and Systems of Thought.* Princeton, NJ: Princeton University Press.

King, Gary, Robert O. Keohane, and Sidney Verba. 1994. *Designing Social Inquiry: Scientific Inference in Qualitative Research.* Princeton, NJ: Princeton University Press.

Lebow, Richard Ned. 2000. "Contingency, Catalysts, and International System Change." *Polit-ical Science Quarterly* 115(4):591–616.

Mackie, John L. 1974. *The Cement of the Universe.* Oxford: Oxford University Press.

Mahoney, James. 2000. "Path Dependence in Historical Sociology." *Theory and Society* 29:507–48.

Mahoney, James, and Dietrich Rueschemeyer, eds. 2003. *Comparative Historical Analysis in the Social Sciences.* Cambridge: Cambridge University Press.

Mahoney, James, and Kathleen Thelen, eds. 2015. *Advances in Comparative-Historical Analy-sis.* Cambridge: Cambridge University Press.

Mandelbaum, M. 1977. *The Anatomy of Historical Knowledge.* Baltimore, MD: Johns Hopkins University Press.

Mann, Michael. 1986. *The Sources of Social Power, Vol. I: A History of Power from the Begin-ning to 1760 AD.* New York: Cambridge University Press.

Marini, Margaret Mooney, and Burton Singer. 1988. "Causality in the Social Sciences." *Sociological Methodology* 18:347–409.

Martin, John Levi. 2011. *The Explanation of Social Action*. New York: Oxford University Press.

Mead, George Herbert. 1932. *The Philosophy of the Present*. Chicago: Open Court.

Menzies, Peter, and Huw Price 1993. "Causation as a Secondary Quality." *British Journal for the Philosophy of Science* 44:187–203.

Mill, John S. [1843] 1950. *A System of Logic*. New York: Harper.

Moore, Barrington Jr. 1958. "Strategy in Social Science." In *Political Power and Social Theory: Six Studies*, 111–59. Cambridge, MA: Harvard University Press.

Morgan, Stephen L., and Christopher Winship. 2014. *Counterfactuals and Causal Inference*. Cambridge: Cambridge University Press.

Mudge, Stephanie L. 2018. *Leftism Reinvented: Western Parties from Socialism to Neoliberalism*. Cambridge, MA: Harvard University Press.

Mumford, Stephen, and Rani L. Anjum. 2011. *Getting Causes from Powers*. Oxford: Oxford University Press.

Nagel, Ernest. [1961] 1979. *The Structure of Science: Problems in the Logic of Scientific Explanation*. New York: Hackett.

Nietzsche, Friedrich W. [1887] 2015. *On the Genealogy of Morals*. New York: Vintage.

Padgett, John F., and Walter W. Powell. 2012. *The Emergence of Organizations and Markets*. Princeton, NJ: Princeton University Press.

Paige, Jeffery M. 1999. "Conjuncture, Comparison, and Conditional Theory in Macrosocial Inquiry." *American Journal of Sociology* 105:781–800.

Pierson, Paul. 2004. *Politics in Time: History, Institutions, and Social Analysis*. Princeton, NJ: Princeton University Press.

Pomeranz, Kenneth. 2001. *The Great Divergence: China, Europe, and the Making of the Modern World Economy*. Princeton, NJ: Princeton University Press.

Popper, Karl. 1963. *Conjectures and Refutations: The Growth of Scientific Knowledge*. London: Routledge and K. Paul.

Psillos, Stathis. 2002. *Causation and Explanation*. Kingston, Ontario, Canada: McGill-Queen's Press-MQUP.

Ragin, Charles C. 1987. *The Comparative Method: Moving Beyond Qualitative and Quantitative Strategies*. Berkeley: University of California Press.

——. 2000. *Fuzzy-Set Social Science*. Chicago: University of Chicago Press.

Reed, Isaac Ariail. 2011. *Interpretation and Social Knowledge: On the Use of Theory in the Human Sciences*. Chicago: University of Chicago Press.

Ricoeur, Paul. 1984. *Time and Narrative*. Chicago: University of Chicago Press.

Ross, Dorothy. 1991. *The Origins of American Social Science*. Cambridge: Cambridge University Press.

Roth, Randolph. 1992. "Is History a Process? Nonlinearity, Revitalization Theory, and the Central Metaphor of Social Science History." *Social Science History* 16:197–243.

Sahlins, Marshall. 1991. "The Return of the Event, Again: With Reflections on the Beginnings of the Great Fijian War of 1843 to 1845 Between the Kingdoms of Bau and Rewa." In *Clio in Oceania*, edited by Aletta Biersack, 37–100. Washington, DC: Smithsonian Institution.

Salmon, Wesley C. 1984. *Scientific Explanation and the Causal Structure of the World*. Princeton, NJ: Princeton University Press.

Sewell, William H., Jr. 2005. *Logics of History: Social Theory and Social Transformation*. Chicago: University of Chicago Press.

Skocpol, Theda. 1979. *States and Social Revolutions: A Comparative Analysis of France, Russia, and China*. Cambridge: Cambridge University Press.

——, ed. 1984. *Vision and Method in Historical Sociology*. Cambridge: Cambridge University Press.

Somers, Margaret R. 1996. "Where Is Sociology After the Historic Turn? Knowledge Cultures and Historical Epistemologies." In *The Historic Turn in the Human Sciences*, edited by Terrence J. McDonald, 53–89. Ann Arbor: University of Michigan Press.

——. 1998. "We're No Angels: Realism, Rational Choice, and Relationality in Social Science." *American Journal of Sociology* 104:722–84.

Steinmetz, George. 1998. "Critical Realism and Historical Sociology." *Comparative Studies in Society and History* 40:170–86.

——. 2004. "Odious Comparisons: Incommensurability, the Case Study, and 'Small N's' in Sociology." *Sociological Theory* 22:371–400.

——. 2014. "Comparative History and Its Critics: A Genealogy and a Possible Solution." In *A Companion to Global Historical Thought*, edited by Prasenjit Duara, Viren Murthy, and Andrew Sartori, 412–36. Chichester, United Kingdom: Wiley-Blackwell.

Stinchcombe, Arthur L. 1978. *Theoretical Methods in Social History*. New York: Academic.

——. 1991. "The Conditions of Fruitfulness of Theorizing About Mechanisms in Social Science." *Philosophy of the Social Sciences* 21:367–88.

Stone, Lawrence. 1972. *The Causes of the English Revolution 1529–1642*. New York: Routledge.

Strand, Michael, and Omar Lizardo. 2022. "Chance, Orientation, and Interpretation: Max Weber's Neglected Probabilism and the Future of Social Theory." *Sociological Theory* 40:124–50.

Stryker, Robin. 1996. "Beyond History Versus Theory: Strategic Narrative and Sociological Explanation." *Sociological Methods and Research* 24(3):304–52.

Thelen, Kathleen. 1999. "Historical Institutionalism in Comparative Politics." *Annual Review of Political Science* 2(1):369–404.

Tilly, Charles. 1984. *Big Structures, Large Processes, Huge Comparison*. New York: Russell Sage Foundation.

——. 1995. "To Explain Political Processes." *American Journal of Sociology* 100:1594–610.

Veyne, Paul. [1970] 1984. *Writing History: Essay on Epistemology*. Manchester: Manchester University Press.

Weber, Max. 1949. *The Methodology of the Social Sciences*. New York: Free Press.

Whitehead, Alfred North. [1929] 1978. *Process and Reality*. New York: Simon and Schuster.

Woodward, James. 2003. *Making Things Happen: A Theory of Causal Explanation*. Oxford: Oxford University Press.

Zhang, Yang. 2007. "Is Falsification Possible in Social Science?" *Sociological Studies* 3:136–53.

——. 2019. "Thinking Counterfactual Sequentially: A Processual View of Counterfactual in Historical Sociology." *Journal of Historical Sociology* 32: e15–e21.

——. 2021. "Why Elites Rebel: Elite Insurrections During the Taiping Civil War in China." *American Journal of Sociology* 127(1):60–101.

Zhang, Yang, and Feng Shi. 2023. "The Micro-foundations of Elite Politics: Conversation Networks and Elite Conflict During China's Reform Era." *Theory and Society*. https://doi.org/10.1007/s11186-023-09530-7.

CHAPTER 12

THE DIALECTICAL COMPARATIVE
METHODOLOGY

REBECCA JEAN EMIGH, DYLAN RILEY,
AND PATRICIA AHMED

We confess that this chapter is written out of frustration. In reviews of our comparative historical papers as well as those of our students and colleagues, we note two common contradictory themes. First, if we have a single case, reviewers focus on "what can be done with a single case" and ask for a comparative case. But if we provide a comparative case based on the most widely used comparative strategies—namely, John Stuart Mill's ([1843] 1974a, VII, 388-396) methods of agreement and difference or most similar/different systems (Przeworski and Teune 1970, 32-35)—the methods are immediately shot down as outdated and invalid. Or, if we use comparison informally but do not explicitly state our methods, the paper is rejected as "methodless." We also note a historical trend over our careers (after all, we are historical comparative sociologists!). With the rise of process tracing and negative case methodology, along with endless, ad nauseum condemnations of Mill, the criticisms of single cases have perhaps declined while the criticism of comparative methods has increased. Bizarrely, many comparative and historical sociologists, despite the official American Sociological Association name of their subfield, now immediately reject comparison. Perhaps there is also a shift toward using the term "historical sociology" without the comparative nomenclature. This problem essentially leaves this important and broad sociological subfield, with its emancipatory project to show how taken-for-granteds became real, without a strong methodological basis.

This tension between cases studies and comparison, moreover, is not just a problem in comparative and historical sociology, although it is discussed most explicitly there. In fact, every study has both a "case study" and a "comparison" problem if the unit of analysis is switched: at a higher level of generality, every study is a single case (i.e., data sets collected in the United States are about the single case of this country); at a more fine-grained level of analysis, every case study is composed of compared units (i.e., an analysis of the United States necessarily compares the individuals living there). Thus, this methodological issue of comparison affects all social science. Furthermore, comparison is central for explanation. It is almost impossible to know anything without comparing one thing, either explicitly or implicitly, to something else in some way (as a proclamation for comparative ethnography extols; Abramson and Gong 2020, 1). Comparison moreover assists theoretical development, which occurs primarily through the construction of better explanatory models in general, and for information gathering, in particular (Arthur 2011, 173; Emigh 1997, 656-57; Gorski 2004, 22; Mora 2014, 203; Ragin 2008, 4). Explanation, the answering of a why question, virtually requires that it be possible to specify why something applies to some topic but not to some other topic. Thus, research getting caught in these crosshairs between case studies and comparison is counterproductive for historical and comparative work in particular and for sociology in general. Indeed, the very distinction between case studies and comparison is a false one, since cases must be cases of something, and therefore can be identified only in a comparative framework. Clearly, both types of work are needed. They simply address different units of analysis of empirical inquiry, although at an epistemological and methodological level, they are both comparative. At the same time, many criticisms of comparative methods have merit.

Here, to find a way forward methodologically, but also taking account of the criticisms, we reformulate formal comparative methods for small N studies. To do so, we draw on the difference between a methodology, which combines a set of techniques, an ontology, and an epistemology, and a method, which is one such concrete technique (Olsen 2007, 2; Roberts 2014, 1-2). We essentially argue that Mill's method (rightly or wrongly) has been cast mostly as a positivist methodology that is inappropriate for comparative historical sociology. Thus, we embed this concrete method of comparison within a methodology based in a philosophy of social science that we call "dialectical realism," with an underlying understanding of social action as "praxis as knowing" (Riley, Emigh, and Ahmed 2021, 331-34). We employ a broad definition of dialectic as the examination of things constituted by social relationships (as is used in, but also beyond, Marxist work to think comparatively and historically in both substantive and methodological terms). We call this new methodology *dialectical comparative methodology* (DCM).

We argue that this is a crucial intervention for comparative historical sociology, as well as for any study that compares a few cases, such as ethnography, because at present there is no widely agreed-upon method for comparing cases with only a few Ns. Mill's methods are best applied to small N research, but they have been discredited. Qualitative comparative analysis (QCA) cannot substitute for Mill's methods for small N research. QCA is generally considered to be optimally effective for intermediate-sized studies with ten to fifty cases (and perhaps for larger N) (Hanckel et al. 2021, 2; Ide and Mello 2022, 9; Rutten 2022, 1212; e.g., Ragin 1987, 88). A few QCA examples exist for studies with five to ten cases (Ragin 1987, 90, 96; Rihoux 2006, 698), but QCA generally is not effective for studies with fewer N (Ide and Mello 2022, 9) (Bayesian techniques can also be effective with an intermediate N; Western 1999, 16). It is notably difficult, however, to understand how variables or factors create patterns of causal mechanisms for large-scale historical processes where the unit of analysis is typically a region-time period (conventionally, a nation-state with a stable government, making a periodization of its history possible) because these units are rare and often incomparable (Becker 2014, 7–8; George and Bennett 2005, 164). Thus, viable small N methods are crucial. Our intervention is also perhaps increasingly urgent as ethnographers turn to comparative historical methods for inspiration and as comparative historical sociologists—like ethnographers—turn to regional units other than nation states, both local and global, or to temporal units (Abramson and Gong 2020, 1–2; Bhambra 2010, 140; Emigh, Ahmed, and Riley 2021, 10; Pacewicz 2020, 935; George 2023, 305; cf. Burawoy 1998, 27–28).

We present an extremely simple methodology of comparison that is easily implemented in any small N research (e.g., comparative, historical, and ethnographic), that requires few assumptions, and that can be used to develop social science theory. And, although we prefer to retain the entire methodology, including the dialectical realist assumptions, we note that the method itself, since it requires virtually no assumptions, can be embedded within the ontological and epistemological rubrics of any methodology where the preconditions for such an embedding hold (so, for example, our method is identical to Mill's methods of difference and agreement where the assumptions for their application hold). We also show how this comparative method combines with existing narrative methods so that the two methods can be used in tandem, either in the same study or across different studies. This provides small N research with easily applied strategies that can be used across a broad range of research and that can be deployed to evaluate theory. These strategies thus increase the range and scope of small N research.

We make this argument in this chapter in the following sections. First, we introduce an empirical example of the difficulties of using Mill's comparative method. Second, we consider how Mill's methods have been cast, more or less, in a positivist methodology. Third, we consider how comparative methods can be recast as a dialectical realist methodology, that is, as DCM. Fourth, we outline the details of DCM. Fifth, we return to the empirical example from our first section to show concretely how DCM can work. Finally, our conclusions suggest how and why DCM can be useful. As we noted earlier, although we contend that dialectical realism provides the best philosophical backing for our comparative method, since it can be deployed from a variety of philosophical perspectives, readers interested in the concrete method or its application can skip straight to the details of the method (in the fourth section) or its application (in the fifth section) and return (or not) to the philosophical details in the other sections at their leisure.

An Example of the Comparative Quandary: Land Surveys

At present, small N comparativists face a quandary. They can leave their comparative methods unstated, but they may get called out for lack of a method. Or, they may try to use, however modified, Mill's methods, but they then risk the onslaught of criticism against it. Small N comparison is attacked from positivist circles as nonscientific, as well as from interpretive, nonpositivist circles as incommensurable (Steinmetz 2004, 372). To deal with this quandary, some authors seem to toss Mill in or mention his methods in passing, perhaps hoping no one will notice (e.g., Anderson 2018, 183; Charrad 2001, 10); others use cases with similarities and differences without explicitly calling attention to their Millian patterns (e.g., Fairbrother 2014, 1336-37; Gorski 1993, 303-4; Hung 2008, 574-75; Lachmann 2000, 14; Tsutsui 2017, 1059-60; cf. Beck 2017, 540). Faced with the same problem, we noted that it is impossible to compare cases without drawing on the logic represented in Mill in some way while also relaxing many of the assumptions thought to apply to the use of his method (Emigh et al. 2021, 19-20; see also, e.g., Bergene 2007, 21-24 for other adaptations). Another approach is simply to tire of the debates about causality and therefore make no claims about it, but instead describe change over time through narrative. These same strategies recur repeatedly in small N studies.

To highlight this quandary, as well as how our new method addresses it, we use an example of our own work. We could use any of the studies cited earlier or, indeed, virtually any small N study, but to illustrate our points most clearly, we draw on our own work, which we understand well and in which we explicitly used Mill's methods, as well as discussed their advantages and disadvantages. Our example also explicitly uses narrative, so it will help to illustrate our point about how narrative and comparison can combine.

We evaluated the influence of three processes—state strength, tacit or local knowledge, and social actors' interests in information gathering—on the completion of land surveys in the United States, Italy, and the United Kingdom (Emigh, Riley, and Ahmed 2019, 407). We provided a short methods section explaining that the empirical cases follow the pattern of Mill's method of difference and agreement (Emigh et al. 2019, 407). This allowed us to create a table summarizing the outcome and possible influences that could be used to assess the explanatory power of state-centered and society-centered theories.

However, immediately after our invocation of Mill, we also distanced our-selves from his method, citing its drawbacks. We noted that this method cannot strictly evaluate causality, as is sometimes claimed. Mill's method provides no information about a causal mechanism, necessary for assessing causality, that a narrative method might provide (Emigh et al. 2019, 407). We also noted that Mill's method is difficult to apply in practice, as empirical cases generally do not conform to the pattern needed to apply it (Emigh et al. 2019, 408). To get around these difficulties, we combined the comparison presented in the table with a more detailed narrative (Emigh et al. 2019, 408). In doing so, we tried to turn a disadvantage into an advantage.

Of course, all methods have disadvantages (Emigh et al. 2019, 407), but our own difficulty in applying what is a widely known and used method seems espe-cially poignant. Though we used a standard method widely used to judge com-parisons, either implicitly or explicitly, we cannot really depend on it because of faulty philosophical underpinnings as well as empirical realities. There are two central problems. Philosophically, Mill's method has been interpreted to rely on a view of causality of constant conjunction, based on induction, without refer-ence to a causal mechanism. In addition, neither reality nor the empirical cases that comparative historical research uses usually conform to the stricture of this philosophical application. We realized that reviewers, themselves familiar with the method and its endless critics, would immediately shoot down Mill's meth-ods as discredited. Nevertheless, we used them, and in doing so, we hoped to provide a useful example of how to combine comparison and narrative. How-ever, the combination was ad hoc, so it provided few explicit cues that could be applied elsewhere. We return to this example later to illustrate how DCM solves these issues.

Can Mill's Methods Be Cast as a Positivist Methodology?

Mill's Methods and Methodologies

Mill ([1843] 1974a, VII, 388–406) developed four (or more, depending on how they are enumerated) methods—namely, the methods of agreement, differ-ence, residues, and concomitant variation—but only the methods of agreement and difference are widely used in sociology, so we focus on them here. Mill's method of agreement searches for cases with the same outcome and then uses this agreement to eliminate all the factors that are different, as these are not causes of the outcome. In contrast, his method of difference searches for cases with a different outcome and explanatory factors that are all similar except for one crucial difference. This difference is the causal one. Mill's joint method of agreement and difference combines these two methods to assess the pattern of the similarities and differences to isolate the single cause. Mill's methods, at some level, are simply that: concrete methods of making comparisons through patterns of difference and similarity. However, to impute causality to a single outcome, the factors have to be independent, they have to be sorted into necessary and sufficient causes, and they have to be subjected to an eliminatory logic, generally through the joint application of the method of agreement and difference. Thus, for causality, the methods have to be turned into a methodology: they have to be embedded into a particular positivist philosophy of science that understands causality as a constant conjunction of a factor with a single outcome. The factors must be concrete entities, empirically observable and independent across cases. The relationship between the factors and the outcome, ideally, should be observable through induction. Positivism, of course, includes a broad set of philosophical tenets that do not always rely on induction and a search for a single cause, but Mill's methods of difference and agreement are generally turned into a methodology on this basis.

It is clear, however, that Mill ([1843] 1974b, VIII, 846-47, 864, 870, 881-84) did not think that the methods of agreement and difference could be deployed in the social sciences as methodologies with this particular positivist philosophical underpinning (Elster 1978, 178-79). He essentially argued that human sciences are different from physical sciences and require different philosophies (Mill [1843] 1974b, VIII, 846-47). Humans are different from physical objects; social phenomena are different from physical ones. The causes of human behavior are incredibly complex, multiple, and variable, and experimentation is generally not possible (Hausman 1992, 14; Mill [1843] 1974b, VIII, 888; Smits 2004, 303). Mill ([1843] 1974b, VIII, 869) called the science of the study of humans "ethology," and interestingly linked it to education. His argument is quite dialectical: humans' circumstances and their characters are linked (Mill [1843] 1974b, VIII, 864). As a consequence, human sciences can only achieve approximate generalizations (Mill [1843] 1974b, VIII, 847, 864). The variability and multiplicity of causes in social sciences mean that only deduction, not induction, can be used (Mill [1843] 1974b, VIII, 865). Sociology, then, is a deductive science and must consider all possible, conjoint causes (Mill [1843] 1974b, VIII, 895).

Mill ([1843] 1974a, VII, 454) argued specifically for a social science deductive method in three stages: direct induction, ratiocination, and verification. His overall deductive method required that general premises be stated in advance; for this to be possible, however, at the first stage, direct induction had to be used to develop these premises (Mill [1843] 1974a, VII, 454). Here, however, Mill ([1843] 1974a, VII, 455) pointed out that the four methods of comparison (difference, agreement, residues, and concomitant variation) were the basis for this induction. This first stage established basic psychological or technical laws

(Hausmann 1992, 14). These established premises were not universal laws—these basic generalizations were instead statements of tendencies. The second stage of the deductive method, ratiocination, was trying to figure out, from these deductive premises, what combination of causes they might produce (Hausman 1992, 14; Mill [1843] 1974a, VII, 458). The final stage in deduction, verification, required empirical observations that confirmed the deduction (Mill [1843] 1974a, VII, 461). Here, Mill ([1843] 1974a, VII, 461) pointed to the role of comparison and, in particular, the method of agreement, in verifying deduction for complex cases. Verification provided the "accordance between its results and those of observation *a posteriori*" (Mill [1843] 1974b, VIII, 897). Verification essentially showed whether the deductions had been correctly made and whether significant causal factors had been left out; however, verification did not provide evidence for initial premises (Hausman 1992, 14). Sociology, then, is a science of "tendencies," not of "positive predictions," since it cannot be a system of deductions *a priori* (Mill [1843] 1974b, VIII, 898). It is clear, then, that even in the deductive method used for social science, comparison has a crucial role—but the basis for using it has a different logic than in the physical sciences. Thus, in his methodological writing, Mill used induction and deduction iteratively and dialectically to generate and evaluate theories empirically.

In his substantive writing, Mill pursued related ideas. Mill's ([1859] 1989, 20) defense of freedom of expression was rooted in the idea that truth is an interactional achievement. Thus, Mill conceptualized truth in a dialogic or dialectical way. Explanation was not just a matter of holding ideas that corresponded to the state of affairs in the world; it required providing reasons for why those ideas were held (Mill [1859] 1989, 37-38; cf. Habermas 1989, 27). Thus, truth claims, to be truth claims, must be contested (Mill [1859] 1989, 53). He even worried that the progress of modern science might lead to a generation of dogmatists as "truth" became more and more established (Mill [1859] 1989, 39-40, 53-54). Pedagogy would then be required to recreate artificially the contested conditions of the original situation (Mill [1859] 1989, 45). Mill distinguished between holding a truth as an opinion and knowing the truth in a living way. This latter truth required discussion: "If the cultivation of the understanding consists in one thing more than another, it is surely in learning the grounds of one's own opinions" (Mill [1859] 1989, 37). Without this dialogic component, truth is "but one superstition the more" (Mill [1859] 1989, 37). In sum, in his substantive writings as well as his methodological ones, Mill clearly understood that social science was based on a different philosophy of science than natural science. Social science deals with a much more complex and indeterminant reality than natural science. In his substantive writings on freedom of expression, he argued that debate and contestation about social reality were crucial. Although Mill's ([1843] 1974b, VIII, 879) somewhat reductionist view of human nature in his methodological writings—that all social-level analysis can be resolved into individual-level analysis—is at odds with a view of sociology as attending to emergent properties, it is clear that Mill did not intend for his methods of agreement and difference to be used with positivist philosophies of social science in sociology.

Skocpol and Somers's Adaptation of Mill's Methods as a Methodology

Skocpol and Somers (1980, 181–83, 195) revived Mill's method of agreement and difference with a specific purpose: they were attempting to show how comparative historical methods could be used to make causal inferences about macrolevel structures by creating approximations to controlled comparisons. They used the method to link theory to data, with an underlying understanding of causality in the sense of a constant conjunction between a temporally ordered antecedent and outcome (stereotypically labeled A and B, with A temporally preceding B) (Skocpol and Somers 1980, 184). Thus, they explicitly applied Mill's methods with an eye for testing hypotheses about theories and generating new theories of historical and macro phenomena (Skocpol and Somers 1980, 182). The factors used in the methods of agreement and difference could be related to the outcome through Millian comparison. The comparison then could demonstrate causality.[1] Thus, essentially, they created a methodology from Mill's methods that drew heavily on a positivist philosophy of social science, at least in principle. Skocpol and Somers's (1980, 181-83) revival of Mill's methods of agreement and difference, which led to their widespread adoption in comparative historical sociology, was in direct contradiction to Mill's own prescription. This is widely known but usually invoked as a confirmation that Mill's methods should not be used in social science (e.g., Goldthorpe 2000, 49–50; cf. Sekhon 2004, 284-86).

There are endless criticisms of Skocpol and Somers's adaptation of Mill's methods, including their reliance on induction, the impossibility of finding cases with the exact combination of similarities and differences, the inability of the method to handle interactions, its search for singular deterministic causes, and the lack of comparability and independence across cases (e.g., Bennett 2004, 31-32; Bergene 2007, 14, 16; Burawoy 1989, 779; Gorski 2004, 22–28; Lieberson 1991, 307; Pacewicz 2022, 936; Sekhon 2004, 281; Sewell 2005, 93-96). Some of these certainly misrepresent Skocpol and Somers's (1980, 195) argument, as they noted many of these problems themselves. For example, although they have been criticized for using induction (e.g., Burawoy 1989, 778; Gorski 2004, 22), they did note that they used comparison "in relation to particular explanatory problems and (one or more) hypotheses about likely causes" (Skocpol and Somers 1980, 182-83), thus suggesting that they were also, at least partially, reframing Mill deductively. They also noted that general theories have to account for "societal dynamics and epochal transformations" (Skocpol and Somers 1980, 196), suggesting that they also realized that Mill's methods alone, based on constant conjunction, do not provide a complete causal explanation. These concessions were not, however, well integrated into Skocpol and Somers's overarching interpretation of Mill. It is important to note that all the criticisms of Skocpol and Somers's interpretation of Mill actually focus on their reframing of Mill's methods as a methodology, rooted, at least largely, in a positivist philosophy of social science, which of course Mill himself never intended. At least in principle, this methodology focuses on using the method of agreement and difference to eliminate all factors except the one that is the singular cause of the outcome through induction. Whether Mill's methods could be turned into a positivist methodology with underpinnings more appropriate for social science and comparative historical sociology (e.g., making use of some of the various components of this methodology, such as multiple conjunctural causes; causal modeling; theories of regularity, inferential, and counterfactual causality; deduction) is of course another question but is beyond the scope of this chapter.

The Retreat from Comparison

Nevertheless, partly (at least) in response to these criticisms of Skocpol and Somers's interpretation of Mill's methods, there was a return to narrative methods that entailed tracing out the sequence or temporal ordering of events and processes (Bhambra 2010, 140; Clemens 2007, 532; Kiser 1996, 249; Lara-Millán, Sargent, and Kim 2020, 351; Sewell 2005, 100). This movement took multiple forms, including studies that emphasized narrative per se in terms of a discursive telling of events as either the explanation or the cause (Griffin 1993, 1096; Sewell 1992, 480; Somers 1994, 614); narrative positivism as a formalization of a sequence of events and social processes to trace their changes and historicity (Abbott 1992, 434; 2016, ix-x; Abell 1993, 94; Glaeser 2005, 16); process tracing as a way to consider causal mechanisms rooted in a positivist but inferential theory of causality (George and Bennet 2005, 6-7); path dependence as a way to understand contingent sequences (Mahoney 2000, 507-8); and negative case methodology as a way to develop the substantive content of theory (Emigh 1997, 649). Here, although the development of narrative methods is not the main focus of our chapter, we describe briefly the two types of narrative that are explicitly intended to highlight causal mechanisms—namely, process tracing and negative case methodology—as we will advocate that they can be used in conjunction with comparison.

Process tracing itself has multiple forms (Crasnow 2017, 7-8), but in general, it is a formalized form of narrative, based on a particular view of causality rooted in a positivist philosophy of science, that searches for causal mechanisms that create associations between the independent and dependent variables, generally in single cases. Thus, it is generally a within-case method for drawing inferences about mechanisms by assessing alternative hypotheses that best explain the outcome (Bennett, Fairfield, and Soifer 2019, 1). While the relationship among variables or factors and outcomes can show a constant conjunction, there must be a causal mechanism that produces the correlation or conjunction (see review in Beach and Pedersen 2019, 1-27). Process tracing, then, tries to identify this mechanism by explicating temporal processes or chains of independent variables that produce particular outcomes within cases (Runhardt 2022, 5), although comparisons are also possible (Bengtsson and Ruonavaara 2017, 45). The process of tracing is done by observing empirical "fingerprints" or "traces" left by the operation of the causal mechanism in a case (Beach and Pedersen 2019, 2). This methodology is, then, not just a descriptive narrative—it seeks causal explanations (Beach and Pederson 2019, 2).

Process tracing is quite valuable but highly confirmatory in the sense that it focuses on explaining why an outcome did occur. It is almost impossible to show why something did not occur empirically, as the point is to find the best explanation for why the outcome did occur. Thus, empirical cases where the outcome did not occur are not generally the focus of process tracing. It tends to then assume that the causal mechanism is effective, or it searches for specific tests of whether or not it is effective. The closest process tracing gets to looking at outcomes that do not occur is looking at deviant cases, where the mechanism breaks down (Beach and Pedersen 2019, 11). But even in these cases, the process is present, so the point is to confirm the importance of the mechanism more generally. It is perhaps for this reason that process tracing often focuses on counterfactuals and hypothetical interventions (Runhardt 2022, 28). They help assess alternative explanations for that same outcome.

Negative case methodology can help prevent some of this confirmation bias that is inherent in process tracing. In contrast to process tracing, it focuses on cases where the outcome did not occur, even when predicted by some theory (Emigh 1997, 649–50). Negative case methodology is rooted in a postpositivist understanding of social science, based on Imre Lakatos, who in many ways anticipated a realist philosophy of science. He focused on how models could be developed to improve their fit with reality, while recognizing that all models simulated reality (Lakatos 1970, 132–35). Furthermore, Lakatos (1970, 132) focused on confirming and disconfirming theories, an approach that has hallmarks of a dialectical philosophy. Consistent with a Lakatosian perspective, negative case methodology builds on the idea that disconfirming evidence can strengthen theories if the evidence is taken seriously as a way to build the content of the theory to improve its fit with reality. Negative case methodology, like process tracing, focuses on tracing the details of the case, but, unlike process tracing, it also focuses on understanding why the theory incorrectly predicted the outcome and on adding theoretical content, whether new theoretical material or a revision of existing material, to explain the case. Negative case methodology assumes the importance of comparison: it deploys comparison among the cases and theories to develop the content of theory. Thus, the Lakatosian approach is easily understood in realist terms: models come closer to reality through increases in knowledge, although they are never reality itself, through a dialectic of confirmation and refutation.

Cases in which the outcome occurs as expected, as analyzed by process tracing, make it possible to trace the causal mechanism and show how it created the outcome. However, cases in which the outcome did occur are not the most powerful ones to develop the substantive content of the theory because it is easy to assume, if the outcome is present, that all the features of the case contributed to the outcome (Emigh 1997, 650). Furthermore, understanding the range of possibility of transformation is possible only if cases where the outcome does not occur are also examined. The cases where the outcome did not occur are generally the more powerful ones for expanding substantive theoretical content, as the missing outcome makes it easier to discriminate between the important and unimportant features of the cases (Emigh 1997, 650, 652, 655; cf. Lachmann 2000, 16; Mill [1843] 1974a, VII, 394; Przeworski and Teune 1970, 34, 35). Thus, negative case methodology is crucial to developing the content of theory and not simply reconfirming over and over again a theory with process tracing. Thus, the narrative methods—process tracing and negative case methodology—must be used in combination both with each other and with comparison.

The increased use of explicit invocations of narrative methods has been quite productive. Clearly, causal explanation is not about the deterministic regularity of patterns and mechanisms (Hu 2018, 122). At the same time, however, the examination of only the causal mechanisms is misleading because these analyses require the identification of the starting and ending points of the causal mechanism, and so the identification of these points is also crucial to analyzing causal mechanisms. Furthermore, comparison is necessary for explanation (cf. critical realism, Danermark, Ekström, and Karlsson 2002, 105). But the explicit rejection of Millian comparison, along with the replacement of comparison with narrative, leaves the field without a useable comparative method for small N cases. At the same time, Mill's comparative methods are, of course, widely used in comparative historical sociology, as we argued earlier, whether or not explicitly cited; despite these criticisms, undoubtedly, as Skocpol and Somers showed, they are quite useful in practice for small N analysis. By reframing comparison in a dialectical realist philosophy of social science, we try to develop a fruitful comparative methodology, one that can be combined with narrative instead of replacing it. The next section creates the philosophical underpinnings of this methodology.

A Dialectical Realist Philosophy to Underpin a Comparative Methodology

Dialectical Realism

Realism is a widespread form of reasoning used in analytic sociology (i.e., analytic realism) and comparative historical sociology (i.e., critical realism, dialectical realism) (Archer 2020, 137; Bergene 2007, 25; Gorski 2009, 180; 2013, 667-68; Hedström and Ylikoski 2010, 58; Riley et al. 2021, 332). Realism is a philosophy based on an ontology specifying that noumena (essences or things in themselves) are different from phenomena (experiences of such essences or things) (Archer 2020, 140; reviews in Jessop 2005, 40-45; Riley et al. 2021, 332). Accordingly, scientific models are different from reality since they represent, at a very general level, an experience of reality, but models are never reality themselves (Bhaskar 1986, 24-25; Gorski 2004, 19; Hacking 1999, 80-84; Hartmann 1921, 43; Pula 2021, 741; Somers 1998, 766). Through empirical and theoretical work, these models can become closer to reality. We understand models in a broad sense as representations of entire theoretical processes, or as representations of parts of them such as factors or variables. Thus, all variables and factors, in the realist understanding, are models derived from conceptual schemes (cf. Roberts 2014, 15). This view of models as necessarily incomplete is shared by many other formal philosophical traditions as well as more informal research strategies, but they do not always share the insistence that social and physical reality are inherently different (e.g., complex systems; Page 2015, 25).

Dialectical realism builds on and improves on critical realism (cf. Jessop 2005, 48-53). First, although it shares with critical realism the idea that the noumena are different from phenomena, dialectical realism has a fuller understanding of their nature and relationship. Implicit in critical realism, but explicit in dialectical realism, is the idea that social reality is composed of "interactive kinds," which are real but also interact with the descriptions that describe them (Collier 2005, 335-36; Engelskirchen 2011, 9, 20, 37, 92; Hacking 1999, 58-59, 103, 106-8; 2002, 2; Riley et al. 2021, 331-32). Because of this interaction, social reality has a potentiality that may or may not be fulfilled (Collier 2005, 335). For positivism, only positive events and things can be analyzed because they are present. For dialectical realism (and critical realism where it draws on dialectical realism), in contrast, causal effects of absences or negations are also real and can be analyzed (Bhaskar 1993, 44-45; Collier 2005, 335-36). Social existence cannot be equated with what "is." Unique to dialectical realism, however, is the rejection of the opposition between "things" and "relations"; things are internally constituted by relations, and relations can exist only among *relata*, that is to say, broadly speaking, things. This conceptualization makes the analysis of the interactive kinds of social reality fully possible because the kinds themselves, their presences and absences, and their relationships, all have causal power.

Second, dialectical realism specifies that knowledge grows though confirmation and refutation, building on the conceptualization of presences and absences. Although critical realism suggests that the improvement of social science models grows through confirmation (Gorski 2004, 22), dialectical realism expands this understanding of the use of evidence to include refutation as well as confirmation. Although theories are unlikely to be definitively confirmed or refuted by a single study (or even several; cf. Gorski 2004, 20–21), empirical studies do provide confirmation or refutation, which, though partial at each step, builds knowledge over time. Furthermore, confirmation implies refutation since a theory can only be confirmed with respect to a well-articulated alternative theory, which itself must be refuted by the same evidence that confirms the original theory (cf. Gorksi 2004, 21). Or, in dialectical terms, a confirmation of one theory is also a refutation of another. In fact, claims about knowledge are inherently polemical since they provide knowledge for a claim and against an alternative one (Gramsci 1971, 330). In addition, as Lakatos (1970, 133-34) noted, refutation is particularly important in developing the content of theory, while confirmation is important in generalizing (Emigh 1997, 665). Thus, for dialectical realism, as for Mill, debate though confirmation and refutation is an absolute necessity.

Third, actors' positionality influences knowledge, and the contestation among the knowledge holders in different social positions is also crucial in developing new knowledge (Emigh, Riley, and Ahmed 2016a, 25). Critical realism, as applied to social science, sometimes lacks an understanding of how positionality affects social action and research outcomes (Sweet 2018, 222–23; cf. Haraway 1988, 581; Smith 1987, 105). If reality is real, and models, though approximations of this reality, move closer toward it, then how does positionality affect research outcomes? Critical realism can answer part of this question by positing domains or dimensions of reality that are more or less concept dependent (see review in Decoteau 2017, 67, 70). However, for dialectical realism, positionality is inherently built into the philosophical apparatus (Emigh, Riley, and Ahmed 2016b, 15-16; Riley et al. 2021, 332). Dialectical realism posits social interactive kinds, which can be present or absent and which necessarily entail positionality because their constitution depends on their social setting. Individuals in different social positions view reality in very different ways (Ollman 2003, 16; Riley et al. 2021, 333; Roberts 2014, 15). Although there is some debate over whether structures and objects have agency (e.g., Gorski 2013, 668-69; Latour 1991, 108), physical reality does not have the same characteristics as social reality because physical reality is not composed of interactive kinds as is social reality. For example, social classes are real regardless of whether people recognize them or not, but social classes that understand themselves as such are a different kind than classes that do not (Riley et al. 2021, 331-32). Thus, social classes that understand themselves have different views of the world than other social classes have. Another example is racism. Structural racism exists whether individuals recognize it or not; part of the point of the civil rights movements and Black Lives Matter is bringing awareness to this racism and what perpetuates it. Standpoints are not impossible to analyze from the critical realist position, but they are inherent in the dialectical realist one.

Fourth, for dialectical realism, this positionality is inherent in the research process as well as social life. Dialectical realism is based on a philosophy of science that assumes the existence of reality separate from humans' apprehension of it. Nevertheless, this reality is very complex and cannot be studied in its entirety (Emigh et al. 2016a, 40; cf. Mill [1843] 1974b, VIII, 924-25). Thus, although social reality, at the ontological level, holds together in a very complicated, interconnected, and holistic way, for any particular research project, specific interdependencies have to be extracted from this whole so that they can be compared and evaluated in concrete ways (Elster 1978, 179; Emigh et al. 2016a, 40; Ollman 2003, 15; Roberts 2014, 3). This makes it possible to compare, with a particular theoretical framework, a finite number of specified factors or variables or different societies (Elster 1978, 179). Different researchers will view and select elements in different ways. These can be combined for fuller views as each one separately is necessarily partial (Riley et al. 2021, 333). Dialectical realism thus concludes that researchers must have some knowledge—that is, positionality—about the causal properties of the whole and contradictory social reality to understand how these properties operate in more concrete settings (Roberts 2014, 17). Thus, researchers from different positionalities will view research projects in different ways because of their social position. For example, that the gendered and racialized nature of knowledge, as well as women's and non-Whites' understandings of it (as well as other positionalities that have been excluded because of ableism, heteronormativity, gender binarism, etc.), were not considered in much of academic science is also understandable from the position of dialectical realism, as it points to the social structures that prevented such knowledge from being heard (cf. epistemic structures and exclusions; Go 2020, 81).

Finally, humans can act reflexively on new knowledge, thus changing the nature of interactive kinds and the relationship among the research and the researchers. This is the essence of praxis (Gramsci 1971, 326-30). For dialectical realism, this is unproblematic. All views of the world are partial, and contestation among the views is crucial for the growth of knowledge (Emigh et al. 2016b, 219-21; Lana and Georgoudi 1983, 481).

Dialectical Causality

Causality is the examination of why something happens. Many philosophical points of view (e.g., theories of causation based on regularity, inference, or counterfactuals), as well as commonsense thinking, are generally based on demonstrative logic, reasoning from known truths and then deriving propositions from them (Lana and Georgoudi 1983, 480; Rychlak 1968, 305). These propositions generally describe how discrete antecedents produce outcomes. In contrast, a dialectical logic explains causality by considering how relationships, not static antecedents, produce change, usually though conflict or contestation (Pascual-Leone 1987, 536; Roberts 2014, 8–9; Rychlak 1968, 305). In dialectical causality, relations produce outcomes even though they may be reified as occurrences or objects. Indeed, relata and relationships are dialectically constituted. Thus, relations are central to dialectical thinking: social elements, and representations of them such factors and variables, themselves are relations, and there are relations among these social elements (Ollman 2003, 26; Roberts 2014, 7; cf. Archer 2020, 147; Jessop 2005, 52). These relationships, as explanantia, have causal influence on outcomes (explananda).

This emphasis on relationship is found in other sociological analysis, but dialectical causality centers it in the analysis of how outcomes occur. Complexity analysis, for example, shows how connectedness or interdependence of the occurrences affects the outcome (e.g., Page 2015, 30–31). Yet, connectedness or interdependence is still theorized as an afterthought, not as intrinsic to the property of occurrences. Relational sociology poses the question in a slightly different language: Is the world conceptualized as "things" or "relations?" (cf. Archer 2020, 147; Somers 1998, 766). Although its answer is the latter—that is, relations—network analysis, one of the preferred techniques for relational sociology (Emirbayer 1997, 298), easily lapses into considering both individuals and the networks in which they belong as the "things" that constitute social structure, with characteristic object-like measures of the network as variables in analyses (cf. Archer 2020, 147-48). In contrast, dialectical causality considers how the relationship itself creates an outcome. From this perspective, relata (substances) and relationships are dialectically constituted. Emirbayer's (1997, 281) distinction between substantive and relational sociology thus undermines itself. Nothing can be "relational all the way down" (Emirbayer and Mische 1998, 974) because substances and relations are dialectically constituted. Without substances, there is nothing to relate.

Although the very term "dialectical" implies two things having a relationship, it is clear that the number is less important than the relationship. For example, Karl Marx rarely specified only two relationships. His analysis of the expropriation of English land considered peasants, landlords, landless laborers, the king, and Parliament, to name a few of the actors, implying multiple relationships (Marx [1867] 1990, 877–78). Georg Hegel ([1820] 1991, 223–24) also referred to sometimes two, three, or four things: for example, the relationship between "the system of needs," the "administration of justice," and "corporations" (review in Maybee 2020). Roy Bhaskar (1993, 3, 29–30) also downplayed the importance of a specific number of elements in dialectical analysis, stressing instead the importance of thinking about distinctions and connections (Creaven 2007, 22). It is also clear that the relationship among the elements in the dialectic do not need to be strictly opposite as in the textbook explanation of thesis, antithesis, and synthesis, but can be conceptualized more generally in terms of conflict, contestation, contradiction, or skepticism (Hegel [1817] 2010, 128; review in Maybee 2020). As we have argued, Mill's framing is also broadly around contestation and, thus, also implicitly dialectical.

In dialectical causality, the relationship—among opposites, in the classic sense—leads to a new outcome that can be positive or negative (present or absent). Dialectical causality is, then, in some sense processual by definition, as it looks at how a relationship creates some new outcome. Thus, like narrative, it traces how something works over time. Therefore, examining causality is a matter of tracing the process of contestation among the relationships of the dialectic. Dialectical causality implies two parts of a theory: first, a set of relationships, and second, the mechanism of conflict or contestation that produces a change in the relationship.

Concretely and empirically, however, to examine this process in detail, these relationships have to be specified and examined. These relationships are often reduced to factors in comparative historical work or variables in quantitative work. From the perspective of dialectical realism, this reduction is just a shorthand; as in all realist thought, complicated social relationships have to be abstracted from the whole of reality for analysis. Factors or variables are themselves relationships at some other level of analysis. However, realist philosophy makes clear that not everything can be examined at the same time. Thus, for any particular analysis, a set of factors or variables is treated as such to consider how the relationship among them works over time. Therefore, a dialectical explanation points to a relationship among a set of factors and variables and suggests that the interrelationship among those factors or variables leads to a new outcome, which is also a new factor or variable, as well as a relationship. Thus, from a dialectical realist perspective, factors and variables are simply models, theory laden, to simplify reality to make possible analysis. Arguing that factors or variables cannot ever be used in social analyses misses the point that they are simply models of reality, not reality itself (cf. Abbott 1992, 435; Emigh 1997, 653). Indeed, since relata and relationships are dialectically constituted, for dialectical realism, factors or variables and relationships must coexist.

For example, Marx specified both factors or variables and a mechanism: the relationships (factors or variables) were classes, and the mechanism or process of change was conflict. In the transition to capitalism, the key classes were peasants and landlords, and the contestation between them over land rights created a new outcome: agricultural capitalists. Of course, Marx knew that classes are not fixed factors. Classes are externally constituted in relations of exploitation, and they are internally constituted by relationships among different parts (e.g., entrepreneurial landlords, rentiers). Furthermore, some classes, but not all, had awareness "for themselves." Thus, classes too were relationships, but this relationality could be "flattened" for epistemological purposes if the analytic task at hand entailed looking at the relationship among classes, rather than relationships within them. Or, the relationality of individuals within classes themselves could be examined by "unflattening" this set of relations.

Dialectic causality has an intrinsically subjective component. Because social reality is composed of interactive kinds, human actions must be understood differently from nonhuman events (Lana and Georgoudi 1983, 482). Humans may provide explanations for behavior that are interpretations of actions or ways of understanding actions (Lana and Georgoudi 1983, 482). A subjective understanding of a situation, in fact, is indeed necessary for social action (Berger and Luckmann 1966, 33; Gramsci 1971, 326–27; Roberts 2014, 4; Schutz 1967, 25; Weber [1922] 1978, 4). Individuals must have an understanding, which can only be gained through interpretation (Garfinkel 1967, 20–21), of the values and theories of reality that animate particular groups of human beings (Berger and Luckmann 1966, 7, 19, 177–79; Bhaskar 1979, 27; Schutz and Luckmann 1973, 67). These interpretations, necessary for engaging in action, are also used to make sense of events and actions after they have happened, which may or may not correspond to the interpretation before the action. However, the interpretation of the action, after it has occurred, may lead to more action, and in this sense is causal. Action, therefore, entails a continuous interpretation that looks forward, or is prospective, and looks backward, or is retrospective. Dialectical causality, then, must take into account this subjectivity and the interpretive dimension of social reality because humans interpret social reality in an ongoing, changing way. That subjectivity stands at the center of social reality is the core reason why positivist ontology is rather unhelpful in this zone of reality. Of course, dialectical causality is not able to prove theories in the way that a positivist causality claims, nor does it predict the future. This is appropriate, however, since social science reality, based on interactive kinds, deals with noumena that change in response to being studied, unlike physical reality, which is inanimate.

The Logic of Analysis

Philosophies of science generally also discuss logic, that is, how theory and evidence fit together. At the broadest level, deduction is arguing from the general to the specifics, whereas induction is arguing from the specifics to the general (cf. Martin 1994, 63). However, in the philosophy of science, deductive inference or deductive logic is a more particular form of deductive reasoning that uses logically interconnected statements to create theories that can be proven to be true or false by means of premises that form syllogisms so that conclusions can be tested precisely (Martin 1994, 63; Olsen 2007, 1). Inductive inference cannot be constructed in exactly the same way because this form of reasoning starts with evidence, which by its very nature is multiple. However, it is also based on premises, surmised from data, that combine to form a general theory or statement. Deductive and inductive inference may also have slightly different functions. Deductive inference is generally assumed to be a way to test existing theory. Because it is generally agreed that it is impossible to "prove" a theory in standard falsificationist fashion, the syllogisms of deductive theory make falsification logically possible. So, with deductive inference, evidence either confirms or falsifies the theory itself. In contrast, induction is supposed to lead to new theories because the evidence is interpreted and analyzed in novel ways. In sociology, this inductive approach, for example, has been implemented through grounded theory, the idea that researchers go to their research sites without preconceived hypotheses and develop theories from the fieldwork that fit to these data (Glaser and Strauss 1967, 33-34). However, both deduction and induction are generally infused with a positivist, demonstrative logic. For example, for deductive inference, the theory specifies a set of hypotheses that can prove or disprove a single cause. Similarly, inductive inference is also supposed to create a single theory. Thus, although induction and deduction can be used in broad ways (i.e., specifics to general; general to specifics), in practice, their application in social science has been much more focused.

Not surprisingly, these specific forms of both inductive and deductive inference work poorly with social science outcomes, which are, as even Mill argued, generally multicausal (cf. Somers 1998, 728). Syllogism is basically impossible with social science phenomena for three reasons: first, they cannot be deduced from each other; second, the elements of subjective interpretation inherent in social kinds means that exact replication is impossible; and third, strict comparability is limited. Strict induction is also impossible, even in principle. In addition, however, in social science, concepts themselves are theory laden, and researchers' subjectivities mean that they enter any empirical research site with presuppositions that make strict induction impossible. Thus, the way that physical sciences use induction or deduction as principles of inference cannot be used in the social sciences.

It is perhaps for this reason that Charles Peirce introduced abduction or retroduction, which are both forms of reasoning that are largely inductive but eliminate the necessity of identifying a single cause (review in Pietarinen and Bellucci 2014, 355-57). There is considerable confusion and disagreement about whether Peirce was using the terms indiscriminately or whether he was distinguishing them in a way that he never fully worked out in his publications (Chiasson 2005, 223-24; Decoteau 2017, 71). Most realists consider that abduction makes it possible to guess at the best explanation, while retroduction makes it possible to point to the most likely causal mechanism (Decoteau 2017, 71-72; Meyer and Lunnay 2013, 1). Both abduction and retroduction involve guessing about the relation between theory and evidence; the theory has no absolutely necessary implication for evidence as in deductive inference. In this sense, both are like induction because they argue from the specifics to the general. Abduction, moreover, has been interpreted to mean a way to produce "novel" theories and thus to have a particular role in discovery (Decoteau 2017, 71-72).

We argue that the terms "abduction" and "retroduction" are unnecessary for dialectical realism, as the logic of inquiry can be understood as dialectically deductive and inductive. First, abduction assumes the use of "surprising" findings to produce new theories (e.g., see Tavory and Timmermans 2014, 36 on ethnography). But findings are surprising only with respect to particular theories, so abduction depends on a prior stage of deduction. Similarly, retroduction depends on the existence of prior theories. Furthermore, neither abduction nor retroduction is generally assumed to involve a single step; they are supposed to be used iteratively to generate ideas about theories and examine them empirically. Thus, although abduction and retroduction are proposed as different logics, they really are just dialectically using deduction and induction without the necessity of finding a single cause through syllogism. The root source of the confusion is simply that they are both rooted in a positivist, demonstrative understanding of causality in the physical sciences that Peirce understood was problematic but did not fully eliminate. Furthermore, their usage in scientific inference conflates two things: first, how the theory relates to data (the logic of explanation), and second, how to do research (the logic of discovery). Both are, in fact, different but dialectical processes.

A much simpler solution is to understand deduction and induction as "loose" forms (i.e., without the use of syllogism) of argumentation (Emigh 1997, 656) that are dialectically related. In this way, the use of these terms can be removed from their positivist and demonstrative origins, where they were posed as unidirectional, and be recast as "loose." This move eliminates the necessity of syllogism, which is generally an impossible and unhelpful representation of social reality. A dialectical framing obviates the necessity of using one or the other or of using them in a particular direction. As Lakatos (1970, 151-52) pointed out, theories produce anomalies; they are incorporated either by other theories or by their rivals in a dialectical process that is also historically specific. Thus, the discovery of new theories before new evidence, or vice versa, is always possible. Consequently, there is no particular reason to trace out elaborate sequences of abduction and retroduction for particular methodologies, although these may be quite helpful heuristics (Decoteau 2017, 71-73).

Finally, as dialectical realism insists, it is not possible to conduct research on a social whole (only selected parts of it), and in this sense, perhaps, deduction is the "thesis" or starting place of the process. All researchers have standpoints as humans that are necessarily located socially in the world, so they will choose different starting points. However, beyond these starting points, induction and deduction will be used iteratively in the research process. Deduction and induction are dialectically related; general theories are revised in light of data; data show how theories must be revised. Thus, the addition of the terms "abduction" and "retroduction" simply captures this dialectical process. We hesitate to coin a new term, but we could perhaps use the term "diduction" to note the dialectical relationship of deduction and induction.

Dialectic and Comparison

As we have argued, dialectical causality is a matter of tracing a relationship over time and showing how it changes through contestation. At first glance, it might seem that understanding dialectical causality, just like using process tracing, requires no comparison because it focuses on how a single relationship changes over time. However, comparison is crucial to any application because it is impossible to know, without comparison, whether the explanation of the relationship is a unique historical explanation or a more general social phenomenon. Marx, for example, used comparison to provide empirical evidence for his theory of capitalism. To show how capitalist surplus-value extraction was based in primitive accumulation, Marx ([1867] 1990, 1082; [1894] 1991, 938-50) compared England, France, and Eastern Europe. In France, peasant rights to land were secure. Smallholding did not provide the right conditions for capitalist surplus extraction to take off because peasants could survive on their own land and did not have to engage in capitalist enterprises to survive. In Eastern Europe, in contrast, landlords held virtually absolute rights over land, so they could reimpose feudalism there. They also did not have to adopt capitalist agriculture to survive until much later in history. In England, there was an intermediate set of property rights: both landlords and tenants had rights, but neither were completely secure. So, in England, capitalist agriculture, dependent upon the market, could take off. Then, once capitalist agriculture was established, capitalist accumulation could occur. Smallholding, feudal, or capitalist agriculture could be described as a "factor" for simplicity, but at another level, it was a relationship among landlords, peasants, and capitalists, as well as legal entities who specified and upheld the rights. So, both for the preconditions of primitive accumulation and the process of surplus extraction, Marx proposed a theory that specified a set of relationships and traced a contested process and then considered whether it held in England, France, or Eastern Europe.[2] The relationships were present in England, but not in France or Eastern Europe, and all three cases gave the predicted outcome.[3] Marx ([1894] 1991, 186) also used comparisons at levels other than the nation-state; for example, he compared the deaths of men and women to argue about health conditions for workers. Thus, as Marx's examples illustrate, the dialectic and comparative methods work together at multiple levels (nation-states did not even exist before the modern period and so should not be taken as the "natural" unit of comparison). All dialectical thinking requires confirmation and refutation, which imply comparison. As Marx's European examples show, comparison provides these opportunities to confirm and refute theories, as well as develop their content and explanatory power.

We also should clarify our understanding of narrative methods of process tracing and negative case methodology. Because we argue that factors and relationships are understood through models, and thus factors can be expanded into relationships or vice versa, we do not have a positivist understanding of narrative methods. Instead, we understand that factors, because they can always be expanded into relationships, hold the potential for a set of outcomes that then may or may not be realized. For example, widespread private property rights to land and local markets may expand into full-scale agrarian capitalism and then into industrial capitalism, as we have already argued that Marx illustrated in England. However, this possibility may be foreclosed, which only a narrative method can show. For example, in Tuscany, widespread private property rights to land and local markets did not lead directly to industrialization because the degree of inequality between rural and urban landowners undermined the continued spread of markets (Emigh 2009, 210). Thus, the dynamic of capitalist agriculture there led to its own collapse. However, it was possible—perhaps given different patterns of international trade or power relations in medieval Europe—that the inequality between the urban and rural sector could have been lower, and thus the original patterns of property rights and local markets could have led to agricultural capitalism that in turn could have led directly to industrial capitalism. In short, we understand that factors, such as private property rights and local markets, are simply shorthands for complex relationships based on substantive social interests and relationships. Their potential may, or may not, be realized. The key is understanding the components of social reality as relationships of interactive kinds at different levels that nevertheless can be modeled in compact ways where necessary for analysis. Comparison and narrative methods complement each other to understand how factors and relationships stand in dialectical relationship.

How Processual and Comparative Methods Combine

Dialectical realism, then, combines narrative and comparison. In fact, a wide range of philosophies of social science, including positivism and realism, suggest that theories have this sort of bipartite structure: first, the specification of a cause and outcome, and second, the description of a mechanism linking them (Abell 1993, 100; Beach 2016, 468; Becker 2014, 61; Bergene 2007, 18; Gorski 2004, 19; Hedström and Ylikoski 2010, 52-53, 59; Kiser and Hechter 1991, 4-5; Mahoney 2004, 461; Maxwell 2012, 37, 118-20). First, entities with certain properties have observable, regular relationships with outcomes (Gorski 2004, 19). These are the endpoints, the cause and effect or outcome, the independent and dependent variables, or the explanans and the explanandum. This part of the explanation is conceptualized in different ways, as causal relations between observables (Kiser and Hechter 1991, 4), as causal agents at specified units of analysis (Mahoney 2004, 461), or as changes in entities and relationships (Gorski 2009, 160). These regular relationships are operationalized so that they can be observed as variables or, more commonly in comparative historical research, factors (Gorski 2009, 182; Kiser and Hechter 1991, 4-5; Mahoney 2004, 462). Second, causal mechanisms create these observable relationships (Gorski 2009, 160; Kiser and Hechter 1991, 5). This second component is the processual element that is generally theorized through inference. Understanding causal mechanisms through process tracing has become de rigueur in comparative historical research that typically uses case studies (Gorski 2009, 167-68).

The two parts of theories described previously produce two common research strategies: the first searches for correlational patterns between variables or factors and outcomes, whereas the second seeks to understand how the mechanism works to produce these patterns (Abend 2008, 177-78; Gorski 2009, 173; Tarrow 2010, 238). In turn, these strategies imply two methodologies: the first attempts to find patterns using statistical or small N analytic techniques, whereas the second uses narrative or process tracing, usually in one or just a few cases, to understand how the mechanism works empirically (reviews in Beach 2016, 464-66; George and Bennett 2005, 205-32; Goertz and Mahoney 2012, 87-88; Tarrow 2010, 238-40). Of course, these two different pieces of the explanation can be, and often have been, posed as opposites (e.g., stereotypically, large N statistical studies as "theoretical" and narrative as "descriptive," or large N statistical studies implying a "constant conjunction" or regularity philosophy of causality and narrative implying a "mechanism" or inferential philosophy of causality) (Hedström and Ylikoski 2010, 54-55, 57; Tarrow 2010, 232). It is more helpful, however, to view them as corresponding to different, but necessary, theoretical components (Ermakoff 2019, 597; Goertz and Mahoney 2012, 96, 103, 110; Janoski and Hicks 1994, 8-9; Maxwell 2012, 34-37). For example, Ide and Mello (2022, 6) argued that QCA, as a cross-case method, can be combined with process tracing as a within-case method. Of course, any particular piece of research may—but more likely may not—deploy both methodologies simultaneously. Similarly, statistical techniques such as regression are generally understood to be inadequate for illustrating causality in the absence of a causal model or understanding of the mechanism that creates the observed association or correlation.

However, as we noted earlier, with Mill's methods being mostly discredited, as least as embedded within a positivist methodology, for small N research, there is no credible way to establish this first part of the theory. Here, then, we have developed this method into a realist methodology. Although realism has been criticized for ignoring methods (review in Decoteau 2017, 59), there have been several attempts to provide a small N methodology, or at least an epistemology, that explicitly draws on critical realism. In historical comparative sociology, Philip Gorski (2004, 17) proposed the idea of identifying two basic patterns of causal influence: wedges that describe the interaction of several causal processes and forks (fan) that explain how a single causal process generates similar outcomes. Danermark et al. (2002, 105) explicitly discussed comparison in terms of using retroduction to compare cases, basically describing Mill's methods of agreement and difference, to develop a theory that includes all the important structural similarities (like the method of agreement) and that finds important mechanisms by looking at different cases (like the method of difference) (Meyer and Lunnay 2013, 3-4). In this way, Danermark et al. (2002, 105) argued that the necessary and constitutive, common, and universal circumstances can be distinguished from the more contingent ones. Ann Bergene (2007, 25) reframed comparison in terms of critical realism, primarily focusing on the dissimilarities among the cases to examine macro social processes. In many ways, ethnography, like historical methods, relies on narrative methods that can also be set in comparative context, and the two methodologies can learn from each other (Abramson and Gong 2020, 1-2; Pacewicz 2022, 935). Claire Decoteau (2017, 59) also provided a critical realist understanding of ethnography, different from other forms of it. Similarly, QCA can also be framed as positivist or realist (Ide and Mello 2022, 4; Ruttan 2022, 1220-21). We expand on these efforts, developing methodological techniques appropriate for dialectical realism.

Dialectical Comparative Methodology

To build the DCM, we start with an exploration of what single cases do through comparison and narrative (table 12.1) and then put these single cases in pairwise comparison (table 12.2). Finally, we show how pairwise comparisons can be combined to assess theoretical expectations (tables 12.3 and 12.4). In the next

TABLE 12.1 The DCM: Explanation of single cases

Case characteristics	Dialectical role in building theory	Methodological heuristic	What cases can do			
			How the single case builds theory	What is not possible with a single case?	What does a different case outcome do?	What does another case with the same outcome do?
Outcome present when it is expected (relationship present) (EP)	Confirmatory	Static and processual	The outcome provides evidence for the theory; process tracing shows how the relationship has an effect.	It provides no idea where this relationship and process might not hold.	It shows the limits on generalizability and expands theory.	It extends generalizability.
Outcome absent when it is expected (relationship present) (UA)	Refutational, potentially reconfiguring	Static and processual	The outcome provides evidence against the theory. Negative case methodology can trace why the relationship did not work as expected and, therefore, reconstruct the theory by adding substantive content.	It provides no idea where this relationship and process might not hold.	It shows whether the theory reconstruction from the negative case methodology holds in another case.	It can confirm the generalizability of the expansion of the theory.
Outcome present when it is unexpected (relationship absent) (UP)	Refutational, potentially reconfiguring	Static	The outcome provides evidence against the theory and redirects the research to some other relationships not originally specified by the theory.	The process cannot be traced, so no information is given about how the process that determined the outcome might work.	It can highlight other relationships in original case that might be important.	It can highlight other relationships in original case and comparison that might be important.
Outcome absent when it is not expected (relationship absent) (EA)	Confirmatory	Static	The outcome provides evidence for the theory. It prevents overgeneralization, overapplication, and confirmation bias.	The process cannot be traced, so it gives no information about it.	It can highlight how other relationships in comparison case might be important.	It extends generalizability.

section, we apply the DCM to the empirical example of land surveys introduced earlier (tables 12.5 and 12.6).

In table 12.1, we present our understanding of how single cases work and then, by extension, what theoretical work comparison and narrative do. This illustrates one of our earlier central methodological points: that comparison and narrative combine for a fuller explanation. In the column that sets up the table, we define these cases as expected or unexpected, and the outcome can be present or absent. (When single cases are used alone, in a positivist framework, one at a time, matching the expected outcome to the independent variables is sometimes called "congruence testing" [Bennett 2004, 24].) As dialectical realism underlies this methodology, we specify the case characteristics as relationships, not factors or variables. The cases can have the following outcomes: expectedly present (EP), unexpectedly absent (UA), unexpectedly present (UP), and expectedly absent (EA). Each of these types of cases has a row in table 12.1 that explains its features. These cases will be important in combining pairwise comparisons, which we turn to later in our exposition.

The columns of table 12.1 give different aspects of theory building. EP cases (row 1) are ones in which some particular relationship and outcome are both present; thus, the cases have a confirmatory nature (row 1, column 1). In this case, the relationship and outcome can be compared statically; in addition, because the relationship is present, the process through which it works can be traced (row 1, column 2). Thus, the case provides evidence for the theory because the relationship and outcome are present, and the presence of the relationship makes it possible to trace how it works through a narrative method (row 1, column 3). In this way, it contributes to theoretical development. However, because it only shows that the relationship holds, it cannot provide any information about where or when it might hold (row 1, column 4). Thus, the addition of a second, different (comparative) case (row 1, columns 5 and 6) can show that the relationship, outcome, and the process that links them are found or not found elsewhere. Of course, adding a comparison necessarily brings in the problem of the comparability of cases. However, even to trace the process, a relationship and an outcome must be identified; otherwise, the process cannot be traced. While finding a comparative case may be fraught with difficulties, these are inherent in any realist conceptualization (because all cases have to be extracted from a larger social reality), not in the logic of comparison.

The other three rows of table 12.1 can be read analogously. In row 2, the UA case is one in which a key relationship is present, but the outcome does not occur. Thus, these cases have a potentially refutational and reconfiguring role in theoretical development (row 2, column 1). Like the EP case in row 1, the UA case has both a static and processual dimension (row 2, column 2). Although the static part of the theory provides evidence against the theory, the processual method—negative case methodology—can trace out why the relationship is not working as expected, and thus can help specify the process (row 2, column 3). It can help reconstruct the theory or provide evidence against it. Again, while valuable on its own, this case alone will not show that the reconstructed case works anywhere else, so it is limited in assessing generalizability (row 2, column 4). Thus, another case can show that the reconstructed theory is supported or not (row 2, columns 5 and 6).

Rows 3 and 4 present the static cases of UP and EA. In these cases, the relationship is absent, although the outcome may be present (UP) or absent (EA), so it is impossible to use a processual method to trace how this particular relationship works to create either outcome. Thus, only the static part can be used (rows 3 and 4, column 2). However, these cases alone provide important checks on the overapplication of the theory. Universality can be an extremely dangerous assumption (Bhambra 2010, 130; Emigh 1997, 666), so these cases are key to showing where and when theories apply. UP cases are refutational and potentially reconfiguring because the outcome is present when the relationship is not (row 3, column 1). UP cases are also important because they help redirect the search to other relationships that might be related to the outcome but are not explained by the relationship (row 3, column 3). EA cases are most helpful in preventing overapplication of theories because they confirm that the outcome did not occur when the relationship was not present (row 4, column 3). Thus, they help to set domain boundaries around the applicability of theories. Again, these UP and EA cases contribute to theory building in and of themselves, but comparison cases help direct the search for other possible explanatory relationships (UP cases, row 3, columns 5 and 6) and generalizability (EA cases, row 4, columns 5 and 6).

Columns 5 and 6 provide only a few suggestions about how comparative cases might be used. Many more uses are possible. A single study is thus very valuable. It can do any of these things illustrated in table 12.1. A comparison will do several at a time. The point is not to rule out studies—a single case may be all that is possible given the difficulties of the research. But table 12.1 contextualizes single cases to show their location in relation to theory as well as narrative methods. In sum, then, table 12.1 summarizes the logic of how single cases, narrative, and comparative cases combine in small N research and what role they play in theory development. The table can thus be used to guide research.

In table 12.2, we illustrate how two concrete cases might be compared and how narrative is related to the comparison, drawing inspiration from the possibilities described in table 12.1. Table 12.2 simply looks at the cross-classification of a relationship (rows), specified by theory, and an outcome (columns) for two cases, A and B. The two cases can be at any social level, or even different time periods, but the level or unit of analysis should be similar in both cases. The relationship, given by the theory, and the cases in which it is found are given in the setup column. The theory may have domain conditions or other initial

TABLE 12.2 The DCM: Case comparison

What relationships are present?	What outcomes are present?		
	Same outcome (case A, outcome present; case B, outcome present)	Different outcome (case A, outcome present; case B, outcome absent)	Same outcome (case A, outcome not present; case B, outcome not present)
Specified relationship present in cases A and B	A (EP) and B (EP) provide evidence for theory; process tracing in A (EP) and B (EP)	A (EP) provides evidence for the theory, process tracing in A (EP); B (UA) provides evidence against the theory, negative case methodology on B (UA)	A (UA) and B (UA) provide evidence against the theory; negative case methodology on A (UA) and B (UA)
Specified relationship present in A, not in B	A (EP) provides evidence for theory, process tracing in A (EP); B (UP) provides evidence against theory	A (EP) and B (EA) provides evidence for theory; process tracing in A (EP)	A (UA) provides evidence against the theory, negative case methodology in A (UA); B (EA) provides evidence for the theory
Specified relationship is not present in A or B	A (UP) and B (UP) provide evidence against the theory	A (UP) provides evidence against the theory; B (EA) provides evidence for the theory	A (EA) and B (EA) provide evidence for the theory

preconditions that must hold. If not, the cases are obviously not comparable at that particular level or unit of analysis (or at all, depending on how the theory is specified). The key relationship is specified, by the theory in question, to have some outcome (the various outcomes will be explored in columns 1, 2, and 3). The key elements are relationships (though of course, this could also be summarized as a factor or a variable), and two cases (A and B) are compared with respect to whether the relationship is present or not in the cases. Table 12.2 also notes whether the cases are classified as UP, UA, EP, or EA, as in table 12.1. Again, we specify the aspects of the cases as relationships, as this is key for dialectical realist theory. This is in some sense, however, a false dichotomy, as a factor in some sense is a label at a particular level that, at another level, could be deconstructed to reveal a relationship.[4]

In the setup column of table 12.2, the possible patterns of comparing the cases are presented. The two cases can have three possible patterns: the key relationship (the explanans) can be present in both cases (row 1), present in one but not the other (row 2), or absent in both (row 3). It is important here to distinguish between two terminologies: the outcome and the prediction from the theory. First, the outcome can be absent or present. Second, the outcome can be predicted by theory or not. In this table, we use the usual convention about the directionality of the theory: the theory predicts that if the relationship is present, then the outcome is also present (e.g., in case A, if the relationship and outcome are present, then we call this case an EP because we are assuming the standard convention: the theory predicts that if the relationship is present, so is the outcome).

Columns 1, 2, and 3 of table 12.2 present the possible patterns in the outcome. First, as shown in the first column, both cases can have the same outcome. Here, because we are specifying that the outcome anticipated by theory is the one where it is present, this same outcome is the one that is anticipated by the theory when the relationship is present. In the second column, the cases have different outcomes: one has the outcome, and the other does not. In the third column, the cases have the same outcome: both are absent. Table 12.2 thus summarizes how two cases may be used together to provide evidence for or against a theory and whether the narrative, processual element can be used. The processual element, either process tracing or negative case methodology, can be used only when the relationship specified by the theory is present. The other case combinations, however, are still useful, as illustrated in table 12.1.

In column 1, both cases have the same outcome. In the first row, the outcome occurs in both cases, as expected (column 1, row 1). This simply confirms the theory. Process tracing can then be used to show how this outcome occurs. This is quite useful but cannot expand the content of the theory in any way (of course, it is possible that process tracing shows that the outcome is produced in different ways in the two cases, which then does lead to theory reformulation). In the second row (column 1, row 2), the outcome occurs in both cases; it occurs as expected in one case with the key relationship (A), but it unexpectedly occurs in the case that has the outcome but for which the key relationship is not present (B). Process tracing can be used in A. Case B provides evidence against the theory, but the relationship is not present, so a narrative methodology cannot be used. In the final example of similar outcomes, in the third row (column 1, row 3), the key relationship is missing in both cases, but the outcomes do occur. These cases provide evidence against the theory, but because the relationships are not present, a processual methodology cannot be used.

In column 2, the cases have different outcomes. In the first row (column 2, row 1), process tracing and negative case methodology can both be used where the outcomes are present (A) and absent (B), respectively. In the second row (column 2, row 2), both cases A and B provide evidence for the theory, and process tracing can be used on case A to show the process. Finally, in the third row (column 2, row 3), the cases provide some evidence for and some evidence against the theory. Although this combination does not use a processual element, the contradictory evidence obviously forces a revaluation of the cases and the theory.

Finally, in the third column, the cases have the same outcome—that outcome is not present in either case. In the first row (column 3, row 1), the cases have the same outcomes, and the key relationship is present in both cases. Here, negative case methodology can be used in both cases to reconstruct the theory, and if the same reconstruction works in them, evidence for that particular reconstruction is developed. In the second row (column 3, row 2), negative case methodology can be used again to reconstruct the theory for case A where the relationship is present, whereas case B provides evidence to confirm the theory; because the relationship is not present, narrative methods cannot be used. In the third row (column 3, row 3), the outcomes are not present and neither are the relationships, so these cases provide evidence for the theory. This is also the classic counterfactual case, where the outcomes do not occur because the specified relationship did not occur (cf. Bennett 2004, 25; Elster 1978, 184-85; Meyer and Lunnay 2013, 3). We argue that this overall conceptualization makes it easier to think of and to use counterfactuals. In general, it is difficult to provide evidence for something that did not occur as predicted because no processual methodology can be used to trace a relationship. Counterfactuals work only through the static comparison. For example, Barrington Moore ([1967] 1993, 61-63) invoked a counterfactual to explain why France could not take a peaceful path to political change if it were to consolidate as a democratic capitalist country. (A nonrevolutionary path was possible for Moore, but it would have led to authoritarianism in the twentieth century.) However, because such a path did not occur, Moore could not directly use a processual narrative about French history to explain this nonoutcome. Instead, he compared French and English history, using the stylized processual narrative of English history, where the outcome did occur, to show what relationship was missing from French society (namely, the enclosure movement) to create the nonoutcome (namely, a peaceful transition to democratic capitalism). Our framework thus provides a concrete way to think about a counterfactual in the context of a set of cases, narrative methods, and theory, making it easier to work with them.

These cells link back to table 12.1. While the single cases in table 12.1 are helpful in building theory, table 12.2 shows how the cases can be linked in a comparative context. For example, in table 12.2, when the relationship is not present in A or B and the cases have different outcomes (row 3, column 2), even though it is not possible to use a processual method, it is virtually impossible to reconcile these tensions without motivating further research with additional cases (cf. table 12.1; UP and EA cases in rows 3 and 4 respectively). In this way, the original cases, as well as the comparison between them, are quite valuable. Tables 12.1 and 12.2 are based on "loose deduction," as the relationship to be considered is given by the theory. The logic of explanation, because it is obviously influenced by researchers' positionality and how they choose the theories, is also based on loose deduction. The methodology of using tables 12.1 and 12.2, however, is diductive (based on diduction), or dialectically inductive and deductive, as the research must move back and forth between theoretical assessment and the evaluation of empirical cases. Furthermore, the logic of discovery is also diductive. As tables 12.1 and 12.2 show, comparative cases can be selected in advance (deductively), or they can be motivated by anomalous, disconfirmatory findings that arise from either single or multiple cases (inductively; even though this inductive stimulus must be theoretically motivated since findings from particular cases are anomalous only in relation to specific articulated or unarticulated theories). Thus, small N researchers, in practice, can use deduction to find theoretically useful cases, and they may also find "interesting research sites" among archival documents, other repositories, or concrete ethnographic locations that may generate trajectories of comparisons not originally anticipated and therefore make use of induction.

Finally, in table 12.3, we can combine insights from tables 12.1 and 12.2, as well as expand the number of cases that can be used. We use the EP, UA, UP, and EA language from tables 12.1 and 12.2 and then use the logic of table 12.2 but apply it for research with multiple cases. While pairs of cases are used in table 12.2 as an example, the comparisons can be iterated—this process can simply be repeated for multiple cases and for multiple key relationships as needed to work through any number of possible combinations. In table 12.3, we specify three relationships and three cases. As in table 12.2, in table 12.3, we use the usual convention that if the relationship is present, then the theory predicts that the outcome will be present as well. Thus, for example, for case C, the empirical findings show that relationship 1 is not present, relationship 2 is not present, and relationship 3 is present. Because the outcome is present, we can classify the cells of table 12.3 for case C (using tables 12.1 and 12.2), as "UP" for relationship 1 (column 1, row 1), "UP" for relationship 2 (column 1, row 2), and "EP" for relationship 3 (column 1, row 3). The rest of the table for cases D and E can be completed analogously. The four types of cases—UP, EP, UA, and EA—have confirmatory or disconfirmatory roles (added to the far right of the column),

TABLE 12.3 **A DCM sample table, example 1**

	Case C	Case D	Case E	**Theoretical evaluation**
Relationship 1	No (UP)	Yes (EP)	Yes (UA)	1 confirmation, 2 disconfirmations
Relationship 2	No (UP)	Yes (EP)	Yes (UA)	1 confirmation, 2 disconfirmations
Relationship 3	Yes (EP)	Yes (EP)	No (EA)	3 confirmations, no disconfirmations
Outcome	Yes	Yes	No	

as explained in tables 12.1 and 12.2. The numbers of these confirmations and disconfirmations can be easily assessed in the last column of table 12.3. The table, although it cannot produce definitive "proof" or "test" a theory in any strict sense, nevertheless provides more evidence, in general, for the theorized effects of relationship 3 than the other ones. The method of reading the table is analogous to reading a regression table: sets of coefficients provide evidence for or against different theories because the theories make predictions about the presence and directionality of a relationship between two variables. Here, analogously, table 12.3 provides evidence about the theoretical expectation between a relationship (factor, variable) and an outcome.

Furthermore, tables 12.1 and 12.2 show where and what sort of narrative methods can be used. For example, in table 12.3, for case C, relationship 3 is present and so is the outcome (EP), so table 12.2 shows that process tracing can be used to understand how relationship 3 has its theorized effect. Table 12.1 provides more detail about EP cases, both alone and in combination with other cases. Similarly, reading these tables together shows that no narrative method can be used in the static EA outcome (case E, relationship 3) in table 12.3. Or, they also show that negative case methodology could be used for any of the UA outcomes (e.g., in case E, for either relationship 1 or 2). We argue that these evaluations are well motivated and backed by a dialectical realist philosophy of social science, based on relationships, confirmation and refutation, diduction, and combining comparison and narrative. To be honest, however, they require few assumptions and so could be used with any philosophy of social science, but we leave the development of those methodologies to scholars who prefer such philosophies.

Of course, the information in table 12.3 can be evaluated as a Millian "truth table." Table 12.3, in fact, presents ideal Millian comparisons. For Mill's method of agreement (comparing cases C and D, with similar outcomes), the outcome occurs when relationship 3—usually specified as a variable or factor in Millian language—is present. In a Millian interpretation, the method of agreement also shows that relationships 1 and 2 are not causal, as they differ in cases C (not present) and D (present), although the outcome is present in both these cases. The method of difference (comparing case D with case E with different outcomes) confirms this finding. Relationship 3 is present only in case D where the outcome is present, but not present in case E where the outcome is not present. In a Millian framework, this would "prove" that relationship 3 is the "causal" factor.

We can easily reconcile this finding to the DCM. The DCM outcomes (UP, EP, UA, EA) are evaluated to consider whether the pattern provides evidence for or against the theory (tables 12.1 and 12.2 explain that the "U" outcomes are disconfirmations, whereas the "E" outcomes are confirmations, and those confirmations and disconfirmations are added to table 12.3). The DCM provides the same information as the Millian comparison, but without the eliminative logic of the Millian framework that seeks to find a single cause. Thus, the DCM explicitly rejects the monocausality often associated with the Millian methodology. It shows that relationship 3, in comparison to relationships 1 and 2, provides the most confirmatory evidence and the least disconfirmatory evidence, which is exactly the same conclusion that a Millian reading of the table would provide. However, with the DCM interpretation, neither the assumption of independence nor a single causal factor is needed. Furthermore, tables 12.1 and 12.2 show how to use narrative with comparison in table 12.3: process tracing can be used with the EP cases, while negative case methodology can be used with the UA cases. The DCM reading of table 12.3 is motivated by a dialectical realist understanding of the relationship between theory and evidence. It shows how comparisons can be built up from multiple cases and used to draw conclusions. This procedure provides no "single causal factor" like a Millian method of difference, but across different iterations, it provides support for and against a theory. Thus, tables 12.1, 12.2, and 12.3 represent methodologies, underpinned by a dialectical realist philosophy of science that we outlined earlier. It combines knowledge based on the components of this dialectical realist philosophy. First, it uses a realist philosophy of science, based on the understanding that reality is complex and can be comprehended in terms of increasingly refined models and research that can be combined for fuller knowledge. Second, it is fully dialectical because it is based on locating and analyzing relationships as explanantia, explananda, and processes. Third, its logic of analysis uses evidence and logic dialectically, that is, by iterating deduction and induction. And, finally, it combines narrative and comparison to conduct empirical analyses.

The DCM, however, is superior empirically to Mill's method because, as we noted in the beginning of this chapter, Mill's method is difficult to apply in practice. We illustrate this in table 12.4. In table 12.4, we replace case C with case F, in which relationship 3 is also not present, although it was present in case C (so, none of the relationships, 1, 2, or 3, are present in case F). Now, Mill's methods cannot be easily applied. The method of agreement now eliminates relationships 1, 2, and 3 because they do not occur in case F, but they all occur in case D. The method of difference still could be used to "prove" that relationship

TABLE 12.4 A DCM sample table, example 2

	Case F	Case D	Case E	Theoretical evaluation
Relationship 1	No (UP)	Yes (EP)	Yes (UA)	1 confirmation, 2 disconfirmations
Relationship 2	No (UP)	Yes (EP)	Yes (UA)	1 confirmation, 2 disconfirmations
Relationship 3	No (UP)	Yes (EP)	No (EA)	2 confirmations, 1 disconfirmation
Outcome	Yes	Yes	No	

3 is the causal factor by comparing cases D and E, but adding case F muddles the conclusion because the method of agreement already eliminated all of the possible causal influences. From the point of view of the Millian framework, there is, then, no straightforward answer as to the causal effect of these three relationships. The DCM—that is, the confirmations and disconfirmations added to the final column of table 12.4—however, suggests that there is more evidence in support of relationship 3. As in table 12.3, the other relationships have some support as well. The DCM, using table 12.1 (row 3, column 5), also suggests that this UP case F should motivate a search for another relationship that is linked to the outcome. Thus, again, the information provided by the Millian method, without the methodological underpinnings, is not incorrect. The interpretation of the table using a positivist Millian methodology is also not necessarily incorrect, but it is not particularly useful. The DCM, based on a dialectical realist philosophy, provides a more useful way to interpret the information, given empirical limitations and the ability to drop the strict assumptions. The DCM provides a way to draw theoretical conclusions: it assesses the evidence for and against the theory using a realist understanding of both theory and evidence.

The difference between the methodologies—the positivist framing of Mill and the dialectical realist framing of the DCM—then, is primarily in how they are conceptualized and evaluated and how easily they are applied empirically. In some sense, this is not surprising. After all, comparison is central to explanation, so, in practice, comparative and historical sociologists simply use comparison to good effect even if they do not explicitly spell out the philosophical underpinnings or if they do not follow these strictures when they are made explicit. Nevertheless, it is much more useful to have an underlying philosophy of social science that is compatible with what researchers actually do, how they understand their analyses, and the data that they actually have. We argue that the DCM is thus much more useful for comparative historical sociologists in these respects than a positivist Millian methodology.

Furthermore, the DCM can easily be used to extend the analyses by using the guidelines in tables 12.1 and 12.2. Other cases and relationships can be added and compared in a similar way into tables such as table 12.3. Or, the cases from different authors and research can be compared in a meta-analysis (e.g., using table 12.3 as a model). Or, any particular paper can compare a single case to a set of cases from previous research (e.g., adding a comparative case with ideas from table 12.1). This method could also be further formalized depending on whether researchers can accumulate enough cases. For example, whether something is confirmed or disconfirmed is a binomial distribution, and, with enough repetitions, the evidence could be used in a statistical test for randomness. Similarly, the number of counts of confirmation and disconfirmation form a Poisson distribution that could be tested for randomness in a similar way. Such distributions could also be used as Bayesian priors. In these ways, small N researchers—comparative, historical, and ethnographic—can easily compare their results and draw conclusions. Moreover, they can easily see how to combine comparison and narrative. Thus, our methods are easily applied to all small N research to build theory.

Although we have framed this method using dialectical realism, as we believe it provides the most realistic model for social science, it can be used under different frameworks as well. For example, with a more positivist understanding of the components of table 12.3 as variables instead of relationships (e.g., Beach 2016, 463), DCM could be understood as testing for causes but without the restrictions of Mill's methods. Formalized methods for choosing the negative cases can also be used within a positivist understanding of Mill's methods (Mahoney and Goetz 2004, 653). Similarly, for use with models of path dependency, the relationships in table 12.3 could be reframed as combinations of "critical junctures" (Bennett and Elman 2006, 253). In process tracing, rival hypotheses, in a positivist understanding, can be developed and "tested" in the cases. Process tracing has been recently increasingly formalized primarily in political science (e.g., Ricks and Liu 2018, 843; Rohlfing 2014, 608), relying heavily on these sorts of positivist assumptions. Ingo Rohlfing (2014, 632), for example, claims to have developed a typology of types of hypotheses intended to create unambiguous causal inference through case selection.

Although such models have high rhetorical appeal as promoting exactness and science, like other positivist models, they are probably unrealistic for what comparative historical sociologists actually do. The suggestion of identifying necessary and sufficient criteria for hypotheses (Rohlfing 2014, 611), in our opinion, simply returns us to a positivist interpretation that is inappropriate for social science research. Although it is obviously beyond the scope of this chapter to reevaluate process tracing more generally and reframe it within a realist framework, we concur with Gorski (2004, 2) and Besnik Pula (2021, 749) that it is unlikely to be fully formalized within a positivist understanding that retains its full utility as a sociological method. We, therefore, advocate for "loose deduction" with respect to process tracing as well (Crasnow 2017, 12-13). Despite our own reservations for highly formalized process tracing, it, or any less formalized version, can be easily incorporated within our method. More generally, we argue that a dialectical realist framing is most appropriate, so we do not undertake the development of such a positivist (or other alternatives, such as analytic realism or pragmatism) philosophical framing here, but we realize that others may want to undertake this work (and perhaps based on some of the previous examples).

Of course, the DCM eliminates none of the problems of comparison (e.g., commensurability and translation; Sewell 2005, 97; Steinmetz 2004, 390). Careful arguments have to be made about what is selected to be compared. Selecting the part out of the whole is problematic, and the choice undoubtedly reflects the positionality of the researcher. It may not be useful to compare at one level or unit of analysis but be useful at another. Cases may be, of course, incomparable at any level or unit. A common criticism directed toward historical comparative research per se is that differences in historical time periods mean that it is impossible to create a model that is valid across multiple time periods. Although it may be more difficult to make a good model across time and space, a dialectical realist understanding suggests that this is possible and, furthermore, that such models can be refined. Furthermore, the claim that models cannot be valid across multiple time periods is internally inconsistent, as the identification of "periods" already implies a theory of periodization that necessarily holds across the periods.

Returning to the Example: Land Surveys

We return to the example of land surveys to show concretely how the DCM solves the analytic problems we discussed earlier. Table 12.5 is adapted from our study of land surveys (Emigh et al. 2019, 407). As we noted, we looked at three relationships to consider whether they were important in creating successful land surveys. In standard Millian method, Italy and the United States are the cases for the methods of agreement, and either case, along with the United Kingdom, is the method of difference. Read in a standard Millian manner, table 12.5 shows that the method of agreement would illustrate that the strong state was not necessary for the completed land survey, as the outcome was present in the two cases without the strong state, and therefore would eliminate that relationship. It would not be "causal" using a positivist interpretation of a Millian truth table. The other two relationships, however, could then be evaluated using the method of difference. However, tacit or local knowledge was present

TABLE 12.5 Influences on land survey completion

	Italy	United States	United Kingdom
Possible influences on the completion of land surveys			
Strong state	No	No	Yes
Tacit or local knowledge	Tacit/yes	Local/yes	Local/yes
Social actors' interests align in information gathering	Partially/yes	Yes	No
Outcome			
Successful land survey	Yes	Yes	No

Source: Adapted from Emigh et al. (2019, 407).

TABLE 12.6 Recasting Emigh et al. (2019) in the DCM

	Italy	United States	United Kingdom	Theoretical evaluation
Possible influences on the completion of land surveys				
Strong state	No (UP)	No (UP)	Yes (UA)	3 disconfirmations
Tacit or local knowledge	Yes (EP)	Yes (EP)	Yes (UA)	2 confirmations, 1 disconfirmation
Social actors' interests align in information gathering	Yes (EP)	Yes (EP)	No (EA)	3 confirmations
Outcome				
Successful land survey	Yes	Yes	No	

in the case of the United Kingdom where the outcome did not occur, so the method of difference would also eliminate it. Thus, the table would "prove" that social actors' interests were the key relationship.

In table 12.6, we just reformat the table for the DCM. Table 12.6 provides the same conclusions as table 12.5: the importance of the strong state has little empirical support, the importance of tacit or local knowledge some support, and the alignment of social actors' interests the most support. As in a regression table, we can "read" off the support for the theories about the relationships from the final column, in terms of confirmations and disconfirmations, to see what theorized relationship has the most support.

Yet, in that paper, we did more than just evaluate the strength of the theory through the comparison alone (as a conventional Millian analysis might do). We also used narrative methods. In the case of the United Kingdom (the negative case, or UA, from the point of view of the theory of the strong state and the theory of local knowledge), we showed that the same actors who held local knowledge—namely, powerful landlords—had strong ties to the state, allowing them to prevent the implementation of a land survey (Emigh et al. 2019, 412). The United Kingdom is the UA case with respect to these relationships, so table 12.2 shows that negative case methodology is indeed helpful in understanding this unexpectedly absent outcome. Thus, we showed how a strong state was blocked in its attempts and why the way in which local knowledge was held was crucial. Furthermore, we explored the differences in local versus tacit knowledge. This difference in the types of knowledge presents a problem for Millian methodology because it makes the cases strictly incomparable so that they cannot be used together with an eliminative logic. However, for the DCM, these two EP cases (Italy and the United States) are ones in which process tracing is useful in showing how the relationship produces the outcome. Tacit knowledge was held in the Italian case, making the entire population more accepting of a land survey, even though they might not have had specific interests in its completion (Emigh et al. 2019, 419–20). In contrast, in the United States, White settlers were highly dependent upon and had a close understanding of how surveyance supported their land rights vis-à-vis the Indigenous population and other settlers (Emigh et al. 2019, 415). Thus, the narrative methods help explain the table, providing an explanation of the mechanisms that underlay why the particular relationships of state strength, lay knowledge, and local actors and their relative power led, or did not lead, to successful land surveys. Although we provided a useful example of how to combine narrative and comparison, we did not analyze this in any formal way, so the DCM makes explicit why it works well, and it provides a useful heuristic to understand how it can be applied more generally. And, in doing so, other authors can apply the method to their own empirical cases more easily. Tables 12.1, 12.2, and 12.3 thus formalize our intuition: the comparison can be evaluated, and narrative methods can be used.

Of course, we never claimed that we found a single cause of land surveys (as a conventional Millian analysis might do), or even to have eliminated the possibility that strong states might, in other instances, facilitate land surveys. We simply claimed to add evidence for the weaknesses of a state-centered approach to information gathering and for the strength of an interactive approach that looked at the interplay of states and societies (Emigh et al. 2019, 420–21). Thus, the analysis of land surveys, while possible in the language of Millian analysis, is also completely, and much more subtly, understood in the language of DCM. As we have shown, we had the right intuition in combining comparison and narrative and in both using and dismissing Millian methods. As we have illustrated, we needed a better and more explicit underlying philosophy of social science and a more flexible way to use empirical evidence.

Furthermore, this example illustrates well other aspects of a dialectical realist philosophy of social science. We explicitly understand our project as fitting into such a dialectical realist philosophy of social science (Emigh et al. 2016a, 40–46; Riley et al. 2021, 331–34). In fact, our land surveys paper probably could have been improved by a more extended discussion of our dialectical realist position: that we were really considering the explanans as relationships, not factors (Emigh et al. 2016a, 43–45); how the selection of the research problem came out of our previous work, thereby illustrating our point about positionality; and how we were using a diductive logic of analysis. These elements are implicit in our land surveys research, but the explicit philosophical points to create a dialectical realist methodology in this paper here would have improved our previous ones. Our land surveys research emerged from our project on censuses as an extension of the theoretical model we developed there to another set of efforts to collect information, that is, land surveys instead of censuses (Emigh et al. 2016b, 221). We used the same heuristic of looking at state and social influences, conceptualizing these influences as relationships (Emigh et al. 2016a, 43-45). The entire project was, of course, diductive, with iterative elements of deduction and induction. For example, the idea of analyzing land surveys came inductively out of our previous project, but the theoretical application to the land surveys was deductive.

As we noted earlier, we chose our specific example of our research on land surveys to illustrate the DCM for concreteness because our paper explicitly used Mill's methods, as well as explicated their advantages and disadvantages, and because we understand the philosophical position we are trying to develop. However, the DCM can be applied equally well to any other small N work, whether framed as comparative, historical, or ethnographic. It can also be applied to studies that use Mill implicitly or explicitly (e.g., the examples from earlier: Anderson 2018, 183; Bergene 2007, 21-24; Charrad 2001, 10; Gorski 1993, 303-4; Hung 2008, 574-75; Lachmann 2000, 14; Tsutsui 2017, 1059-60; for a temporal application see Emigh et al. 2021, 10). Not only does it help evaluate the comparison, but it also guides the selection of the form of narrative (process tracing versus negative case methodology). Finally, although we have argued that the method fits well with the philosophy of dialectical realism because the method focuses on relationships and provides confirmatory and disconfirmatory evidence, to be honest, it can also be used with any underlying philosophy of science (although we leave others to implement such a methodology if they want).

✳ ✳ ✳

In this chapter, we reformulated comparative methods in a new way, as a methodology underpinned by a philosophy of social science of dialectical realism. From this perspective, theories are just models of the world: sociologists can refine these models by providing evidence that supports or refutes these theories. This process never aligns theories completely with reality but does provide better models. From this perspective, comparison does the same: it can provide evidence for or against the theories. Comparison works in tandem with narrative methods (e.g., process tracing, negative case methodology). Comparison points to patterns of connections among relationships (the explanans) and outcomes (the explanandum); narrative shows why those patterns exist by tracing out processes over time. Thus, comparison and narrative are not opposite strategies—they are complementary.

The dialectical comparative methodology—DCM, as we have called it— works with single or multiple cases, either developed from scratch by the researcher or pulled from across previous research. The entire comparative process can be used with two or more cases, and single cases can still be analyzed within this overall framework (although obviously the whole methodology cannot be used). It is loosely deductive—it specifies a theoretical relationship that should produce some outcome, and then looks empirically to see whether the relationship and outcome are present or not. Depending on whether the relationship is present or absent, a narrative method can then be used to show why the relationship has a particular outcome. Process tracing can be used where the outcome is present to show why it occurred. Negative case methodology can be used to show why an expected outcome does not occur and thus expand the content of the theory. Although we emphasize that the logic of explanation, as well as researchers' positionality, is loosely deductive, we argue that every other step in the process of explanation, as well as the logic of discovery, is dialectically deductive and inductive (diductive). The method is extremely simple, with a wide application to comparative and historical work as well as ethnography.

These comparisons provide the same substantive conclusions as Millian comparisons, but they require none of the assumptions of independence, induction, or eliminative logic that are necessary to identify a single cause. Of course, by dropping these assumptions, DCM does not "prove" or "disprove" a single cause like Mill's methods of agreement and difference or show that particular factors are necessary or sufficient "causes" of outcomes; this, however, is its advantage, as it is generally agreed that Mill's method cannot be applied inductively in the social sciences to isolate a single cause. It is wildly unrealistic to think that any particular factor could be a singular "cause" of complex social reality. DCM in no way eliminates the possibility of using Mill's method, QCA (qualitative comparative analysis) or Boolean analysis, or any other form of statistical analysis, where the assumptions hold for their application, and where the researcher can accumulate enough appropriate cases for their application. However, DCM requires none of the assumptions that these other methods require and that generally do not hold for comparative and historical sociology or ethnography, and it can be used on small N research with only a few cases (even too few, for example, for QCA). Similarly, DCM does not falsify a theory in the Popperian sense, but then it is also widely agreed that pieces of fragmentary evidence do not hold such power over theories. Thus, the DCM is a much more realistic way to provide evidence for theories, as well as to expand their content by noting where narrative methods apply and which ones to use (process tracing or negative case methodology). Our method is fully dialectical: it can provide evidence for or against theories and trace processes that are expected or unexpected. Because much process tracing is focused on showing why something occurred and when it occurred, it tends to confirm findings. This approach, used in isolation, leads to bias. A full examination of cases where the outcomes do not occur or do occur when unexpected helps eliminate this bias.

We argue that this method stands at the center of a dialectical realist research agenda (Riley et al. 2021, 331-34). This research agenda provides a reasonable philosophy of social science that meshes with how social science research is actually done and a method that can actually be used within this philosophy. It provides a flexible, yet meaningful, way of comparing research, which is both essential and crucial to developing better theories.

Acknowledgments
We would like to thank Andrew Herman, Johanna Hernández Pérez, Charles Kurzman, Kyle Nelson, Tala Oszkay, Caroline Reilly, Gabriel Locke Suchodolski, and the many anonymous reviewers for their comments, and Corey O'Malley and Michelle Marinello for their research assistance. This work was funded by a University of California, Los Angeles faculty senate grant.

Notes

1. Przeworski and Teune (1970, 32-35) formulated a similar method, although without explicitly referencing Mill.

2. Marx used other comparisons of France and England. To illustrate his more general theory of capitalist accumulation, Marx ([1867] 1990, 1075-79) used France and England as examples of the different levels of concentration of the means of production, showing that they were much more highly concentrated in England than in France. He linked this plethora of small, undercapitalized factories back to the parcelization of landholdings in France and the relative consolidation of holdings in England. Here, French and English "industry" and "landholdings" are described as factors, for comparison, to understand the general theoretical point. Yet, it is also clear that both were relationships in and of themselves, composed of capitalists and laborers. Thus, Marx was considering a theory that specified a set of relationships and seeing whether it held in England or France or not. In this case, it was present in England and not in France, and both cases gave the theoretically correct outcome.

3. Marx also compared these cases to northern Italy, although much more briefly. The case of northern Italy, however, is a negative case where, to a large extent, the preconditions for capitalist agriculture did exist, but the transition to capitalism was delayed (Emigh 2009, 19-20; 1998, 351; Marx [1867] 1990, 876; [1894] 1991, 937). A close examination of the Tuscan case in northern Italy, through the use of negative case methodology, however, shows that Marx's explanation, that sharecropping was just another form of peasant possession or that urbanites exploited the countryside, is empirically and theoretically inadequate. Instead, sharecropping was in fact a capitalist form of land tenure, and the high degree of inequality, spurred by capitalism, not feudalism or smallholding, prevented further capitalist development there (Emigh 2009, 221-24). From the point of view of Marx's theory, then, given that sharecropping was a capitalist form of agriculture, the transition to capitalism should have occurred there. Tuscany, then, is a negative case, where the theoretically expected outcome did not occur. Marx was incorrect because he only took formal property rights into account. In Tuscany, inequality was so high that formal property rights were insufficient to assure the spread of an operational

market. This negative case of Tuscany, through the application of negative case methodology, provides many theoretical insights, including that substantive properties of property rights (including individuals' subjective orientation toward them), not just the formal properties that Marx considered, must be considered to understand theories of capitalism. It also shows that the attainment of working-class consciousness is not the only way—as Marx suggested—that capitalist accumulation can be halted. High inequality can itself reverse capitalist accumulation.

4. It is compatible with Mill as well. Mill ([1843] 1974, VIII, 888) specified that in the social sciences, all causes will be multiple. Instead, then, of thinking of these as multiple, unrelated causes, we think of them as relationships.

References

Abbott, Andrew. 1992. "From Causes to Events: Notes on Narrative Positivism." *Sociological Methods and Research* 20(4):428–55.

——. 2016. *Processual Sociology*. Chicago: University of Chicago Press.

Abell, Peter. 1993. "Some Aspects of Narrative Method." *Journal of Mathematical Sociology* 18(2–3):93–134.

Abend, Gabriel. 2008. "The Meaning of 'Theory.'" *Sociological Theory* 26(2):173–99.

Abramson, Corey M., and Neil Gong. 2020. "Introduction: The Promise, Pitfalls, and Practicalities of Comparative Ethnography." In *Beyond the Case: The Logics and Practices of Comparative Ethnography*, edited by C. M. Abramson and N. Gong, 1–27. Oxford: Oxford University Press.

Anderson, Elisabeth. 2018. "Policy Entrepreneurs and the Origins of the Regulatory Welfare State: Child Labor Reform in Nineteenth-Century Europe." *American Sociological Review* 83(1):173–211.

Archer, Margaret Scotford. 2020. "The Morphogenetic Approach; Critical Realism's Explanatory Framework Approach." In *Agency and Causal Explanations in Economics*, edited by P. Róna and L. Zsolnai, 137–50. Cham, Switzerland: Springer.

Arthur, Mikaila Mariel Lemonik. 2011. "The Neglected Virtues of Comparative-Historical Methods." In *New Directions in Sociology: Essays on Theory and Methodology in the 21st Century*, edited by I. Zake and M. DeCesare, 172–92. Jefferson, NC: McFarland.

Beach, Derek. 2016. "It's All About Mechanisms: What Process-Tracing Case Studies Should Be Tracing." *New Political Economy* 21(5):463–72.

Beach, Derek, and Rasmus Brun Pedersen. 2019. *Process-Tracing Methods: Foundations and Guidelines*. 2nd edition. Ann Arbor: University of Michigan Press.

Beck, Colin J. 2017. "The Comparative Method in Practice: Case Selection and the Social Science of Revolution." *Social Science History* 41(3):533–54.

Becker, Howard S. 2014. *What About Mozart? What About Murder? Reasoning from Cases.* Chicago: University of Chicago Press.

Bengtsson, Bo, and Hannu Ruonavaara. 2017. "Comparative Process Tracing: Making Historical Comparison Structured and Focused." *Philosophy of the Social Sciences* 47(1):44–66.

Bennett, Andrew. 2004. "Case Study Methods: Design, Use, and Comparative Advantages." In *Models, Numbers, and Cases: Methods for Studying International Relations*, edited by D. F. Sprinz and Y. Wolinsky-Nahmias, 19–55. Ann Arbor: University of Michigan Press.

Bennett, Andrew, and Colin Elman. 2006. "Complex Causal Relations and Case Study Methods: The Example of Path Dependence." *Political Analysis* 14(3):250–67.

Bennett, Andrew, Tasha Fairfield, and Hillel David Soifer. 2019. "Comparative Methods and Process Tracing." American Political Science Association Organized Section for Qualitative and Multi-Method Research, Qualitative Transparency Deliberations, Working Group Final Reports, Report III.1 (January 2019). https://ssrn.com/abstract=3333405 or http://dx .doi.org/10.2139/ssrn.3333405.

Bergene, Ann Cecilie. 2007. "Towards a Critical Realist Comparative Methodology: Context-Sensitive Theoretical Comparison." *Journal of Critical Realism* 6(1):5-27.

Berger, Peter L., and Thomas Luckmann. 1966. *The Social Construction of Reality: A Treatise in the Sociology of Knowledge*. Garden City, NY: Doubleday.

Bhambra, Gurminder K. 2010. "Historical Sociology, International Relations and Connected Histories." *Cambridge Review of International Affairs* 23(1):127-43.

Bhaskar, Roy. 1979. *The Possibility of Naturalism: A Philosophical Critique of the Contemporary Human Sciences*. Atlantic Highlands, NJ: Humanities Press.

——. 1986. *Scientific Realism and Human Emancipation*. London: Verso.

——. 1993. *Dialectic: The Pulse of Freedom*. London: Verso.

Burawoy, Michael. 1989. "Two Methods in Search of Science: Skocpol Versus Trotsky." *Theory and Society* 18(6):759-805.

——. 1998. "The Extended Case Method." *Sociological Theory* 16(1):4-33.

Charrad, Mounira M. 2001. *States and Women's Rights: The Making of Postcolonial Tunisia, Algeria, and Morocco*. Berkeley: University of California Press.

Chiasson, Phyllis. 2005. "Abduction as an Aspect of Retroduction." *Semiotica* 153(1/4):223-42.

Clemens, Elisabeth S. 2007. "Toward a Historicized Sociology: Theorizing Events, Processes, and Emergence." *Annual Review of Sociology* 33:527-49.

Collier, Andrew. 2005. "Philosophy and Critical Realism: Critical Realism." In *The Politics of Method in the Human Sciences: Positivism and Its Epistemological Others*, edited by G. Steinmetz, 327-45. Durham, NC: Duke University Press.

Crasnow, Sharon. 2017. "Process Tracing in Political Science: What's the Story?" *Studies in History and Philosophy of Science* 62:6-13.

Creaven, Sean. 2007. *Emergentist Marxism: Dialectical Philosophy and Social Theory*. London: Routledge.

Danermark, Berth, Mats Ekström, and Jan Ch. Karlsson. 2002. *Explaining Society: Critical Realism in the Social Sciences*. London: Routledge.

Decoteau, Claire Laurier. 2017. "The AART of Ethnography: A Critical Realist Explanatory Research Model." *Journal for the Theory of Social Behavior* 47(1):58-82.

Elster, Jon. 1978. *Logic and Society: Contradictions and Possible Worlds*. Chichester, United Kingdom: Wiley.

Emigh, Rebecca Jean. 1997. "The Power of Negative Thinking: The Use of Negative Case Methodology in the Development of Sociological Theory." *Theory and Society* 26(5):649-84.

——. 1998. "The Mystery of the Missing Middle-Tenants: The 'Negative' Case of Fixed-Term Leasing and Agricultural Investment in Fifteenth-Century Tuscany." *Theory and Society* 27(3):351-75.

——. 2009. *The Undevelopment of Capitalism: Sectors and Markets in Fifteenth-Century Tuscany*. Philadelphia: Temple University Press.

Emigh, Rebecca Jean, Dylan Riley, and Patricia Ahmed. 2016a. *How Societies and States Count. Vol. 1, Antecedents of Censuses from Medieval to Nation States*. Basingstoke, United Kingdom: Palgrave Macmillan.

——. 2016b. *How Societies and States Count. Vol. 2, Changes in Censuses from Imperialist to Welfare States*. Basingstoke, United Kingdom: Palgrave Macmillan.

——. 2019. "Toward a Sociology of Knowledge of Land Surveys: The Influences of Societies and States." *Journal of Historical Sociology* 32(4):404–25.

Emigh, Rebecca Jean, Patricia Ahmed, and Dylan Riley. 2021. *How Everyday Forms of Racial Categorization Survived Imperialist Censuses in Puerto Rico*. Cham, Switzerland: Palgrave Macmillan.

Emirbayer, Mustafa. 1997. "Manifesto for Relational Sociology." *American Journal of Sociology* 103(2):281–317.

Emirbayer, Mustafa, and Ann Mische. 1998. "What Is Agency?" *American Journal of Sociology* 103(4):962–1023.

Engelskirchen, Howard. 2011. *Capital as a Social Kind: Definitions and Transformations in the Critique of Political Economy*. London: Routledge.

Ermakoff, Ivan. 2019. "Causality and History: Modes of Causal Investigation in Historical Social Sciences." *Annual Review of Sociology* 45:581–606.

Fairbrother, Malcolm. 2014. "Economists, Capitalists, and the Making of Globalization: North American Free Trade in Comparative-Historical Perspective." *American Journal of Sociology* 119(5):1324–79.

Garfinkel, Harold. 1967. *Studies in Ethnomethodology*. Englewood Cliffs, NJ: Prentice-Hall.

George, Alexander L., and Andrew Bennett. 2005. *Case Studies and Theory Development in the Social Sciences*. Cambridge, MA: MIT Press.

George, Kristin. 2023. "'Ministering at the Altar of Slavery': Religious Slavery Conflict and Social Movement Repression." *Social Science History* 47(2):299–323.

Glaeser, Andreas. 2005. "On Ontology for the Ethnographic Analysis of Social Processes: Extending the Extended-Case Method." *Social Analysis* 49(3):16–45.

Glaser, Barney G., and Anselm L. Strauss. 1967. *The Discovery of Grounded Theory: Strategies for Qualitative Research*. Chicago: Aldine.

Go, Julian. 2020. "Race, Empire, and Epistemic Exclusion: Or the Structures of Sociological Thought." *Sociological Theory* 38(2):79–100.

Goertz, Gary, and James Mahoney. 2012. *A Tale of Two Cultures: Qualitative and Quantitative Research in the Social Sciences*. Princeton, NJ: Princeton University Press.

Goldthorpe, John H. 2000. *On Sociology: Numbers, Narratives, and the Integration of Research and Theory*. Oxford: Oxford University Press.

Gorski, Philip S. 1993. "The Protestant Ethic Revisited: Disciplinary Revolution and State Formation in Holland and Prussia." *American Journal of Sociology* 99(2):265–316.

——. 2004. "The Poverty of Deductivism: A Constructive Realist Model of Sociological Explanation." *Sociological Methodology* 34(1):1–33.

——. 2009. "Social 'Mechanisms' and Comparative-Historical Sociology: A Critical Realist Proposal." In *Frontiers of Sociology*, edited by P. Hedström and B. Wittrock, 147–94. Leiden, Netherlands: Brill.

——. 2013. "What Is Critical Realism? And Why Should You Care?" *Contemporary Sociology* 42(5):658–70.

Gramsci, Antonio. 1971. *Selections from the Prison Notebooks of Antonio Gramsci*. Edited and translated by Q. Hoare and G. N. Smith. New York: International Publishers.

Griffin, Larry J. 1993. "Narrative, Event-Structure Analysis, and Causal Interpretation in Historical Sociology." *American Journal of Sociology* 98(5):1094–133.

Habermas, Jürgen. 1989. *The Structural Transformation of the Public Sphere: An Inquiry Into a Category of Bourgeois Society*. Translated by Thomas Burger, with the assistance of Frederick Lawrence. Cambridge, MA: MIT Press.

Hacking, Ian. 1999. *The Social Construction of What?* Cambridge, MA: Harvard University Press.

——. 2002. *Historical Ontology*. Cambridge, MA: Harvard University Press.

Hanckel, Benjamin, Mark Petticrew, James Thomas, and Judith Green. 2021. "The Use of Qualitative Comparative Analysis (QCA) to Address Causality in Complex Systems: A Systematic Review of Research on Public Health Interventions." *BMC Public Health* 21:877. https://doi.org/10.1186/s12889-021-10926-2.

Haraway, Donna. 1988. "Situated Knowledges: The Science Question in Feminism and the Privilege of Partial Perspective." *Feminist Studies* 14(3):575-99.

Hartmann, Nicolai. 1921. *Grundzüge einer Metaphysik der Erkenntnis*. Berlin: Walter de Gruyter.

Hausman, Daniel M. 1992. *Essays on Philosophy and Economic Methodology*. Cambridge: Cambridge University Press.

Hedström, Peter, and Petri Ylikoski. 2010. "Causal Mechanisms in the Social Sciences." *Annual Review of Sociology* 36:49-67.

Hegel, Georg Wilhelm Friedrich. [1820] 1991. *Elements of the Philosophy of Right*. Edited by A. W. Wood and translated by H. B. Nisbet. Cambridge: Cambridge University Press.

——. [1817] 2010. *Encyclopedia of the Philosophical Sciences in Basic Outline. Part I: Science of Logic*. Translated by K. Brinkmann and D. O. Dahlstrom. Cambridge: Cambridge University Press.

Hu, Xiaoti. 2018. "Methodological Implications of Critical Realism for Entrepreneurship Research." *Journal of Critical Realism* 17(2):118-39.

Hung, Ho-fung. 2008. "Agricultural Revolution and Elite Reproduction in Qing China: The Transition to Capitalism Debate Revisited." *American Sociological Review* 73(4):569-88.

Ide, Tobias, and Patrick A. Mello. 2022. "QCA in International Relations: A Review of Strengths, Pitfalls, and Empirical Applications." *International Studies Review* 24(1): viac008. https://doi.org/10.1093/isr/viac008.

Janoski, Thomas, and Alexander M. Hicks. 1994. "Methodological Innovations in Comparative Political Economy: An Introduction." In *The Comparative Political Economy of the Welfare State*, edited by T. Janoski and A. M. Hicks, 1-27. Cambridge: Cambridge University Press.

Jessop, Bob. 2005. "Critical Realism and the Strategic-Relational Approach." *New Formations: A Journal of Culture / Theory / Politics* 56(Autumn):40-53.

Kiser, Edgar. 1996. "The Revival of Narrative in Historical Sociology: What Rational Choice Theory Can Contribute." *Politics and Society* 24(3):249-71.

Kiser, Edgar, and Michael Hechter. 1991. "The Role of General Theory in Comparative-Historical Sociology." *American Journal of Sociology* 97(1):1-30.

Lachmann, Richard. 2000. *Capitalists in Spite of Themselves: Elite Conflict and Economic Transitions in Early Modern Europe*. Oxford: Oxford University Press.

Lakatos, Imre. 1970. "Falsification and the Methodology of Scientific Research Programmes." In *Criticism and the Growth of Knowledge*, edited by I. Lakatos and A. Musgrave, 91-196. Cambridge: Cambridge University Press.

Lana, Robert E., and Marianthi Georgoudi. 1983. "Causal Attributions: Phenomenological and Dialectical Aspects." *Journal of Mind and Behavior* 4(4):479-89.

Lara-Millán, Armando, Brian Sargent, and Sunmin Kim. 2020. "Theorizing with Archives: Continency, Mistakes, and Plausible Alternatives." *Qualitative Sociology* 43(3):345-65.

Latour, Bruno. 1991. "Technology Is Society Made Durable." In *A Sociology of Monsters: Essays on Power, Technology and Domination*, edited by J. Law, 103-31. London: Routledge.

Lieberson, Stanley. 1991. "Small N's and Big Conclusions: An Examination of the Reasoning in Comparative Studies Based on a Small Number of Cases." *Social Forces* 70(2):307-20.

Mahoney, James. 2000. "Path Dependence in Historical Sociology." *Theory and Society* 29(4):507-48.

——. 2004. "Revisiting General Theory in Historical Sociology." *Social Forces* 83(2):459–89.

Mahoney, James, and Gary Goertz. 2004. "The Possibility Principle: Choosing Negative Cases in Comparative Research." *American Political Science Review* 98(4):653–69.

Martin, Robert. 1994. *The Philosopher's Dictionary.* 2nd edition. Peterborough, Ontario, Canada: Broadview.

Marx, Karl. [1867] 1990. *Capital: A Critique of Political Economy.* Vol. 1. Translated by B. Fowkes. London: Penguin.

——. [1894] 1991. *Capital: A Critique of Political Economy.* Vol. 3. Translated by D. Fernbach. London: Penguin.

Maxwell, Joseph A. 2012. *A Realist Approach for Qualitative Research.* Thousand Oaks, CA: Sage.

Maybee, Julie E. 2020. "Hegel's Dialectics." *Stanford Encyclopedia of Philosophy* (Winter 2020 Edition), edited by E. N. Zalta. https://plato.stanford.edu/archives/win2020/entries/hegel-dialectics/.

Meyer, Samantha B., and Belinda Lunnay. 2013. "The Application of Abductive and Retroductive Inference for the Design and Analysis of Theory-Driven Sociological Research." *Sociological Research Online* 18(1):12. https://doi.org/10.5153/sro.2819.

Mill, John Stuart. [1859] 1989. *On Liberty with the Subjection of Women and Chapters on Socialism.* Edited by S. Collini. Cambridge: Cambridge University Press.

——. [1843] 1974a. *A System of Logic Ratiocinative and Inductive: Being a Connected View of the Principles of Evidence and the Methods of Scientific Investigation.* Vol. VII, *Collected Works of John Stuart Mill.* Edited by J. M. Robson. Toronto: University of Toronto Press.

——. [1843] 1974b. *A System of Logic Ratiocinative and Inductive: Being a Connected View of the Principles of Evidence and the Methods of Scientific Investigation.* Vol. VIII, *Collected Works of John Stuart Mill.* Edited by J. M. Robson. Toronto: University of Toronto Press.

Moore, Barrington, Jr. [1967] 1993. *Social Origins of Dictatorship and Democracy: Lord and Peasant in the Making of the Modern World.* Boston: Beacon.

Mora, G. Cristina. 2014. "Cross-Field Effects and Ethnic Classification: The Institutionalization of Hispanic Panethnicity, 1965 to 1990." *American Sociological Review* 79(2):183–210.

Ollman, Bertell. 2003. *Dance of the Dialectic: Steps in Marx's Method.* Urbana: University of Illinois Press.

Olsen, Wendy. 2007. "Critical Realist Explorations in Methodology." *Methodological Innovations Online* 2(2):1–5. https://doi.org/10.4256/mio.2007.0007.

Pacewicz, Josh. 2022. "What Can You Do with a Single Case? How to Think About Ethnographic Case Selection Like a Historical Sociologist." *Sociological Methods and Research* 51(3):931–62.

Page, Scott E. 2015. "What Sociologists Should Know About Complexity." *Annual Review of Sociology* 41:21–41.

Pascual-Leone, Juan. 1987. "Organismic Processes for Neo-Piagetian Theories: A Dialectical Causal Account of Cognitive Development." *International Journal of Psychology* 22(5–6):531–70.

Pietarinen, Ahti-Veikko, and Francesco Bellucci. 2014. "New Light on Peirce's Conceptions of Retroduction, Deduction, and Scientific Reasoning." *International Studies in the Philosophy of Science* 28(4):353–73.

Przeworski, Adam, and Henry Teune. 1970. *The Logic of Comparative Social Inquiry.* New York: Wiley-Interscience.

Pula, Besnik. 2021. "The Logico-Formalist Turn in Comparative and Case Study Methods: A Critical Realist Critique." *International Journal of Social Research Methodology* 24(6):739–51.

Ragin, Charles C. 1987. *The Comparative Method: Moving Beyond Qualitative and Quantitative Strategies*. Berkeley: University of California Press.

——. 2008. *Redesigning Social Inquiry: Fuzzy Sets and Beyond*. Chicago: University of Chicago Press.

Ricks, Jacob I., and Amy H. Liu. 2018. "Process-Tracing Research Designs: A Practical Guide." *PS: Political Science and Politics* 51(4):842-46.

Rihoux, Benoît. 2006. "Qualitative Comparative Analysis (QCA) and Related Systemic Comparative Methods: Recent Advances and Remaining Challenges for Social Science Research." *International Sociology* 21(5):679-706.

Riley, Dylan, Patricia Ahmed, and Rebecca Jean Emigh. 2021. "Getting Real: Heuristics in Sociological Knowledge." *Theory and Society* 50(2):315-56.

Roberts, John Michael. 2014. "Critical Realism, Dialectics, and Qualitative Research Methods." *Journal for the Theory of Social Behaviour* 44(1):1-23.

Rohlfing, Ingo. 2014. "Comparative Hypothesis Testing via Process Tracing." *Sociological Methods and Research* 43(4):606–42.

Runhardt, Rosa W. 2022. "Concrete Counterfactual Test for Process Tracing: Defending an Interventionist Potential Outcomes Framework." *Sociological Methods and Research*. https://journals.sagepub.com/doi/epub/10.1177/00491241221134523.

Rutten, Roel. 2022. "Applying and Assessing Large-N QCA: Causality and Robustness from a Critical Realist Perspective." *Sociological Methods and Research* 51(3):1211-43.

Rychlak, Joseph F. 1968. *A Philosophy of Science for Personality Theory*. Boston: Houghton Mifflin.

Schutz, Alfred. 1967. *The Phenomenology of the Social World*. Translated by G. Walsh and F. Lehnert. Evanston, IL: Northwestern University Press.

Schutz, Alfred, and Thomas Luckmann. 1973. *The Structures of the Life-World*. Translated by R. M. Zaner and H. T. Engelhardt Jr. Evanston, IL: Northwestern University Press.

Sekhon, Jasjeet S. 2004. "Quality Meets Quantity: Case Studies, Conditional Probability, and Counterfactuals." *Perspectives on Politics* 2(2):281-93.

Sewell, William H., Jr. 1992. "Introduction: Narratives and Social Identities." *Social Science History* 16(3):479-88.

——. 2005. *Logics of History: Social Theory and Social Transformation*. Chicago: University of Chicago Press.

Skocpol, Theda, and Margaret Somers. 1980. "The Uses of Comparative History in Macrosocial Inquiry." *Comparative Studies in Society and History* 22(2):174-97.

Smith, Dorothy E. 1987. *The Everyday World as Problematic: A Feminist Sociology*. Boston: Northeastern University Press.

Smits, Katherine. 2004. "John Stuart Mill and the Social Construction of Identity." *History of Political Thought* 25(2):298-324.

Somers, Margaret R. 1994. "The Narrative Constitution of Identity: A Relational and Network Approach." *Theory and Society* 23(5):605-49.

——. 1998. "'We're No Angels': Realism, Rational Choice, and Relationality in Social Science." *American Journal of Sociology* 104(3):722-84.

Steinmetz, George. 2004. "Odious Comparisons: Incommensurability, the Case Study, and 'Small N's' in Sociology." *Sociological Theory* 22(3):371-400.

Sweet, Paige L. 2018. "The Feminist Question in Realism." *Sociological Theory* 36(3):221–43.

Tarrow, Sidney. 2010. "The Strategy of Paired Comparison: Toward a Theory of Practice." *Comparative Political Studies* 43(2):230-59.

Tavory, Iddo, and Stefan Timmermans. 2014. *Abductive Analysis: Theorizing Qualitative Research*. Chicago: University of Chicago Press.

Tsutsui, Kiyoteru. 2017. "Human Rights and Minority Activism in Japan: Transformation of Movement Actorhood and Local-Global Feedback Loop." *American Journal of Sociology* 122(4):1050–103.

Weber, Max. [1922] 1978. *Economy and Society: An Outline of Interpretive Sociology.* Edited by G. Roth and C. Wittich and translated by E. Fischoff et al. Berkeley: University of California Press.

Western, Bruce. 1999. "Bayesian Analysis for Sociologists: An Introduction." *Sociological Methods and Research* 28(1):7–34.

AFTERWORD

PHILIP GORSKI

For five years, from 2013 to 2018, I directed a project on critical realism (CR) and the social sciences.[1] We organized numerous seminars, workshops, and conferences attended by hundreds of social scientists. Among them was a working group on comparative historical sociology. This volume emerged out of their discussions, which I joined on several occasions.

The original goal of the CR project was to build a CR movement within American sociology and, eventually, the neighboring social sciences. This goal quickly proved much too ambitious. While a few of the participants were wholly persuaded by CR, most were not. A good number did find some of the realist parts of CR convincing, particularly its accounts of "mechanisms" and/or "emergence." But relatively few accepted the critical part of CR: its account of "human flourishing." Almost all did share CR's misgivings about the enduring influence of positivism on the practice of social science in the United States. But some also felt that other philosophies such as American pragmatism provided a better alternative than CR. All of these positions are represented in the present volume.

In this afterword, I sketch out my own position. It is a version of CR that tries to respond to some of the critiques of CR that arose during these discussions. Let's call it "neo-CR" (NCR). In what follows, I outline some of its core ideas and sketch out its implications for the practice of comparative and historical social science. I begin by briefly reviewing what I take to be the four core ideas of classical CR: mechanisms, emergence, openness, and flourishing.

I then discuss four key tenets of neo-CR: ontological heterogeneity, causal complexity, historical contingency, and ethical naturalism. This leads in turn to some "dos and don'ts" for the practice of social science. The "dos" are describe, explain, critique, and evaluate. The "don'ts" are determinism, reductionism, universalism, and relativism. It is my insistence on the ethico-political dimension of comparison that most clearly separates my views from those of other contributors to the volume.

Realism, Mechanisms, Emergence, and Flourishing

CR is a perennial position in modern philosophy. Ever since Immanuel Kant first elaborated his "critical philosophy" in response to David Hume's skeptical empirical philosophy some 250 years ago, various thinkers have adopted the CR label to describe their views, often in opposition to Kant's and/or Hume's, though rarely in relationship to one another (Broad [1934] 2014; Sellars 1916). "CR," in this sense, is not a philosophical tradition that developed continuously over time; it is rather a philosophical stance that has been repeatedly reinvented and reasserted vis-à-vis empiricist and idealist philosophies (Losch 2009).

The sociological version of CR that concerns us here first emerged in the late 1970s in Great Britain (Archer 1998). It initially took shape within an interdisciplinary circle of scholars that included philosophers and economists as well as sociologists. It eventually came to be centered within British sociology, with outposts in Scandinavia, Italy, and now the United States.[2] British CR positioned itself as a *via media* between two then-powerful currents within Anglophone philosophy and social science: "logical positivism" (also known as "logical empiricism") and "social constructionism"—which is to say, two contemporary versions of empiricism and idealism.

Today, "positivism" is more of an epithet than a position in sociology. But in the mid-twentieth century, positivism was still an influential and prestigious movement within Anglophone philosophy (Hanfling 2003). It originally crystallized within the German-speaking "Vienna Circle," which then included well-known luminaries such as Karl Popper (Stadler 2015). It subsequently found its way into English and then American philosophy during World War II, when its champions were forced to emigrate to the United Kingdom and the United States. After the war, positivism penetrated into American social science via the writings of Carl Hempel and Karl Popper and their sociological admirers, such as Paul Lazarsfeld of Columbia (Hempel 1965; Lazarsfeld 1958; Popper 1959). Within philosophy proper, however, the positivist movement was short-lived; the movement died quickly and was eventually pronounced dead by its favorite son, A. J. Ayer (Baggini 2019). Not so in the social sciences.

Echoes of positivism can still be heard even today in the language of "hypothesis testing" and "falsifiability."

Early CR took issue with various aspects of logical positivism (Archer 1995; Bhaskar 1975, 1979; Lawson 1997). For present purposes, four are key: radical empiricism, regularity causation, methodological individualism, and value subjectivism.

Radical empiricism presumes that scientific knowledge is based solely on "observation" of "the phenomena." It also posits an "observation language" that is wholly distinct from any "theoretical concepts" (Neurath 1934; for a trenchant critique, see Hesse 2020). CR's reasons for rejecting radical empiricism are two. First, science does not just passively "observe" the world. It engages with and intervenes in the world (Dreyfus and Taylor 2015; Hacking 1983). For example, laboratory work typically involves experimental closure and strategic manipulation. Second, scientific knowledge is not limited to the "empirical" description of observable "phenomena." Scientific theories often postulate so-called nonobservables, that is, entities and processes that cannot be *directly* observed with the unaided senses but that can be observed *indirectly* with scientific instruments and/or methods and whose structure and powers we must *theorize and conceptualize.* CR is a form of what is sometimes called "depth ontology" (Singh 2018). On this view, scientific knowledge consists of theoretical descriptions of "underlying structures and processes," which brings us to the thorny question of causation.

Logical positivism is typically paired with what philosophers call a "regularity theory of causation" (Mumford and Anjum 2013; Psillos 2009). On this view, we can say that A "causes" B if and only if we perceive that B regularly follows A in time. "Regularly" originally meant "always." Hempel later redefined "regularity" in statistical terms to mean "with probability X." In the regularity theory, any causal account can and must be rendered either as a "law-like statement" or, alternatively, as a "probabilistic statement" with a (NB!) precise coefficient. Early CR rejected the regularity theory for two reasons: first, because the social sciences have never generated any such "laws" (NB: a regression coefficient is *not* a probabilistic law!), second, because even within the physical sciences, "general laws" typically only obtain within the "closed system" of a laboratory and even there only imperfectly (Cartwright 1983). Instead, early CR advanced a mechanismic approach to causation, in which directly observable effects ("the actual") are caused by underlying structures and processes ("the real"). On this view, the goal of social science—of science *tout court*—is to understand the "mechanisms" of which the world is comprised rather than to discover the "universal laws" that (supposedly) govern it. The ongoing failure of the social sciences to discover any (nontautological) laws is due not only to the complexity of the social world but also to the "openness of the social system" and to the "emergence" of new social "things" over time.

Within the social sciences, logical positivism often goes together with an affinity for "methodological individualism" and a suspicion of sociological realism (Hedström 2005; Popper 1957). Why? Because individual human beings are middle-sized objects that can be directly observed with the unaided senses, whereas social structures and collectivities (like genes and quarks) are not and cannot. Persons seem "observable" and "empirical" in a way that institutions and groups do not. So, how can we know that the latter are really "real"? And even if they are real, how they can possibly be objects of "scientific knowledge"? To these questions, classical CR offers two answers. First, individual human beings are themselves "structures," specifically, "bio-psycho-social structures" whose "parts" (e.g., their DNA, thoughts, and intentions) cannot be directly observed. Human bodies may be directly observable; human persons are not. Second, like other structures, human persons have emergent causal powers and properties, such as "consciousness," "desires," and "identities," among others. In plain language, emergence simply means that wholes can sometimes be greater than the sums of their parts, in the sense of having causal powers and properties that their parts do not have in isolation from one another (Bedau and Humphreys 2008; Bunge 2001; Elder-Vass 2010; Sawyer 2005; Wimsatt 1997).

The fourth and final dogma of logical positivism is what we might call value subjectivism. It is closely connected to positivism's atomistic picture of the social world. If human individuals are the elementary particles of that world, then "values" (or "preferences") must simply be their internal states and their "actions" the effect of these states (Gorski 2017). Early CR rejected this dogma as well and on two grounds. First, it was rejected because there are some things that are objectively good for human beings such as food, shelter, and health. Humans cannot help but value or prefer these things, even in the breach. Second, it was rejected because human beings are not physical particles but conscious agents with the potential for self-determination (i.e., "freedom"). They cannot help but value this as well, *especially* in the breach. CR therefore argued that social science can and should be oriented toward the goals of human flourishing and universal emancipation. Social science should be "critical" of society, as well as realist about science. It can be "objective" but not "value free" (Gorski 2019).

The CR critique of logical positivism was quite extensive. Its critique of social constructionism was much less so. It was not really targeted at "social constructionism" in the broadest sense, but at what might be called "discursive constructionism." On this "deconstructionist" or "postmodernist" view, which was not uncommon in fields such as comparative literature and science studies at the time, the social and even the natural worlds were said to be "constructed" by "language" or "discourse." In Derrida's oft-quoted (if mistranslated) phrase, "there is nothing outside of the text." Now, classical CR acknowledged the role of language in the construction of reality. Social structures and processes are said to be "concept dependent" in the sense that terms like "class" or "state" help to constitute the things that they name. CR therefore affirmed social constructionism in this more limited sense. What CR emphatically rejected was a radical idealism that claims, or at least implies, that there is no reality apart from our concepts.

Before moving on, let us briefly sum up. Classical CR positioned itself vis-à-vis logical positivism as follows. It rejected (1) radical empiricism in favor of depth realism; (2) the regularity theory of causality in favor of a focus on "causal mechanisms"; (3) "methodological individualism" and other forms of reductionism in favor of "emergent causal powers and properties"; and (4) value subjectivism in favor of a positive account of "human flourishing" and "emancipation." At the same time, it also positioned itself vis-à-vis radical forms of social constructionism that suggested that social reality was nothing but an "effect of discourse."

Heterogeneity, Complexity, Pluralism, and Naturalism

The practice of social science has changed a great deal since the emergence of classical CR during the late 1970s. Among other things, (1) the old language of "observation" now competes with an emphasis on "interventions" and the use of (quasi) experimental methods and analysis of "big data" (Grimmer, Roberts, and Stewart 2022; Morgan and Winship 2015; Pearl 2009; Woodward 2004); (2) talk of "causal mechanisms" has gone from the margins to the mainstream in sociology and in the social sciences more generally (Gross 2009; Hedström and Swedberg 1998; Tilly 2000); (3) "methodological individualism" has gone out of fashion again, except in economics (Achen and Bartels 2017); and (4) the normative is no longer entirely taboo: psychologists do research on "flourishing," cognitive scientists on "morality," sociologists on "happiness," and anthropologists on "ethics" (Johnson 2021; Keane 2015; Seligman 2012; Veenhoven 2003). Meanwhile, radical forms of linguistic constructionism have given way to a renewed concern with "materiality" and "iconicity" (Fox and Alldred 2020; Tilley et al. 2006). In sum, many of the core claims of classical CR have now been at least partially vindicated.

But they have also been critiqued—and not just by diehard positivists. During the five years of the CR project and in ongoing conversations since then, it became clear to many of the participants that certain tenets of classical CR needed revision and elaboration. This is particularly true of its accounts of ontology, causality, methodology, and flourishing. What follows is my own account of what a reconstructed CR or "NCR" might look like.

One of the hallmarks of classical CR, especially in its philosophical guise, has always been a focus on ontology. There is nothing magical or mysterious about ontology. It is just systematic reflection on "what is" (Mumford 2012). Mainstream, analytic philosophers also study it (Simons 2013). But "epistemology" is much more central to the history of modern philosophy. Since Descartes, and even more since Kant, Western philosophy has been far more concerned with how we can know anything than what we can have knowledge of. CR intentionally reversed this emphasis. Instead of asking how we know, it asked what the world must be like for us to have the kinds of knowledge that we do have. For example, CR asks why natural laws can only be observed under conditions of experimental closure and why social science has failed to discover any laws at all. It also asks why scientific knowledge is organized into specialized disciplines, which resist theoretical unification. The basic answer that CR gives is that the world is an open system composed of numerous "layers" or "strata" (very roughly, physical, biological, and social).

Classical CR assumed a "materialist" ontology, partly because of its roots in British neo-Marxism. But this ontological materialism—the view that the social world was ultimately made of material "stuff"—was hard to square with CR's *social* ontology. Recall the claim that social structures are "concept dependent." CR likewise argued that social structures are "activity dependent" (i.e., re/produced through human action). These two claims made CR vulnerable to interpretivist critiques that insist on the relative autonomy of culture and also to pragmatist and culturalist critiques that insist on the creativity and meaningfulness of human action (Gross 2017; Reed 2021).

One possible response to these tensions and critiques is to acknowledge the *ontological heterogeneity* of the social world (Little 2016). Or, more plainly, to recognize that the social is composed of very different sorts of "stuff," some of which is not "material" in any straightforward sense. I have argued elsewhere that all social structures capable of reproducing themselves are comprised of three basic types of "things": the material, the symbolic, and the human (Gorski 2016). The material elements may be natural, artifactual, or both. The symbolic elements may be linguistic, ritual, or both. And the human element is minds and bodies or, more simply, persons.

The materialist view of social structures and causal mechanisms is also problematic in another respect. It implies that the relations between the parts of a structure or mechanism are purely spatial or physical (Gorski 2015). But this is clearly not the case. Like the parts themselves, the relations that conjoin them are also heterogeneous. Consider just one very simple example: the relation of a person to their own body (Archer 2000). Someone may relate to their body as a natural object, something to be sustained or repaired (e.g., with food or medicine). Or, they may relate to it as an artifactual creation, something to be made and remade (e.g., through diet or surgery). Or they may relate to it as a symbolic expression (e.g., through clothing or bodily hexus). The upshot: ontological heterogeneity is relational as well as substantive.

The ontological heterogeneity of the social world has various implications. One has already been hinted at: *methodological pluralism*. Because social structures and processes are "concept" and "agency dependent," for example, social analysis and critique inevitably involve the interpretation of social action. As Weber argued long ago, any sociological explanation must be interpretively as well as empirically adequate. It is not enough to correctly "predict" a "behavior"; one must also convincingly "understand" its meaning and motivation. This is why the various interpretive methods developed by sociologists (e.g., interviews, ethnography, cultural sociology) are an indispensable part of the disciplinary toolkit and always will be.

However, because social structures and processes also have emergent powers and properties of their own that constrain and enable those of individual actors, interpretive methods alone will never suffice. Supra-individual or "macro" structures and processes (e.g., organizations and markets) must also be studied in their own right. Formal methods such as network analysis, organizational ecology, and field theory are helpful tools for understanding such macro-level effects (Abbott 2005; Fligstein and McAdam, 2011; White 2008). It is worth noting, *en passant*, that comparative and historical methods are a crucial tool for understanding how and why new structures emerge (Hirschman and Reed 2014).

A second consequence of ontological heterogeneity is *causal complexity*. It comes in at least two distinct forms. First, there are different *types* of causation at work in the micro level of social interaction. Human actions are often oriented toward some final end or goal. In philosophical terms, this means that reasons can be causes, at least in the social world (Darwall 2003). Actions may also be enabled (or constrained) by material resources or artefacts, such as money or technologies (Giddens 1984). Further, they may be triggered (or impeded) by the actions of other actors—action frequently involves interaction. Finally, they may be guided by a frame, script, or schema. These four examples roughly correspond to Aristotle's famous fourfold typology of causation: final, material, efficient, and formal (Sachs 1995).

Third, there are different *levels* of causation at work in the social world. Macro structures such as social networks or formal organizations may have causal dynamics that operate quite differently than those at the individual level (Boccaletti et al. 2014; Powell and Padgett 2012). What's more, the macro may impinge on the micro, and vice versa. There is "downward" as well as "upward" causation. On the one hand, human actions may be constrained or enabled by meso- or macro-level structures or processes of which the actors themselves may or may not be fully aware. On the other hand, "small" causes at the micro level may have "large" effects at the macro level. Perhaps the most obvious example is interpersonal dynamics between powerful actors who control large organizations such as corporations, parties, or governments (e.g., Jeff Bezos, Donald Trump, and MBS).

A fourth and final aspect of NCR, somewhat distinct from the other three, is *ethical naturalism* (Gorski 2013). It is "natural" in the sense that all human cultures develop ethical systems (i.e., rules, rituals, and practices governing individual and collective life) (Keane 2015; Murdoch 1971). And it is "ethical" in the sense that it concerns "the good" rather than "the right," that is, how to "live well" rather than how to "act justly" (Murdoch 1971; Taylor 1989). Ethics themselves are "natural" to the extent that they are delimited by certain biological or psychological needs and capabilities, if not determined by them in any straightforward sense (Flanagan 2009). Some of these needs and capabilities, such as nurturance of the young and play, are shared with many other mammals (Bellah 2011). Others, such as meaning and speech, are not fully shared with any other species, if also not uniquely human (MacIntyre 1999; Taylor 2016).

It is important to stress that ethical naturalism does not make claims about "human nature," "ultimate purpose," or "the highest good." Human needs and capabilities are plural and heterogeneous (Nussbaum 2000). What is "good" for one person will not be identical to what is "good" for another. This is because individual needs and capabilities vary a good deal and also because there is considerable variation in the ways and degrees to which they are and can be realized in a particular culture. Humans and other social mammals have a shared capability for "play," for example, but they do not all play the same games, nor does their well-being depend upon playing any particular game (Bellah 2011). In sum, the "human good" may not be "completely subjective." But there is also no such thing as "the human good" or "the good society." And because "freedom" is also part of the human good, ethical naturalism does not provide a political justification for imposing a particular view of the good on others. At most, it provides a warrant for guaranteeing that certain basic resources and opportunities be provided to all members of a society.

What Makes Good Theory Good

Classical CR sought to be three things all at once: a philosophy of science, a theory of society, and a method of social research (see, e.g., Archer 1995; Bhaskar 1979; Danermark, Ekstrom, and Jakobsen 2005). NCR is somewhat less ambitious; it only tries to be two things: (1) a theory of theory or "metatheory" that generates (2) some general methodological dos and don'ts. Put more plainly, it is a theory of what good social theory does and also a set of caveats about what makes bad research bad. In other words, it has a positive as well as a negative side.

Let's begin with the positive metatheory. In NCR, social theories can do as many as four different things: describe, explain, critique, and evaluate. They need not do all these things at once. But good theories usually do at least one of them well, and usually more.

"Mere" description is often contrasted with "high" social theory. This makes sense if by "description" one means something like "common sense descriptions based on direct personal observations." Descriptions of this sort can of course serve as a form of evidence. But there is another form of description that is inherently theoretical: the description of social "nonobservables." Many and indeed most of sociology's research objects are nonobservable in this sense: states and nations, social collectivities and cultural boundaries, economic institutions, social networks, and so on. We do not observe them directly with our unaided senses. Note that "nonobservable" does not mean "unobservable," just "not *directly* observable." Descriptions of this sort may take various forms, including ideal types, formal models, and data visualizations. Some of the most important theoretical breakthroughs are in fact just theoretical descriptions of new or hitherto "invisible" social structures, objects, or practices (e.g., "cultural capital" or "gender performances").

Theories also explain. In classical CR, to explain was to invoke a "causal mechanism." In neo-CR, to explain is to identify causation of any kind. And because there are different types of causation, there will be different forms of explanation as well. The previous section distinguished six different forms of causation: efficient, material, formal, final, downward, and upward. Most sociological explanations are of course mixtures of these various forms. And many debates within sociology can be understood as debates about which type of explanation is most appropriate or powerful in any given case or in general. Progress in social science, on this account, consists in refining and combining the different forms of explanation for particular cases or classes of phenomena (e.g., "the French Revolution" or "social revolutions"; Gorski 2018).

I expect that most sociologists would gladly accept the previous two claims. The claim that social theory can or should be "critical" is probably more controversial. Classical CR claimed that social science was inherently critical and for two reasons. First, insofar as social science explains a "social ill" or "oppression" (i.e., a social structure or mechanism that inhibits flourishing and/or freedom), it also explains, or at least suggests, how the ill might be alleviated or the oppression removed. Second, insofar as social science explains the mechanism whereby the causes of an ill are obscured or misrecognized, it identifies and critiques an ideological formation as well.

Neo-CR does not reject these two forms of social critique. It simply adds to them, based on its core principles of ontological heterogeneity and causal pluralism. In principle, it would be possible to elaborate a complex typology of different forms of social critique corresponding to the different elements of social structure and the various forms of social causation. But that is beyond the scope of this essay. In the present context, two examples must suffice. Both are common in comparative and historical sociology. Comparison is often used to rebut the fatalistic claims of conservative ideologues who insist that "there is no alternative" to a particular institutional arrangement. Comparative work on political economy or social provision is a common example, as in comparisons of (meager) American and (generous) Scandinavian welfare states (Esping-Andersen 1990). Historical accounts are also often mobilized to challenge regimes of collective memory that support the privileges of powerful groups. Historical work on "racial capitalism" or "settler colonialism" that foregrounds the role of oppression and expropriation in economic development and challenges claims of just deserts or cultural superiority is an excellent example (Hannah-Jones 2021). Both are examples of broader strategies of "denaturalizing" and "genealogical" critique that span the social sciences and humanities.

Where "critique" focuses on causes, "evaluation" emphasizes effects. Like critique, evaluation can take many different forms. The most common highlights "unintended consequences," especially ones sharply at odds with the stated aims of key actors. Democratic revolutions that result in authoritarian regimes, as in Tocqueville's analysis of the French case, are a classic example (Skocpol 1979; Tocqueville 2011). "Law and order" policies that lead to extrajudicial killings and marital and family disruption are a contemporary one (Hinton 2017). A more subtle, but less common, form of social evaluation concerns heterogeneous consequences, particularly ones that are seemingly at odds with each other. A classic example, also from Tocqueville, is the way that social equality simultaneously strengthens individualism and conformity (Tocqueville 1988). A more contemporary example would be the way that the internet simultaneously accelerates flows of information and misinformation.

Good comparative and historical social science can and does do all four of these things. But it rarely does them explicitly and self-consciously. One reason for this is that positivism equated theory with explanation by eliding the difference between them: in this perspective, a theory just was an explanation, nothing more and nothing less. Another is that positivism insisted that science must be "objective" and "value free." As a result, description is devalued, and critique and evaluation rendered off limits. Sociologists of race and gender rejected these positivist dogmas long ago (Collins 2000; Harding 1987). Comparative and historical sociologists would do well to follow their lead. This is not to say that politics and activism should replace theory and method, only that they can and should be linked (Burawoy 2005). Nor is this to say that every scholar should always make this link in their research, only that some should do so some of the time. There may be no such thing as "value-free research," but neither is there any such thing as "fact-free values." Debates about values are also tethered to debates about facts, whether this is acknowledged or not (Gorski 2019). Good social science does not sever the tether; it heightens the tension.

What Makes Bad Theory Bad

So much for the "positive" side of NCR; now for its "negative" injunctions. NCR does not privilege a particular social science methodology, nor does it advance any methodological "gold standard." However, it does lead quite directly to four methodological prohibitions. Let's call them—tongue in cheek—the Four Commandments of NCR:

1. Thou shalt not engage in determinism.
2. Thou shalt not engage in reductionism.
3. Though shalt not engage in universalism.
4. Thou shalt not engage in relativism.

Like the Biblical commandments, they require some explication.

1. Thou Shalt Not Engage in Determinism

Determinism comes in stronger and weaker forms. There are two common forms of strong determinism: monocausal and reductionistic. In monocausal determinism, one type of cause is held to be decisive "in the last instance" (e.g., "material" causes). In reductionistic determinism, one level of reality is held to be "fundamental" (e.g., "physical") in the last instance. Some forms of Marxism and rational-choice theory are deterministic in both senses. But few if any contemporary sociologists are strong determinists in either sense. Most would recognize that social effects have multiple causes just as they would reject the view that sociological phenomena can ever be fully accounted for by, say, physics or genetics.

However, some sociologists are still attracted to weaker forms of determinism. Let's call them exhaustive and probabilistic. Exhaustive determinism presumes that fully exhaustive explanations are possible, at least in principle—that is, explanations that identify *all* of the causes of a given phenomenon, or at least all of the "necessary and/or sufficient causes" (Skocpol 1984). But this is possible if and only if the social world has temporal and spatial limits that create a stopping point for historical regress and social contextualization. NCR rejects this possibility on the grounds that the social world is an open system.

Probabilistic determinism presumes that numerically precise explanations are possible (Lieberson 1991). On this account, statistical parameters such as "odds ratios" or "likelihoods" are at least tacitly treated as sociological constants that are analogous to physical constants. NCR also rejects probabilistic determinism and on much the same grounds: the fundamental openness of the social world means that the *ceterus paribus* principle never holds and that external validity is always a problem even in the most rigorous of social experiments. This is not to say that a statistical measures and experimental results are not informative or useful, only that they are neither precise nor constant in the sense that a strict probabilism requires.

2. Thou Shalt Not Engage in Reductionism

Reductionism comes in two different forms that are not always clearly distinguished: ontological and methodological. Ontological reductionism is the claim that there is some fundamental level of reality to which all others can ultimately be reduced (Kim 2005). More plainly, it is the claim that the behavior of the whole can always be understood in terms of its parts, and exhaustively so. Methodological reductionism is the claim that the behavior of the whole can often be better understood by examining its parts, especially when that behavior appears puzzling or anomalous.

Neo-CR rejects all forms of ontological reductionism on the grounds that wholes can have emergent properties and powers that are not possessed by their parts in isolation. This is not to deny that closer study of the parts may shed light on why a whole has the powers and properties that it does and which parts do or do not contribute to those powers and properties. It is only to insist that reductive analyses are not always necessary and rarely sufficient to understand the behavior of wholes. What is more, the behavior of the parts can be, and often is, enabled or constrained by the structure of the whole. Causation may be "downward" as well as "upward." For these reasons, the categorical imperative of "methodological individualism"—"Show me your microfoundations!"—can often be ignored, as can the more polite request to "Show me your bathtub model, please" (Coleman 1990).

3. Thou Shalt Not Engage in Universalism

"Universalism" is used here in an ontological rather than an ethical sense. It is the claim that there can and should be universal theories that are equally applicable in all times and places. Like the other "isms" catalogued here, universalism comes in strong and weak forms in the social sciences. The strong form is theoretical universalism. It claims all phenomena can and should always and everywhere be adequately explained in terms of one theoretical framework (Kiser and Hechter 1991). Rational-choice theory is of course the best contemporary example. The weak form is historicist universalism. It is a second-order form of universalism that claims that all societies must necessarily pass through a series of developmental stages on its way to "modernity," even if the "laws" governing each stage are different (Gilman 2003).

NCR rejects both forms of universalism, as indeed do most contemporary sociologists. While rational-choice theory briefly became the dominant paradigm within political science, it never made significant or lasting inroads into sociology. Cultural sociologists and other interpretivists rejected its emphasis on self-interest. Historical sociologists and other institutionalists rejected its insistence on micro-foundations. And many sociologists saw rational-choice theory as an avatar of neoliberalism. Meanwhile, stage theories were subjected to withering critiques, first by historical sociologists who rejected the "tradition/modernity" dichotomy and more recently by postcolonial theorists who reject Eurocentric accounts of economic and political "development."

4. Thou Shalt Not Engage in Relativism

Whereas the first three commandments regarding determinism, reductionism, and universalism probably command relatively broad assent within sociology, the fourth is much more controversial. Thus, it is particularly important to be clear about what it does and does not mean. The first distinction to make is between epistemological and ontological relativism. One of the three cardinal principles of classical CR is "epistemological relativism." Another is "ontological realism." At first glance, these two principles may seem at odds with each other. How can one be a relativist and a realist at the same time? Classical CR's answer was a form of what we now call "standpoint theory": what you see depends on where you stand. To this, NCR simply adds a corollary: what you see also depends on what methods you are using.

The fourth commandment concerns ethical relativism. By this I mean the view, already discussed earlier, that there are no objective goods, only subjective ones. As the economists say, *de gustibus non est disputandum!* It's all just a matter of "personal preferences" (Becker 1996). Many sociologists would reluctantly agree, albeit for somewhat different reasons. Because they are inclined to prize emancipation and oppose domination, sociologists are generally hesitant to make explicitly normative claims for fear of infringing on others' autonomy or violating the principle of "value freedom." Instead, they make implicitly normative claims. For example, they analyze inequality because they believe in equality, or they work on nationalism because they believe in cosmopolitanism, and so forth.

NCR rejects the view that there are no objective human or social goods. It embraces the form of ethical naturalism developed by Martha Nussbaum and Amartya Sen under the rubric of "the capabilities approach" (Nussbaum 2000;

Nussbaum and Sen 1993; Sen 1999). On this view, human beings are variously endowed with certain "capabilities" or "functions" that it is good for them to develop and exercise. On Nussbaum's account, these include necessary conditions of personal development such as "a long life," "physical health," and "bodily integrity," which are preconditions for higher-order human capabilities such as "play," "relationships," "emotions," "imagination," and "spirituality." It is worth noting that some human goods are also *common goods*, that is, goods that cannot be achieved by a single individual in isolation from others. "Team sports," "interpersonal relationships," "good conversation," or "social rituals" are examples. Note that these goods are "multiply realizable"—that is, they can take many different forms that may vary across cultures.

It might be objected that claims about objective goods are really veiled efforts to dominate others. And of course they can be. Consider the example of sports programs in authoritarian societies such as Russia or China. There, individuals with athletic abilities are often compelled and/or incentivized to develop those abilities by the state as opposed to those abilities they themselves might choose to cultivate. Nussbaum therefore tempers the capabilities approach with a commitment to "political liberalism" (Rawls 2005). In a liberal society, all individuals must be free to choose which of the capabilities they do or do not wish to develop. By this logic, a gifted gymnast cannot be compelled to become an Olympic gymnast if they are more interested in becoming, say, a pastry chef.

By the same token, however, a gifted gymnast should not be denied the opportunity to become an Olympic gymnast. To that end, they should have access to gymnastics instruction and equipment, as indeed should anyone who is interested in gymnastics. A good society on this account is therefore one that provides the shared infrastructure that individuals need to develop their capabilities. The capabilities approach does not provide clear guidelines about what sorts of infrastructure to prioritize, given limited resources (e.g., clean water versus medical care). But it does create a framework for thinking about such decisions that goes beyond aggregative measures such as gross domestic product or per capita income.

What Is Comparison Good For?

In the old Millian-Skocpolian dispensation that has dominated and legitimated "comparative historical sociology" since the mid-1980s, comparison has been widely understood as a strategy for validating explanations (Skocpol 1984). During the early days of the "second wave," there was much talk of "the logic of comparison." That logic was double. On the one hand, it was "deductive," or at least pretended to be. In a conciliatory gesture to positivist dogma, comparative historical explanations were supposed to be presented in the form of a law-like proposition such as: "if state-breakdown and peasant revolt, then social revolution." Of course, this "law" really only applied to a relatively small number of hand-selected cases. In this sense, on the other hand, the logic also had to be "inductive." The cases in the study had to be selected so as not to violate the major premise of the deductive statement. Constructing a comparative historical analysis was a bit like piecing together the pieces of a puzzle. Alas, as critics were quick to note, with their small numbers of pieces, such analyses were more akin to children's puzzles than the grown-up puzzles that social demographers preferred to work on.

And yet, despite the dismissive comments of some of their more quantitatively inclined colleagues, practitioners of qualitative historical comparison persisted, even as they sometimes struggled to justify their methodological practices in the quasi-positivist terms that still dominate many regions of the social sciences. It is high time to give up that struggle, not only because it has proven unhelpful but also because the most sophisticated quantitative methodologists have themselves moved past it. On the one hand, old-school regression analysts must now defend their work against "experimentalists" who question the value of "observational" studies. They must now frame their analyses in "counterfactual" that mimic "interventions" and uncover "mechanisms" (Morgan and Winship 2015). On the other hand, the new-school text-as-data analysts confront many of the same issues as second-wave comparative analysts: like social historians and historical sociologists, they generally work with "found" data that others have produced for other purposes, using "custom" measures that are suited to that data but not widely used by others (Grimmer et al. 2022). As a result, they run into the same questions of "validity" and "replicability" that have long dogged qualitative researchers.

The essays in this volume catalogue and make explicit some of the ways that skilled practitioners of comparison have come to understand their own practices. NCR provides one possible framework for systematizing some of these insights, although surely not the only one. In CR, theory and method have always been understood as closely and tightly connected. Thus, the dos and don'ts of theory sketched earlier also provide a beginning for thinking about the various uses of comparison.

Let's begin with the four "dos" of good theory: description, explanation, critique, and evaluation. One of the very first steps in any comparative analysis is to compare descriptions of the cases with an eye to similarities, differences—and surprises. Initially, the descriptions in question are often historical narratives written by specialists, most often historians. The goal at this stage is usually to identify variations in social structures or event sequences that demand explanation and challenge extant accounts. The number of cases considered often outstrips the number of cases that will eventually be included. In the next stage, the descriptions often take the form of "case studies" or, rather, rough drafts thereof. Here, the goal is to determine whether the structural variations and processual dynamics that underpin an explanatory account yield a narrative that is coherent and plausible. They are like the initial data runs of a statistical analyst trying to figure out which models work and which ones don't. And, like those initial models, they go through multiple revisions and much fine-tuning. Or they are simply discarded.

It is not really possible to draw a sharp line between description and explanation, especially in historical work. Narrative description is just one form of historical explanation. Of course, it is not the only form. Structural analyses (e.g., of social collectivities and boundaries or political institutions or practices) are another, and a particularly important one in historical social science. However, explanations that lean too hard in the direction of structure can be too static to be considered properly "historical." Good historical analysis always attends to social process, too. Weaving together structural and processual analyses in a balanced—and readable—fashion is one of the organizational and rhetorical challenges of comparative work. Some measure of structural analysis is required to validate claims about the constitutive elements of particular structures and the causal powers attributed to them. But some measure of processual analysis is also required to show these powers in action, that is, qua "mechanisms." One of the appeals of the "mechanisms" metaphor is that it combines structure and process into one master term. Good comparative work typically includes both structural and processual comparisons, at least implicitly. But it is nonetheless helpful to be more explicit about the kind of work that comparison does in historical and sociological explanation.

Neither is it possible to draw a sharp line between explanation and critique, and for several reasons. If the social world is open and contingent, as historical sociologists (and NCR) insist it is, then to explain why something is the way it is is also to ask how it could have been different. And those differences are never really "value neutral." Asking why fascists came to power in some parts of interwar Europe but not in others is not a "value-neutral" question, any more than asking why social democrats came to power in some parts of postwar Europe but not in others (Luebbert 1991; Mann 2004). The critique is implicit in the question. Cross-spatial comparisons such as these can also provide the starting point for transtemporal ones. Asking whether Trumpism is a form of fascism is certainly not "value neutral," any more than asking whether multiculturalism is a form of "soft tyranny" (Rahe 2009; Stanley 2020). In these sorts of comparisons, the critique is quite explicit. There is nothing new about this. On the contrary, one could argue that comparative analysis originated as a form of social critique. Kant's writings on "anthropology" and Hegel's discourses on "history" were, among other things, critiques of non-Western societies and assertions of Western cultural superiority (Hegel 2004; Kant 2006). So were the writings of many colonial anthropologists and sociologists during the early twentieth century and of postcolonial modernization theorists after World War II (Steinmetz 2013). Even such self-consciously "value-neutral" works of comparative analysis like Weber's "Collected Essays on the World Religions" are susceptible to this charge (Weber 1964). This is no doubt why so many contemporary sociologists are loathe to advance comparative critiques except between Western countries. In so doing, however, they have simply ceded the field to economists, who have no such hesitations (Robinson and Acemoglu 2012). Nussbaum's synthesis of political liberalism and the capabilities approach provides one possible framework for a comparative sociology that dares to be critical again.

Comparison can also contribute to evaluation. As defined here, "evaluation" concerns the likely consequences of various courses of action in relation to individual or collective goods or values, particularly when they are potentially in conflict with one another. Consider the example of inequality. Based on comparative research, we feel confident that high levels of social inequality usually lead to low levels of happiness, not only on average, but even among the better-off members of a society. In other words, we know that decreasing inequality is objectively good. But we also know that attempts to eliminate equality altogether often lead to objective bads, such as a loss of political free-dom or declines in economic output. Nor is socioeconomic inequality the only form of inequality. Class inequality intersects with race and gender inequality in complex ways. And we know that efforts to mitigate class inequality can actually reinforce race and gender inequality. Trade unions and closed shops boosted wages but primarily for white men. Social insurance schemes built around a "male breadwinner norm" tended to lock women out of the labor force and into household labor. Comparison can be a powerful tool for think-ing about social policy and political action more broadly.

Conclusion: Many Things Go!

The anarchist philosopher, Paul Feyerabend, famously proclaimed that "Anything goes!" in science. If NCR had a motto, it would be more modest: "Many things go!" In this, NCR steers a *via media* between Feyerabend's methodological anarchism and positivism's one-method-fits-all authoritari-anism. The positivist account is much too constricting. It advances a narrow vision of natural science based on physics and seeks to impose this vision on all of the sciences. In that vision, the goal of science is the discovery of laws, and the means to that end is experiments. As we have seen, the social sciences have other ends and other means. Social science seeks to describe, critique, and evaluate, not just explain. And it has invented various method-ological means to these ends. These methods are various because the social world is heterogeneous. Symbols, artifacts, and persons are not made of the same sort of "stuff" and cannot be probed with the same tools. Nor can the social world be reduced to the "elementary particles" of individual action. It is characterized by emergence and openness. Neither does "anything go" in a normative sense. To be sure, the same basic human and social goods can be achieved in many, different ways. "Play" and "friendship" can take numerous forms. But humans are not infinitely malleable either. Although there is admittedly a great deal of within-species variation, humans are nonetheless one species, whose needs and capabilities vary widely but within certain limits. A just society provides the resources and infrastructure that individuals need to flourish and guarantees the freedom they require to choose how to flourish.

Comparison can play many different roles in social science. It can help us to craft better descriptions, ones that adequately capture the distinguishing features of our objects of analysis. It can help us to assemble better explanations, ones that adequately account for the parallels and divergences we seek to track. These are the two ways in which comparison has most often been used by contemporary social scientists. But the classical social theorists also employed comparison for normative purposes, to critique exploitation and anomie and to warn about the consequences of equality and rationalization. Perhaps it is time for historical sociology to reclaim this classical legacy.

Notes

1. The results of that project, including blogs, reading lists, and introductory videos, can be found at criticalrealismnetwork.org.
2. The three best-known proponents of critical realism in American sociology today are Doug Porpora, George Steinmetz, and Christian Smith.

References

Abbott, Andrew. 2005. "Linked Ecologies: States and Universities as Environments for Professions." *Sociological Theory* 23(3):245–74.

Achen, Christopher H., and Larry M. Bartels. 2017. *Democracy for Realists*. Princeton, NJ: Princeton University Press.

Archer, Margaret S. 1995. *Realist Social Theory: The Morphogenetic Approach*. New York: Cambridge University Press.

——. 1998. *Critical Realism: Essential Readings*. New York: Routledge.

——. 2000. *Being Human: The Problem of Agency*. New York: Cambridge University Press.

Baggini, Julian. 2019. "The Influential Wrongness of AJ Ayer." *Prospect*, May 19. https://www .prospectmagazine.co.uk/ideas/philosophy/42582/the-influential-wrongness-of-aj-ayer.

Becker, Gary S. 1996. *Accounting for Tastes*. Cambridge, MA: Harvard University Press.

Bedau, Mark A., and Paul Humphreys. 2008. *Emergence: Contemporary Readings in Philosophy and Science*. Cambridge, MA: MIT Press.

Bellah, Robert N. 2011. *Religion in Human Evolution*. Cambridge, MA: Harvard University Press.

Bhaskar, Roy. 1975. *A Realist Theory of Science*. London: Verso.

——. 1979. *The Possibility of Naturalism: A Philosophical Critique of the Contemporary Human Sciences*. Atlantic Highlands, NJ: Humanities Press.

Boccaletti, S., Bianconi, G., Criado, R., del Genio, C. I., Gómez-Gardenes, J., Romance, M., Sendiña-Nadal, I., Wang, Z., and Zanin, M. 2014. "The Structure and Dynamics of Multilayer Networks." *Physics Reports* 544(1):1–122.

Broad, C. D. [1934] 2014. *The Mind and Its Place in Nature*. London: Routledge.

Bunge, Mario. 2001. "Systems and Emergence, Rationality and Imprecision, Free-Wheeling and Evidence, Science and Ideology: Social Science and Its Philosophy According to van den Berg." *Philosophy of the Social Sciences* 31(3):404–23.

Burawoy, Michael. 2005. "For Public Sociology." *American Sociological Review* 70(1):4–28.

Cartwright, Nancy. 1983. *How the Laws of Physics Lie*. New York: Oxford University Press.

Coleman, James S. 1990. *Foundations of Social Theory*. Cambridge, MA: Harvard University Press.

Collins, Patricia Hill. 2000. *Black Feminist Thought: Knowledge, Consciousness, and the Politics of Empowerment*. Revised 10th anniversary edition. New York: Routledge.

Danermark, Berth, Mats Ekstrom, and Liselotte Jakobsen. 2005. *Explaining Society: An Introduction to Critical Realism in the Social Sciences*. New York: Routledge.

Darwall, Stephen. 2003. "Desires, Reasons and Causes." *Philosophy and Phenomenological Research* 67(2):436–43.

Dreyfus, Hubert, and Charles Taylor. 2015. *Retrieving Realism*. Cambridge, MA: Harvard University Press.

Elder-Vass, Dave. 2010. *The Causal Power of Social Structures: Emergence, Structure and Agency*. New York: Cambridge University Press.

Esping-Andersen, Gøsta. 1990. *The Three Worlds of Welfare Capitalism*. Princeton, NJ: Princeton University Press.

Flanagan, Owen. 2009. *Varieties of Moral Personality: Ethics and Psychological Realism*. Cambridge, MA: Harvard University Press.

Fligstein, Neil, and Doug McAdam. 2011. "Toward a General Theory of Strategic Action Fields." *Sociological Theory* 29(1):1–26.

Fox, Nick J., and Pam Alldred. 2020. *New Materialism*. London: Sage.

Giddens, Anthony. 1984. *The Constitution of Society: Introduction of the Theory of Structuration*. Berkeley: University of California Press.

Gilman, Nils. 2003. *Mandarins of the Future: Modernization Theory in Cold War America*. Baltimore, MD: Johns Hopkins University Press.

Gorski, Philip. 2013. "Beyond the Fact/Value Distinction: Ethical Naturalism and the Social Sciences." *Society* 50:543–53.

——. 2015. "Causal Mechanisms: Lessons from the Life Sciences." In *Generative Mechanisms Transforming the Social Order*, edited by Margaret Archer, 27–48. Cham, Switzerland: Springer.

——. 2016. "The Matter of Emergence: Material Artifacts and Social Structure." *Qualitative Sociology* 39(2):211–15.

——. 2017. "From Sinks to Webs: Critical Social Science after the Fact-Value Distinction." *Canadian Review of Sociology/Revue canadienne de sociologie* 54(4):423–44.

——. 2018. "After Positivism: Critical Realism and Historical Sociology." In *Critical Realism, History, and Philosophy in the Social Sciences*, 23–45. Leeds, United Kingdom: Emerald.

——. 2019. "Ontic Webs: A New Framework for Public Sociology." In *Religion, Humility, and Democracy in a Divided America*, 151–68. Leeds, United Kingdom: Emerald.

Grimmer, Justin, Margaret E. Roberts, and Brandon M. Stewart. 2022. *Text as Data: A New Framework for Machine Learning and the Social Sciences.* Princeton, NJ: Princeton University Press.

Gross, Neil. 2009. "A Pragmatist Theory of Social Mechanisms." *American Sociological Review* 74(3):358–79.

——. 2017. "Reconstructing Sociology: The Critical Realist Approach." *American Journal of Sociology* 123(1):297–301.

Hacking, Ian. 1983. *Representing and Intervening: Introductory Topics in the Philosophy of Natural Science.* New York: Cambridge University Press.

Hanfling, Oswald. 2003. "Logical Positivism." In *Routledge History of Philosophy Volume IX,* 231–51. New York: Routledge.

Hannah-Jones, Nikole. 2021. *The 1619 Project: A New Origin Story.* New York: One World.

Harding, Sandra G. 1987. *Feminism and Methodology: Social Science Issues.* Bloomington: Indiana University Press.

Hedström, Peter. 2005. *Dissecting the Social: On the Principles of Analytical Sociology.* Cambridge: Cambridge University Press.

Hedström, Peter, and Richard Swedberg. 1998. *Social Mechanisms: An Analytical Approach to Social Theory.* New York: Cambridge University Press.

Hegel, Georg Wilhelm Friedrich. 2004. *The Philosophy of History.* Translated by J. Sibree. Minneola, NY: Dover.

Hempel, Carl G. 1965. *Aspects of Scientific Explanation and Other Essays in the Philosophy of Science.* New York: Free Press.

Hesse, Mary B. 2020. *The Structure of Scientific Inference.* Berkeley: University of California Press.

Hinton, Elizabeth. 2017. *From the War on Poverty to the War on Crime: The Making of Mass Incarceration in America.* Cambridge, MA: Harvard University Press.

Hirschman, Daniel, and Isaac Ariail Reed. 2014. "Formation Stories and Causality in Sociology." *Sociological Theory* 32(4):259–82.

Johnson, Mark. 2021. *Morality for Humans: Ethical Understanding from the Perspective of Cognitive Science.* Chicago: University of Chicago Press.

Kant, Immanuel. 2006. *Kant: Anthropology from a Pragmatic Point of View.* New York: Cambridge University Press.

Keane, Webb. 2015. *Ethical Life: Its Natural and Social Histories.* Princeton, NJ: Princeton University Press.

Kim, Jaegwon. 2005. *Physicalism, or Something Near Enough.* Princeton, NJ: Princeton University Press.

Kiser, Edgar, and Michael Hechter. 1991. "The Role of General Theory in Comparative-Historical Sociology." *American Journal of Sociology* 97:1–30.

Lawson, Tony. 1997. *Economics and Reality.* New York: Routledge.

Lazarsfeld, Paul F. 1958. "Evidence and Inference in Social Research." *Daedalus* 87(4):99–130.

Lieberson, Stanley. 1991. "Small N's and Big Conclusions: An Examination of the Reasoning in Comparative Studies Based on a Small Number of Cases." *Social Forces* 70(2):307–20.

Little, Daniel. 2016. *New Directions in the Philosophy of Social Science.* Lanham, MD: Rowman and Littlefield.

Losch, Andreas. 2009. "On the Origins of Critical Realism." *Theology and Science* 7(1):85–106.

Luebbert, Gregory M. 1991. *Liberalism, Fascism, or Social Democracy: Social Classes and the Political Origins of Regimes in Interwar Europe.* New York: Oxford University Press.

MacIntyre, Alasdair C. 1999. *Dependent Rational Animals: Why Human Beings Need the Virtues.* Chicago: Open Court.

Mann, Michael. 2004. *Fascists*. New York: Cambridge University Press.

Morgan, Stephen L., and Christopher Winship. 2015. *Counterfactuals and Causal Inference*. New York: Cambridge University Press.

Mumford, Stephen. 2012. *Metaphysics: A Very Short Introduction*. Oxford: Oxford University Press.

Mumford, Stephen, and Rani Lill Anjum. 2013. *Causation: A Very Short Introduction*. Oxford: Oxford University Press.

Murdoch, Iris. 1971. *The Sovereignty of Good*. New York: Schocken.

Neurath, Otto. 1934. "Radikaler Physikalismus und 'Wirkliche Welt.'" *Erkenntnis* 4:346–62.

Nussbaum, Martha C. 2000. *Women and Human Development: The Capabilities Approach*. New York: Cambridge University Press.

Nussbaum, Martha C., and Amartya Sen. 1993. *The Quality of Life*. New York: Clarendon.

Pearl, Judea. 2009. *Causality: Models, Reasoning, and Inference*. 2nd edition. New York: Cambridge University Press.

Popper, Karl R. 1957. *The Poverty of Historicism*. Boston: Beacon.

——. 1959. *The Logic of Scientific Discovery*. New York: Basic Books.

Powell, Walter W., and John F. Padgett, eds. 2012. *The Emergence of Organizations and Markets*. Princeton, NJ: Princeton University Press.

Psillos, Stathis. 2009. "Regularity Theories." In *The Oxford Handbook of Causation*, edited by Helen Beebee, Christopher Hitchcock, and Peter Menzies, 111–37. Oxford: Oxford University Press.

Rahe, Paul A. 2009. *Soft Despotism, Democracy's Drift: Montesquieu, Rousseau, Tocqueville, and the Modern Prospect*. New Haven, CT: Yale University Press.

Rawls, John. 2005. *Political Liberalism*. Expanded edition. New York: Columbia University Press.

Reed, Isaac Ariail. 2021. *Interpretation and Social Knowledge*. Chicago: University of Chicago Press.

Robinson, James A., and Daron Acemoglu. 2012. *Why Nations Fail: The Origins of Power, Prosperity and Poverty*. London: Profile.

Sachs, Joe. 1995. *Aristotle's Physics: A Guided Study*. New Brunswick, NJ: Rutgers University Press.

Sawyer, R. Keith. 2005. *Social Emergence: Societies as Complex Systems*. New York: Cambridge University Press.

Seligman, Martin E. P. 2012. *Flourish: A Visionary New Understanding of Happiness and Well-Being*. New York: Simon and Schuster.

Sellars, Roy Wood. 1916. *Critical Realism: A Study of the Nature and Conditions of Knowledge*. New York: Rand McNally.

Sen, Amartya K. 1999. *Development as Freedom*. Oxford: Oxford University Press.

Simons, Peter. 2013. "Metaphysics in Analytic Philosophy." In *The Oxford Handbook of the History of Analytic Philosophy*, edited by M. Beaney, 709–28. Oxford: Oxford University Press.

Singh, Sourabh. 2018. "Anchoring Depth Ontology to Epistemological Strategies of Field Theory: Exploring the Possibility for Developing a Core for Sociological Analysis." *Journal of Critical Realism* 17(5):429–48.

Skocpol, Theda. 1979. *States and Social Revolutions: A Comparative Analysis of France, Russia, and China*. New York: Cambridge University Press.

——, ed. 1984. *Vision and Method in Historical Sociology*. New York: Cambridge University Press.

Stadler, Friedrich. 2015. *The Vienna Circle: Studies in the Origins, Development, and Influence of Logical Empiricism*. Vol. 4. New York: Springer.

Stanley, Jason. 2020. *How Fascism Works: The Politics of Us and Them*. New York: Random House.

Steinmetz, George. 2013. *Sociology and Empire: The Imperial Entanglements of a Discipline*. Durham, NC: Duke University Press.

Taylor, Charles. 1989. *Sources of the Self: The Making of the Modern Identity*. Cambridge, MA: Harvard University Press.

——. 2016. *The Language Animal*. Cambridge, MA: Harvard University Press.

Tilley, Chris, Webb Keane, Susanne Küchler, Mike Rowlands, and Patricia Spyer, eds. 2006. *Handbook of Material Culture*. London: Sage.

Tilly, Charles. 2000. "Processes and Mechanisms of Democratization." *Sociological Theory* 18(1):1.

Tocqueville, Alexis de. 2011. *Tocqueville: The Ancien Régime and the French Revolution*. Translated by Arthur Goldhammer. New York: Cambridge University Press.

——. 1988. *Democracy in America*. Translated by J. P. Mayer. 1st Perennial library edition. New York: HarperPerennial.

Veenhoven, Ruut. 2003. "Happiness." *Psychologist* 16:128–29.

Weber, Max. 1964. *From Max Weber: Essays in Sociology*. Edited and translated by H. H. Gerth and C. W. Mills. New York: Oxford University Press.

White, Harrison C. 2008. *Identity and Control: How Social Formations Emerge*. Princeton, NJ: Princeton University Press.

Wimsatt, William C. 1997. "Aggregativity: Reductive Heuristics for Finding Emergence." *Philosophy of Science* 64: S372–S384.

Woodward, James. 2004. "Counterfactuals and Causal Explanation." *International Studies in the Philosophy of Science* 18(1):41–72.

CONTRIBUTORS

Patricia Ahmed is Assistant Professor of Sociology and Criminology at South Dakota State University. Her research interests include comparative historical sociology, cross-cultural sociology, and globalization. Her recent publications include works on census categorization in Puerto Rico and the sociology of knowledge (with Rebecca Jean Emigh and Dylan Riley).

Natalie B. Aviles is Assistant Professor of Sociology at the University of Virginia. She is a pragmatist sociological theorist whose empirical research explores how federal laboratories in the U.S. National Cancer Institute have guided scientific and public policy innovation from the postwar period to the present day. Her book, *An Ungovernable Foe: Science and Policy Innovation in the U.S. National Cancer Institute*, is forthcoming from Columbia University Press.

Stefan Bargheer is a Distinguished Fellow at the Max Weber Centre for Advanced Cultural and Social Studies at the University of Erfurt. His work focuses on the historical sociology of morality and on the sociology of science, knowledge, and technology. He is the author of *Moral Entanglements: Conserving Birds in Britain and Germany* (University of Chicago Press, 2018).

Rebecca Jean Emigh is Professor of Sociology at the University of California, Los Angeles. She is a comparative historical sociologist who specializes in long-term social change. She is the author of multiple prize-winning articles and books on a range of topics, including capitalism, censuses, social theory, and historical demography. She is the past chair of the Comparative-Historical Section of the American Sociological Association and is currently the coeditor of *Social Science History*.

Laura R. Ford is Associate Professor of Law at Faulkner University's Jones School of Law. Her work focuses on law and religion, Weberian sociological theory, and the history of sociology. She is the author of *The Intellectual Property of Nations: Sociological and Historical Perspectives on a Modern Legal Institution* (Cambridge University Press, 2021).

Philip Gorski is the Frederick and Laura Goff Professor and Chair of the Sociology Department at Yale University. His research focuses on religion and politics in early modern and modern Europe and North America. He is the author, most recently, of *The Flag and the Cross: White Christian Nationalism and the Threat to American Democracy* (Oxford University Press, 2022).

Damon Mayrl is Associate Professor of Sociology at Colby College. His research interests include religion and politics, American statecraft, and comparative and historical methods. He is the author of *Secular Conversions: Political Institutions and Religious Education in the United States and Australia, 1800–2000* (Cambridge University Press, 2016).

Simeon J. Newman is a political and historical sociologist with interests in social theory and the philosophy of the social sciences. He earned his PhD from the University of Michigan's Department of Sociology in 2023 and is currently a postdoctoral fellow at the Max-Weber-Institut für Soziologie at Universität Heidelberg.

Josh Pacewicz is Associate Professor of Sociology at Brown University. He is broadly interested in the political economy of the United States, particularly as it pertains to the root causes of issues like political party breakdown, failures of urban governance, policing for profit, and political polarization across American states. His first book received the ASA Theory Award, and he has also won a Guggenheim Fellowship, the Charles Tilly Prize, the Jane Addams Award (twice), and the *Socio-Economic Review* Best Paper Award. His new book project, *Architects of the Divided States*, draws on interviews with the advocates, lobbyists, bureaucrats, and legislators who create a diverging landscape of public health, social services, and civil rights in red and blue America.

Dylan Riley is Professor of Sociology at the University of California, Berkeley, and author of *The Civic Foundations of Fascism in Europe* (Johns Hopkins University Press, 2010/Verso, 2019) and (with Rebecca Jean Emigh and Patricia Ahmed) *Antecedents of Censuses* and *Changes in Censuses* (Palgrave, 2016).

George Steinmetz is the Charles Tilly Collegiate Professor of Sociology at the University of Michigan. His work focuses on the historical sociology of states, colonies, empires, and knowledge, as well as social theory and epistemology. He is the author of *The Colonial Origins of Modern Social Thought: French Sociology and the Overseas Empire* (Princeton University Press, 2023) and *The Social Sciences in the Looking-Glass: Studies in the Production of Knowledge* (Duke University Press, 2023).

Jonah Stuart Brundage is Assistant Professor of Sociology at the University of Michigan. His research interests include empire, state formation, the history of capitalism, and historical and comparative methods. He is currently working on a book entitled *Performing World Order: British Diplomats and the Politics of Recognition Among Empires, 1688–1815.*

Nicholas Hoover Wilson is Associate Professor of Sociology at Stony Brook University. His work focuses on the historical sociology of corruption and empire, as well as the sociology of science, morality, and knowledge. He is the author of *Modernity's Corruption: Empire and Morality in the Making of British India* (Columbia University Press, 2023).

Xiaohong Xu was Assistant Professor of Sociology at the University of Michigan. His research interests included revolutions, social movements, state formation, family and gender politics, and colonialism and nationalism in modern China, East Asia, and Southeast Asia. He has published his research in *American Sociological Review*, *Critical Historical Studies*, and *Sociological Theory* and was writing a book on the Chinese Cultural Revolution and the political origins of Reform China. Xiaohong tragically succumbed to cancer in 2023.

Yang Zhang is Assistant Professor in the School of International Service at American University. His research interests include historical and political sociology of the state, empire, contentious politics, and elite politics, as well as social network analysis and social science philosophy. He has published in *American Journal of Sociology, Theory and Society, Journal of Historical Sociology,* and *Mobilization* and is completing a book entitled *Empire and Its Enemies: Ethnicity, Religion, and Rebellions in Mid-19th-Century China.*

INDEX

GPSR Authorized Representative: Easy Access System Europe, Mustamäe tee
50, 10621 Tallinn, Estonia, gpsr.requests@easproject.com